THE CAMBRIDGE COMPANION TO WOMEN'S WRITING IN THE ROMANTIC PERIOD

The Romantic period saw the first generations of professional women writers flourish in Great Britain. Literary history is only now giving them the attention they deserve, for the quality of their writings and for their popularity in their own time. This collection of new essays by leading scholars explores the challenges and achievements of a fascinating set of women writers, including Jane Austen, Mary Wollstonecraft, Ann Radcliffe, Hannah More, Maria Edgeworth, and Mary Shelley, alongside many lesser-known female authors writing and publishing during this period. Chapters consider major literary genres, including poetry, fiction, drama, travel writing, histories, essays, and political writing, as well as topics such as globalization, colonialism, feminism, economics, families, sexualities, aging, and war. The volume shows how gender intersected with other aspects of identity and with cultural concerns that then shaped the work of authors, critics, and readers.

DEVONEY LOOSER is Professor of English in the Department of English, Arizona State University. She is the author of *Women Writers and Old Age in Great Britain, 1750–1850* (2008) and *British Women Writers and the Writing of History, 1670–1820* (2000), co-editor of *Generations: Academic Feminists in Dialogue* (1997), and editor of *Jane Austen and Discourses of Feminism* (1995).

A complete list of books in the series is at the back of this book.

D1595610

THE CAMBRIDGE
COMPANION TO
WOMEN'S WRITING
IN THE
ROMANTIC PERIOD

EDITED BY
DEVONEY LOOSER

CAMBRIDGE
UNIVERSITY PRESS

CAMBRIDGE
UNIVERSITY PRESS

University Printing House, Cambridge CB2 8BS, United Kingdom

Cambridge University Press is part of the University of Cambridge.

It furthers the University's mission by disseminating knowledge in the pursuit of education, learning and research at the highest international levels of excellence.

www.cambridge.org
Information on this title: www.cambridge.org/9781107602557

© Cambridge University Press 2015

First published 2015

Printed in the United States of America by Sheridan Books, Inc.

A catalogue record for this publication is available from the British Library

Library of Congress Cataloguing in Publication data
The Cambridge companion to women's writing in the romantic period / edited by Devoney Looser.
pages cm. – (Cambridge companions to literature)
Includes bibliographical references and index.
ISBN 978-1-107-01668-2 (hardback) – ISBN 978-1-107-60255-7 (pbk.)
1. English literature–Women authors–History and criticism. 2. Women and literature–Great Britain–History–19th century. I. Looser, Devoney, 1967– editor.
PR111.C36 2015
820.9'9287–dc23   2014043075

ISBN 978-1-107-01668-2 Hardback
ISBN 978-1-107-60255-7 Paperback

CONTENTS

List of illustrations   *page* vii
Notes on contributors   viii
Preface   xiii
Acknowledgments   xix
Chronology   xxi

1   Poetry   1
     STEPHEN C. BEHRENDT

2   Fiction   16
     ANTHONY MANDAL

3   Drama   32
     CATHERINE BURROUGHS

4   Essays and political writing   44
     ANNE K. MELLOR

5   The Gothic   58
     ANGELA WRIGHT

6   Travel writing   73
     ELIZABETH A. FAY

7   History writing and antiquarianism   88
     CRYSTAL B. LAKE

8   Writing in wartime   101
     CATHERINE INGRASSIA

9 Enlightenment feminism and the bluestocking legacy   115
   CAROLINE FRANKLIN

10 The global context   129
   DEIRDRE COLEMAN

11 Social, familial, and literary networks   145
   JULIE A. CARLSON

12 The economics of female authorship   158
   JACQUELINE M. LABBE

13 Age and aging   169
   DEVONEY LOOSER

14 National identities and regional affiliations   183
   FIONA PRICE

15 Sexualities   198
   JILLIAN HEYDT-STEVENSON

   Guide to further reading   213
   Index   226

ILLUSTRATIONS

1 Production of New Fiction, 1780–1829, Anthony Mandal. Data drawn from the printed bibliography *The English Novel, 1770–1829* (2000) and the online database *British Fiction, 1800–1829* (2004) *page* 22

2 Authorship of New Fiction by Gender, 1780–1829, Anthony Mandal. Data drawn from the printed bibliography *The English Novel, 1770–1829* (2000) and the online database *British Fiction, 1800–1829* (2004) 27

3 Most Prolific Authors of New Fiction, 1780–1829, Anthony Mandal. Data drawn from the printed bibliography *The English Novel, 1770–1829* (2000) and the online database *British Fiction, 1800–1829* (2004) 28

4 Robert Jacob Hamerton, *Lady Hester Lucy Stanhope, c.* 1830s. © National Portrait Gallery, London 82

5 "XXXIX: The Seven Ages of Man," *Joh. Amos Comenii Orbis sensualium pictus* (New York, 1810), p. 61. Reprinted by permission of Library Special Collections, Charles E. Young Research Library, UCLA 172

CONTRIBUTORS

STEPHEN C. BEHRENDT is University Professor and George Holmes Distinguished Professor of English at the University of Nebraska. He has published widely on both canonical and extra-canonical British Romantic literature and culture and has edited several collections of essays, as well as two electronic textbase collections of poetry by Irish and Scottish Romantic-era women writers (Alexander Street Press, 2001, 2007). He is the author of *British Women Poets and the Romantic Writing Community* (Johns Hopkins University Press, 2009). He is also a widely published poet; his fourth collection, *Refractions* (2014), is published by Shechem Press.

CATHERINE BURROUGHS is the Ruth and Albert Koch Professor of English at Wells College and a visiting lecturer at Cornell University. In addition to her many articles on British Romantic theatre and drama, her publications include *Reading the Social Body* (co-ed., University of Iowa Press, 1993); *Closet Stages: Joanna Baillie and the Theater Theory of British Romantic Women Writers* (University of Pennsylvania Press, 1997); and *Women in British Romantic Theatre: Drama, Performance, and Society, 1790–1840* (ed., Cambridge University Press, 2000). A member of Actors' Equity Association, Burroughs has also co-edited a book for the Modern Language Association's Options for Teaching Series, *Approaches to Teaching Early British Women Playwrights* (2010).

JULIE A. CARLSON is Professor of English at the University of California, Santa Barbara. She is the author of *In the Theatre of Romanticism: Coleridge, Nationalism, Women* (Cambridge University Press, 1994) and *England's First Family of Writers: Mary Wollstonecraft, William Godwin, Mary Shelley* (Johns Hopkins University Press, 2007), is guest-editor of *Domestic/Tragedy* (*South Atlantic Quarterly*, 1997), and co-editor with Elisabeth Weber of *Speaking about Torture* (Fordham University Press, 2012). She is the Keats–Shelley Association of America Distinguished Scholar of 2010 and has written articles on Romantic-era theater, literature and radical culture, and literary modes of attachment. Currently she is writing a book on books and friends in post-1790s British radical culture.

DEIRDRE COLEMAN is the Robert Wallace Chair of English at the University of Melbourne. Her research centers on eighteenth-century literature and cultural history, focusing in particular on racial ideology, colonialism, natural history, and the anti-slavery movement. She has published in *ELH*, *Eighteenth-Century Life*, and *Eighteenth-Century Studies*, and is the author of *Romantic Colonization and British Anti-Slavery* (Cambridge University Press, 2005), and co-editor (with Hilary Fraser) of *Minds, Bodies, Machines, 1770–1930* (Palgrave Macmillan, 2011).

ELIZABETH A. FAY is Professor of English at the University of Massachusetts, Boston. She is the author of five books, and has also co-edited two essay volumes and one edition. Her most recent publications are *Fashioning Faces: The Portraitive Mode in British Romanticism* (2010) and a co-edited volume, *Urban Identity and the Atlantic World* (University of New Hampshire Press, 2013). She served six years as editor of *Literature Compass Romanticism* (Wiley Blackwell) and is currently book series editor of "The New Urban Atlantic" (Palgrave Macmillan). She also helped found the Research Center for Urban Cultural History at UMass Boston and served eight years as its first director.

CAROLINE FRANKLIN is Professor of English and Director of the Centre for Research into Gender and Culture in Society at Swansea University. Her most recent publications are *The Female Romantics: Nineteenth-Century Women Novelists and Byronism* (Routledge, 2012) and *The Longman Anthology of Gothic Verse* (Pearson, 2010). She is the leader of the AHRC-funded Elizabeth Montagu Correspondence project, which is preparing an online scholarly edition of Bluestocking letters from the archives at www.elizabethmontagunetwork.co.uk.

JILLIAN HEYDT-STEVENSON teaches in the English Department and in the Program for Comparative Literature at the University of Colorado, Boulder. Her primary scholarly interests radiate from topics in British and French Romanticism. She has published on narrative theory, fashion, cosmopolitanism, ruins and landscape architecture, literature and film, and focused on such authors as Austen, Wordsworth, Coleridge, Edgeworth, Burney, and Bernardin de St. Pierre. She has published *Austen's Unbecoming Conjunctions: Subversive Laughter, Embodied History* (Palgrave Macmillan, 2005); co-edited *Recognizing the Romantic Novel: New Histories of British Fiction, 1780–1830* (with Charlotte Sussman; Liverpool University Press, 2008); and was associate editor of *Last Poems of William Wordsworth: 1821–50* (Cornell University Press, 1999). Her current book project is *Belongings: Things in Nineteenth-Century French and British Literature*.

CATHERINE INGRASSIA is Professor of English at Virginia Commonwealth University. She is author of *Authorship, Commerce, and Gender in Eighteenth-Century*

England (Cambridge University Press, 1998), editor of *Anti-Pamela/Shamela* (Broadview, 2004) and *The Cambridge Companion to Women's Writing in England, 1660–1789* (2015), and co-editor of *British Women Poets of the Long Eighteenth Century* (Johns Hopkins University Press, 2009), *The Blackwell Companion to the Eighteenth-Century Novel and Culture* (2005), and *"More Solid Learning": New Perspectives on Pope's Dunciad* (Bucknell University Press, 2000).

JACQUELINE M. LABBE is Professor of Romantic-Period Literature and Pro-Vice-Chancellor for Arts and Humanities at the University of Sheffield. She is the author of several monographs, including *Writing Romanticism: Charlotte Smith and William Wordsworth, 1784–1807* (Palgrave Macmillan, 2011); the editor of several collections, including *The History of British Women's Writing, 1770–1830* (Palgrave Macmillan, 2010); and has written many articles on the poetry and fiction of the Romantic period. She is currently working on a study of the writerly entanglements between Smith and Jane Austen and is planning a book on Smith's novels.

CRYSTAL B. LAKE is an Assistant Professor of English at Wright State University. Her work on historiography, objects, and eighteenth- and nineteenth-century British literature has appeared in *ELH*, *Modern Philology*, and the *Review of English Studies*. Her research has been supported by fellowships from the Lewis Walpole Library, the Yale Center for British Art, and the Centre for the Study of Early Women Writers at Chawton House. She is completing a study of eighteenth-century and Romantic representations of archaeological artifacts in literature, art, and popular culture.

DEVONEY LOOSER is Professor of English at Arizona State University. She is the author of *Women Writers and Old Age in Great Britain, 1750–1850* (Johns Hopkins University Press, 2008) and *British Women Writers and the Writing of History, 1670–1820* (Johns Hopkins University Press, 2000). She edited *Jane Austen and Discourses of Feminism* (Palgrave Macmillan, 1995) and co-edited (with E. Ann Kaplan) *Generations: Academic Feminists in Dialogue* (University of Minnesota Press, 1997). Looser is working on two projects, a study of Jane Austen's reception and a biography of the sister novelists Jane and Anna Maria Porter.

ANTHONY MANDAL is Reader in Print and Digital Cultures, and Director of the Centre for Editorial and Intertextual Research at Cardiff University. He is the author of articles, books and digital resources on nineteenth-century fiction, the gothic and the history of the book, including *The English Novel, 1830–36* (Cardiff University, 2003), *Jane Austen and the Popular Novel: The Determined Author* (Palgrave Macmillan, 2007), and *The Reception of Jane Austen in Europe* (Bloomsbury, 2007, 2014). He has published a scholarly edition of Mary Brunton's

Self-Control for Pickering & Chatto (2014) and is also one of the General Editors of *The New Edinburgh Edition of the Works of Robert Louis Stevenson* (39 vols., 2014–).

ANNE K. MELLOR is Distinguished Research Professor of English at UCLA and the author of numerous books and articles on Romantic-era male and female writers, including *Blake's Human Form Divine* (University of California Press, 1974), *English Romantic Irony* (Harvard University Press, 1980), *Mary Shelley: Her Life, Her Fiction, Her Monsters* (Methuen, 1988), *Romanticism and Gender* (Routledge, 1993), and *Mothers of the Nation* (Indiana University Press, 2000). She has edited many volumes, including *Romanticism and Feminism* (Indiana University Press, 1988), *The Other Mary Shelley* (Oxford University Press, 1993), *British Literature, 1780–1830* (Harcourt Brace, 1996), *Wollstonecraft's Rights of Woman and Wrongs of Woman* (Pearson Longman, 2007), and *Lucy Aikin's Epistles on Women* (Broadview, 2010). She is currently working on the fiction of Jane Austen.

FIONA PRICE is Reader in English Literature at the University of Chichester and author of *Revolutions in Taste 1773–1818: Women Writers and the Aesthetics of Romanticism* (Ashgate, 2009). She has edited two historical novels: Jane Porter's *The Scottish Chiefs* (1810; Broadview Press, 2007) and Sarah Green's *Private History of the Court of England* (1808; Pickering & Chatto, 2011). She has written widely on women's writing, historical fiction, and the aesthetics of political change. She is currently working on a book on nation, liberty, and the historical novel from Walpole to Scott and is co-editor, with Ben Dew, of *Historical Writing in Britain, 1688–1830: Visions of History* (Palgrave Macmillan, 2014).

ANGELA WRIGHT is Professor of Romantic Literature at the University of Sheffield and co-President of the International Gothic Association. She is the author of *Gothic Fiction* (Palgrave Macmillan, 2007), *Britain, France and the Gothic: The Import of Terror* (Cambridge University Press, 2013) and co-editor (with Dale Townshend) of *Ann Radcliffe, Romanticism and the Gothic* (Cambridge University Press, 2014). Current projects include a study of Mary Shelley for the University of Wales Press series *Gothic Literary Authors* and preliminary research for her next project, provisionally titled *Fostering Romanticism*.

The Romantic period – often defined as beginning in 1780, 1789, or 1798 and ending in 1830, 1832, or 1837 – was a watershed moment for British women's writing.[1]

That statement now seems so self-evident and inarguable that it is difficult to believe that, just a few decades ago, it was neither. The Romantic period has long been characterized as a time of innovation and change in both literary form and content, as well as a momentous era of new political thought and social upheaval. But for most of the twentieth century, the term "Romantic" did not serve to plumb the depths of that innovation and change. Instead, it focused on a small number of writers said to be the greatest ones. The Romantic period separated out the writings of what came to be called the Big Six male poets – William Blake, Samuel Taylor Coleridge, William Wordsworth, Percy Bysshe Shelley, John Keats, and Lord Byron – placing them at the center of a new tradition.

Despite our pigeonholing them in this way, the Big Six penned more than poetry, and most did not imagine themselves as in league with each other. Writers we now call part of the Romantic period in Great Britain certainly did not label themselves Romantics. That labeling came into wide use later, as critics looked back on this period of literary history. Other so-called minor male writers also came to be considered Romantic, among them Thomas De Quincey, William Hazlitt, Leigh Hunt, and Robert Southey. But prior to the 1980s, as Stephen C. Behrendt's chapter in this book carefully describes, the study of British Romanticism did not encompass many – or sometimes any – women writers. This is strange, because, as Behrendt notes, between 1770 and 1835, there were at least 500 women publishing poetry in Great Britain. This number does not include those who circulated their poems, perhaps deliberately and widely, in manuscript, rather than seeking print – a then common practice that scholars have come to call manuscript circulation or scribal publication. The figure of 500 also leaves out women who did not seek a wider audience for their verse and those who wrote in genres other than poetry.

The shift from our slighting of Romantic women writers' contributions to including them in our conversations can be measured in many ways. It is evident in the changing tables of contents of literature textbooks. These anthologies provide collective assessments of the writings that make up our literary canon. Prior to the 1980s and even into the 1990s, female authors were poorly represented. Although the first edition of *The Norton Anthology of Literature by Women* was published in 1985, it was skewed toward representing women who published after 1830.[2] Today that anthology has grown to two volumes, with approximately twenty Romantic-era women writers featured among its 219 authors.[3] Some may argue that this is still not sufficient as a percentage of the total contents, but it is at least a move toward greater representation. *The Norton Anthology of English Literature* went from virtual absence to greater inclusion for women writers in its updated contents. (Authors who have been newly included – and dropped – in the *Norton Anthology* can be tracked on the publisher's website.) Women's writings are now much better represented in the pages of that anthology. By design, these oft-used textbooks feature but a fraction of known authors of any given period. We are still in the process of discovering and documenting the full range of women writers and their published and unpublished texts in the Romantic era.

Even in the case of the most familiar Romantic female authors, reputations have changed profoundly. Jane Austen was among the few read widely from the late nineteenth century forward, but she was not imagined as Romantic until the late 1970s. Instead, she was grouped with eighteenth-century novelists, a classification said to be more in keeping with her Augustan (or neo-classical) literary sensibilities. Feminist philosopher and novelist Mary Wollstonecraft (1759–97) was absent from classrooms and textbooks until second-wave feminist literary critics successfully brought her back into our conversations in the 1970s. Formerly, when Wollstonecraft's daughter, Mary Wollstonecraft Shelley (1797–1851), was mentioned, it was as the wife of Percy Bysshe Shelley and as the author of one novel, *Frankenstein* (1818). She was rarely considered, as she is today, as a prolific and notable novelist, short story writer, biographer, and travel writer. Similarly, Dorothy Wordsworth (1771–1855) was not taken seriously as a writer in her own right. She was condescended to as her famous brother's helpmate, muse, or inspiration, rather than as the original creative force we now know her to be from her journals.

Austen, Wollstonecraft, Shelley, and Wordsworth were, and remain, the most recognized female names in British Romanticism, but hundreds of others were active. Cataloguing them and assessing their contributions in aggregate is a project that scholars are now vigorously engaged in, as Anthony Mandal's chapter on fiction shows. Still, accurately counting these writers remains a difficult task. Among other things, it presents us with a problem of categorization. What is a "Romantic" woman writer? Do we consider a woman writer to belong to the Romantic period if she died in the early 1790s, or if she didn't start publishing until the late 1830s? Do her birth and death dates matter most, or is it the dates of her published works, or might it be some other qualities of her career or writings that lead us to describe her as Romantic? Placing women writers in the traditional literary categories of eighteenth-century, Romantic, nineteenth-century, or Victorian literature is definitely not an exact science. Lives and careers are rarely so neat. Most authors from the period straddle more than one chronological category (e.g. eighteenth century and Romantic, or Romantic and Victorian), but we tend to label them as belonging to just one group, making it difficult to envision and attend to the entirety of their careers.

Compounding the problem of hazy chronology is the question of the sex of unmarked or ambiguously marked authors. A portion of authors in this period, male and female, published anonymously or used pseudonyms. Even in the case of those who identified their anonymous authorship by gender, we may never know with certainty whether their claims were truthful. A text said to have been written "by a lady" may or may not have been authored by a female. Jane Austen published her first work, *Sense and Sensibility* [1811] as "By a Lady" – an accurate claim. But *Confessions of an Old Maid* (1828), once believed to have been written by a woman, was later revealed as the work of a man, Edmund Frederick John Carrington (1804–74). Anonymous and pseudonymous mysteries aside, it is clear that this period saw the first generations of professional women writers to flourish in larger numbers. We often encounter Aphra Behn (*c.* 1640–89) being labeled as the first professional woman writer, the first to make her living by writing. But if this is an accurate claim – and stories of origins always deserve our skepticism! – then Behn made a living by authorship at a time when there were just a handful of literary women actively publishing. A century later, more women were trying than ever before to make a living by the pen. Some were financially successful, and some were not, as Jacqueline M. Labbe's chapter on the economics of authorship shows. The number of women writers making the attempt had unquestionably swelled.

Once-celebrated Romantic female authors have made a forceful return to our textbooks, syllabi, classrooms, and scholarship, among them Joanna Baillie, Anna Letitia Barbauld, Frances Burney, Maria Edgeworth, Felicia Dorothea Hemans, Letitia Elizabeth Landon (popularly known as L. E. L.),

Hannah More, Ann Radcliffe, Mary Robinson, and Charlotte Smith. All of these, and many others who remain lesser known, are discussed in the chapters of this book. Behrendt and Mandal consider them as poets and fiction writers respectively. Catherine Burroughs looks at women as contributors to British drama, and Anne K. Mellor – in focusing on Wollstonecraft, More, Mary Hays, and Anna Letitia Barbauld – looks at women's essays and political writings. Angela Wright unpacks female-authored Gothic texts, and Elizabeth A. Fay considers women travel writers, whose contributions remain less frequently examined. Crystal Lake explores the innovations in history writing and the vogue for antiquarian pursuits by women writers during the period, and Catherine Ingrassia focuses on women, particularly poets, who were actively writing about war during this tumultuous time. Caroline Franklin's essay makes sense of the ways in which mid- to late eighteenth-century feminists (particularly in what is called the Bluestocking Circle) established political and social ideas and ideals that endured into the nineteenth century. Deirdre Coleman looks at how British women writers entered a literary marketplace shaped by global concerns, including imperialism and colonialism. Julie A. Carlson helps us to understand the ways that writers functioned within familial and literary networks and relations. Jacqueline M. Labbe's chapter examines women writers' financial circumstances, particularly the financial challenges they faced in producing profitable, publishable writing, using Charlotte Smith as a focal point. My chapter investigates the role that age and aging played in a woman writer's life, career, and reception by readers and critics during this pivotal period in literary history. Fiona Price considers national identities and regional affiliations as they shaped female authors' sense of themselves, their readers, and the circulation of their writings. Finally, Jillian Heydt-Stevenson looks at sexual expression and sexualities in a range of Romantic-era women's texts.

The longstanding neglect of the fascinating, pioneering group of women writers of the Romantic period is now a thing of the past. This *Cambridge Companion* devoted to studying them is a testament to that fact. It is, at the same time, evidence that our merely recognizing their existence does not mean that our work is done. Some accomplished Romantic-era women writers already have extensive entries in the *Oxford Dictionary of National Biography*, the *Cambridge Orlando Women's Writing* database, *The Literary Encyclopedia* online, or the less reliable, ever-changing *Wikipedia*. The project of adding more trustworthy, well-documented introductory information about this group of British women writers is a noble goal. Simply put, we need more introductions, as well as full-scale biographical studies. In the case of many of these women, there is as yet no book-length work devoted to them or their writings. Or, if there is one, it was often published half a century or more ago and may have drawn on partial, outdated, or even incorrect information or assumptions. As the essays in this *Companion* show, continuing biographical neglect of this body of women writers does not arise from a lack of interesting subjects. Burroughs's description of playwright Hannah Cowley, Fay's discussion of traveler and travel writer Hester Stanhope, and Heydt-Stevenson's assessment of lesbian diarist Anne Lister will no doubt leave many wondering not if, but when, further biographies, literary studies, and even biopic films may appear.

More Romantic-era women writers and writings seem poised for revivification. Nevertheless, in our era of "big data" and more precise large-scale claims to measure impact – made possible by online databases like *British Fiction, 1800–1829* – some critics and readers may remain skeptical about whether women writers *deserve* greater notice.[4] Old debates have prompted new questions. How ought we to gauge Romantic-era women writers' noteworthy successes and high visibility in their own day? Does extensive publication point to greater significance, or might quantity here be just quantity, rather than quality or importance? (I certainly believe we will conclude that it means more than mere quantity.) In short, what makes Romantic women writers worthy of rereading and worthy of further study? The question may turn on how these women writers' first critics and readers valued them. It may turn on whether critics and readers of today do so. We may choose to read these authors because of their literary importance, their historical importance, or their social importance – or some combination of these factors. Such debates will certainly continue and are helpful in propelling our scholarship forward.

Some have questioned whether we ought to continue to study women's writings separately from men's. I believe there is value in doing so. When we look at Romantic-era women's writings in aggregate, we stand to gain new perspectives and notice different patterns of self-presentation and critical reception based on sex. These patterns shaped how women writers wrote and how all readers read. They created the conditions for what we came to call male or female – or, more properly, masculine or feminine – in literary terms. If we do not continue to study and read women writers as a group, both in comparison and contrast, we risk misconstruing the reach and implications of these gendered patterns in literary history, as well as how such patterns led the way to where we are now.

Whether today's readers think so or not, most eighteenth- and nineteenth-century readers and writers believed that the author's sex mattered. How and why it mattered – how gender shaped writing and reception – is worth knowing, particularly as it intertwined with other aspects of identity that are explored in this book, including class, race, nation, age, and sexuality. Genres were seen as having gendered dimensions, which no doubt had an impact on authors, readers, critics, and publishers, whether they acceded to or defied such stereotyping. Certain kinds of diction and rhetoric were imagined as gendered. How did writers and readers respond to female authors who either followed or flouted what was expected of them in their writings, based on their sex? This *Companion* sets out to convince you that we stand to gain vital knowledge by looking at Romantic-era women writers *en masse*.

Regardless of where your opinion ultimately falls on these questions, the asking of them – and seeking better answers to them – is crucial to creating more nuanced literary histories in generations to come. Today's students and scholars who seek to gain expertise in the Romantic era are rightly *expected* to read once-celebrated women writers' once-famous texts, just as educated readers would have done when these texts were first published. Rereading Romantic-era women writers – and reading about them – helps us to interrogate what our literary values are and were. In the course of rereading these and other female-authored texts, two centuries hence, all of us take part in the project of building and rebuilding a significant body of knowledge.

Devoney Looser

NOTES

1 A quick word about the Romantic period may be needed. When "Romantic" is defined as beginning in 1789, it marks the beginning of the French Revolution. When 1798 is used, it is to reference the publication of the "Preface to *Lyrical Ballads*," a groundbreaking piece of writing about changes in poetic form and content. When the Romantic period is said to end in 1832, it marks the passing of the first Reform Bill, and when 1837, Queen Victoria's coming to the throne. The choice of 1780 or 1830 reflects our desire to delimit periods using beginnings of decades.

2 Sandra Gilbert and Susan Gubar, eds., *The Norton Anthology of Literature by Women: The Tradition in English* (New York: W. W. Norton, 1985).

3 Sandra Gilbert and Susan Gubar, eds., *The Norton Anthology of Literature by Women: The Traditions in English*, 3rd edn. (New York: W. W. Norton, 2007).

4 Peter Garside et al., *British Fiction, 1800–1829: A Database of Production, Circulation, and Reception.* Cardiff: Cardiff University Center for Editorial and Intertextual Research, 2004–14. www.british-fiction.cf.ac.uk.

ACKNOWLEDGMENTS

Editors incur many debts. My greatest thanks are to Linda Bree, for entrusting me with a subject that means so much to us both. I am grateful for her guidance throughout the editorial process, as well as for her vision, generosity, patience, and friendship. The contributors to this volume have been a pleasure to work with. I appreciate their insights and their willingness to tackle matters large and small, over a longer period of time than they or I anticipated. Anna Bond at Cambridge University Press has been unfailingly helpful, as has Arizona State University English PhD student and research assistant Emily Zarka.

There are many whose encouragement and support makes doing scholarly work that much more meaningful. Several deserve mention for assistance during the completion of this *Companion*. The members of the 2012 National Endowment for the Humanities Seminar on Jane Austen and her Contemporaries at the University of Missouri and its coordinator Caitlin Kelly continue to energize and sustain me. Calinda Shely, Stacy Kikendall, and the organizers of the British Women Writers Conference held in Albuquerque in 2013 are inspiring as emerging scholarly leaders, as is Heather Dundas at USC. Gillian Dow and Jennie Batchelor, co-organizers of the tenth-anniversary conference, Pride and Prejudices: Women's Writing of the Long Eighteenth Century, held at Chawton House Library in July 2013, are models of brilliance, professionalism, rigor, and aplomb. My profound gratitude also goes to Paula Backscheider, Janine Barchas, Ron Broglio, Tina Brownley, Antoinette Burton, the CoMo Derby Dames, Al Coppola, Jeff Cox, Frances Dickey, Leigh Dillard, Tom DiPiero, Alistair Duckworth, Elizabeth Eger, Margaret Ezell, Emily Friedman, Catherine Ingrassia, Steve Karian, Ruth Knezevich, Crystal Lake, Mark Lussier, Teresa Mangum, Bob Markley, Nick Mason, Michelle Masse, Anne Myers, Chris Nagle, Megan Peiser, Claude Rawson, Alexander Regier, Angela Rehbein, Joe Roach, Donelle Ruwe, Peter Sabor, Clifford Siskin, Rajani Sudan, Ed White, and

Jeff Williams for their support and encouragement above and beyond the call of collegial duty. I'm grateful to Lowell Justice for being in training with me and to Carl Justice for his wish that, if I must mention him, I ought to make a joke about his behaving just well enough to allow for the book's completion. Finally, and as ever, George L. Justice helps me to redefine both the Romantic and the romantic as they evolve in our lives and work.

CHRONOLOGY

1741	Foundling Hospital established in London Hester Lynch Piozzi and Sarah Trimmer born
1742	Anna Seward born
1743	Anna Letitia Barbauld and Hannah Cowley born
1745	Hannah More born
1749	Charlotte Smith born
1750	Sophia Lee born
1752	Frances Burney born
1753	Elizabeth Inchbald and Ann Yearsley born
1754	French and Indian War begins
1755	Anne MacVicar Grant born
c. 1756	Elizabeth Hamilton born
1757	William Blake, Ellis Cornelia Knight, Harriet Lee, and Mary Robinson born
1758	Jane West born
1759	Mary Hays, Helen Maria Williams, and Mary Wollstonecraft born
1760	George III becomes King of Great Britain
1762	Jean-Jacques Rousseau, *Emile* Joanna Baillie born
1763	Seven Years War/French and Indian War ends with signing of treaty in Paris

1764   Mary Lamb, Ann Radcliffe, and Regina Maria Roche born
       Horace Walpole, *The Castle of Otranto*

1766   Eliza Fenwick born

1768   Maria Edgeworth born

1769   Amelia Opie born

1770   William Wordsworth born

1771   Dorothy Wordsworth born

1772   Lord Mansfield's ruling declares that there is no legal basis for
       slavery in England
       Samuel Taylor Coleridge and Mary Tighe born

1773   Anna Letitia Barbauld, *Poems*

1775   Start of American Revolutionary War or the American
       Rebellion
       Jane Austen born

1776   Hannah Cowley, *The Runaway*
       Declaration of Independence of American Colonies
       Jane Porter baptized

c. 1778   Sydney Owenson, Lady Morgan, likely born, although later
       claiming a birthdate of 1785

1778   Britain declares war on France
       Mary Brunton born
       Frances Burney, *Evelina*

1779   Mary Robinson acting as Perdita catches eye of 17-year-old
       Prince of Wales
       Frances Trollope born

1780   Elizabeth Inchbald makes her London stage debut
       Charlotte Cowley, *The Ladies History of England*
       Hannah Cowley, *The Belle's Stratagem*
       Sophia Lee, *The Chapter of Accidents*
       Sarah Trimmer, *An Easy Introduction to the Knowledge of
       Nature ... Adapted to the Capacities of Children*

1781   Lucy Aikin born
       Anna Seward, *Monody on Major André*

1782   Susan Ferrier born

Frances Burney, *Cecilia*
Hannah More, *Sacred Dramas*

1783   Treaty of Paris signed, ending the war and establishing the
United States of America as its own country
Sophia Lee, *The Recess, or A Tale of Other Times* (1783–5)

1784   First manned hot air balloon flight made in England
Hannah More, *The Bas Bleu, or Conversation*
Anna Seward, *Louisa: A Poetical Novel in Four Epistles*
Charlotte Smith, *Elegiac Sonnets*

1785   Clara Reeve, *The Progress of Romance*
Ann Yearsley, *Poems, on Several Occasions* (with help and
patronage of Hannah More)
Lady Caroline Lamb born

1786   Helen Maria Williams, *Poems*

1787   Mary Wollstonecraft, *Thoughts on the Education of Daughters*

c. 1787 Jane Austen begins her juvenile writings

1788   United States constitution is ratified and comes into effect
George III's first signs of mental illness appear
George Gordon, Lord Byron born
Hannah More, *Slavery, a Poem*
Hester Lynch Piozzi, *Letters to and from the Late Samuel
Johnson*
Charlotte Smith, *Emmeline*
Mary Wollstonecraft, *Mary: A Fiction*
Ann Yearsley, *A Poem on the Inhumanity of the Slave Trade*

1789   Storming of the Bastille (July 14); mob forces Louis XVI out
of Versailles and to Paris; Declaration of the Rights of Man
George Washington elected president of the United States of
America
Elizabeth Inchbald retires from acting to concentrate on
writing
William Blake, *Songs of Innocence*

1790   Ellis Cornelia Knight, *Dinarbus*
Catharine Macaulay, *Letters on Education*
Helen Maria Williams, *Letters Written in France*
Mary Wollstonecraft, *A Vindication of the Rights of Men*

1791   Anne Lister born
Elizabeth Ogilvie Benger, *The Female Geniad*
Elizabeth Inchbald, *A Simple Story*
Thomas Paine, *The Rights of Man*

1792   Overthrow of French monarchy
Proclamation against seditious writings, made by George III;
Paine charged with sedition
Percy Shelley born
Mary Wollstonecraft, *A Vindication of the Rights of Woman*
Charlotte Smith, *Desmond*

1793   Execution of Louis XVI and Marie Antoinette in France
France declares war on Britain
Felicia Hemans born
Anna Maria Porter, *Artless Tales*

1794   End of the Reign of Terror and execution of Robespierre in
France
William Blake, *Songs of Experience*
Ann Radcliffe, *The Mysteries of Udolpho*

1795   Food riots in Britain
John Keats born
Maria Edgeworth, *Letters for Literary Ladies*
Eliza Fenwick, *Secresy, or The Ruin on the Rock*
Hannah More, *Cheap Repository Tracts* (1795–8)

1796   Frances Burney, *Camilla*
Elizabeth Hamilton, *Translations of the Letters of a Hindoo
Rajah*
Mary Hays, *Memoirs of Emma Courtney*
Mary Robinson, *Hubert de Severac*
Regina Maria Roche, *Children of the Abbey*
Charlotte Smith, *Marchmont*
Jane West, *A Gossip's Story, and A Legendary Tale*
Napoleon begins his campaign in Italy; French forces attempt
to invade Ireland
Mary Lamb stabs her mother to death in a fit of insanity

1797   Coleridge walks 40 miles to meet the Barbaulds
Mary Wollstonecraft dies in childbirth; Mary Wollstonecraft
Godwin (later Mary Shelley) born
Ann Radcliffe, *The Italian*

Harriet Lee, *The Canterbury Tales* (later with Sophia Lee, 1797–9)

1798   Samuel Coleridge and William Wordsworth, *Lyrical Ballads*
Joanna Baillie, *Plays on the Passions*
Mary Hays, *Appeal to the Men of Great Britain in behalf of Women*
Mary Wollstonecraft, *Maria, or The Wrongs of Woman*, published posthumously
Rev. Richard Polwhele, *The Unsex'd Females*
Irish Rebellion; French army lands in Ireland

1800   Maria Edgeworth, *Castle Rackrent*
Elizabeth Hamilton, *Memoirs of Modern Philosophers*
Mary Robinson, *Lyrical Tales*
Wordsworth and Coleridge, expanded second edition of *Lyrical Ballads*, with Preface
Mary Robinson dies
Act of Union between Great Britain and Ireland

1801   Maria Edgeworth, *Belinda*

1802   Letitia Elizabeth Landon (L. E. L.) born
Mary Hays, *Female Biography*
Amelia Opie, *Poems*
Hester Piozzi, *Retrospection*

1803   Louisiana Purchase doubles the territory of the United States
Jane Porter, *Thaddeus of Warsaw*

1804   Napoleon crowns himself Emperor of the French
Amelia Opie, *Adeline Mowbray*

1806   Sydney Owenson (Lady Morgan), *The Wild Irish Girl*
Elizabeth Barrett Browning born
Charlotte Smith and Ann Yearsley die

1807   Anne MacVicar Grant, *Letters from the Mountains*
Charles and Mary Lamb, *Tales from Shakespear*, published under Charles's name
Charlotte Smith, *Beachy Head, Fables, and other Poems* (published posthumously)
Abolition of the slave trade in Great Britain (but not of slavery itself, which continues in the British colonies)

1808   Felicia Browne (later Hemans), *Poems*
        Hannah More, *Coelebs in Search of a Wife*

1809   Hannah Cowley and Anna Seward die

1810   Lucy Aikin, *Epistles on Women*
        Jane Porter, *The Scottish Chiefs*
        Mary Tighe and Sarah Trimmer die

1811   Regency begins, as George III is deemed mentally unfit to rule
        Jane Austen, *Sense and Sensibility*
        Anna Letitia Barbauld, *The Female Speaker*
        Mary Brunton, *Self-Control*
        Lord Byron, *Childe Harold's Pilgrimage* (first two cantos)
        Mary Tighe, *Psyche* (after private printing, 1805)

1812   War of 1812; United States declares war on the British
        Charles Dickens born

1813   Jane Austen, *Pride and Prejudice*

1814   Napoleon abdicates and is exiled
        Jane Austen, *Mansfield Park*
        Frances Burney (Madame D'Arblay), *The Wanderer*
        Sir Walter Scott, *Waverley*
        Maria Edgeworth, *Patronage*

1815   Battle of Waterloo, ending Napoleonic wars
        Louis XVII installed as King of France
        Napoleon escapes from exile, briefly returns to power, and is
        exiled again

1816   Jane Austen, *Emma*
        Lady Caroline Lamb, *Glenarvon*
        Charlotte Brontë born
        Elizabeth Hamilton dies

1817   Jane Austen dies
        Maria Edgeworth, *Harrington*
        Felicia Hemans, *Modern Greece: A Poem* (anonymously)

1818   Mary Shelley, *Frankenstein, or The Modern Prometheus* (published anonymously)
        Jane Austen, *Northanger Abbey* and *Persuasion* (posthumous publication)

Susan Ferrier, *Marriage*
Mary Brunton dies

1819   Peterloo Massacre; a large public demonstration in Manchester seeking reform in parliamentary representation results in citizens being attacked by troops
Queen Victoria born
Lord Byron, *Don Juan* (1819–24)
Felicia Hemans, *Tales and Historic Scenes in Verse*

1820   Death of George III; accession of Regent as King George IV

1821   Letitia Elizabeth Landon, *The Fate of Adelaide*
Napoleon, Elizabeth Inchbald, John Keats, and Hester Piozzi die

1822   Percy Shelley dies

1823   Second edition of *Frankenstein*, published with author's name, Mary Shelley
Ann Radcliffe dies

1824   Lord Byron, Sophia Lee, and Jane Taylor die

1825   Anna Letitia Barbauld dies

1826   Mary Shelley, *The Last Man*
First photograph taken (c. 1826–7)

1827   Helen Maria Williams dies

1828   Repeal of Test and Corporation Acts; Dissenters now able to hold government posts
Felicia Hemans, *Records of Woman with Other Poems*
Lady Caroline Lamb dies

1829   Catholic Emancipation Act ends ban on suffrage and allows the ownership of property and the holding of public office

1830   Death of George IV; his brother, King William IV, enthroned
Manchester and Liverpool Railway opened
Christina Rossetti born

1832   First Reform Act passed; extends voting rights to some previously disenfranchised men
Frances Burney (Madame D'Arblay), *Memoirs of Doctor Burney*
Frances Trollope, *Domestic Manners of the Americans*

1833   Slavery Abolition Act outlaws slavery in the British Empire

Factory Act limits children under 12 to 48-hour work week and stipulates that young children must be permitted to leave work for two hours a day to attend school
Hannah More dies

1834   Poor Law Amendment Act establishes system of workhouses
Maria Edgeworth, *Helen*

1835   Felicia Hemans dies
Dorothy Wordsworth contracts a form of dementia, adding to her *Journal* only sporadically hereafter

1837   King William IV dies; reign of his niece, Queen Victoria, begins (d. 1901)
Civil List Act establishes pensions for needy authors; Sydney Owenson, Lady Morgan becomes the first woman writer to receive an annual pension of £300
Charles Dickens, *Oliver Twist*
Ellis Cornelia Knight dies

1838   Anne MacVicar Grant and Letitia Elizabeth Landon (L. E. L.) die

1840   Anne Lister and Eliza Fenwick die
Queen Victoria marries her first cousin, Prince Albert

1843   Mary Hays dies

1845   Regina Maria Roche dies

1846   Commercial telegraph service established

1847   Emily Brontë, *Wuthering Heights*; Charlotte Brontë, *Jane Eyre*
Mary Lamb dies

1848   Maria Edgeworth, *Orlandino*

1849   Maria Edgeworth dies

1850   William Wordsworth dies
Elizabeth Barrett Browning, *Sonnets from the Portuguese*

1851   Joanna Baillie, *Dramatic and Poetical Works of Joanna Baillie*
Joanna Baillie, Harriet Lee, and Mary Shelley die

1852   Jane West dies

1853   Amelia Opie dies

1854   Susan Ferrier dies

1855   Dorothy Wordsworth dies

1859   Sydney Owenson, Lady Morgan dies

1863   Frances Trollope dies

1864   Lucy Aikin dies

I

STEPHEN C. BEHRENDT

Poetry

For much of the two centuries following the Romantic era, its poetry was defined largely, if not exclusively, by the work of male poets: William Wordsworth, Samuel Taylor Coleridge, Lord Byron, Percy Bysshe Shelley, and John Keats, with William Blake added regularly after the mid 1950s. This "canon" was variously augmented by other male poets including Robert Burns, George Crabbe, Walter Scott, Leigh Hunt, Walter Savage Landor, and Samuel Rogers, and since the 1980s especially, John Clare. Conspicuously absent was Robert Bloomfield, whose *The Farmer's Boy* (1800) enjoyed great circulation but whose laboring-class origins and life-style relegated him to the margins of a literary-historical account dominated by more patrician tastes.

The greatest exclusions from the canon, though, involved women, whose names and poetry were largely absent from discussions of Romantic poetry for most of the twentieth century. Felicia Hemans (1793–1835), the most commercially successful Romantic-era woman poet on both sides of the Atlantic, became by the twentieth century a talisman for condescending notions of women as poets of hearth, home, heart, and shallow sentimentality: her celebrated contemporary, Letitia Elizabeth Landon ("L. E. L.") (1802–38), fared little better in a literary history of Romantic-era Britain that was written almost exclusively by, for, and about men – and particularly academic men, scholars and students alike. When it appeared at all in twentieth-century anthologies, women's poetry was relegated to dismissive sub-categories such as minor poets or lyric poets that resolutely kept women poets *outside* of the canonical company, even while claiming to include them.

Exclusions of this sort went virtually unchallenged in a society (on both sides of the Atlantic) in which women did not in fact enjoy anything like equal status. Their exclusion was perpetuated through the trickle-down enculturation produced by male-dominated academic institutions where (typically male) scholars and teachers set the (also typically male) curriculum that was passed down as literary canon law to generations of aspiring teachers (many of them, ironically, female) who in turn passed it along to the students of both sexes with whose education they were charged. It might seem superfluous to retrace this history now in the twenty-first century, when women are far more prominent both in academic institutions and in the curricula devised and promulgated there, and not just in literary studies but indeed in almost all the disciplines. But history reminds us that encultur-ated errors, misperceptions, and misrepresentations become more resistant to revision the more often and widely they are repeated. The less narrowly gendered roster of Romantic-era poets to which students and scholars alike now revert is a relatively new configuration that is still evolving as revision-ist literary and cultural scholarship operates upon the growing body of pri-mary material – both original poetry and related biographical, cultural, and demographic information that now constitutes the field of Romantic poetry.

This sea change dates especially to the 1980s, when critical and schol-arly attention turned to the extraordinarily diverse body of poetry produced during the Romantic era by women. Stuart Curran's landmark 1988 essay, "Romantic Poetry: The I Altered," eloquently made the case for the recovery and reassessment of this poetry, a view that has gained wide acceptance over the past several decades, urged along by the work of many other scholars.[1] Subsequent scholarship has furnished new insights reflecting the perspec-tives not just of feminist critical theory but also of revisionist literary history. Anthologies of Romantic-era women's poetry followed, the most exten-sive edited by Paula Feldman and Duncan Wu, and the increased availability of primary texts has stimulated still further critical reassessment.[2] Broadly inclusive books by Paula Backscheider and Stephen Behrendt surveyed the recovered ground from multiple angles including genre, theme, poetic form, and cultural function in their respective efforts to remap the literary land-scape of eighteenth- and early nineteenth-century Britain.[3] Together with new scholarly editions of the work of poets such as Anna Letitia Barbauld, Charlotte Smith, Mary Robinson, Mary Tighe, Hemans, and Landon, new bibliographical and reference resources – especially electronic ones – have provided access to works that can now be consulted online. Electronic databases that aim to be comprehensive, like *Scottish Women Poets of the Romantic Period* and *Irish Women Poets of the Romantic Period*, make available many such texts while also reminding us how many more active women poets there actually were than traditional literary history has usu-ally thought it worthwhile to record or remark. The large body of poetry by women published before 1800 is available through *Eighteenth Century Collections Online* (*ECCO*), while post-1800 works are appearing on an ever-expanding array of websites and electronic archives, including *Nineteenth Century Collections Online* (*NCCO*).

Revisionist literary history once more credits Romantic-era women poets with the visibility, authority, and influence they enjoyed during the period. However grudging was the critical approval granted their writing, and however condescending or belittling was the gendered commentary to which it was subjected, then and afterward, the cultural *currency* of that writing is now acknowledged. In 1793, for example, Mary Robinson's *Three Poems* was widely celebrated in the press when it was released in July; even the *Morning Post*, which then barely noticed any literary publication, puffed the poems and published extracts, while on 27 November the Tory ministerial paper *The True Briton* called Robinson not just "the *first Poet* now living" but, more emphatically, the *first Poet*, period. Meanwhile, the Irish poet Lady Catherine Rebecca Manners was prominently advertised (and excerpted) by her publisher, John Bell, in the *Oracle, or Bell's New World*. While some of this publicity owed to aggressive marketing by enterprising publishers like Bell or partisan periodicals like *The True Briton*, some of it stemmed directly from the poetry's public appeal. Charlotte Smith's slim 1784 volume, *Elegiac Sonnets, and Other Essays*, originally published at her own expense by the staid London publisher James Dodsley, attracted so many readers (and subscribers) that it had gone through ten editions and grown to two substantial volumes by the time of her death in 1806.

Later, sales of Felicia Hemans's poems rivaled those of Byron, who first admired her poems and then petulantly denigrated her in 1820 to his publisher (and hers), John Murray, as "Mrs. Hewoman." That the successful and powerful Murray was publishing both poets testifies to both the reputation and the market value that Hemans had acquired already by 1820. And at what we usually think of as the very end of the Romantic era, there was no doubting the public fascination with the powerful and shrewd Letitia Elizabeth Landon: poet, editor, *mysterieuse*, and celebrity. Indeed, it is safe to say no English writer of the later 1820s and 1830s was better known or more popular than L. E. L. No female *or male* poet surpassed Landon in reputation or (presumably) sales – not even Byron. (Traditional literary history has routinely dubbed Byron a perennial bestseller, more so than Walter Scott and before Charles Dickens.) Like other women poets of her generation, Landon contributed repeatedly and conspicuously to the legions of literary annuals (like *The Keepsake* and *The Amulet*) and gift books that emerged in the 1820s. Unlike them, however, she went on to edit two such annuals herself, most notably *Fisher's Drawing-Room Scrap Book*, over which she exerted virtually full editorial control and for which she regularly composed poems (referred to on the title pages as "poetical illustrations") to accompany engraved pictures that she herself selected. Landon was perhaps the most powerful and influential female presence in the later Romantic literary scene; her success and fame attests to the visibility of women poets during the time and makes all the more remarkable their erasure from subsequent generations of literary and cultural history.

This is not to say that engaged and influential literary women like Landon were late arrivals on the scene. Quite the reverse. Mary Wollstonecraft, though not a poet, was a regular critical contributor to Joseph Johnson's periodical, the *Analytical Review*, beginning in the later 1780s. The anti-war poet Elizabeth Moody reviewed for the *Monthly Review* from 1789 through 1808. And Mary Robinson succeeded Robert Southey in October 1799 as poetry editor for the *Morning Post*. Moreover, Charlotte Smith's influence extended everywhere, her visibility increased by the self-dramatizing prefaces she added to her novels and to later editions of the *Elegiac Sonnets*. This influence was marked both explicitly and implicitly by women and men poets alike. The obscure but talented sonneteer Mariann Dark invoked Smith in two sonnets from her 1818 *Sonnets and Other Poems*, "On Reading Mrs. Smith's Sonnets" and "On Reviewing the Preceding." In the second sonnet Dark ruefully juxtaposes Smith's inspirational but intimidating fame with her own obscurity, hidden away in rural Britain without patrons or public: "I strike the lyre unknown! My very name / Will soon be blotted from this wretched earth."[4] Others appropriated Smith less explicitly. Martha Hanson, for example, opened her two-volume *Sonnets and Other Poems* (1809), with "To the South Downs," a lyric with unmistakable echoes of Smith's well-known sonnet of that name. Other poems by Hanson rehearse familiar Smith imagery, tropes, and language to reprise the distinctive aesthetics of melancholy with which Smith had been associated, while "Stanzas, Occasioned by the Death of Mrs. Charlotte Smith," the long poem that opens Hanson's second volume, recounts the soothing but inspiring effects of Smith's poems on Hanson's own youth.[5] Like other Romantic-era women poets, Hanson treats a female predecessor as an exemplary role model both of achievements amid adversity and of consoling presence for the later poet whose accomplishments (and reputation) fail to match Smith's. Poems like these underscore the poetic sisterhood that is commemorated repeatedly among the era's women poets.

Smith's influence is apparent in the poems of both female and male contemporaries and successors, from Helen Maria Williams, Anne Bannerman, and Amelia Opie among the women to Sir Samuel Egerton Brydges, James Lacey, and John Taylor among the men. There are thematic echoes, of course, but also stylistic and generic similarities including an emphasis upon the sonnet, Smith's signature poetic form. William Wordsworth referred to her in 1833 as "a lady to whom English verse is under greater obligations than are likely to be either acknowledged or remembered," but twenty-five years earlier Thomas Gent had already included a memorial sonnet in the 1808 edition of his *Poetic Sketches*.[6] There Gent assures Smith's audience (and his own) that the "thoughtless world" of 1808 that fails to acknowledge her greatness will give way in time to a more appreciative one. This sense of merit denied – or at least deferred – recurs in early anthologies like the Reverend Alexander Dyce's 1825 *Specimens of British Poetesses*, where Smith is represented by nine pages of poems and where Dyce observes that as a poet Smith "has been excelled by few of her countrywomen."[7]

Smith offers a conspicuous example of how women poets (and their works) functioned in often elaborate communities of readers, sister poets and women generally, whether authors or not. In fact, this sense of community is one of the rhetorical hallmarks of Romantic-era women poets, traceable alike in their published poems and their private letters and journals. More so than their male contemporaries, and perhaps because they were so acutely aware of their ambivalent cultural status as publishing *women* poets, women expressed their sense of a distinct (and distinctive) sisterhood even as they composed and published poems that placed them within (and therefore in implicit competition with) historically masculinist British poetic genres and their traditions and conventions. Backscheider details the attraction for eighteenth-century women poets of genres like the verse epistle, the elegy, and especially the sonnet, where the implied competition with male poets was understood to be less aggressive, and these genres remained of interest to their Romantic-era successors, as Behrendt also demonstrates. But their poetry explored new directions, new genres, including the long narrative poem and a variety of poems that are conspicuously anti-war in nature.

As already indicated, the sonnet enjoyed particular favor among women poets, but along with the inherent community (both literary and gender-focused) that the shared experience of sonnet writing fostered came a measure of territoriality. Anna Seward's notorious antipathy to Charlotte Smith, and to Smith's sonnets in particular, testifies to how much some authors felt was at stake in publishing their work. Seward considered Smith's sonnets derivative in subject and language and deficient in execution, faulting her for easy sentimentality on the one hand and failure to adhere to the ostensible structural conventions of the legitimate sonnet form on the other. Seward's objections highlight the dilemma that confronted many women poets who chose poetic forms and conventions whose exemplars were almost exclusively male.

Indeed, the issue of what was – and was not – the proper subject matter, authorial attitude, and generic choices provided fodder for both the champions (of both sexes) of women poets and their denigrators. Among the latter, reactionary critics like T. J. Mathias and the Rev. Richard Polwhele attempted in print to impose or reinforce boundaries upon women's literary production that were invariably tied to gendered notions of morality and propriety. Polwhele, for instance, branded socially or politically activist poets like Barbauld, Smith, and Robinson as "Unsex'd Females," as he called them in 1798 in his hostile poem *The Unsex'd Females*. Women poets' apparent debarment from both political activism and sophisticated intellectual and philosophical discourse generally was a critical commonplace. Some two decades after Polwhele's blast, Hemans published *Modern Greece: A Poem* (1817) without her name. The reviewer for the *British Review* wrote in January 1820, "we conceived it to be the production of an academical, and certainly not a female, pen."[8] The reviewer singles out for special praise the poem's "elaborate finish" (p. 299). Such finish, the reviewer declared, was conspicuously absent from the poetry of most women because "the mind of women is not usually favourable to that deep-toned emotion which constitutes the very essence of the higher kinds of poetry" (p. 300). Indeed, the poem's "classical" texture had already misled the *Eclectic Review*'s critic in December 1818 to call *Modern Greece* "the production of a man [*sic*] of genuine talent and feeling," ironically underscoring the routine association of "classical" art with maleness.[9]

Relatively undeterred by such persistent critical resistance and bias, women poets continued to expand both their own numbers and the range of forms and subjects about which they wrote. Between 1770 and 1835, according to the bibliography compiled by J. R. de J. Jackson, no fewer than 400 women were actually *publishing* their poetry in England proper.[10] When the number is adjusted to include Scotland and Ireland, it rises to well over 500. These numbers include everything poetic, of course, including hymns and devotional verse, verse for children (like the collections by Ann and Jane Taylor that saw literally dozens of editions during the period), and translations (many women, including Smith, began their literary careers as translators). But the range of subjects, themes, and forms expanded exponentially as the period progressed, in part because innovations and improvements in printing and publishing (or, more properly, bookselling) made it possible to produce ever greater numbers of books at ever lower cost to publisher and purchaser alike, which in turn generated ever larger and more diverse readerships.

Given war's omnipresence in Europe for the quarter century plus that culminated in 1815 at Waterloo, it is little surprise that women poets had much to say about war, warmaking, and their effects, toward which their culture expected women to adopt a sentimental, subjective approach. While society expected women to participate in Britain's defense, their role was customarily defined along traditional gendered lines as wife, mother, sister, or nurse and caretaker. The discourse for which their voices were culturally sanctioned was therefore that of loyal civic support for militarism and its male protagonists. They were expected to document the pathos of war for a beleaguered nation and to celebrate triumphant British militarism with nationalistic pride. Some did just that: Maria de Fleury (*British Liberty Established*, 1790), Barbara Hoole ("Verses on the Threatened Invasion, Written in July, 1803" [1805]), and Isabella Lickbarrow ("Invocation to Peace" [1814]) proclaimed England's divinely sanctioned special status as "favour'd Queen of Isles, / Long kindly foster'd by thy Maker's hand" and confidently assured war-weary citizens of the cultural and economic rewards of Britain's inevitable victory, when "arts and manufactures would revive, / And happy Industry rejoice again; / [and] friendly Commerce would unfurl her sails."[11] Other poets celebrated the lives, triumphs, and deaths of military heroes like Admiral Nelson (killed at Trafalgar in 1805) and Sir John Moore (fallen in Spain at Corunna in 1809).

Not surprisingly, war touched many women poets personally. The longest poem in Felicia Hemans's *The Domestic Affections, and Other Poems* (1812), for example, is "War and Peace – A Poem, Written at the age of Fifteen." Painfully immature, it nevertheless captures the war-weary nation's distress nearly twenty years into the seemingly endless conflict with France that was draining the national treasury of both gold and the blood of the nation's young men. The poem's nationalistic militarism is characteristic of many poems of the period: "Then wave, oh, Albion! wave thy sword again, / Call thy brave champions to the battle-plain!"[12] Hemans recites the familiar roster of fallen heroes like Nelson and Moore whose losses the nation (figured in the emblematic weeping Britannia) mourns. But she focuses on the survivors of the fallen, particularly the mothers, wives, sisters, and daughters of the less celebrated soldiers and sailors whose loss is made doubly terrible by the resulting destitution during an era that offered little or no social safety net for such survivors beyond an often meager parish charity. Hemans had two brothers serving in the Peninsular War (*The Domestic Affections* contains poems to both), and so her poetic anxiety mirrored a personal anxiety that would have resonated with her female readers in particular.

Jane Alice Sargant, too, was from a military family; her brother, Sir Henry (Harry) Smith, had risen from yeoman cavalryman in 1804 to lieutenant colonel of the Ninety-fifth Regiment Riflemen. Her military-family background informs many of the poems in her *Sonnets and Other Poems* (1817), whose subscribers included numerous military men, including some explicitly identified with the Rifle Brigade. Not surprisingly, then, many of

Sargant's poems involve sabre-rattling appeals to national solidarity in the face of war's rigors. Some, however, like "The Disbanded Soldier's Lament," disquietingly explore the difficult circumstances faced by returning veterans amid the economic depression and the socio-political volatility that characterized post-Waterloo Britain.

Women poets' overtly nationalistic effusions were warmly welcomed by the critical establishment no less than by the political one. Pro-war poetry by women reinforced the values and expectations of contemporary male culture by casting women in supportive roles, whether as spouses or kin, or as propagandists and publicists for British military enterprise generally. Some women poets, though, explicitly advocated redress of the widespread social distress that war produces, composing tales of war widows, bereft mothers and sisters, and mourning daughters that drew upon the later eighteenth-century vein of elegiac verse that had become a sub-specialty of women poets. Amelia Opie's 1802 *Poems* contains a particularly poignant poem, "Lines Written at Norwich on the First News of the Peace" (the short-lived peace produced in 1802–3 by the Treaty of Amiens). Among the celebrating citizens of Norwich, where Opie was born, appears one "poor mourner" whose emotional suffering is embodied in her "shrunk form" and who ruefully congratulates her townsfolk on the real or impending restoration of their soldiers and sailors before concluding with her frantic declaration that "Alas! Peace comes for me too late, ... / For my brave boy in Egypt died!"[13] Especially for women, the poetic evidence suggests, the restoration of others' loved ones is salt to the wounds of those whose loved ones have died. Women's poetry concerning war and its effects, therefore, exhibits a troubling mixture of pain and celebration, an ambivalence that voices the broader cultural ambivalence of the nation more tellingly than the writing of these poets' male contemporaries, including even those who likewise opposed war.

Particularly when writing about war and its victims, women poets employed straightforward forms (like the ballad stanza) and quotidian language familiar to readers from religious hymns, didactic verse, and popular songs. Poems in this idiom appeared regularly in the periodical press and represented a populist poetics unlike the staid, stiff formality of the classical-leaning commemorative poems that typically marked major public events, happy or otherwise. Long accustomed to the unaffected discourse of friendship, candor, and sincerity that characterized personal correspondence (the genre historically ceded to women as their literary domain), poets infused this discursive model with sentimentality and pathos especially well suited to tales of war's victims. Shrewdly appropriating the social and linguistic conventions of the masculinist majority culture to engage and subvert that culture and its assumptions, they generated community not only with one another (as poets and writers) but also with British women generally, whose experiences they related in affectingly familiar ways. Inevitably, this inscribed network of shared experience empowered authors and readers alike, for in articulating the ideas and emotions of the women about whom (and to whom) they wrote their poems they reminded their readers of the community (often a community of suffering) that they shared and whose individual, private circumstances might otherwise remain largely invisible to the broader public community.

Women's more overtly oppositional voices and poems often incurred the conservative moral and political establishment's wrath, as noted earlier. A particularly notable example was the sensation surrounding the publication of Anna Letitia Barbauld's *Eighteen Hundred and Eleven* (1812). Barbauld was by 1812 a respected elder poet, critic, and educator who had published widely in verse and prose for adults and younger readers alike and who had produced critical editions of British poets and essayists in addition to a fifty-volume edition of novelists. A Dissenter who had argued in print against slavery, religious intolerance, and war, she was admired by authors as diverse as Frances Burney, Hannah More, and William Wordsworth (despite his reservations about her Dissenter connections). But *Eighteen Hundred and Eleven*, which predicts Britain's demise as a world power and its replacement by the New World (figured both as the young American nation and the emerging republics of South America) was deemed shockingly "unfilial" in its post-imperial view of Britain. Publishing the poem when the outcome of the Napoleonic Wars remained undecided and when Britain was again at war with its former colonies struck many of Barbauld's contemporaries as treacherous, as the brutal response in the periodical press illustrates. That the poem elicited such widespread response from all quarters – including poetic rejoinders like Anne MacVicar Grant's reactionary *Eighteen Hundred and Thirteen* (1814) – indicates how widely women's poetry was being read, taken seriously, and debated publicly – in person and in print – by the Regency period.

Barbauld composed *Eighteen Hundred and Eleven* in heroic couplets, the verse form still considered the appropriate vehicle for elevated discourse on momentous subjects. Other women poets employed the heroic couplet for comparable encomiastic or hortatory purposes. Lucy Aikin (Barbauld's niece), for example, chose heroic couplets for her remarkable *Epistles on Women, Exemplifying Their Character and Condition in Various Ages and Nations* (1810). Taking as its point of departure Alexander Pope's slighting portrayal of women in his "Epistle to a Lady" (the second of his *Moral Essays*), Aikin's poem undertakes an epic survey of women from Eve through the present, documenting women's historical oppression while affirming their cultural centrality not in traditional gendered terms but rather as full intellectual, emotional, and physical partners – even equals – to their male counterparts. Some two decades earlier the Dublin Quaker Mary Birkett had likewise employed heroic couplets for her long two-part *Poem on the African Slave Trade* (1792), which was, as its title page explicitly announces, addressed to her own sex and which followed by a year Barbauld's shorter heroic-couplet "Epistle to William Wilberforce, Esq. On the Rejection of the Bill for Abolishing the Slave Trade" (1791).

Women's involvement in the abolitionist debate furnished them with opportunities to direct politically inflected interventionist poetry toward a public that was inclined (or simply chose) to hear in their voices the humanitarian impulses traditionally associated with women's gendered socio-political role. Even the anger that suffuses Hannah More's 1788 *Slavery, A Poem* (also cast in heroic couplets) is couched in rhetoric calculated to invoke woman's "natural" (nurturant) feelings in the oppressed slaves' cause. As these three poems (and others like them) demonstrate, though, that rhetoric could also serve the cause of women, caught up as they were in a historically oppressive social structure to which the slaves' plight furnished a clear analogy. This point was not lost on the conservative establishment (which included both men and women), and it undoubtedly contributed to the suspicion among that establishment about women's increasing involvement in the 1790s in other revisionist social, political, and intellectual causes. It is important to remember today that much of the reactionary resistance to the increasingly apparent activism informing women's public discourse – including the poems they published – stemmed from a systemic fear of the social and political power toward which their activity *as writers* seemed to many of their contemporaries inexorably to be leading them.

But women also used the heroic couplet for long narratives. In 1822, Eleanor Anne Porden, who specialized in long, learned, and weighty tales, used them for her multi-volume *Cœur de Lion, or The Third Crusade: A Poem, in Sixteen Books.* They were also the vehicle of choice for national tales in verse like the title poem in Anne MacVicar Grant's *The Highlanders, and Other Poems* (1808), which offered an intimate and sympathetic view of a populace and way of life unfamiliar to English readers, much as poems by Sydney Owenson (later Lady Morgan) and Thomas Moore did for Ireland. Catherine Luby, too, employed heroic couplets in *The Spirit of the Lakes, or Mucruss Abbey* (1822), an Irish Gothic romance set among the medieval ruins of County Kerry that is as much a descriptive poem as a narrative one and that reveals the unmistakable influence of Ann Radcliffe's immensely successful novels.

Indeed, the long narrative tale in verse emerged after 1800 as a favorite among women poets, perhaps because it seemed more flexible and less cumbersome than the novel. Moreover, poetry presumed a more refined and sophisticated readership (of both sexes) than that which was widely associated with the supposedly less reputable novel, a readership capable of appreciating verse's greater verbal artistry. Luby's *Spirit of the Lakes* reflects this deliberate refinement in its subtle texturing of descriptive and narrative details, and in the variations it works upon familiar conventions of the Gothic tale. Its structure is less rigorously uniform than that of the conventional heroic-couplet poem, though. Each of the three cantos is composed of separately numbered subsections of varying length, lending the narrative an almost respiratory nature and affording Luby the relative narratorial leisure to build slowly to the unhappy climax that situates her poem within the cynical, proto-Byronic world of post-Waterloo disenchantment. Hannah Maria Bourke's *O'Donoghue, Prince of Killarney* (1830), another long verse narrative (in seven cantos), also numbers its cantos' subsections, as Luby had done, but substitutes an octometric line for the heroic couplet's pentameters. Unlike Luby, whose genuine affection for both her tale and the nation in which it is set is immediately evident, Bourke adopts a detached antiquarian attitude toward her subject and story that has the curious effect of pushing the reader *away* from emphatic engagement with the tale.

Quite the reverse is the case with the majority of long verse narratives, which often employ familiar paradigms of social or cultural experience to engage their readers, and which demonstrate great variety in their versification and verse forms, often juxtaposing passages of strict exposition with others of intense lyricism or deliberately heightened pathos. In *Ellen Fitzarthur: A Metrical Tale* (1820), Caroline Bowles Southey addressed the familiar plight of the impulsive woman who runs off with a soldier, against the will of her parent (typically, as here, an elderly widower), only to find herself abandoned, impoverished, and shunned by polite society. *Ellen Fitzarthur* is a poetic variation on the model furnished by Amelia Opie's popular and widely influential novel *The Father and Daughter* (1801) and revisited in other novels of the period, including Jane Austen's *Pride and Prejudice* (1813), where it is reprised in the persons of Lydia Bennet and George Wickham. Verse narratives like *Ellen Fitzarthur*, their melodrama and predictable moral agendas notwithstanding, served women writers and readers in ways that scholarship has only recently begun to appreciate. These tales resonated with countless women who had been victimized by the era's masculinist culture, which frequently stripped them not just of legal and civil status but also of property, privacy, and personhood. Writing (and publishing and reading) tales of this sort validated the existence of an extensive female community to whom the experiences recounted in the tales were familiar in their general outlines and often in their particular details, in the process permitting female readers to transcend, if only imaginatively, the narrow boundaries of their individual personal circumstances. Not always the sentimental escapist indulgences for which they are occasionally mistaken, many of these verse narratives are in fact gestures in print that aimed at raising a collective consciousness of shared experience, shared aspiration, and shared community.

Community is constructed in many ways, of course. One is physical and immediate, involving individuals who are personally acquainted. Collections often contain numerous poems to or about friends and acquaintances, many of them named either explicitly or with elided identifying letters. These naming protocols invite writer, reader, and subject into a shared community mediated on the printed page, as when the Irish nationalist poet Henrietta Battier shared with readers of *The Protected Fugitives* (1791) her verse correspondence with her friend Eliza Ryan.

Another sort of community revolves around correspondence: individuals who are physically separated inscribe a network through letters and journals that record both their own one-on-one relationships and the extended communities that radiate from each writerly center. The correspondence of literary friends like Barbara Hofland and Mary Russell Mitford documents each writer's extensive social contacts and provides a site for sharing these connections with their correspondents. Melesina Trench, who wrote both verse and socially committed prose during the 1810s but actually *published* little of it in the usual sense, nevertheless shared that writing. She apparently had numerous works printed but kept many if not most copies for private distribution to friends and acquaintances, often inserting corrections, emendations, and explanatory notes (not always the same from copy to copy). On the title pages of many of these copies, Trench wrote "not published." This practice suggests an intimacy that recalls the Bluestocking Circle of the previous century, while the variations among copies and their annotations likewise suggest the spontaneity of gift-giving, rather than publishing in the usual sense. For Trench, as for many of her female contemporaries, poetry functioned not just as personal expression but also as broader social communication and identity. Trench corresponded extensively with other women writers, especially the reclusive Irish Quaker Mary Leadbeater, who had witnessed the slaughter of Irish insurgents at Ballitore in 1798 and who, in one of her *Poems* (1808), laments that after the bloody suppression of the Irish Rising of 1798, the Muses had dropped their lyres and fled the grisly scene. Ironically, she commemorates this abandonment of poetry *in a poem*, a rhetorical gesture that mirrors many comparable gestures of self-erasure that women poets make *in poems that they then publish*, as Mariann Dark does in the sonnet mentioned earlier.

Indeed, many Romantic-era women's poems exhibit their authors' awareness of their ambivalent and often contested position in the literary and cultural scene. Simultaneously present and absent, technically included but culturally excluded, women inscribed an affiliation of shared experience through poems to which they assumed that other women would be especially responsive, like their many intensely personal elegiac poems. War and the dawn of modern alienation yielded casualties at all levels of society. They were in turn commemorated by countless elegies published both in the daily or periodical press and (often subsequently) in books. Elegies by Romantic-era women poets tended generally to memorialize not the heroic figures of the public arena but rather the beloved members of the private circle. Encomiums on the dead may elicit a generalized pathos, but a more moving *and intimate* pathos arises from elegies on deaths within the domestic circle.

A third sort of community takes the more immediately public form of print discourse, including both individually authored books intended for public sale and, especially after 1820, literary annuals, gift books, and the like in whose pages women and men both were published. Because these books were aimed principally at an emerging market of middle-class women readers, many of the women's poems published in annuals like the *Forget Me Not*, *The Amulet*, and *Fisher's Drawing-Room Scrap Book* tended toward the sentimental and the domestic associated with the increasingly pejorative term "poetess" that has in recent years been contested. But the presence of women and men in the same company *in print* reinforced the growing public awareness of their shared status as writers. Indeed, while we may debate whether to call William Wordsworth the first to define being a poet as a *profession*, there is no disputing the extent to which the Romantic era witnessed the professionalization of writing, including the writing of poetry. The growing presence, visibility, and cultural influence of women poets is a testament to their enduring contribution to the democratization of the arts during the era. The presence of male and female poets together in the profitable annual and gift books graphically documents the dissolution of gendered cultural practices that had historically enforced separate spheres for them.

Publication in annuals and gift books could prove quite profitable, making them attractive venues for writers of both sexes, while their great press runs ensured that women's poetry became increasingly visible to their emerging bourgeois readerships. Interestingly, Hemans's tribute to Mary Tighe,

"The Grave of a Poetess" (1827–8), semantically mediates the personal role of one single woman writer and the public persona of "a poetess," since the seemingly innocent article – "a" – identifies not *the* poetess but rather *a* presumably representative poetess who stands (or stands in) for all. In fact, Hemans's poem balances the life of the unseen poetess between Tighe's actual public life as writer and her actual private life as woman. Like Landon later in her "Stanzas on the Death of Mrs. Hemans" (1835), Hemans constructs a sort of balance sheet that reckons the woman poet's accomplishments in the public sphere against what those achievements have cost her in the private one. Far more than their male counterparts, women poets were scrutinized in these terms by both women and men alike, for although society was becoming more enlightened about literary production, the emerging Victorian cultural values nevertheless reinforced earlier periods' conceptions of the appropriate venues and vehicles for each sex's literary efforts. Old ideas, old ways, have always died hard.

NOTES

1 Stuart Curran, "Romantic Poetry: The I Altered," in *Romanticism and Feminism*, ed. Anne K. Mellor (Bloomington: Indiana University Press, 1988), pp. 185–207.

2 Paula R. Feldman, ed., *British Women Poets of the Romantic Era: An Anthology* (Baltimore: Johns Hopkins University Press, 1997); Duncan Wu, ed., *Romantic Women Poets: An Anthology* (Oxford: Blackwell, 1997).

3 Paula R. Backscheider, *Eighteenth-Century Women Poets and their Poetry: Inventing Agency, Inventing Genre* (Baltimore: Johns Hopkins University Press, 2005); Stephen C. Behrendt, *British Women Poets and the Romantic Writing Community* (Baltimore: Johns Hopkins University Press, 2009).

4 Mariann Dark, *Sonnets and Other Poems* (London: S. Curtis, 1818), p. 42.

5 Martha Hanson, *Sonnets and Other Poems* (London: J. Mawman, 1809), Vol. II, pp. 1–13.

6 William Wordsworth, *The Poetical Works of William Wordsworth*, ed. E. De Selincourt and Helen Darbishire, 5 vols. (Oxford: Clarendon Press, 1947), Vol. IV, p. 403 n.

7 Rev. Alexander Dyce, *Specimens of British Poetesses: Selected and Chronologically Arranged by the Rev. Alexander Dyce* (London: T. Rodd and S. Prowett, 1825), p. 254.

8 Review of *Modern Greece* by Felicia Hemans, *British Review* 15 (January 1820); *Eclectic Review*, n. s. 10 (December 1818), p. 299. Subsequent references cited parenthetically in the text.

9 Review of *Modern Greece* by Felicia Hemans, *Eclectic Review*, n. s. 6 (December 1818), p. 598.

10 J. R. de J. Jackson, *Romantic Poetry by Women: A Bibliography 1770–1835* (Oxford: Clarendon Press, 1993).

11 Isabella Lickbarrow, *Poetical Effusions* [1814] (Oxford: Woodstock Books, 1994), p. 20.
12 Felicia Dorothea Browne [Hemans], *The Domestic Affections, and Other Poems* (London: T. Cadell and W. Davies, 1812), p. 95.
13 Amelia Opie, *Poems* (London: Longman, Hurst, Rees, and Orme, 1802), p. 74.

2

ANTHONY MANDAL

Fiction

Until relatively recently, the significance of women's fiction in the Romantic era has been sorely neglected by literary historians. Scholarship typically defined the period's literature by its poetical outputs – namely those of the Big Six (Blake, Wordsworth, Coleridge, Byron, Shelley, Keats). What scant attention was paid to the novel characterized it as the "Age of Austen and Scott," and it was not until the later 1970s that other names began to receive due attention: Frances Burney, Maria Edgeworth, Sydney Owenson (Lady Morgan), all of whom published bestsellers in their lifetimes. A defining moment in this reconstitution of women's writing was Marilyn Butler's *Jane Austen and the War of Ideas* (1975), which signaled the commencement of a sustained effort to correct what had been a distorted view of Romantic literary output.[1] Butler's efforts have been extended over the succeeding decades in monographs and edited collections, which continue to excavate the complex relationships between women writers and the literary marketplace.

This critical labor has been augmented in the past fifteen years by scholarship that offers a more complete bibliographical record of the production of fiction. Landmark reference works such as the third edition of the *Cambridge Bibliography of English Literature* (1999) record the extent to which women participated in the literary marketplace. Subscription-based digital archives like Gale's *Eighteenth* and *Nineteenth Century Collections Online* (*ECCO/NCCO*), alongside open-access collections like *Google Books* and the *Internet Archive*, now enable scholars to read virtually all the novels published during the Romantic period.[2] Without a doubt, however, the single most significant bibliographical act of recuperation is *The English Novel, 1770–1829* (2000), edited by Garside, Raven, and Schöwerling. Based on the identification of some 3,677 titles, approximately 90 percent of which have been examined at first hand, *The English Novel* offers both a general overview of fiction production during the period (through its comprehensive introductions, tables, charts, and indexes) and granular detail about each title (identifying provenance and authorship, recording title pages and imprints, supplying location information, and tracing the afterlives of works through further editions and translations).[3] As a result, scholars now have a robust empirical basis from which to challenge or confirm long-held ideas about the Romantic novel market.

Building on these moments of recovery, this chapter explores the dynamics of Romantic women's fiction. My discussion concentrates on the Romantic novel, typically in the form of newly published "triple-deckers" (that is, one novel published in three volumes) aimed at a polite audience made up of the aristocracy, gentry, and middling classes. Of course, fiction circulated in myriad other forms (chapbooks and bluebooks, magazine publications, increasingly cheap reprints, and, later on, gift books), which shared a symbiotic relationship with the multi-volume novel. What remains most remarkable about this period, however, is the rapid expansion of, and appetite for, new novel-length works published in multiple volumes.

The literary marketplace

The emergence of women's fiction during the Romantic period resulted from the convergence of three factors: legal changes that fundamentally reshaped the commercial principles of the publishing market; technological developments that made the production of fiction increasingly affordable for publishers; and an expanding and receptive female readership, which in turn generated a burgeoning cohort of women writers. Without the confluence of these legal, technological, and social transformations, the economic conditions that stimulated the expansion of Romantic fiction would not have existed.

The convoluted legislation regarding copyright of the eighteenth century was perhaps the single most significant factor in transforming the Romantic literary marketplace. Since its consolidation in the sixteenth century, publishing in Britain had been mainly restricted to a small cartel of London-based booksellers, primarily achieved by the continuing protection of perpetual copyright. This resulted in a conservative literary marketplace, in which booksellers relied on strictly regulated reprints of popular works, leaving little impetus to innovate through speculation on untested writers, while curtailing the efforts of newer publishers more willing to take such risks. During the middle of the eighteenth century, the London hegemony was challenged by a number of Scottish booksellers, who began publishing unauthorized reprints of English titles. As a result of their distinct traditions, the republication of English works in Scotland was perfectly legal, as English copyright legislation had no authority north of the border. However, what *was* illegal was traversal of these cheaper Scottish reprints into the English marketplace, which undermined sales of author-ized originals.

The English trade responded with litigation, and a series of landmark cases inexorably signaled the end of the old prerogatives – in particular *Donaldson v. Becket*, a case taken by the London-based Thomas Becket to prevent the Donaldsons of Edinburgh from reprinting James Thomson's *The Seasons* in 1771. The case reached the House of Lords by 1774, in which perpetual copyright was deemed against the public interest. The term was now limited to a maximum period of twenty-eight years, after which a text would enter the public domain. John Feather notes: "The London booksell-ers ... had been comprehensively challenged by the Scottish entrepreneurs. It was their response to that challenge which saw the emergence of the pub-lisher as the dominant figure in the trade of printed books in Britain."[4] Once their statutory term expired, texts could be republished by anyone, which led to the inception of cheap and vibrant reprint series. As they could no longer depend on their existing copyrights, the metropolitan firms had little choice but to adopt the ethos of the free market by seeking out new works to maintain their revenues:

> After 1774 a huge, previously suppressed, demand for reading was met by a huge surge in the supply of books, and was caught up in a virtuous cycle of growth ... The decision of 1774 transferred, through lower prices, a huge quantum of purchasing power from book producers to book buyers.[5]

From *book producers* to *book buyers*: as the century drew to its close, the literary marketplace was driven increasingly by the demands of readers, both for new, exciting publications and for cheap reprints of established classics. This was abetted in no small measure by the expansion of the pro-vincial publishing trade, which itself became part of a larger network linked to the metropolitan nexus, thus ensuring the dissemination of print to read-ers in both town and country.

Despite the stimulation given to the trade, books remained expen-sive items to produce, as far as both materials and labor were concerned. Fiction publication in particular was a speculative enterprise, given that novels were lengthy items that tended to be read a few times at best. Of all the material costs of producing a book, the most basic – paper – was also the most expensive, constituting between half and two thirds, as it was typically handmade from linen rags imported mainly from Europe. Printing processes themselves had changed little since the invention of the moveable-type printing press by Gutenberg in the 1450s, with printers rely-ing on wooden hand presses to transfer an impression of inked type onto the page. The invention of the iron press by the Earl of Stanhope around

1800 accelerated the process of printing and improved clarity of text, but the setting, or "compositing," of type remained a time-consuming operation that required a highly skilled workforce. Owing to such costs, typical print runs for novels averaged around 500–750 copies per edition, perhaps 1,000–1,500 for established authors. If a work's popularity required further editions, the text would have to be set from scratch once again. Thus, printing a novel was time-consuming labor: it might take two pressmen working on a triple-decker 960 pages long two months to set and run off around 1,000 copies.[6] Consequently, novels were expensive products to purchase, something reflected by their price, which during the Regency period (1811–20) was approximately 17s. 6d. (about half a week's wages for a skilled workman). Despite their costliness, few novels enjoyed longevity in a literary marketplace that demanded volume and variety of output. Less than a third of new fictions published during the 1800s appeared in further editions; instead, the majority were ephemeral, formulaic works intended to pass through readers' hands in short shrift.

Given the expenses attached to making and purchasing novels, the primary market lay not with individual consumers but the proprietors of circulating libraries – one of the major success stories of the Romantic era. Circulating libraries allowed patrons who paid a membership fee to borrow a certain number of books over a set period of time. Owing to their bulk, but moreover to assist in distributing a small number of copies to a large readership, novels were generally published in multiple volumes – most often in the form of the "triple-decker," a term that became synonymous with "novel." In this way, a library proprietor could purchase a few copies of a popular novel, but loan out each volume to individual patrons, thus maximizing the profitability of the book. Anecdotal information cited by Cheryl Turner suggests that around 40 percent of a print run might be bought by the library market.[7] Owners of circulating libraries could make a significant income from the demand for the latest works, as attested to by the immense fortunes of the Noble brothers, William Lane's Minerva Library, and Henry Colburn's English and Foreign Circulating Library.

The production of fiction

The fortunes of circulating libraries and novels were inextricably linked, often to the detriment of both: the former decried as sites of inappropriate class and gender mixing, of improper flirtations and illicit seductions; the latter vilified as purveying bad morals and unrealistic romances that would corrupt their young (female) readers. According to the conservative propagandist Hannah More, the novel was "one of the most universal as well as most pernicious sources of corruption among us."[8] More's comments typify the dominant view of novels as a degrading, even illicit, form of literary enterprise, with one reviewer likening them to "buzzing insects which [have] received a temporary life from the warmth of the circulating library," and others bewailing, "when will the dreary prospect be enlivened again by a work of real genius?"[9] Even Frances Burney, whose fortunes were heavily imbricated with the vagaries of novel publishing, prevaricated when working on her third novel, *Camilla*, in June 1795: "I own I do not like calling [*Camilla*] a *Novel*: it gives so simply the notion of a mere love story, that I recoil a little from it. I mean it to be *sketches of Characters & morals, put in action*, not a Romance."[10] Similarly, Charlotte Smith often prefaced her novels with addresses to the reader that stressed the strain and anxiety she felt in professing herself a novelist, which has led Jennie Batchelor to speak of "the tangled web of contradictions and possibilities conjured for the professional woman writer by the question of woman's work."[11]

One of Jane Austen's earliest extant letters, dating from 1798, facetiously reflects on how the troubled status of the novel could even confound library proprietors themselves:

> As an inducement to subscribe Mrs Martin tells us that her Collection is not to consist only of Novels, but of every kind of Literature &c &c – She might have spared this pretension to *our* family, who are great Novel-readers & not ashamed of being so; – but it was necessary I suppose to the self-consequence of half her Subscribers.[12]

Austen's observations encapsulate that *other* view of fiction – as something that could be enjoyed openly and without shame – a perspective she would more trenchantly address through her defense of the novel in the fifth chapter of *Northanger Abbey* (1818). But even conservative writers, like the Presbyterian Mary Brunton, attempted to ameliorate the seeming conflict between rectitude and fiction, enquiring in 1814:

> Why should an epic or a tragedy be supposed to hold such an exalted place in composition, while a novel is almost a nickname for a book? Does not a novel admit of as noble sentiments – as lively description – as natural character – as perfect unity of action – and a moral as irresistible as either of them?[13]

A complex response to the novel emerges, then, from the mouths of novelists themselves, who ambivalently construct oppositions between "popular" fictions on the one hand and "improving" tales on the other.

Despite such mixed attitudes toward and the high costs of fiction, the market for new titles expanded quickly and responsively during the Romantic era, as illustrated in Figure 1, which charts the output of 3,378 new novels published between 1780 and 1829. An exponential leap in production occurs in the imprint year 1788, rising from fifty-one new titles in 1787 to eighty, the result of a number of factors: an expanding market for female authors and readers; increasing translations of continental works (which represented 15 percent of the new novels published during the 1790s and 1800s); and the proliferation of circulating libraries and the expansion of newly formed publishing concerns stimulated by the 1774 ruling. The bulk of fiction published during the 1780s and 1790s consisted of sentimental novels of various kinds, which shared a number of motifs: the troubled plight of youthful figures, often victimized young women, persecuted by an uncaring world, separated from their loved ones, threatened with (and sometimes suffering) death. The longest-lived comprised epistolary works that drew on patterns established by Richardson and Sterne; from the 1790s onwards, however, novels-in-letters had declined irrevocably in popular taste, becoming perceived as outmoded and clumsy. Late-century sentimental fiction also took inspiration from the continental novels of Rousseau, Goethe, and De Saint Pierre, enjoying sustained popularity from the 1770s until the end of the century. A final variant, driven by a new generation of female novelists and predominantly written in direct narrative, explains the surge from the later 1780s, with key exponents including Anna Maria Bennett, Mary Robinson, and Charlotte Smith.

As well as being one of the most prolific novelists of the period, Smith is noteworthy for the way in which authorship formed her principal means of generating an income. During a twenty-two-year literary career, Smith published twelve novels, which deploy typically sentimental paradigms (*Emmeline*, 1788; *Celestina*, 1791), occasionally verge on the Gothic (*The Old Manor House*, 1793), and engage polemically with the plight of women in the Revolutionary era (*Desmond*, 1792; *The Young Philosopher*, 1798). Despite a small output in comparison (*Evelina*, 1778; *Cecilia*, 1782; *Camilla*, 1796; *The Wanderer*, 1814), Burney was one of the most successful novelists of the day, whose works combine sentimental motifs with social comedy to recount the stories of orphaned young women cast into a hostile and superficial world. Notwithstanding this period of increased productivity and some innovations, however, sensibility as a form could not outlast the turn of the century. Not only was it being replaced by newer fictions, most notably the Gothic: it became increasingly intertwined with the "war of ideas" that occurred in the wake of the French Revolution. Inspired by the possibilities promised by the revolution, "Jacobin" novelists explored the tensions between individual freedoms and social oppression: these were given a potent female slant by Eliza Fenwick, Elizabeth Inchbald, Mary Hays, and Mary Wollstonecraft. Leveled against such works were equally polemical reactionary titles penned by "Anti-Jacobins" such as Elizabeth

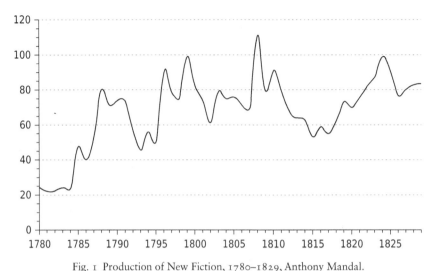

Fig. 1 Production of New Fiction, 1780–1829, Anthony Mandal.
Data drawn from the printed bibliography *The English Novel, 1770–1829* (2000)
and the online database *British Fiction, 1800–1829* (2004)

Hamilton, Mary Ann Hanway, and Jane West, who warned against the dangers of harboring radical ideas and their pernicious effects on the lives of suggestible young women.

In fact, the counter-revolutionary reaction was partly responsible for a slight drop in output of new fiction at the turn of the century. Still, the appetite for novels continued unabated through the 1800s, which saw a 10 percent increase in production compared to the 1790s. The Gothic novel rocketed in popularity in Britain from the mid 1790s to the 1800s, superseding sensibility as the dominant fictional mode. According to Peter Garside, over a quarter of new novels published during the 1800s can be identified as Gothic (Garside et al., *The English Novel*, Vol. II, p. 56). Of course, given the originary role of sensibility in history of the Gothic, it is difficult to say where the former ends and the latter begins, as evidenced in the "dark sensibility" of Fenwick, Robinson, and Smith, and the "sentimental Gothic" of Ann Radcliffe and Regina Maria Roche. In fact, Radcliffe's novels capture the anxious uncertainties, but also the imaginative possibilities, of the literary landscape in the immediate wake of the French Revolution. Setting female innocence against the tyranny of male persecutors, most particularly in *The Mysteries of Udolpho* (1794) and *The Italian* (1797), Radcliffe's geographies of terror interweave concerns about the marginalization of women with anxieties over the political radicalism of the *fin de siècle*. The brief period of dominance by the Gothic was marked by both innovation and derivation, although it was the latter that prevailed, tipping the genre into programmatism and exhaustion. So the 1800s enjoyed a soaring output of fiction, while suffering a nadir in quality, typically comprising salacious works meant to titillate and feed the consumptive appetite of voracious readers.

Nevertheless, serious experimentation with the form was being undertaken at this time, principally in the form of the national tale. Pioneered by Maria Edgeworth, the national tale explores the complex, often-fraught relationship between Ireland and England following the 1801 Act of Union, which absorbed the former into the United Kingdom of Great Britain and Ireland. Beginning with *Castle Rackrent* (1800), and continuing with *The Absentee* (1809) and *Ormond* (1817), Edgeworth's national tales portray a world marked by the decline of a feudal Irish landscape, the absenteeism of English landlords, and colonial exploitation. Edgeworth's perspective is a rational (and often wry) one, rendering the complicated dynamics of the Anglo-Irish relationship unsentimentally, and exhibiting in the words of one reviewer, "admirable pictures, delineated ... with perfect accuracy and truth of character."[14] If Edgeworth takes a rational view of Anglo-Irish relations, her romantic counterpart is Sydney Owenson (Lady Morgan), who translated "national tale" into "national romance," imbricating sentimental narrative and topographical description within a Romantic national context. Inaugurated by her third novel, *The Wild Irish Girl* (1806), and continued through works such as *Woman, or Ida of Athens* (1809) and *O'Donnel: A National Tale* (1814), Morgan's romances explored the emergent national identities that were being formulated across Europe during the Romantic period. Complementing Morgan's fictions are those of the Swiss–French writer Germaine de Staël, whose *Delphine* (1802) and *Corinne* (1807) offer continental inflections of the national romance as a rejection of Napoleonic Europe. Generating both popular success and virulent rejections in equal measure, national romances challenged contemporary formulations of cultural identity and political structures in gendered terms, contrasting the colonizer who leaves the modern metropolis (signified by the male protagonist) with the idyllic, hermetically sealed colony (enacted through the female heroine).

Productivity during the 1810s dropped considerably, constituting only 86 percent of that during the 1800s, reined in by the economic impact of the Napoleonic wars, a fall in foreign translations (from 15 percent in the 1800s to 5 percent) and the serious turn in fiction that followed in the wake of the Evangelical revival. As the Regency began, a shift can be traced toward a more domestic inflection, and religious, most notably Evangelical, writers embarked upon novel-writing with a purpose in mind: to tame the novel and to educate its readers. Inaugurating this turn, Hannah More's best-selling celebration of homely virtues, *Coelebs in Search of a Wife* (1808), supplies a programmatic Evangelical story about a bachelor who visits various circles of acquaintance seeking a suitably Christian wife. Disappointed by the modern women he meets, he finally settles upon the accomplished but demure Lucilla Stanley, who hides her talents behind veils of modest silence. Key to the Evangelical tale was its self-aware simplicity of approach, which eschewed the baroque accoutrements of contemporary genres such as the Gothic and scandal novel. Evangelical novels deal with the conflict between the evanescent values of the *beau monde* and the more enduring principles inspired by religion and self-discipline. Following *Coelebs*, a spate of Evangelically influenced novels appeared from the late 1800s, among them Mary Brunton's *Self-Control* (1811), Laetitia-Matilda Hawkins's *The Countess and Gertrude* (1811), and Amelia Opie's *Temper, or Domestic Scenes* (1812). This kind of moral-didactic fiction, aimed at and representative of the emergent middle classes, was popular throughout the Regency period, although by the 1820s, Evangelical writers redirected their efforts toward a younger audience. The novel was under reform, transforming into a vehicle that could articulate serious issues while avoiding the more hysterical polemicism of the Jacobin era.

It is in this context that we should place Walter Scott's appearance in the novel market in 1814 with the publication of *Waverley, or 'tis Sixty Years Since*. Literary criticism has traditionally posited the historical novel as a fundamentally masculine form initiated by Scott and emerging in the crucible of the Napoleonic wars. However, historical romances had been in existence years earlier, ranging from Sophia Lee's *The Recess* (1783) to Jane West's *The Loyalists* (1812). Perhaps the most significant female writers of historical fictions, however, were the Porter sisters, Anna Maria and Jane, whose trans-European romances were published from 1793 to 1834. In fact, Jane Porter's *The Scottish Chiefs* (1810), a fictionalized account of the life of William Wallace, was one of the most reissued titles from the decade. Nevertheless, Scott's fictions were indeed a catalyst that enabled the successful appropriation of the historical novel as a male model of fiction. Scott's meditations on the relationship between the past and present attempted to subsume the cultural, political, and religious disparities that faced nineteenth-century Britain, through a conciliatory myth of historicized and unifying "Britishness." Despite its largely innovative nature, *Waverley* nevertheless references contemporary fiction in its paratextual "bookend" chapters. While the "Introductory" chapter dismisses the popular models of sentimental, Gothic, and fashionable fiction as formulaic and exhausted, the "Postscript" explicitly invokes female forms as sources of inspiration, in particular the national tales of Maria Edgeworth. Indeed, that the Regency period was a singularly significant moment in the history of women's writing is signaled by the experiences of Jane Austen. She had previously been unsuccessful in her attempts to publish in 1797 and 1803 and was able to bring her novels to market in the 1810s. Published between 1811 and 1817, Austen's six novels engage with the vibrant market for women's fiction in all its configurations. Despite her relatively small output compared to her peers, Austen nonetheless can be seen as responding to the discrete imperatives of the Romantic novel, through sophisticated intertextual practices that encapsulate women's fiction in all its configurations. Such was the popularity of the novel following this period of consolidation, principally by the hands of women writers, that by the 1820s, fiction exceeded poetry as the dominant literary form.

Gender and genre

During the Romantic period, women were the primary consumers, experimenters, and producers of fiction. This market was an expanding one, driven by the needs of an emergent readership drawn from the middling ranks, comprised in large numbers by women who experienced increased amounts of leisure time. As well as generating demand for new works, women were responsible for meeting it, acting as both originators of new titles and translators of foreign works. Alongside this world of demand was an economy of laboring women that resulted from the widening gulf between the possibilities unlocked by their education and the limited financial opportunities available to them. Turner points to "a flexible, at times desperate, at times highly successful accommodation of pressing need and inadequate resources. In this context, the value of authorship as a new occupation was immense, and the persistence with which these women pursued it is not at all surprising" (Turner, *Living*, p. 82). Figure 2 plots the production of new titles by gender for the period 1780–1829. As the chart makes clear, increased production in the 1790s was led by the efforts of female novelists (responsible for 41.5 percent of new titles, compared to 32 percent by men). The 1800s were a period of roughly even gender distribution of authorship, in no small part the result of the public taste for Gothic romances and fashionable *romans-à-clef*. By the 1810s, however, the shift toward domesticity was the product of female activity that exceeded that of the 1790s, with women producing in excess of half the new novels. Nevertheless, even in the midst of this highpoint, the turning tide was signaled by the appearance of Scott's *Waverley*. Sensing what this presaged, Jane Austen jokingly complained that "Walter Scott has no business to write novels, especially good ones. – It is not fair. – He has Fame & Profit enough as a Poet, and should not be taking the bread out of other people's mouths" (Le Faye, *Austen's Letters*, p. 289). Indeed, her forebodings proved accurate, as the 1820s saw fiction pass into the purview of male writers, who wrote over 51.5 percent of new titles. Flocking to the post-Waterloo market in the wake of Scott, these male novelists redirected the now respectable genre toward historical, militaristic, and fashionable "silver-fork" novels.

Broad statistical patterns of this kind, although helpful in delineating the contours of the novel market, can only tell us so much. While it is true that the period saw a variety of novels by a plethora of female authors (at least 1,449 of the 3,378 titles), what is notable is the number of individually prolific female novelists in addition to the proliferation of many female novelists. Figure 3 lists twenty-six authors who published ten or more titles between 1780 and 1829, among whom women outnumber men four to one, producing 303 titles compared to ninety-three. What is particularly striking, though, is how *unrecognizable* most of these prolific female authors are within the majority of today's academic curricula (with the exceptions perhaps of Amelia Opie, Regina Maria Roche, and Charlotte Smith). Those who *do* fall within the remit of sustained academic teaching published significantly fewer novels in comparison: Maria Edgeworth (nine), Sydney Owenson (eight), Ann Radcliffe (six), Jane Austen (five), Frances Burney (three), Mary Shelley (three), and Mary Wollstonecraft (three). In fact, the most prolific novelist of the period, "Mrs. Meeke," has been a resistant figure for whom the details were scant, leading to much speculation and little certainty. Meeke wrote a range of titles between 1795 and 1823, fashioning works to meet the changing tastes of her reading public, be they sentimental melodramas, Gothic suspense, or fashionable mysteries. For a long time tentatively identified as the wife of a clergyman, very recent scholarship has made a convincing case that she was actually Elizabeth Meeke, the stepsister of Frances Burney.[15] While a fuller record exists for other prolific novelists such as Barbara Hofland, Eliza Parsons, and Amelia Opie, the fact remains that the act of recuperating their work has been the work of the past few decades, and there is still a much fuller story to tell.

If there were so many (female) novelists occupying the novel market, the question remains, "Was it a profitable enterprise?" Excluding a few exceptional successes, the simple answer is "No." The most successful single profit made by a female novelist in the period was that by Burney, who earned £2,000 from the first edition of *Camilla*; in fact, she made a mere £250 from selling her first two novels. Similarly, Radcliffe outshone her peers, earning sums of £500 for *The Mysteries of Udolpho* and £800 for *The Italian*, while Scott was able to use the fortune gleaned from his literary outputs to build his manorial pile at Abbotsford. But such instances remained the exception

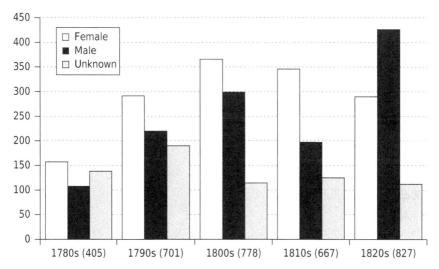

Fig. 2 Authorship of New Fiction by Gender, 1780–1829, Anthony Mandal.

Data drawn from the printed bibliography *The English Novel, 1770–1829* (2000) and the online database *British Fiction, 1800–1829* (2004)

rather than the rule: James Raven surmises that most sales would be in the range of five to one hundred guineas for the sale of copyright, with most transactions tipping toward the lower end of the scale (Garside et al., *The English Novel*, Vol. 1, p. 54). Even the literary earnings of today's most recognizable Romantic-era novelist, Jane Austen, amounted to £1,600, more than half of which was generated posthumously.

It becomes clear that producing work after work was no guarantee of lasting posterity: indeed, it could signal the opposite, an evanescent moment, followed by further such moments. For most, the reality of authorship consisted less of participating in the genteel republic of letters, than of laboring for measly sums doled out by the booksellers. Many Romantic authors were amateurs who wrote as a pastime, but the majority were trade hacks who operated as cogs in great novel-producing machines like the Minerva Press. For instance, Eliza Parsons, the author of nineteen titles, found herself forced to appeal for assistance to the Royal Literary Fund (RLF) early in her career:

> I have finished Another Novel now in the Press, but Incapable of Soliciting Subscriptions in Person I fear my Advantages will be Very Small and at this time I am in the most alarming situation from the certainty of being drag[g]ed to a prison Miserable Cripple as I am if I do not raise near Twenty Pounds by Christmas besides little wants that will Oppress me till next March.[16]

Author	Titles	Vols.	Notes
Mrs. Meeke	26	95	Excludes 4 translations (11 vols.).
August Lafontaine	23	60	
Sir Walter Scott	22	70	
Stéphanie de Genlis	22	57	
Barbara Hofland	21	46	
Francis Lathom	20	59	
Eliza Parsons	19	61	
Sarah Green	17	47	
Catherine George Ward	17	24	
John Galt	16	28	
Anna Maria Porter	15	43	Includes 2 titles (5 vols.) written with Jane Porter.
Regina Maria Roche	15	30	Includes 1 widely, but uncertainly, attributed title.
Louisa Stanhope	14	52	
Anne Hatton ("Ann of Swansea")	13	60	
Anna Maria Mackenzie	13	35	
Charlotte Smith	12	44	
"Anthony Frederick Holstein"	12	41	Holstein is most likely a pseudonymous figure.
Jane Harvey	12	37	
Amelia Opie	12	33	Includes 2 titles attributed uncertainly to Opie.
Henrietta Rouviere Mosse	11	40	Includes 1 title attributed uncertainly to Mosse.
Regina Maria Roche	11	39	Includes 1 title attributed uncertianly to Roche.
Elizabeth Gunning	11	36	Excludes 2 translations (6 vols.).
Mrs. E. M. Foster	11	25	
Mary Pilkington	11	14	
Elizabeth Thomas	10	33	
Isabella Kelly	10	31	

Fig. 3 Most Prolific Authors of New Fiction, 1780–1829, Anthony Mandal.
Data drawn from the printed bibliography *The English Novel, 1770–1829* (2000) and the online database *British Fiction, 1800–1829* (2004)

Regina Maria Roche, at one time seen as second only to Radcliffe, found herself similarly circumstanced near the end of her life. According to an appeal to the RLF, the paralysis of her husband in 1825, combined with a Chancery suit, led to a "state of miserable destitution" for her "unhappy family" at the hands of an unrelenting creditor.[17] As attested to by numerous case files in the RLF archives, for every success story like those of Burney or Radcliffe, there remain hundreds that tell of woe and penury to rival the very novels these authors wrote to entertain their readers.

If the majority of authors failed to profit from the demand for fiction during the period, publishers were its clearest beneficiaries, able to generate huge fortunes on the back of their publications. Founded in 1773, William Lane's Minerva Press became synonymous with fictional potboilers, issuing new novels at almost industrial levels (819 new titles between 1780 and 1829). A cursory examination of Minerva's lists indicates the firm's responsiveness to public tastes, crowded as they are with such chilling pleasures as *The Horrors of Oakendale Abbey* (1797), *More Ghosts!* (1798), and even a *Minerva Castle* (1802)! Contextualizing the role of Lane's firm, Feather observes that "the 'Minerva Press novel' became almost as much of a descriptor as 'Mills and Boon' was to be of popular romantic novels in the second half of the twentieth century" (Feather, *History*, p. 78). A shrewd entrepreneur, Lane actively solicited new authors, particularly female ones, and promoted their works through the catalogues of his Minerva Library and in the lists of "Works Just Published" that were appended to his novels (Turner, *Living*, p. 91). In fact, Meeke published her entire fictional output with Lane throughout her twenty-eight-year career, suggesting the symbiotic relationship that existed between Lane and many female trade novelists.

If the Minerva Press pitched its wares squarely to the mass market, the second most prolific publishers, Longmans, maintained a steady course. Founded in 1724, the venerable firm dealt in works aimed at a polite audience, with output increasing gradually rather than dramatically during the period (220 titles between 1787 and 1829). Longmans titles are more sedate, while representative authors include the Porter sisters, as well as Amelia Opie and Barbara Hofland, both of whom were able to negotiate the transition from sentimental melodramas toward more didactic, domestic forms from the 1810s and 1820s respectively. If Minerva was "trade" and Longmans was "polite," then the third most prominent publisher of fiction during the period, Henry Colburn, was unequivocally "flash." Colburn entered the market considerably later than Minerva and Longmans, trading from 1807 in francophone publications and translations of foreign works into English. It wasn't until the 1810s that Colburn made a serious impression on the market with forty-three new titles, which proportionately doubled in the 1820s to 104. Colburn was initially drawn to high-profile female writers, among them De Staël, Owenson, and Lady Caroline Lamb (author of the scandalous *Glenarvon* in 1816, based on Lamb's love affair with Byron). Sensing the turning tide in the post-Scott era, Colburn turned his attentions toward male authors in a very marked way: while 58 percent of his new fiction was female authored during the 1810s, by the 1820s this had fallen to just over 18 percent. Just as Lane had capitalized on the penchant for women's writing in the earlier part of the era, Colburn similarly profited from and stimulated the swing toward male authorship from the later, metonymically reflecting the waning dominance of women in the novel market.

Conclusion

In a recent essay on women and print culture between 1780 and 1830, Michelle Levy has imbricated the emergence of fiction as the dominant genre of the early nineteenth century with the pivotal role played by women novelists as only the beginning of a vital project of recuperation: "It has taken feminist scholars thirty years to repopulate the literary landscape with forgotten female authors; in the decades to come, we should seek to develop an even broader understanding of women's thorough enmeshment in the material history of print."[18] And it is through this prism that we should view the development of the novel during the Romantic period: as the result of the efforts of numerous women writers who drove many of its innovations. Notwithstanding their positions on either side of the conservative/feminist divide, of their anxious responses toward fame and profit, and their doubts about the morality and utility of their efforts, without the vital intercession of women authors during the Romantic era, the novel as we recognize it today would simply not have existed. Certainly, the genre itself would have been impoverished were it not for the underpaid and undervalued, but invaluable and formative, labors of these female novelists during a watershed period in the history of British literature.

NOTES

The data used to generate the two charts and table that accompany this chapter, as well as many of the statistics supplied in my discussion, draw upon research for two projects in which I was involved: the printed bibliography *The English Novel, 1770–1829* (2000) and the online database *British Fiction, 1800–1829* (2004).

1 Marilyn Butler, *Jane Austen and the War of Ideas* (Oxford: Clarendon, 1975).

2 NCCO, for instance, includes digital copies of the anglophone holdings of the Corvey Library, which comprises around 80 percent of all British fiction published between 1796 and 1834.

3 Peter Garside, James Raven, and Rainer Schöwerling, eds., *The English Novel, 1770–1829: A Bibliographical Survey of Prose Fiction Published in the British Isles*, 2 vols. (Oxford University Press, 2000).

4 John Feather, *A History of British Publishing*, 2nd edn. (London and New York: Routledge, 2006), p. 68. Subsequent references cited parenthetically in the text.

5 William St. Clair, *The Reading Nation in the Romantic Period* (Cambridge University Press, 2004), p. 115.

6 Garside, Raven, and Schöwerling, eds., *The English Novel*, Vol. II, p. 39. Subsequent references cited parenthetically in the text.

7 Cheryl Turner, *Living by the Pen: Women Writers in the Eighteenth Century* (London: Routledge, 1994), p. 134. Subsequent references cited parenthetically in the text.

8 Hannah More, *Strictures on the Modern System of Female Education*, 5th edn., 2 vols. (London: Cadell and Davies, 1799), Vol. I, p. 191.

9 Anon., Review of *Eliza Cleland* (1788), *Critical Review*, 65 (June 1788), p. 486; Anon., Review of *The Triumphs of Constancy*, *Critical Review*, n. s. 1 (April 1791), p. 471.

10 Joyce Hemlow, et al., eds., *The Journals and Letters of Fanny Burney (Madame D'Arblay)*, 12 vols. (Oxford: Clarendon Press, 1972–84), Vol. III, p. 117.

11 Jennie Batchelor, *Women's Work: Labour, Gender, Authorship, 1750–1830* (Manchester University Press, 2010), p. 68.

12 Deirdre Le Faye, ed., *Jane Austen's Letters*, 4th edn. (Oxford University Press, 2011), p. 27. Subsequent references cited parenthetically in the text.

13 Alexander Brunton, Memoir in Mary Brunton, *Emmeline: With Some Other Pieces ... to Which Is Prefixed a Memoir of her Life* (Edinburgh: Manners and Miller, 1819), p. lxxiv.

14 *Monthly Review*, 2nd ser. 32 (May 1800), p. 91.

15 Simon Macdonald, "Identifying Mrs. Meeke: Another Burney Family Novelist," *Review of English Studies* (RES), 2/205 (Feb. 2013), pp. 67–85.

16 Eliza Parsons, letter to Dr. Dale, December 17, 1792; British Library, Loan 96 RLF 1/21/1.

17 Edward Popham and Cornelius Bolton, letter to Sir Benjamin Hobhouse, February 23, 1827; British Library, Loan 96 RLF 1/590/2.

18 Michelle Levy, "Women and Print Culture, 1750–1830," in Jacqueline M. Labbe, ed., *The History of British Women's Writing, 1750–1830* (Basingstoke and New York: Palgrave Macmillan, 2010), p. 42.

3

CATHERINE BURROUGHS

Drama

By the late eighteenth century, women were regularly making rich contributions to the British professional stage as playwrights, actors, critics, theorists, translators/adaptors, and managers. That the dramas produced by women between 1780 and 1830 are relatively unfamiliar today to students of British literature says less about their quality and more about the ways in which performance history (and the anthologies that become carriers of that history) keeps alive the drama created – or fails to do so. Nineteenth-century drama by women was, until recently, omitted from our critical histories and our anthologies, even from anthologies that specifically collected Romantic-era plays. It is true that the same may be said for much of the dramatic writing produced by men of the Romantic era. Unless a particular playscript endures over time – to be read or staged and evaluated in different eras and venues with different actors and a wide variety of spectators – it is certainly less likely to retain value, except as a relic or as a bridge to other periods that produced more enduring dramas.

When one looks closely at the plays from the late eighteenth century that have become part of the performance canon of Western drama, only a few titles – by women or men – stand out: Oliver Goldsmith's *She Stoops to Conquer* (1773) and Richard Brinsley Sheridan's *The Rivals* (1775). Although the nineteenth century saw the staging of hundreds of plays, in an atmosphere that relished theater in all sorts of spaces and modes, only a few, such as Oscar Wilde's *The Importance of Being Earnest* (1895), have attained canonical status. Instead of focusing on what is in (or might yet deserve to be in) the literary canon, we might shift our perspective to explore performance in the Romantic period as it was important in repertoire or was flourishing in practice. Using this as a starting point, this essay does not argue that Romantic drama by women ought to be revived or, in some cases, staged for the first time. Rather, I seek to paint a clear picture of the contributions made to drama and theater by British Romantic women writers so that what came before and after them can be rendered with more nuance.

Focusing on those contexts that throw into relief the significance of Romantic women writers' accomplishments as produced and published playwrights, I start by providing a brief narrative of the history of women writing for the theater in Great Britain before 1780, one that I would have appreciated when I began my own explorations of this period. Tracing the series of "firsts" for women in British drama establishes some of the traditions and themes that Romantic women writers would subsequently follow and consciously eschew. Though less a progress narrative than an acknowledgment of derivation, consistency, or comparability, this essay nevertheless notes "originality, innovation, and marked changes" to contextualize the significance of the achievements and continuities of women writers during the Romantic period.[1]

Women were responsible for many milestones in dramatic history. A sixteenth-century woman was the first person to provide a translation of Euripides for English readers: Jane (Joanna) Lumley's (1537–78) *Iphigeneia at Aulis*. Mary Sidney, Countess of Pembroke (1561–1621), printed (as opposed to staged) a translation of Robert Garnier's drama based on Antony and Cleopatra, *Antonius* (1592). She also wrote historical closet drama that would be developed throughout the eighteenth century and into the Romantic period by both men and women. Moreover, Sidney influenced Shakespeare when he adapted her words and characters in his *Anthony and Cleopatra* (c. 1603–7; pub. 1623).

The first original play in English written by a woman was arguably Elizabeth Cary's *The Tragedy of Mariam*, published in 1613, but written possibly as early as 1602. Katherine Philips's translation of Pierre Corneille's *La Mort de Pompée* (1644; rev. 1660; pub. 1667) was also a women's literary history landmark. It was performed at the Theatre Royal in Dublin in February 1663, making Philips the first woman to have a play staged in Great Britain. Margaret Cavendish wrote nineteen dramas; seven of them were ten acts long and were ultimately published in two volumes, *Playes* (1662) and *Plays Never Before Printed* (1668). She appears not to have sought production for them, but she never claims she meant them merely to be read.

After centuries of transvestite theater, female actors were finally performing the female parts on commercial stages beginning with the Restoration of the monarchy in 1660, although women had certainly acted in a number of venues before this time. This fact influenced the dramaturgy of staged plays, since the live body of a female actor was now available to interpret the part and arrest an audience accustomed only to imagine the gender of Elizabethan and Jacobean female characters. The first professional female playwright was Aphra Behn, whose *The Forc'd Marriage* – which opened on September 20, 1670 and had six performances – unleashed a career of more than twenty dramatic compositions, many of which were staged to full houses and which continue to be performed today. Frances Boothby and Elizabeth Polwhele also had public performances of their respective plays, *Marcelia* (1669) and *The Faithful Virgins* (1671).

Between 1690 and 1780, one finds clusters of women playwrights whose work was staged, none more notable than the group satirized as "The Female Wits" in an anonymous comedy of 1696: Mary Pix, Catharine Trotter, and Delarivier Manley. Each of these writers debuted a play at professional theaters in London between 1695 and 1696. These three dramatists would have more than eighteen professional productions between them, including tragedies, comedies, and farces. While it is true that immediately after the Restoration, it was more common for aristocratic women to write for private audiences – notably Anne Wharton, Anne Finch, Countess of Winchilsea, and Lady Mary Wortley Montagu – Aphra Behn's success ensured that, throughout the eighteenth century, theater managers would make it more common to stage a play by a woman even as they rationed, in effect, the number of spots available to women writers in the repertoire.

With the first of the Hanoverian kings, George I, the make up of those writing for the stage shifted. Actors attempted playwriting, as did actresses, including Susanna Centlivre, Eliza Haywood, Charlotte Charke, Jane Egleton, Susannah Cibber, and Kitty Clive. For both men and women, "access to the stage usually required recommendation through an intermediary, such as an influential patron, playwright, or actor or a direct approach to a theater-manager" and, for this reason, Jane Milling cautions us to resist thinking of women dramatists before 1750 "as lone, literary figures"; instead, they were just as often "active participants in the commercial networks and conversations of the theater industry."[2] The same is true for men. However, even with patronage or connections, women playwrights throughout the eighteenth century and the Romantic period were tied to men's authoritative theatrical influence and power.

In the late seventeenth century, plays by women or plays based on works by women made up a third of those staged. Thereafter, the numbers dropped. There was an initial decline in the early eighteenth century, and after that, the numbers stayed steady at 7 to 10 percent of plays produced, both in the United States and Great Britain, into the 1980s. As one scholar quipped, it is almost "as if an unofficial quota had been imposed."[3]

The several decades preceding the 1780s mark the nadir of women writing for the British stage. This period has been described as hostile to women, and publishing a play anonymously was still a common practice. Even closet plays – traditionally a mode for women (and men) with little appetite for or access to the stage – were few. In 1763, Drury Lane Theatre, one of the two licensed commercial stages in London, mounted productions of three plays by Kitty Clive and Frances Sheridan. Two years later, Elizabeth Griffith, who was to have five successful comedies produced between 1765 and 1779, also began her career. Playwrights who would become important in the late eighteenth century, Hannah More and Hannah Cowley, began writing professionally in the 1770s. We can locate the return in the 1780s of a robust atmosphere for play composition by women in England and Ireland. This included closet plays, staged dramas, and private theatricals.

By the 1790s, more than twenty-six women had their plays published and/or performed. In 1799, twenty titles by women – labeled as translations, closet plays, or private productions – are recorded. An irony is that, later in the eighteenth century, there was a forgetting of most women playwrights who had come before, with the exception of Susanna Centlivre. Some critics have seen this as a backlash against Restoration and early eighteenth-century plays, which were judged as morally loose or too playful where gender is concerned.

It also took some time to adjust to a major piece of legislation that created an atmosphere inimical to creativity in both drama and theater: the Stage Licensing Act of 1737. This act gave more teeth to the judgments of the Lord Chamberlain, who was responsible for licensing (in effect, approving) those plays that would be inoffensive to the government and powers that be. The Licensing Act also confined the production of the spoken drama – or those plays in the British repertoire, including Shakespeare – to two playhouses that increased in size over the next decades in order to accommodate the large audiences that flocked to the theater. Along with the increasing democratization of these patent playhouses, a two-tiered system of theatrical spaces developed – described as legitimate and illegitimate – which would initiate some of the trends that infused the Victorian theater with such variety and vigor after the Licensing Act was repealed in 1843. (The position of Lord Chamberlain remained, however, until 1968.) The patent theaters, perhaps because and in spite of their monopoly, had audiences of 3,000-plus and became the site of some of the greatest acting in the history of British theater.

The most acclaimed actress of the early Romantic period, Sarah Siddons, had apprenticed to David Garrick in her younger years and, along with her brother, John Philip Kemble, established a mode of performance that would alternately be celebrated and critiqued. This mode was later contrasted to the fiery and more spontaneously oriented Edmund Kean, who debuted as Shylock in 1814. Siddons knew how to rivet audiences with a blend of what appeared then as a more psychologically "real" form of line delivery but which, coupled with her bodily presence, inspired comparisons to awe-inspiring Greek statuary. Siddons specialized in tragedy, and, when Sir Joshua Reynolds made his famous portrait in 1784, he sat her in a chair and labeled her the "tragic muse." As Elizabeth Eger writes, "By 1789 Siddons's status was such that her roles included serving as the symbol of the entire nation, dressed as Britannia at the service in St. Paul's to celebrate the recovery of George III from his madness."[4] Her most celebrated roles were those of feminine strength and pathos, something that critics have seen as having an influence on contemporary attitudes to the female sex. These included Calista and Jane Shore – from two of Nicholas Rowe's early eighteenth-century "she-tragedies" – and Euphrasia from Arthur Murphy's she-tragedy *The Grecian Daughter* (1772). Siddons was also acclaimed for her Lady Macbeth. Because she often chose to embody characters of dignity underscored by her "noble" performance style, Siddons positioned herself as a kind of "mother of the nation" (Anne K. Mellor's phrase), and the result was to increase respect for acting in general, particularly for the woman on stage.

Even though actors were, in legal terms, not considered different from vagrants until 1843, Siddons's dignified and powerful performances of tragic heroines did much to raise the stature of the actress – even as audiences relished the conflation of the role with the performer, a blurring that began from the moment that England permitted women to take female parts on the public stage in 1661. It was Nell Gwynn, the lover of Charles II and one of the first English actresses, who established what one critic has called "the role of the ultimate English sexual Cinderella."[5] This practice of actresses performing royalty and aristocracy on stage and then being elevated into these ranks in real life through marriage or mistresshood continued into the Romantic period, with actresses Eliza O'Neill, Elizabeth Farren, Anna Maria Crouch, and Mary Robinson each becoming either an aristocrat or royal lover.

Mary Robinson (1758–1800) is particularly interesting. Not only was she celebrated for creating the role of Victoria in Hannah Cowley's popular play *Bold Stroke for a Husband* (1783), but her role as Perdita in *The Winter's Tale* also earned her that nickname with the public, as she became the first mistress of the Prince of Wales. While Robinson was notorious in London, frequently mentioned in the periodical press in gossip about who might have been her lover, whether she had taken ill, how she was conveyed about town, or what she was wearing, she was also an author of note. Her first play, a farce called *The Lucky Escape* (1778), was included as an afterpiece on her benefit night, May 30, 1778. A second satiric farce, *Nobody*, appeared at Drury Lane in 1794 (unpublished); and a tragedy, *The Sicilian Lover* (1796), was published but not performed. Robinson also wrote fiction and was a member of the "Della Cruscans" poetry circle. Robinson's *Memoirs*, published after her death in 1801, offers an example of the ways in which the "backstage" life of a writer, but especially an actress, forecast the modern obsession with celebrity magazines and biographies.

Despite Siddons's determination not to incur a whiff of scandal, the sexualization of other actresses was abetted by the tradition of women performing breeches parts, a feature of female performance that, aside from affording a view of the legs, was used by them to compete with men for the choicest stage roles. Dorothy Jordan (the era's most celebrated comic actress and lover of the future king William IV, bearing him ten children) was well known for these kinds of breeches roles, which continued to complicate the degree to which an actress should be regarded as a prostitute or a lady, even as eighteenth-century culture began to expect bourgeois propriety. Even so, the public appetite for memoirs of both actresses and prostitutes was great, and the two genres began to seem very much alike. The theater also offered opportunities for women of shaken sexual reputation to maintain independence and to lead seemingly glamorous lives. In late eighteenth-century plays, prostitutes and actresses are depicted as experts in performing the arts of pleasing, rather than as examples of excessive female desire.

A growing area of scholarship in theater history is the retrieval of the names and contributions of women who managed theaters, especially after 1800. But even throughout the eighteenth century, actresses served as theater-managers, whether officially or unofficially. Some did so very successfully, some in strolling and fairground companies. Both Siddons and Jordan started out as strolling players. This was advantageous work when patent houses were closed in the summer time, and it also afforded employment to those who couldn't find roles at those theaters.

The surging theatrical vitality of the Romantic period led to "hybridity" in playwriting, a strategy for getting around the restrictions created by the theater monopoly and the British government's fears about the effects of the French Revolution. Mixed genres allowed women writers to join political debates of the day, as long as they worked to distance themselves from any political intentions. Lines from Shakespeare or other Jacobean and Restoration writers could be slipped into prologues or after-pieces or other modes in which these lines were sung. Thus, the Romantic period, while still producing new plays modeled on the five-act tradition in both classical comedy and tragedy, was invigorated by equestrian and nautical dramas (in which the stars were horses, spectacular effects, and other stage scenery); Gothic dramas translated from the German and sentimental comedies from the French, along with English originals in these modes; harlequinades; pantomime; farces; romances; musical entertainments, including comic operas and burlettas; and melodramas, which were emerging in the early nineteenth century. Jane Scott prolifically developed melodrama as a genre in the theater she managed after 1809, the Sans Pareil (later the Adelphi). Moreover, an interest in verse tragedies was the product of renewed national pride in Shakespeare that began during the eighteenth century – at the level of criticism and staging – driven by David Garrick, who dominated the theater culture until his death in 1776.

In addition to performances in major London playhouses or those royal theaters so designated around the country – such as in Bath and Norwich – there was the phenomenon of private theatricals, which were plays acted at the estates of aristocrats and usually managed/produced by women. For instance, Lady Elizabeth Craven, the Margravine of Anspach, made Brandenburgh House the site of a private theater that hired both professional and amateur actors to perform original and tested plays. As indicated by the invaluable website *British Women Playwrights around 1800*, a number of plays by women went unacted, which indicates that, while many women were engaged in writing plays, finding a production – private or public – was continually a difficult business.[6]

This brings up the tradition of closet play as distinct from the unacted drama. As more innovation in theatrical genres characterized the era, the split between closet and stage grew because the spoken word was becoming but a stagehand to special effects and scenic awe. Both Lord Byron and Joanna Baillie reacted against this trend, even as both wrote formidable plays whose dramaturgy invites consideration of how stages and staging might be conceived anew in order to allow for more psychological subtlety and intellectual drama in the theater itself. Among these closet dramatists were Mary Eleanor Bowes, Sarah Kirby Trimmer, Anne Hughes, Margaret Turner, Elizabeth Pinchard, Jane West, Mary Deverell, Elizabeth Helme, Lady Sophia Burrell, Maria Edgeworth, Fanny Holcroft, Susan Fraser, Ann Gittins Francis, Ann Wilson, Sarah Richardson, Barbara Hoole Hofland, Charlotte Nooth, Mary Hornby, Isabel Hill, Charlotte de Humboldt, and Mary G. Lewis.

We can make some general observations about the content of the plays produced between 1780 and 1830 at the patent theaters. Certainly there was a tendency to create female characters that would reflect more positively on women as wives, mothers, and daughters – and to construct a dramaturgy that tests the legal limits on female power through negotiating (marital) relationships promising a degree of autonomy. One of the prominent themes in comedy stretching back to Shakespeare and Ben Jonson was how to negotiate marriages and maintain class hierarchies through economic gatekeeping. Increasingly, the plays of the Romantic era were preoccupied with nationalist and mercantile projects in an age of increasing travel and colonization, especially in India. Mariana Starke, for instance, author of the tragedy *The Widow of Malabar* (produced at Covent Garden in 1791), has received recent critical attention for the degree to which she succeeded commercially with a play that was imbued with politics, especially political content that was relevant to contemporary culture.

Between 1772 and 1829, more than fifteen comedies by women were produced at the patent playhouses in London. Those from the 1770s include Elizabeth Griffith's *A Wife in the Right* (1772); Charlotte Lennox's *Old City Manners* (1775); Hannah Cowley's *The Runaway* (1776) and *Who's the Dupe?* (1779); and Elizabeth Richardson's *The Double Deception* (1779). In the 1780s, we find Lady Elizabeth Craven's *The Miniature Picture* (1780); Sophia Lee's *The Chapter of Accidents* (1780) and *The Assignation* (1807); sister Harriet Lee's *The New Peerage* (1787); Lady Eglantine Wallace's *The Ton* (1788); and Mariana Starke's *The Sword of Peace* (1788). Quite a gap occurs before the next mainstream comedy, Marie Thérèse De Camp Kemble's *First Faults* (1799), which was followed by Mary Berry's *The Fashionable Friends* (1802), Marianne Chambers's two plays, *The School for Friends* (1805) and *Ourselves* (1811), and Alicia Sheridan Lefanu's *The Sons of Erin* (1812).

Two comic playwrights stand out in the late Georgian period because of their sustained commercial success: Hannah Cowley (1743–1809) and Elizabeth Inchbald (1753–1821). Cowley has been called the most successful female playwright after Centlivre, enjoying 118 performances before 1800, some of which took place on the early American stage. While Cowley wrote a tragedy – *Albina* (1779) – comedies were her forte. Her first play, *The Runaway* (1776), starring Sarah Siddons, had nineteen performances in its first season and saw ten subsequent productions over the next twenty-five years. Her most popular work is *The Belle's Strategem*; it was revived in 2005 at the Oregon Shakespeare Festival – the first full staging of the comedy at a major theatre in well over a century.

Inchbald was unusual in that she was both an actress and a playwright. Her 1780 London debut "marks the beginning of the most commercially successful career of any woman dramatist in the late eighteenth century," indicated by the fact that she "left an estate of over £6,000 at her death."[7] Her career spans the years between 1784 and 1805 during which time seventeen of her more than twenty plays were successfully staged. Half of her plays were original, and the other half were audience-friendly adaptations from French and German playwrights. Inchbald is also distinctive for being the first woman to write critical prefaces (a prolific 125) for a series of anthologies of British drama (1806–9), advancing a lineage of female writers who wrote about drama and theater – a legacy that can be traced back to Margaret Cavendish in the 1660s, Eliza Haywood in the 1740s, and Frances Brooke and Charlotte Lennox in the 1750s up through Elizabeth Montagu (the 1760s), Elizabeth Griffith (the 1770s), and Joanna Baillie (from 1790 to 1830).

Inchbald's accomplishment as a critic/theorist reminds us that the playwright of the era, Joanna Baillie – considered a kind of "female Shakespeare" of the age – is today highly regarded for the extensive writing she produced about what playwriting and theater might do in an age held captive by a vigorous but also stifling commercial stage. The many and deeply thoughtful prefaces that she attached to the volumes of plays she published between 1798 and 1836 – most notably the prefatory essays she composed for the three volumes of what we now call *Plays on the Passions* (1798, 1802, 1812) – describe a vision of plays that might deepen the humanity of their spectators, whether in England, Scotland, Sri Lanka, or the United States. In writing about the theory behind the staging of her plays, Baillie focused on the ways in which major human "passions" – such as fear, hate, anger, greed, and lust – required, in her view, particular reforms or innovations in stagecraft, including the size of the theaters, the lighting of the stage, and the style of acting. Though only seven of Baillie's twenty-seven plays were staged during her lifetime, they received major productions with first-rate actors (Siddons, John Philip Kemble, Edmund Kean) in London, Glasgow, New York City, and Philadelphia. And today Baillie's plays are receiving staged readings and performances in the kind of intimate theaters she originally envisioned for her work, garnering attention for their potential to explore with subtlety and depth the psychological dramas of her tragic and comic characters.

Baillie's interest in theater as a site of instruction for teaching her audiences what she defined as "sympathetick curiosity" was shared by a variety of women writers who wrote history plays as a way to educate spectators. As Greg Kucich argues,

> For women writers of the romantic era, the appealing concept of historical drama as a "National School" [Hannah Cowley's phrase] emerged out of a wider, intensive cultural dispute about the present epoch's relation of Britain's illustrious literary traditions and the attendant question of any remaining creative opportunities following the exhaustive accomplishments of the past.[8]

Especially in their history plays, Romantic women writers often suggest a sense of not belonging to a tradition. Their female characters are outsiders, and their plays use the past to comment critically on the present. Two such practitioners were Hannah Brand, who had two historical tragedies – *Huniades* and *Agmunda* – produced within a month at Drury Lane in 1792, and Sophia Lee, whose *Almeyda* was also performed there in 1796. A group of history plays set in Anglo-Saxon times included Ann Yearsley's *Earl Goodwin* staged at the Theatre Royal in Bristol in 1789 and printed the same year.

By far the most successful of those writers interested in the Anglo-Saxon period was Hannah More, who created a tragedy, *Percy* (1777), which became the most frequently performed tragic drama by a woman of the era. More's work provides another example of the trend among women and men of the Romantic period to write in a wide range of genres, even as they explored the stage. One of the most influential and commercially successful writers of her time, More not only produced poems, plays, essays, tracts, novels, and conduct literature, but she also worked on behalf of the abolition of the slave trade and advanced efforts to educate those in poverty. By 1800 she was distancing herself from theater as a site for moral reform and advocating for closet drama instead. This was the result of Hannah Cowley's accusing More of plagiarizing Cowley's *Albina* in *The Fatal Falsehood*, which opened in July of 1779 but is said to have been written three years earlier. More benefited for a time from David Garrick's mentorship. Indeed, Drury Lane dominates in producing women playwrights between 1747 and 1776; there were 292 performances of plays by women as compared to 111 for Covent Garden.

Of special significance during this period is a sub-category of the history play, called the siege drama. Between 1760 and 1830, more than twenty plays (some written for closet and others for the stage) used the word "siege" in their titles. Frances Brooke (*c.* 1724–89) was an early practitioner of this mode – her play *The Siege of Sinope* was staged at Covent Garden in 1781 – and she was, like many of her contemporaries, interested in exploring multiple genres, having earlier published a novel called *The Excursion* (1777), which features a female character who encounters difficulties having her play produced. In addition, Brooke also produced thirty-seven issues of the periodical *The Old Maid* (1755–6) – which included her theater reviews – under the pseudonym "Mary Singleton, Spinster"; managed King's Theatre, London, between 1773 and 1777; published a popular translation of Madame Riccoboni's novel *Les Lettres de Juliette Catesby* (1759) into English; and wrote her own epistolary novel, *The Letters of Julia Mandeville* (1763).

Felicia Hemans (1793–1835), a professional poet who also wrote "siege drama," achieved distinction by adapting European Romantic literature for a British context. Hemans has been said to engage directly with Schiller in her plays *Vespers of Palermo* (1823) and *The Siege of Valencia* (1823), rewriting his drama in British feminist terms. In addition to admiring Joanna Baillie, Hemans also appreciated the historical drama of Mary Russell Mitford (1787–1855); when Mitford's *Rienzi: A Tragedy* was first staged at Drury Lane on October 11, 1828, it became "the most popular and successful dramatic work by a woman playwright on the later Romantic-period stage," [9] running thirty-four performances and later being performed at the Chatham Theatre in New York City. Like Baillie's dramas, Mitford's plays were ushered onto the commercial stage with the best actors of the day. In 1823, William Charles Macready starred in *Julian* at Covent Garden, and Charles Kemble played the lead in *The Foscari* in 1826. The Lord Chamberlain refused to license another of Mitford's plays, *Charles the First*, but it was eventually performed in 1834 at the Surrey Theatre.

As the Romantic period gave way to the vigorous entertainments of the Victorian theater, several playwrights began to establish themselves and, to some extent, straddle the imaginary lines between one era and another. Frances Anne Kemble (1809–93) is notable for having been an accomplished actress (she was the niece of Sarah Siddons) who also wrote several plays, including *Francis the First* (1832) and *The Star of Seville* (1837). Later, she published *An English Tragedy* (1863) a verse drama that, quite boldly, explores explicit sexual themes such as brother–sister incest and marital infidelity. Catherine Gore (1799–1861) was a prolific novelist and author of eleven plays (starting in 1824) who made melodrama more sophisticated and therefore of greater appeal to the upper classes.

The story of women's contributions to British drama continues to the present day. As a result of the ongoing recovery work of the past several decades, we have reached the point at which it is unthinkable that women's dramatic contributions could be erased from the record, as has happened in the past. But this fact does not so much underscore the increasing visibility of British women playwrights today as it highlights the commitment of theater scholars who study women dramatists and women in theater from the seventeenth century to the present. Scholars continue efforts to make more accessible and enduring the narrative of British women's myriad accomplishments and contributions to the stage in the Romantic era, as well as before and after it.

NOTES

1 Tracy C. Davis, "Introduction," in *The Broadview Anthology of Nineteenth-Century British Performance*, ed. Tracy C. Davis (Peterborough, Ontario: Broadview Press, 2012), p. 13.
2 Jane Milling, "Working in the Theater: Women Playwrights, 1660–1750," in *Teaching British Women Playwrights of the Restoration and Eighteenth*

Century, ed. Bonnie Nelson and Catherine Burroughs (New York: The Modern Language Association of America, 2010), pp. 20, 22.

3 Ellen Donkin, *Getting into the Act: Women Playwrights in London, 1776–1829* (London and New York: Routledge, 1994), pp. 186–9, 189.

4 Elizabeth Eger, "Spectacle, Intellect and Authority: The Actress in the Eighteenth Century," in *The Cambridge Companion to the Actress*, ed. Maggie B. Gale and John Stokes (Cambridge University Press, 2007), p. 43.

5 Gilli Bush-Bailey, "Revolution, Legislation and Autonomy," in *The Cambridge Companion to the Actress*, ed. Maggie B. Gale and John Stokes (Cambridge University Press, 2007), p. 15.

6 Thomas C. Crochunis and Michael Eberle-Sinatra, eds., *British Women Playwrights Around 1800*. www.etang.umontreal.ca/bwp1800.

7 Misty Anderson, "Women Playwrights," in *The Cambridge Companion to British Theatre, 1730–1830*, ed. Jane Moody and Daniel O'Quinn (Cambridge University Press, 2007), pp. 153, 147.

8 Greg Kucich, "Baillie, Mitford, and the 'Different Track' of Women's Historical Drama on the Romantic Stage," in *Women's Romantic Theatre and Drama: History, Agency, and Performativity*, ed. Lilla Maria Crisafulli and Keir Elam (Burlington, VT: Ashgate, 2010), p. 23.

9 Diego Saglia, "When Mitford Met Baillie: Theatre, Sociability, and the Networks of Women's Romantic Drama," in *Women's Romantic Theatre and Drama: History, Agency, and Performativity*, ed. Lilla Maria Crisafulli and Keir Elam (Burlington, VT: Ashgate, 2010), p. 125.

4

ANNE K. MELLOR

Essays and political writing

By the end of the eighteenth century, women writers were participating fully in the discursive public sphere and were as central to the formation of public opinion as other disenfranchised members of the body politic (Dissenters, Catholics, working-class men, etc.). The new print culture and the lending libraries guaranteed women access to print – both as writers and as readers – through publication and circulation of ideas, values, and sentiments in all literary genres, including non-fictional prose genres such as history, philosophy, science, didactic and pedagogical tracts, literary reviews, and political treatises. They engaged fully in bourgeois "civil society," that public space where the common good is debated and promoted and where public opinion based not on status or traditions but on free and rational communication of ideas is developed.

These Romantic-era female writers emphasized *rational exchange* among women. In political tracts, essays, published letters, literary criticism, and reviews, they engaged with burning political issues of the day: the French Revolution, rights of women, rights of oppressed minorities (especially religious minorities), and campaigns to abolish the slave trade and slavery in the British colonies. In this essay, I focus on the most influential female prose writers of the 1790s – Mary Wollstonecraft, Mary Hays, Hannah More, and Anna Letitia Barbauld – and the enduring contributions each made to political and cultural debates.

Wollstonecraft began her career as a political theorist and pamphleteer. In a passionate defense of the rights of the working classes, she responded to Edmund Burke's defense of the French monarchy following the storming of the Bastille prison on July 14, 1789, and the beginning of the French Revolution. Burke's defense of the French king Louis XVI, the hereditary principle of succession, the necessary alliance between church and state, and the restriction of political power to men "of permanent property" was published in London in November, 1790, as *Reflections on the Revolution in France, and on the Proceedings in Certain Societies in London, Relative to that Event.* Burke argued that we "derive all we possess as an *inheritance from our forefathers*" and that men have equal rights "but not to equal things," using inflammatory images of revolutionary France as a female prostitute and of Queen Marie Antoinette as an innocent and pure young damsel, forced to flee "almost naked" from her bed pursued "by a band of cruel ruffians and assassins."[1] In three weeks Wollstonecraft rushed to print with *A Vindication of the Rights of Men* (November, 1790), insisting that political authority rest on reason and justice. She demanded people be entitled to enjoy and dispense the fruits of their own labors, that inequality of rank be eliminated and independent understanding and sound judgment replace exaggerated respect for the authority of "canonized forefathers." Burke imagined the nation as a ravished wife in need of virile protection, but Wollstonecraft presented it as a benevolent family educating its children for mature independence, motivated by "natural affections" to ensure the welfare of its members.[2] She laid out an early version of what political theorists now call a socialist or communitarian state.

Believing the French Revolution would establish an enlightened, socialist republic that would respect the natural rights of all, Wollstonecraft was appalled to read that the new French minister of education proposed public education for *men only*. She composed a response to the author of the *Rapport sur l'Instruction Publique, fait au nom du Comité de Constitution* (Paris, 1791), the former Bishop of Autun, Charles Maurice de Talleyrand-Perigord. Wollstonecraft perceived that the gender inequality at the core of the revolutionary French nation and of British society threatened developing democracy. She recognized that denying an equal education to women was tantamount to denying their personhood, their full participation in natural and civil rights.

Wollstonecraft initiated her own revolution, "a REVOLUTION in female manners."[3] Following Catharine Macaulay's *Letters on Education* (1790), which she had reviewed enthusiastically for the *Analytical Review*, Wollstonecraft attacked her society's definition of females as innately emotional, intuitive, illogical, and capable of moral sentiment, but not rational understanding. *A Vindication of the Rights of Woman* proposed a model of what we would now call "equality" or "liberal" feminism. Grounded on affirming universal human rights endorsed by such Enlightenment thinkers as Voltaire, Rousseau, and John Locke, underpinning both the American Revolution (1776) and the French Revolution (1789), Wollstonecraft argued that females and males are in some important aspects the same, both possessing the same souls and mental capacities and thus human rights. The first edition of the *Vindication* (January, 1792) attributed physical superiority to males, acknowledging their ability to overpower females with greater brute strength. Only six months later, in the second edition of 1792, Wollstonecraft denied the significance and necessary existence of male physical superiority. She reduced physical differences between males and females:

> In the government of the physical world it is observable that the female in point of strength is, in general, inferior to the male. This is the law of nature, and does not appear to be suspended or abrogated in favour of women. A *degree* of physical superiority cannot, therefore, be denied – and it is a noble prerogative!
>
> (*Vindication*, 24, italics added)

She then insisted women's virtues – "strength of mind, perseverance and fortitude" – are the "same in kind" if not yet in "degree" (*Vindication*, 55). She adamantly denied "the existence of sexual virtues, not excepting modesty" (*Vindication*, 71), erasing essential differences between males and females. She concluded by suggesting that if females were allowed the same exercise as males, they would arrive at "perfection of body" that might erase any "natural superiority" of the male body (*Vindication*, 111).

On this philosophical assumption of sexual equality and potential sameness, Wollstonecraft mounted her campaign for the reform of female education, arguing that girls should be educated in the same subjects and by the same methods as boys. She advocated a revision of British law to enable a new, egalitarian marriage in which women would share equally in the management and possession of household resources. British women in 1790 lived under the legal condition of *couverture* (being "covered" by the body of another), which meant they could not own or distribute property, even their own body, or possess custody of their children. To Wollstonecraft, legal *couverture* was tantamount to female slavery. Women, she argued, possessed the same souls and natural rights as men and should hold the same civil and legal rights. She demanded that women be paid – equally – for their labor, gaining civil and legal rights to possess and distribute property, and admission to prestigious professions. She argued that women (and all disenfranchised men) should be given the vote: "I really think that women ought to have representatives, instead of being arbitrarily governed without any direct share allowed them in the deliberations of government" (*Vindication*, 179).

To defend her utopian vision, Wollstonecraft described the errors and evils of society's definition of females as subordinate helpmates of males. Referring to Milton and Rousseau, she sardonically attacked their portrayals of women. Milton tells us, "That women are formed for softness and sweet attractive grace" (*Paradise Lost*, Book IV, lines 297–9). Wollstonecraft wrote with sarcasm in response, "I cannot comprehend his meaning, unless, in the true Mahometan strain he meant to deprive us of souls, and insinuate that we were beings only designed to gratify the senses of man when he can no longer soar on the wing of contemplation" (*Vindication*, 36). She saved her bitterest attacks for Rousseau, whose gender policies contradicted his politics of individual choice and the social contract. She was critical of the picture of the ideal woman that Rousseau drew in his novel *Emile*. Portraying Sophie ("female wisdom") as submissive, loving, and ever faithful, Rousseau asserted:

> The first and most important qualification in a woman is good nature or sweetness of temper: formed to obey a being so imperfect as man, often full of vices, and always full of faults, she ought to learn betimes even to suffer injustice, and to bear the insults of a husband without complaint.
>
> (*Vindication*, 108)

Much of *A Vindication* is devoted to illustrating the damage wrought by this definition of women's nature and social role. Upper- and middle-class girls were taught to become adept at arousing and sustaining (but never fully satisfying) male sexual desire to capture husbands upon whom their financial welfare depended. (It was not considered "respectable" for women to work for money.) They were obsessed with personal appearance, beauty, and fashion. Encouraged to be "delicate" and refined, many were what we now recognize as anorexic or bulimic. This model of "good" femininity encouraged, argued Wollstonecraft, hypocrisy and insincerity. Women were taught to arouse male sexual desire by allowing "innocent freedoms" or "liberties," but were forbidden to show sexual desire. They received no rational or useful education but were trained only in "female accomplishments" (penmanship, sewing, dancing, foreign languages, singing, sketching). Women were kept "in a state of perpetual childhood" (*Vindication*, 25). They were "slaves" to fathers and husbands, but, in revenge, cruel and petty tyrants to their own daughters and servants (continuing to use sexual "wiles" to manipulate husbands).

Wollstonecraft insisted the revolution in female manners would change both genders. It would produce sincerely modest, chaste, virtuous, and Christian women, who acted with reason, prudence, and generosity. It would produce men who – rather than being petty household tyrants over "house-slaves" (*Vindication*, 122) – would treat women with respect and act toward all with benevolence, justice, and sound reason. It would eliminate the "want of chastity in men," a depravity that in Wollstonecraft's view was responsible for unmanly "equivocal beings" (*Vindication*, 170). It would produce egalitarian marriages based on compatibility, mutual affection, and respect. These would be marriages of *rational love*, not erotic passion. Insisting that sexual passion does not last, she argued that "the one grand truth women have yet to learn, though most it imports them to act accordingly" is "that in the choice of a husband, they should not be led astray by the qualities of a lover – for a lover the husband, even supposing him to be wise and virtuous, cannot long remain" (*Vindication*, 148). Wollstonecraft was condemned by twentieth-century feminists as hostile to female sexual desire, but she did not mean that women should foreswear sexual passion. As her own life suggests, she embraced sexual desire. She felt strongly, however, that women channel sexual passion toward a person they rationally deemed a suitable partner, with shared interests and values. "Women as well as men ought to have the common appetites and passions of their nature," she insisted, emphasizing, "they are only brutal when unchecked by reason" (*Vindication*, 161), and concluding

> we shall not see women affectionate till more equality be established in society, till ranks are confounded and women freed, neither shall we see that dignified domestic happiness, the simple grandeur of which cannot be relished by ignorant or vitiated minds; nor will the important task of education ever be properly begun till the person of a woman is no longer preferred to her mind.
>
> (*Vindication*, 228)

Wollstonecraft advocated what we might call "family politics," where the relationship between the sexes in the home models political relationships between rulers and ruled and relationships between nation states. She may have been the first to articulate how the personal is the political. By conceiving egalitarian families as prototypes of democracy, where husbands and wives regard each other as equals in intelligence, sensitivity, and power and participate equally in childcare and decision making, Wollstonecraft envisioned a revolutionary society. Sharing the French Enlightenment *philosophes'* affirmation of reason and wit, sound moral principles, and good taste grounded on wide learning, she contested traditions of the father as the ultimate social, political, and religious authority. Where Enlightenment thinkers and nonconformist writers such as Voltaire, Thomas Paine, and Thomas Jefferson challenged the authority of the father in the name of the younger son, or challenged the authority of the king in the name of the self-made common man, Wollstonecraft challenged the rights of males in the name of all females. She even suggested that rational women might possess a greater capacity than men for virtue and the performance of moral duty, and thus for political leadership.

During the heady days of the early 1790s, as the workers and middle classes overthrew the *ancien régime* in France, Wollstonecraft's call for a revolution in female manners was immediately taken up by several female compatriots. Her close friend Mary Hays, the daughter of middle-class London Dissenters and the author of a spirited defense of the Unitarian church, *Cursory Remarks on an Enquiry into the Expediency and Propriety of Public or Social Worship* (London, 1791), sprang to the defense of Wollstonecraft's feminist program. Hays's *Letters and Essays, Moral, and Miscellaneous* (London, 1793) eloquently attacked the

> mental bondage … the absurd despotism which has hitherto, with more than gothic barbarity, enslaved the female mind, the enervating and degrading system of manners by which the understandings of women have been chained down to frivolity and trifles, have increased the general tide of effeminacy and corruption.[4]

Hays further endorsed Wollstonecraft's most radical claim, "the idea of there being no sexual character," arguing that the opposite opinion has caused far more dangerous social extremes; moreover, "similarity of mind and principle is the only true basis of harmony." She concluded, "the rights of woman, and the name of Woollstonecraft [sic], will go down to posterity with reverence, when the pointless sarcasms of witlings are forgotten" (*Letters*, 37–8). In her letter to the Dissenting *Monthly Magazine* for March 2, 1797, published under the running head "Improvements Suggested in Female Education," Hays invoked Wollstonecraft before concluding that, "Till one moral mental standard is established for every rational agent, every member of a community, and a free scope afforded for the exertion of their faculties and talents, without distinction of rank or sex, virtue will be an empty name, and happiness elude our most anxious research."[5]

Hays's most radical feminist claims appeared in her *Appeal to the Men of Great Britain in Behalf of Women*, a tract she wrote before reading Wollstonecraft's *Vindication* but did not publish until 1798. Hays was far more critical of men than was Wollstonecraft, insisting on the primary equality of women, arguing that "God created mankind male and female, different indeed in sex for the wisest and best purposes, but equal in rank, because of equal utility."[6] It is men who have defied God, Hays charged, by refusing to educate women, keeping them in "subjection and dependence" (*Appeal*, 68), in a state Hays memorably defined as "PERPETUAL BABYISM" (*Appeal*, 97). Prostitution is caused not by female vice but by "the base arts used by profligate men, to seduce innocent and unsuspecting females," and fallen women are thus "more objects of pity than blame" (*Appeal*, 235–6). And it is men who prefer "folly, vice, impertinence of every kind," who desire women to be solely "their amusement, their dependent; and in plain and unvarnished terms their slaves," because they are terrified that their unearned claims of sexual superiority could be overthrown, terrified "of the frightful certainty of having women declared their equals, and as such their companions and friends" (*Appeal*, 116).

Hays continued her campaign for liberal feminism after Wollstonecraft's death, although she was forced to speak more circumspectly because of the public denunciation of Wollstonecraft sparked by Godwin's ill-judged publication of his *Memoirs of the Author of the Vindication of the Rights of Woman* in 1798. (Hays's *Appeal* was published anonymously.) In 1803 she published her six-volume collation of 305 mini-biographies of famous women, *Female Biography, or Memoirs of Illustrious and Celebrated Women, of all Ages and Countries*, designed to inspire her female contemporaries to "a worthier emulation."[7] Hays omitted a biography of Wollstonecraft, although she included biographies of earlier feminists Mary Astell, Catharine Macaulay, and Madame Roland. Hays's actions remind us of just how dangerous it had become by 1800 for a woman who hoped to be published and taken seriously to identify openly with Wollstonecraft *as a person*. Wollstonecraft was demonized after her death. Nonetheless, many women writers who did not wish to be tarred with the blackened brush of Wollstonecraft's reputation still continued to invoke and espouse her ideas. As the nineteenth century wore on, numerous women writers and thinkers once again openly invoked Wollstonecraft as their noble precursor, in private letters and in print.

Reaffirming her commitment both to the education of women and to the importance of the feelings in social intercourse, Hays prefaced her *Female Biography* thus:

> My pen has been taken up in the cause, and for the benefit, of my own sex. For their improvement, and to their entertainment, my labours have been devoted. Women ... require pleasure to be mingled with instruction, lively images, the graces of sentiment, and the polish of language. Their understandings are principally accessible through their affections: they delight in minute delineation of character; nor must the truths which impress them be either cold or unadorned.
>
> (p. iv)

Hays moved beyond her earlier arguments for the equality of the sexes to suggest that females might be superior to males: "A woman who, to the graces and gentleness of her own sex, adds the knowledge and fortitude of the other, exhibits the most perfect combination of human excellence" (*Female*, v). In her final work, *Memoirs of Queens Illustrious and Celebrated*, however, Hays returned to Wollstonecraft's equality feminism:

> I maintain ... that there is, there can be, but *one moral standard of excellence for mankind*, whether male or female, and that the licentious distinctions

[between the sexes] made by the domineering party, in the spirit of tyranny, selfishness, and sexuality, are at the foundation of the heaviest evils that have afflicted, degraded, and corrupted society: and I found my arguments upon nature, equity, philosophy, and the Christian religion.[8]

In the 1790s, several women endorsed the program of liberal feminism that Wollstonecraft, Catharine Macaulay, and Mary Astell had developed, although none so rigorously or wholeheartedly as Hays.

In *The Female Advocate, or An Attempt to Recover the Rights of Women from Male Usurpation* (London, 1799), Mary Anne Radcliffe, evoking her personal experiences as a landed Scottish heiress whose ne'er-do-well husband had lost all their money, leaving her destitute and in ill health, bitterly attacked the lack of suitable employment for women. The poet and novelist Mary Robinson, writing as Anne Frances Randall, in her *Thoughts on the Condition of Women, and on the Injustice of Mental Subordination* (1799), attacked the sexual double standard, directly repeating Wollstonecraft's and Hays's argument that male hypocrisy was primarily responsible for female prostitution. At the same time, she celebrated accomplished female writers, philosophers, historians, translators, and artists, including both Mrs. Wollstonecraft [sic] and Miss Hayes [sic]. After calling for a university for women, Robinson turned her attention to women's writing, arguing that by 1790 the novel had become a feminine genre:

> The best novels that have been written, since those of Smollett, Richardson and Fielding, have been produced by women: and their pages have not only been embellished with the interesting events of domestic life, portrayed with all the elegance of phraseology, and all the refinement of sentiment, but with forcible and eloquent political, theological, and philosophical reasoning.[9]

At the conservative end of the feminist spectrum in Wollstonecraft's day stood Hannah More, a prolific writer of poems, plays, religious and political tracts, and ballads and fiction. So opposed to Wollstonecraft was More that she refused even to read the *Vindication of the Rights of Woman*. Often dismissed by scholars and critics as a reactionary thinker dedicated to upholding the status quo, More developed a feminist program of her own, one based on a theoretical basis different from Wollstonecraft's. More and Wollstonecraft arrived at surprisingly similar conclusions. More's career is central to understanding the full participation of women in the discursive public sphere. Famously included in Richard Samuel's group portrait of *The Nine Living Muses of Great Britain* in 1778, More was arguably the most influential woman living in England during the Romantic era. Through her writings, political actions, and personal relationships, she carried out a radical program for social change from *within* the existing social and political order, calling for a "revolution in manners"[10] or cultural mores, a radical change in the moral behavior of the nation as a whole. In contrast to Wollstonecraft's "revolution in female manners," which aimed at transforming the education and behavior of women in particular, More attempted to change the behavior of *all* the subjects of the British nation, aristocrats, clergy, the middling classes, workers, and women of all classes. Because Wollstonecraft's efforts to change the social construction of gender entailed a change in the attitudes and daily practices of men as well as women, these two "revolutions in manners" came to work toward very similar feminist goals.

More's writings contributed significantly to the prevention of a French-style, violent political revolution in England. They did so by helping to reform, rather than subvert, the existing social order. More's reform efforts were aimed in four directions: the moral and financial irresponsibility of the aristocracy, the laxness of the Anglican clergy, the immorality and economic bad management of the working classes, and the flawed education and frivolous behavior of women of all classes. What More sought was to create a new British national identity, one based on a shared value system grounded on the Christian virtues of rational benevolence, honesty, personal virtue, the fulfillment of social duty, thrift, sobriety, and hard work.

Fundamental to More's project was a transformation of the role played by women in British moral and political culture. Unlike Wollstonecraft, More insisted on the innate difference between the sexes. To women she assigned a greater delicacy of perception and feeling and a greater moral purity and capacity for virtue. Men, in More's view, had better judgment, based on wider experience of the public world; at the same time their manners are coarse, with "rough angles and asperities."[11] Wollstonecraft looked equally to men and to women to institute her new systems of co-education and egalitarian marriage; More's "revolution in manners" must be carried out primarily by women.

First, women must be educated to understand their proper function in society. More's *Strictures on the Modern System of Female Education* (1799) laid out her program for the education of "excellent women" (III: 200): a systematic development of the innate female capacity for virtue and piety through a judicious reading of the Bible, devotional tracts, and serious literature, extended by rational conversation, and manifested in the active exercise of compassion and generosity. The goal of More's educational project for women was a cultural redefinition of *female virtue*. As summed up in that "pattern daughter … [who] will make a pattern wife," Lucilla Stanley, the heroine of More's novel *Coelebs in Search of a Wife* (1808),[12] female virtue was equated by More with rational intelligence, modesty, and chastity, a sincere commitment to spiritual values and the Christian religion, an affectionate devotion to one's family, active service on behalf of one's community, and an insistence on keeping promises. In More's words:

> I call education, not that which smothers a woman with accomplishments, but that which tends to consolidate a firm and regular system of character; that which tends to form a friend, a companion, and a wife. I call education, not that which is made up of the shreds and patches of useless arts, but that which inculcates principles, polishes taste, regulates temper, cultivates reason, subdues the passions, directs the feelings, habituates to reflection, trains to self-denial, and, more especially, that which refers all actions, feelings, sentiments, tastes and passions to the love and fear of God.
>
> (*Coelebs*, 13)

More's concept of female virtue – like Wollstonecraft's concept of the rational woman – stood in contrast to her culture's definition of the ideal woman as possessing beauty and accomplishments, whose object in life was to entice a man into marriage.

Embedded in More's ideas was a new career for upper- and middle-class women, a sustained and institutionalized effort to relieve the sufferings of the less fortunate. As the novel's Mrs. Stanley says, "Charity is the calling of a lady; *the care of the poor is her profession*" (*Coelebs*, 138; More's italics). More did not endorse Wollstonecraft's view that women should enter the professions (Wollstonecraft had singled out business, medicine, and education as particularly suited to female talents). But More conceptualized the "social worker" and the organized and corporate practice of philanthropy. As embodied in Lucinda Stanley, it involved spending one day each week collecting "necessaries" for the poor – food, clothing, medicine – and two evenings visiting them in their cottages to best determine "their wants and their characters" (*Coelebs*, 63).

More advocated for women's participation in institutionalized philanthropy, a "regular systematical good" resulting in a "broad stream of bounty ... flowing through and refreshing whole districts" (*Strictures*, III: 270). She urged working aggressively in organizing voluntary benevolent societies and founding hospitals, orphanages, Sunday schools, and all-week charity or "ragged" schools for the poor. Her call was heard: thousands of voluntary societies sprang up in the early nineteenth century to serve the needs of many groups of sufferers. More's Evangelical demand that women demonstrate commitment to God through active service gave her upper- and middle-class sisters a new mission in life, to personally and financially support institutionalized charities, from orphanages, workhouses and hospitals to asylums and prisons. As F. K. Prochaska documented, these philanthropic activities contributed directly to the increasing social empowerment of women by teaching them to run complex financial institutions.[13]

More believed women were suited to charity work because of their sexual difference, possessing greater sensibility than men. More defined sensibility as an active sympathy for the sufferings of others, immediately attempting to relieve the misery it perceives. As she wrote in an early poem,

> Sweet Sensibility! thou keen delight!
> Thou hasty moral! sudden sense of right!
> Thou untaught goodness! Virtue's precious seed!
> Thou sweet precursor of the gen'rous deed![14]

Women were more versed in what More called "practical piety," the assessment and relief of the day-to-day requirements of the poor, sick, and dying. Women who learned how to manage a household properly could extend those skills to the Sunday school, the workhouse, or the hospital. By assigning to women – and their mentor Eve – the capacity to develop and execute a plan of management for the physical, emotional, and religious needs of the household (servants as well as family members), More defined women as the best managers of the national estate, as the true patriots. More proposed "a practical politics of domestic reformation, which is national in the ambitious scope of its campaign and personal in its focus on the woman in her family as the source of this larger regeneration," as Kathryn Sutherland argues.[15]

It is in the role of mother that More's ideal of the well-educated, fiscally responsible, and morally pure woman finds fulfillment. It is crucial to recognize that More's mother is the mother, not just of her own family, but of the nation. More implicitly endorses Wollstonecraft's "family politics," seeing the well-managed, co-parented, and egalitarian family as providing a model for governing the state. As More wrote,

> The great object to which you, who are or may be mothers, are more especially called, is the education of your children. If we are responsible for the use of influence in the case of those over whom we have no immediate control, in the case of our children we are responsible for the exercise of acknowledged power: a power wide in its extent, indefinite in its effects, and inestimable in its importance. On YOU depend in no small degree the principles of the whole rising generation ... To YOU is made over the awfully important trust of infusing the first principles of piety into the tender minds of those who may one day be called to instruct, not families merely, but districts; to influence, not individuals, but senates. Your private exertions may at this moment be contributing to the future happiness, your domestic neglect, to the future ruin, of your country.

> (*Strictures*, III: 44)

As Anne Stott has argued, Hannah More was the "first Victorian," the thinker who promoted the domestic ideology that came to dominate the later nineteenth century.[16] More's vision was more radical than her followers recognized. She would insist, not on the doctrine of the separate spheres associated with Victorian concepts of the "angel in the house," but on the empowerment of women as the Mothers of the Nation.

In making the private middle-class household the model for the national household, as had Wollstonecraft, More erased meaningful distinctions between the private and public sphere. Both More and Wollstonecraft agreed that women, not men, were most responsible for carrying out moral reforms and advancing the progress of civilization. As More put it, "The general state of civilized society depends more than those are aware who are not accustomed to scrutinize into the springs of human action, on the prevailing sentiments and habits of women, and on the nature and degree of the estimation in which they are held" (*Strictures*, III: 12). Insisting on the primary role of women in establishing "true taste, right principle, and genuine feeling" in the culture of a nation, both More and Wollstonecraft claimed for women the dominant role in the civilizing process.

Between these two camps of feminist reform, Wollstonecraft's overtly political "revolution in female manners" based on an assertion of sexual equality and universal human rights and More's more restrictively cultural "revolution in manners" based on sexual difference and the essential moral superiority of women, other women writers took up more moderate feminist positions. Most notable in their efforts to find a middle ground were the Dissenters, women whose religion (Quaker, Unitarian, or Methodist) granted them a degree of sexual equality based on their capacity for virtue, rationality, and religious leadership.

The Unitarian Anna Letitia Barbauld was inspired by her education at the leading Dissenting academy, Warrington Academy, where her father was the tutor in Classics and Belles Lettres. She argued for the equal rights of all British religious subjects in her fiery denunciation of the government's refusal to repeal the Corporation and Test Acts, which prohibited non-members of the Church of England from holding political office or attending the established universities. This was in her political pamphlet *Appeal to the Opposers of the Repeal of the Corporation and Test Acts* (1790). Barbauld became the leading female literary critic of her day. She assembled the first "canon" of the British novel, a reprinted series of eighteenth- and early nineteenth-century novels. In her essay *On the Origin and Progress of Novel-Writing* (1810) that prefaces these fifty volumes, she argued for the superiority of the genre of fiction over poetry and drama, claiming the novel better represented the probability of everyday life as well as the moral developments and failures of human beings. After insisting that the majority of the best fiction writers of her day were "ladies," invoking Frances (Burney) D'Arblay, Maria Edgeworth, Elizabeth Inchbald, and Ann Radcliffe, she concluded that novelists were central to the formation of shared cultural beliefs and moral codes: "It was said by Fletcher of Saltoun, 'Let me make the ballads of a nation, and I care not who makes the laws.' Might it not be said with as much propriety, Let me make the novels of a country, and let who will make the systems?"[17]

Barbauld insisted that since mothers were the primary educators of young children, they should guide their reading to inculcate rational thought and moral sensibility. Every mother becomes a literary critic. She promoted the rational religious education of children in her *Hymns in Prose for Children* and was a leading advocate for the abolition of slavery, writing poems and tracts, including *Sins of Government, Sins of the Nation, or A Discourse for the Fast* (1793). She attacked the British slave trade, slavery in the British colonies, and the growing corruption of government and commerce as the British empire extended to India and the Pacific Islands. "Are there not some *darker-coloured* children of the same family, over whom we assume a hard and unjust control?" she asked, and concluded, "if such enormities ... are still sanctioned by our legislature, defended by our princes – deep indeed is the colour of our guilt."[18]

Intellectual disagreements and psychological tensions existed between the leading women political essayists in England in the Romantic era. Although all advocated for improved education of women and increased female control over domestic, social, cultural, and political life, they held distinctly different views as to how women could best exercise that new cultural authority. Wollstonecraft, Hays, and Mary Robinson would have women fulfill the social and political roles currently played by men, Barbauld would have women enter the literary realm as didactic writers, educators, and critical judges, while More would have women engage in a life of active service for the welfare of others.

NOTES

1 Edmund Burke, *Reflections on the Revolution in France and on the Proceedings in Certain Societies in London, Relative to that Event* (November, 1790), ed. Thomas H. D. Mahoney (New York: Liberal Arts Press, 1955), pp. 35, 67, 82.
2 Mary Wollstonecraft, *A Vindication of the Rights of Men* (London, 1790), facsimile edition with introduction by Eleanor Louise Nicholes (Gainesville, FL: Scholars' Facsimiles & Reprints, 1960), pp. 41, 52.
3 Mary Wollstonecraft, *A Vindication of the Rights of Woman and The Wrongs of Woman, or Maria*, ed. Anne K. Mellor and Noelle Chao (New York: Longman

Cultural Edition, 2007), p. 230. Subsequent references cited parenthetically in the text.

4 Mary Hays, from *Letters and Essays, Moral, and Miscellaneous*, reprinted in *British Literature, 1780–1830*, ed. Anne K. Mellor and Richard Matlak (Fort Worth, TX: Harcourt Brace / Thomson Learning, 1996), p. 37. Subsequent references cited parenthetically in the text.

5 [Mary Hays], "Improvements Suggested in Female Education," *Monthly Magazine* 3 (1797): 195.

6 Mary Hays, *Appeal to the Men of Great Britain in Behalf of Women* (1798), introduction by Gina Luria (New York and London: Garland, 1974), p. 21. Subsequent references cited parenthetically in the text.

7 Mary Hays, *Female Biography, or Memoirs of Illustrious and Celebrated Women, of All Ages and Countries* (London: R. Phillips, 1803), p. vi. Subsequent references cited parenthetically in the text.

8 Mary Hays, *Memoirs of Queens Illustrious and Celebrated* (London: T. and J. Allman, 1821), p. vi.

9 [Mary Hays], *Thoughts on the Condition of Women, and on the Injustice of Mental Subordination*, 2nd edn. (London: Longman and Rees, 1799), p. 95.

10 Hannah More, *The Works of Hannah More*, 6 vols. (London: H. Fisher, R. Fisher and P. Jackson, 1834), Vol. II, p. 316. Subsequent references are to this edition and are cited parenthetically in the text.

11 Hannah More, "Introduction," in *Essays on Various Subjects, Principally Designed for Young Ladies* (London: J. Wilkie and T. Cadell, 1777), p. 13.

12 Hannah More, *Coelebs in Search of a Wife* (London, 1808; repr. Bristol: Theommes Press, 1995), p. 246. Subsequent references are cited parenthetically in the text.

13 F. K. Prochaska, *Women and Philanthropy in Nineteenth-Century England* (Oxford: Clarendon Press, 1980), p. 227 and passim.

14 Hannah More, *Sacred Dramas: Chiefly Intended for Young Persons: The Subjects Taken from the Bible; To which is Added, Sensibility: A Poem* (London: T. Cadell, 1782), p. 282.

15 Kathryn Sutherland, "Hannah More's Counter-Revolutionary Feminism," in *Revolution in Writing: British Literary Responses to the French Revolution*, ed. Kelvin Everest (Milton Keynes and Philadelphia: Open University Press, 1991), p. 36.

16 Anne Stott, *Hannah More: The First Victorian* (Oxford University Press, 2003).

17 Anna Letitia Barbauld, "On the Origin and Progress of Novel-Writing," Introduction to *The British Novelists*, 50 vols. (London: Rivington, 1810), Vol. I, p. 33.

18 [Anna Letitia Barbauld], *Sins of Government, Sins of the Nation, or A Discourse for the Fast* (London: J. Johnson, 1793), p. 20.

5

ANGELA WRIGHT

The Gothic

For those unfamiliar with the Gothic, picking one's way across the literary and critical terrain can be a fraught task. As an analytical and historical term, "Gothic" has been applied to a style of architecture, a Germanic tribe, a form of British patriotism, reactionary thought, and last, but not least, to a burgeoning literary form in the eighteenth century and Romantic period. It comes as little consolation to discover that all of these meanings were in circulation during this time, and that of this range of definitions, the least recorded usage applied to the burgeoning literary genre, the Gothic.

Horace Walpole's second edition of his novel *The Castle of Otranto* (1765) was the first to use the subtitle "A Gothic Story," followed in the next decade by Clara Reeve's *The Old English Baron: A Gothic Story* (1778), originally published under the title *The Champion of Virtue* (1777). After the examples of Walpole and Reeve, however, the taking up of the term "Gothic" was slow and reluctant. Nonetheless, even if authors and readers of the Romantic period did not use the word Gothic freely to define the form of writing that we now know by that term, they had the contours of that literary form firmly in their minds. Poet and novelist Charlotte Smith articulated those contours quite clearly in the lighthearted complaint that she launched in the Preface to Volume 2 of *The Banished Man*:

> For my part, who can now no longer build chateaux even en Espagne, I find that Mowbray Castle, Grasmere Abbey, the castle of Rock-March, the castle of Hauteville, and Rayland Hall, have taken so many of my materials to construct, that I have hardly a watch tower, a Gothic arch, a cedar parlour, or a long gallery, an illuminated window, or a ruined chapel, left to help myself. Yet some of these are indispensably necessary; and I have already built and burnt down one of these venerable edifices in this work, yet must seek wherewithal to raise another.
>
> But my ingenious contemporaries have fully possessed themselves of every bastion and buttress – of every tower and turret – of every gallery and gateway, together with all their furniture of ivy mantles, and mossy battlements;

tapestry, and old pictures, owls, bats, and ravens – that I had some doubts whether, to avoid the charge of plagiarism, it would not have been better to have *earthed* my hero, and have sent him for adventures to the subterraneous town on the Chatelet mountain in Champagne, or even to Herculaneum, or Pompeii, where I think no scenes have yet been laid, and where I should have been in less danger of being *again* accused of borrowing, than I may perhaps be, while I only visit "The glympses of the moon."[1]

Smith's claim for innovation in the burgeoning genre of what we now appreciate as Gothic writing is remarkable for its confident articulation of the challenges associated with that form. Using the first-person pronoun with frequency, Smith moves between the architectural tropes of the Gothic and the languages of French and English, and plays with alternative European locations for her future novels. As a discussion of contemporaneous fictional practice, it is a remarkable expression of certain uncertainty. Smith confesses quite openly that she has "hardly a watch tower ... left to help myself" and that she has "doubts whether, to avoid the charge of plagiarism" she should instead send her hero to sites of archaeological interest (Pompeii and Herculaneum) that had captured public imagination in the late eighteenth century.[2] With an eye upon her readership's appetite, Smith's debate upon whether to relocate her fiction at a safe distance from the increasingly popular Gothic is responsive to the competing and often conflicting demands of authorship and readership.

Smith acknowledges that the architecture of the castle is "indispensably necessary" to her economic and socio-political purposes, drawing attention to a rare consonance in the reading marketplace between catering to an audience's appetite and writing about what mattered. Castles may seem, at first glance, to be flights of fancy, far removed from the commercial and social demands of the 1790s, but the frequent invocation of them by Smith and her many contemporaries indicated a shared concern about issues surrounding the ownership and exploitation of property. Ann Radcliffe, Maria Regina Roche, Charlotte Smith, Mary Robinson, and Eliza Parsons were some of the most popular female authors of the 1790s. Their works consistently and seriously addressed themes of women being dispossessed of their rightful property. That contested property was figured through the structure of the castle.

The combination of a heroine and a castle formed a stable combination of features that critics such as Ellen Moers, Kate Ferguson Ellis, Anne Williams, and Diane Long Hoeveler have located within a specifically female tradition of Gothic composition. Writing in the late 1970s, Ellen Moers first coined the term "Female Gothic," which bonded the gender of the author with her subject matter.[3] As a category of research that has since been strongly contested, "Female Gothic" did succeed in placing the question of gender at the heart of any critical analysis of this body of fiction. Since Moers's formative work, others have chosen to foreground the Gothic's uncanny ability to pinpoint the contradictions between the feminine domestic space and the male public sphere. Recent studies attest to the vibrancy of Gothic fiction, a body of writing that still remains overlooked. In what follows, I demonstrate the similarities and crucial diversity of Gothic writing by women during the Romantic period, exploring how female authors negotiated a marketplace that viewed them with skepticism, and describing how several became successful authors who were able to negotiate large sums of money for their work.

A "feminine fiction"?

As the parameters of Gothic fiction came to be recognized in the 1790s, so too did they come to be understood, rather disparagingly and misleadingly, as "feminine." The Gothic novel's "feminine" form accommodated its female authorship, the fictional tropes of the heroine fleeing the tyrant, and the gender of its readership. For the anti-Jacobin Reverend T. J. Mathias in *The Pursuits of Literature* (1794–7), the Gothic tended to "turn our girls heads wild with impossible adventures."[4] Many a satirical recipe produced in the periodical press of the 1790s regurgitated this view. Mathias included both Charlotte Smith and Mary Robinson in his list of "*unsexed* female writers" who "now instruct, or confuse, us and themselves in the labyrinths of politics or turn us wild with Gallic frenzy."[5] The anonymous author of "The Terrorist System of Novel Writing" in *The Monthly Magazine* of 1797 also worried about his daughters' unbridled consumption of Gothic fiction as events across the channel in France became increasingly violent.[6] Catherine Morland in Jane Austen's *Northanger Abbey* (composed *c.* 1797, published posthumously in 1818) also confuses revolution with novelistic events. "Fashion" was emphasized derogatively in many of these satires. The anonymously composed "Terrorist Novel Writing" (1798), for example, complained of a "great quantity of novels … in which it has been the fashion to make *terror the order of the day*, by confining the heroes and heroines in old gloomy castles, full of spectres, apparitions, ghosts, and dead men's bones. This is now so common," the writer concluded, "that a Novelist blushes to bring about a marriage by ordinary means."[7] The blushes of the novelist hinted toward the gender of that author, connecting the vogue for ghosts, heroes, and heroines irrevocably to female authorship. Specters, dead men's bones, castles, and heroines: women's Gothic writing during the Romantic period was all too easily caricatured for its reputedly stable set of ingredients. "Terrorist Novel Writing" implicitly connected this to a feminine form of fiction both in terms of form and readership. It complained of the "dresses and decorations of a modern novel" (1798) and the paucity of education that such feminine embellishment would offer a "young lady," before concluding with a satirical recipe for composing a Gothic novel. These recipes cropped up frequently in the periodical press of the 1790s; they were later transformed into novelistic satire of Gothic writing in the 1810s, with Eaton Stannard Barrett's *The Heroine, or Adventures for the Romance Reader* (1813), Thomas Love Peacock's *Nightmare Abbey* (1818), and Jane Austen's posthumously published *Northanger Abbey* seemingly satirizing both the female consumption and production of Gothic fiction.

As early as 1794, Smith's "Avis au Lecteur" in *The Banished Man* can be seen to anticipate and play with these concerns of a "feminine" fiction. Interspersing her English with occasional French phrases, castles become "chateaux en Espagne," playfully alluding to the effeminized values associated with France and with the Gothic. What is more, Smith's "ingenious contemporaries" are without a doubt female. Women's Gothic writing during the Romantic period thus comes to epitomize the anxieties of the decade in which it became truly popular. The political anxieties of the 1790s could not and did not accommodate such a burgeoning authorship and readership with complacency. The generic features of the Gothic – castles, imprisoned heroines, rapacious and tyrannical villains – came perilously close to the unfolding revolutionary events in France. Associated with France and Catholic continental Europe, women's Gothic writing became synonymous with cultural treason. What better way, then, to dismiss the subject matter of this literature as lightly "feminine," in order to dismiss their consistently serious engagement with revolutionary politics? This "feminization," I argue, is something that Charlotte Smith and many others embraced, for it suited their economic and social purposes.

Revolutionary engagements

The interconnections between women's Gothic writing in the 1790s and revolutionary discourse began with the formative debate conducted between Edmund Burke and Mary Wollstonecraft in 1790. In responding to Burke's *Reflections on the Revolution in France* (1790) in *A Vindication of the Rights of Men* (1790), Wollstonecraft decried Burke's "gothic notions of beauty" and "Gothic materials," connecting them explicitly with his effeminized idolatry of the fallen French queen Marie Antoinette and his denigration of the unfolding events in France. Burke's veneration of the Gothic castle, for Wollstonecraft, became associated with his urge to defend the outdated values of the English constitution. "Why was it a duty to repair an ancient castle, built in barbarous ages, of Gothic materials?" Wollstonecraft demanded of Burke. Burke's urge to preserve the Gothic castle of the English constitution was further flawed, in Wollstonecraft's estimation, by his lament for the "idle tapestry that decorated a gothic pile."[8] The movement from the architectural features of Burke's conservatism to its decorative embellishment by the "idle tapestry" was a vital sign, to Wollstonecraft, of Burke's elision of indulgent sentiment with constitutional debate.

It comes as no surprise, then, to see these concerns writ large in women's Gothic writing of the Romantic period. If we return to Smith's "Avis au Lecteur," we see these concerns between architectural and decorative features figured quite precisely. The architectural features of Smith's Mowbray Castle from *Emmeline, the Orphan of the Castle* (1788) and Grasmere Abbey from *Ethelinde* (1789) comprise Gothic arches, "cedar parlours," "illuminated windows," and "ruined chapels."[9] By 1794, these had been used quite extensively by Smith, Radcliffe, and Parsons. A closer reading, however, tells us that the architectural figuring of the castle is not Smith's immediate concern; rather, it is the hackneyed embellishment of the "gallery and gateway," the "ivy mantles, and mossy battlements, old pictures, owls, bats, and ravens" that Smith claims her "ingenious contemporaries" had embraced so fulsomely. The more organic life forms (ivy, owls, bats, and ravens) that decorated the castles of Smith's contemporaries had, in her estimation, diminished the potential political and socio-economic resonances of the castle. The castle had offered up the space in which authors, both male and female, could, like Burke and Wollstonecraft, debate the English constitution, but as we have seen, its sensational embellishments were decried by critics as symptomatic of a decline in literary values.

For many critics, however, Ann Radcliffe was exempted from the charge sheet of female subversives. T. J. Mathias exonerated her with the observation, "Not so the mighty magician of The Mysteries of Udolpho, bred and nourished by the Florentine muses, in their sacred, solitary caverns, amid the paler shrines of Gothic superstition."[10] Recording possibly one of the earliest usages of the term "Gothic" in relation to Radcliffe, Mathias seemed inclined, one might argue, to associate Radcliffe with a more masculine tradition of writing. Engaging with more proper, classical sources, Radcliffe was the "mighty magician" in Mathias's version. Her place in the canon was secured by her engagement with Tasso, Ariosto, Edmund Spenser, William Shakespeare, James Thomson, and Thomas Gray, whereas Smith's and Robinson's more contemporaneous versions of war-torn revolutionary France (in Smith's *Desmond* [1792] and Robinson's *Hubert de Sevrac* [1796]) divested them of the garments of their sex.

In other words, in Mathias's flawed readings, Smith and Robinson were "unsexed" due to their improper incursions into the realm of the contemporary political landscape, in which they dared to portray views that were sympathetic to the ideals of the French Revolution, whereas Ann Radcliffe succeeded by self-consciously aligning herself with a more remote, classical, masculine tradition of composition. Her exceptionalism was also foregrounded in masculine terms in Nathan Drake's oft-cited anointment of Radcliffe as "the Shakspear [sic] of Romance writers" in *Literary Hours* (1798).[11] By defining Radcliffe as *the* Shakespeare, Drake not only placed her at the pinnacle of the genre of romance in the 1790s; he also naturalized her supremacy as a masculine achievement.

The origins and iterations of Radcliffean success

Radcliffe's growing economic success was an important factor in the composition of Charlotte Smith's "Avis au Lecteur." Such a preface was, in many ways, an astute maneuver upon Smith's part as she came to appreciate the commercial potential of Gothic fiction. The year 1794 saw the fourth publication of Ann Radcliffe's four-volume *The Mysteries of Udolpho*, which made its author one of the most famed and well-paid writers of the eighteenth century. It was the first novel that Radcliffe did not publish anonymously, indicating a growing confidence in the readership, payment, and reception of her work. Radcliffe's first novel, *The Castles of Athlin and Dunbayne* (1789), situated, as the title suggests, in Scotland, had been published anonymously by Hookham. The two novels that followed, *A Sicilian Romance* (1790) and *The Romance of the Forest* (1791), moved her fiction to continental, Catholic locations, but trading upon the small amount of success that her first novel had enjoyed, they were advertised to the public as being by the "authoress" of her preceding work. Only in the second edition of *The Romance of the Forest* (1792) did Radcliffe acknowledge her authorship.

The Mysteries of Udolpho is a testament to the resolution of both publisher and author, for on the title page of its first edition, Radcliffe's name stood prominent: "The Mysteries of Udolpho; A Romance; interspersed with some pieces of poetry. By Ann Radcliffe, Author of the Romance of the Forest, etc. In Four Volumes." The title page drew attention to the generic diversity of the work; the "romance" was to be "interspersed" with "some pieces of poetry." Its atmospheric qualities were further emphasized by the poetic fragment that stood as epigraph to the novel:

> Fate sits on these dark battlements, and frowns,
> And, as the portals open to receive me,

> Her voice, in sullen echoes through the courts,
> Tells of a nameless deed.[12]

This irregular fragment offers a metaphor for what is to follow, not just at the level of story, but also in terms of the relationship between the novel and the reader. The "portals" are opening, transporting the nameless character into the castle as they transport the young reader across the threshold of the novel. "Portals" give no hint as to what truly lies inside either the novel or the castle beyond; by their very nature they are a threshold. They simulate a sublime and rather breathless response, mirrored in the irregularity of the meter here. At the level of story, this also foregrounds key elements with the emphasis upon subjectivity (the unnamed "me"): the personification of fate and the dimly anticipated threat of the castle. The castle's portals open only to admit the unidentified "me." But Fate, personified as a female, tells the tale of a "nameless deed." That deed is articulated only through its uncertainty; we do not know where the deed was committed, or indeed what it was. The "nameless deed" mirrors the nameless protagonist, deliberately anonymous, one imagines, so that the reader can anticipate and imagine her tale herself. Further, if the heroine is without name, then so too can any crime committed against her remain unnamed. In the compressed space of four irregular poetic lines, Radcliffe foregrounds some key aspects of her craft. Atmosphere, anticipation, imagination, female subjectivity, female sorority, and the uncharted but dreaded "deed" are features that became crucial to the fiction of Radcliffe and her 1790s contemporaries Maria Regina Roche, Eliza Parsons, Eleanor Sleath, and Mary Robinson, to name but a few.

In *The Mysteries of Udolpho*, which earned Radcliffe the impressive sum of £600 in 1794, the heroine Emily St. Aubert is first presented to the reader with both a mother and father, who rear her in pastoral seclusion at La Vallée in Gascony in France. It is not long, however, before the sentimental education that both parents offer is torn away from the heroine, and she is transported into an environment where careless, unfeeling relatives expose her to danger. Montoni, the villain of the novel who imprisons her in the Castle of Udolpho, will sneer at Emily St. Aubert as he tries to force her to sign away her birthright, "You speak like a heroine, we will see whether you can suffer like one" (381). His threats remain largely empty. The precise nature of Montoni's villainy is undetermined. Instead, it is the threat of the castle, which, to Emily's imagination, "seemed to stand the sovereign of the scene, and to frown defiance on all, who dared to invade its solitary reign" (277). It is the impenetrability, the indefinability of that edifice that is "vast, ancient and dreary," that is the locus of the heroine's terror. Castles and monastic edifices can conceal and protect tyrannical figures who usurp ownership, abuse guardianship, and abrogate moral authority. This was a theme that was present in the first examples of the Gothic tradition, by Horace Walpole and Clara Reeve. Walpole's *Castle of Otranto* (1764) and Reeve's *The Old English Baron* (first published under the title *The Champion of Virtue* in 1777) both presented usurpers who tried to deny rightful male heirs their birthright. By the time of Reeve's example, legal, social, and economic matters had become the central concerns of the Gothic plot, relegating the villain's guilt (in Reeve's case Lord Lovel) and the use of the supernatural to supporting roles.

As Charlotte Smith's "Avis au Lecteur" implicitly acknowledges, Radcliffe's and Smith's female contemporaries further exploited the theme of the usurping, sometimes lecherous villain who would test the heroine's mettle. The supernatural's already auxiliary function was dispensed with by women authors who followed in the wake of Walpole and Reeve. Sophia Lee, whose three-volume historical novel *The Recess* was composed between the years of 1783 and 1785, imagined fictive twin daughters of Mary, Queen of Scots, who are protected in an underground asylum from the machinations of a paranoid Queen Elizabeth I. Described as an early example of both Gothic and historical fiction in England, Lee's novel yoked the epistolary sentimental tradition to a terrifying exploration of the possible fates of women who have no parental or legal protection. This was no ghost story, but it did invoke the word "spectre" several times in relation to the guilt that the villain (Elizabeth I) feels when she is confronted by the wronged daughters of her arch-enemy, Mary, Queen of Scots. Ellinor, the second sister, loses her sanity in the face of the pressures that the sisters encounter, and is described by another woman as a "fair spectre, which once was Ellinor."[13] In Lee's account, Matilda and Ellinor become the return of the repressed, there to remind Elizabeth of the wrongs that she has committed against their mother. The supernatural is no longer necessary, as the story's female protagonists have become the forgotten and neglected in place of ghosts.

The Recess remains difficult to pigeonhole purely as Gothic romance due to its generic hybridity. Its internalization of the supernatural, however, was crucial to the more recognizable Gothic productions of the authors who followed. One such legacy was the strange lights and noises from an uninhabited part of a castle that Ann Radcliffe's two sister characters, Julia and Emilia, fear must come from a ghost in *A Sicilian Romance* (1790). The noises emanate, it transpires, from their own mother who has been imprisoned there by her ruthless and dissipated husband for fifteen years.

The Castle of Wolfenbach: A German Story by Eliza Parsons, published in two volumes by William Lane in 1793, tells a similar tale of marital neglect. True to the spirit of the developing tradition of Gothic romance, a servant warns a young unprotected lady against taking shelter in a neighboring castle: "O! dear madam, why it is haunted; there are bloody floors, prison rooms, and scriptions, they say, on the windows, to make a body's hair stand on end."[14] As with Lee and Radcliffe, terror for Parsons lies not in the supernatural, but in a tyrannical character (in this instance, a husband) who imprisons his wife. Once she is released, by the discovery of the younger woman Matilda, Parsons's tale moves abruptly and quickly away from its Gothic location and tropes to a more sentimental novel of manners that is set in England.

The castle also contains the same source of terror for Radcliffe's most popular contemporary of the 1790s. Although Regina Maria Roche remains relatively understudied, her popularity during the 1790s was on a par with Radcliffe's. Roche's 1796 novel *The Children of the Abbey* was one of only fifty-six novels published in the British Isles that ran to more than five editions before 1801. It was also translated into French within a year of its appearance, published as *Les Enfans de l'Abbaye* in Paris in 1797. Roche's next novel, *Clermont* (1798), may not have enjoyed quite the same level of runaway success as *The Children of the Abbey*, but it was memorialized as one of the "horrid" novels that Catherine Morland and Isabella Thorpe breathlessly read in Austen's *Northanger Abbey* (1818). Like Smith's *Ethelinde* (1789), Radcliffe's *Castles of Athlin and Dunbayne* (1789) and *The Mysteries of Udolpho* (1794), Roche's *Clermont* offers up two versions of castles, the Chateaux de Merville and de Montmorenci. In these spaces, the heroine Madeline must confront the tyrannical terrors of the D'Alemberts. Their capacity for cruelty is confirmed by the buildings that they choose to inhabit:

> The vast magnitude and decaying grandeur of the chateau, impressed Madeline with surprise and melancholy; which were almost heightened to awe and veneration on entering a gloomy-vaulted hall of immense size, with small arched windows, and supported by stone arches, ornamented with rude sculpture, and hung with rusty coats of armour.[15]

Here, the adjectival embellishment is as important as the architectural structure of the castle; the sculptures must be "rude" and the coats of armour "rusty" in order to illustrate the feudal tastes of its owner.

The two-castle model used by Smith, Radcliffe, Roche, and many others was in some instances substituted for two monasteries or two convents. Radcliffe's penultimate novel, *The Italian* (1797), for example, offered up two versions of convents, with the arbitrary tyranny of the first being counterbalanced by the mercy and toleration shown in the second, Santa Maria della Pièta. The focus upon monastic or conventual tyranny was something that Mary Robinson also exploited in her three-volume novel

Hubert de Sevrac (1796), where the heroine Sabina de Sevrac must confront and overcome monastic tyranny as a priest attempts to manipulate her marital choice.

Critical exhaustion?

To return to this essay's opening quotation, it seems prescient of Charlotte Smith to have identified the coherence of a Gothic tradition in the "Avis au Lecteur." It was also premature of her to complain of the critical exhaustion of Gothic tropes at this stage, for many of my examples, and certainly the bestselling ones, come from after 1794. Perhaps due to the advent of critiques such as "The Terrorist System of Novel Writing," the year 1798 seems to be the watershed moment in which critical complaints of imitation and plagiarism really become prominent. By 1796, many women authors (including Roche and Robinson) published under their own names. This confidence may in itself have attracted greater censure, as they were compared unfavorably with the works of Radcliffe. Of Robinson's *Hubert de Sevrac* (1796), for example, the *Critical Review* observed that "It is an imitation of Mrs. Radcliffe's romances, but without any resemblance that may not be attained by a common pen."[16] Of Roche's *Clermont*, the same periodical complained, "This tale reminds us, without any great pleasure, of Mrs. Radcliffe's romances. In Clermont mystery is heaped upon mystery, and murder upon murder, with little art, and great improbability."[17] As these reviews indicate, Radcliffe was frequently singled out as being the exception to the rule of the species of Gothic romance writing, which she had pioneered in creating. When reviewing Radcliffe's penultimate romance *The Italian*, the *Critical Review* woefully prophesied that "the constitution" of "*modern romance* would degenerate into repetition, and would disappoint curiosity."[18]

Such a prediction appeared to be supported by the spate of parodies of the 1810s – Barrett's *The Heroine*, Peacock's *Nightmare Abbey*, Austen's *Northanger Abbey* – that seemingly insisted upon the formulaic and derivative nature of Gothic writing by women, and the dangerously overheated responses of its female readership. One must be careful with this assessment for several reasons, however. First of all, it is important to acknowledge, as Austen does in *Northanger Abbey* (1818), that neither the readership nor the authorship of Gothic romance was straightforwardly female. Austen's Henry Tilney confesses to Catherine Morland that his "hair [stood] on end the whole time" he read Radcliffe's *Mysteries of Udolpho*.[19] A particularly engaging letter that Jane Austen sent to her sister Cassandra sounds a further note of caution when she makes the complacent observation that

"My father is now reading the 'Midnight Bell', which he has got from the library."[20] The fact that Austen's clerical father reads a Gothic novel, and one by an anonymous author whose work reappears on Catherine Morland and Isabella Thorpe's reading list in *Northanger Abbey*, is not a subject of particular censure by her in 1798. But this anecdote adds a further layer of complexity to the gendering of the authorship and readership of Gothic fiction during the Romantic period. *The Midnight Bell*, as it happens, was composed by a man named Francis Lathom. His first novel, *The Castle of Ollada*, had been published by the Minerva Press in 1795; *The Midnight Bell: A German Story, Founded on Incidents in Real Life* was Lathom's second anonymously published work. As a year, 1798 reveals a high number of Gothic fictions that were published anonymously, but which in fact turned out to be by male authors who were perhaps keen to exploit the commercial potential of Gothic fiction but unwilling to run the risk of critical opprobrium that their female contemporaries attracted. It is also worth bearing in mind, too, that Percy Shelley's first book was a Gothic novel, *Zastrozzi: A Romance*, published almost anonymously with only his initials P. B. S. in 1810.

There is a second note of caution to sound about the thematic, gendered, and generic homogeneity of women's Gothic writing during the Romantic period. "Gothic" moved beyond the confines of the heroine escaping the clutches of the villain before the end of the 1790s. Joanna Baillie's first volume of *Plays on the Passions*, for example, first published in 1798, sought not to explore the psychology of a heroine, but to take a passion, and to demonstrate how it functions in the formation and agency of character. Baillie chose not to confine these explorations to female character alone. One of her first and most chilling tragedies, *De Monfort*, focused upon the workings of envy in a male character, De Monfort, who is curiously drawn towards his arch-enemy Rezenvelt. A few months after Baillie had composed *Count Basil, The Tryal,* and *De Monfort*, she wrote a lengthy "Introductory Discourse" which set out her theorization of our "sympathetick curiosity":

> Our love of the grand, the beautiful, the novel, and above all of the marvellous, is very strong; and if we are richly fed with what we have a good relish for, we may be weaned to forget our native and favourite aliment. Yet we can never so far forget it, but that we will cling to, and acknowledge it again, whenever it is presented to us. In a work abounding with the marvellous and the unnatural, if the author has anyhow stumbled upon an unsophisticated genuine stroke of nature, we will immediately perceive and be delighted with it, though we are foolish enough to admire at the same time, all the nonsense with which it is surrounded. After all the wonderful incidents, dark mysteries, and secrets revealed ... after the beautiful fairy ground, and even the grand

and sublime scenes of nature with which descriptive novel so often enchants us; these works which most strongly characterize human nature ... will ever be the most popular.[21]

Derived in part from Adam Smith's *Theory of Moral Sentiments* (1759), Baillie's discourse insisted that human beings all shared the quality of "sympathetick curiosity."[22] At first glance, the passage quoted here seems to take a sideswipe at the Radcliffean school of romance, dismissing the "fairy ground" and "grand and sublime scenes of nature," but I do not think that this is the case. "Stumbl[ing] upon" a "stroke of nature," Baillie suggests, is a genuine, legitimate, and rare discovery that must be celebrated. For Baillie's own dramas do not dispense with the Gothic mode; in fact, quite the opposite. *De Monfort* (1798) concludes with the eponymous anti-hero being taken to a neighboring monastery after he has murdered his enemy. The closing scenes of *De Monfort* are replete with atmospheric music and Gothic architecture; her later tragedy *Orra* (from the third and final volume of the *Plays on the Passions*, published in 1812) finds a young girl imprisoned in a castle, subject to the manipulations of those around her. The Gothic architecture serves only to illuminate the natural and all too human passions to which Baillie's protagonists are subject.

Joanna Baillie's Gothic dramas were not unique; Harriet Lee's *The Mysterious Marriage, or The Heirship of Roselva* was in fact composed earlier, in 1795, published in 1798, but never performed, as London theater managers refused to stage it due to its potent combination of ghosts, murder, and bad marriage. Theater managers and reviewers gradually became more sanguine about women's Gothic drama as the decades progressed and the plays proliferated. Of Elizabeth Polack's later *St Clair of the Isles* (1838), for example, one anonymous reviewer remarked of its opening evening, "We are free to confess that we anticipated a milk and water concern, but Miss Polack, the fair authoress of St. Clair of the Isles, agreeably disappointed us."[23] Polack's exceptionalism came from the fact that her heroine was in fact a villainess who outwitted the male characters in her drama.

Women's Gothic dramaturgy, in part pioneered by Joanna Baillie and then embraced by many other authors, marked a subtle shift of direction in some (but certainly not all) women's Gothic writing. Poet and novelist Charlotte Dacre, for example, reprised the theme of the passions in her four Gothic novels, composed between 1805 and 1811, *Confessions of the Nun of St. Omer* (1805), *Zofloya* (1806), *The Libertine* (1807), and *The Passions* (1811). Her most famous, *Zofloya*, began with a similar emphasis to that of Baillie, asserting that the historian of human nature "must ascertain causes, and follow progressively their effects."[24] And indeed Dacre called her 1811 novel *The Passions*, emphasizing the plurality and diversity of human emotion and interaction. Dacre's heroines are quite the opposite, one might argue, of the controlled and seemingly victimized female subjectivities of Radcliffe's heroines. Dacre's heroines are fully aware of their desires, willing to act upon them, and in consequence, owe more to Matthew Lewis's demonic avatar Matilda from *The Monk* (1796), whose name clearly inspired Dacre's pen name, Rosa Matilda. Dacre's analysis of her female characters contained the same trace of scientific enquiry as that of Baillie. Her narrative's pseudo-scientific approach in *Zofloya*, however, is rendered almost redundant by the unbridled passions of Victoria de Loredani. "'Ah! what means *can* I pursue?' she cried aloud ... 'how satisfy my destroying passion?'"[25]

From Radcliffe's poetic fragment at the opening of *The Mysteries of Udolpho*, which plays so carefully to her reader's anticipation, to Henry Tilney's admission in Austen's *Northanger Abbey* that he read *Udolpho* with his "hair standing on end," to Dacre's representation of the processes of thinking disordered by passion, in the Gothic novel, emotion was created both in character representation and in the response of readers. Moving beyond the generic boundaries of fiction, Gothic gradually came to inhabit the prose, poetry, and dramaturgy of the Romantic period. While the Gothic novel was without a doubt the most successful container for the Gothic, large numbers of women also followed the example of Radcliffe's poetic fragments, Smith's sonnets, and Baillie's dramaturgy. Before she composed *Frankenstein* (1818 and 1831) in the famous ghost story challenge that Lord Byron organized at the Villa Diodati on Lake Geneva, Mary Shelley was an enthusiastic and frequent consumer of the Gothic. Her anxiety about commencing her own tale, which she records in the 1831 edition, conveys a sense of impossibility. She wishes, she records, to "make the reader dread to look round, to curdle the blood, and quicken the beatings of the heart."[26] This is no easy accomplishment in an age where pulses had been raised for close to fifty years. It comes as little surprise, then, to find *Frankenstein* so far removed from the traces of the Radcliffean Gothic in its first iteration. Mary Shelley was weighed down not just by the tradition of well-executed and popular Gothic writing of men and women, but also by the critical opprobrium that women's Gothic writing in particular attracted in the 1810s. Still, in that first edition of 1818, we find that both Walton the explorer and Victor Frankenstein are avid readers of romance and adventure themselves, and it is their reading matter that sparks their Promethean ambitions. This theme is sharpened in the 1831 edition of *Frankenstein*, where in the second letter to his sister, Robert Walton's anticipation of his journey, the "trembling sensation, half pleasurable and half fearful" is ascribed to the following confession:

> There is something at work in my soul which I do not understand. I am prac-
> tically industrious – painstaking, a workman to execute with perseverance and
> labour – but besides this there is a love for the marvelous, a belief in the mar-
> velous, intertwined in all my projects, which hurries me out of the common
> pathways of men.[27]

Walton's asseverations of his love of the marvelous are too painstaking to ignore. Emblematic, perhaps, of Mary Shelley's love of the much-denigrated Gothic romances that had preceded her, here Shelley defined her own author-ial attempts to strike a critical balance between the "love for the marvelous" with "the common pathways of men." From their successes in combining temporally and geographically remote tales with contemporaneous, human concerns, Radcliffe, Roche, Baillie, Dacre, and countless others had, without a doubt, taught Mary Shelley much.

NOTES

1 Charlotte Smith, "Avis au Lecteur," in *The Banished Man*, 4 vols. (London: Cadell, 1794), Vol. II, pp. iii–v.
2 Smith, "Avis au Lecteur," p. iv.
3 Ellen Moers, *Literary Women* (1976), introduction by Helen Taylor (London: The Women's Press, 1986).
4 Reverend Thomas James Mathias, *The Pursuits of Literature* (1794–7), 8th rev. edn. (London: T. Becket, 1798), Book I, p. 56.
5 Mathias, *The Pursuits of Literature*, Book IV, p. 258.
6 Anon., "The Terrorist System of Novel Writing," *Monthly Magazine*, 21/4 (August 1797), p. 102.
7 Anon., "Terrorist Novel Writing," in *Spirit of the Public Journals for 1797*, Vol. I (London, 1798), pp. 223–5.
8 Mary Wollstonecraft, *A Vindication of the Rights of Men* (1790) in *Political Writings*, ed. Janet Todd (Oxford University Press, 1993), p. 41.
9 Charlotte Smith, *Emmeline, the Orphan of the Castle* (London: T. Cadell, 1788) and *Ethelinde, or The Recluse of the Lake* (London: T. Cadell, 1789).
10 Mathias, *The Pursuits of Literature*, p. 58.
11 Nathan Drake, *Literary Hours, or Sketches Critical and Narrative* (1798), 2 vols., 2nd edn. (London: J. Burkitt, 1800) Vol. I, p. 354.
12 Ann Radcliffe (1794), *The Mysteries of Udolpho, a Romance: Interspersed with Some Pieces of Poetry*, ed. Bonamy Dobrée (Oxford University Press, 1980), p. xvi. Subsequent references cited parenthetically in the text.
13 Sophia Lee, *The Recess, or A Tale of Other Times* (London: T. Cadell, 1783–5), Vol. III, pp. 220–1.
14 Eliza Parsons, *The Castle of Wolfenbach: A German Story* (London: William Lane, 1793), Vol. I, p. 4.

15 Maria Regina Roche, *Clermont: A Tale* (London: William Lane, 1798), Vol. I, p. 104.

16 *Critical Review*, 23 (1798), p. 472.

17 *Critical Review*, 24 (1798), p. 356.

18 *Critical Review*, 23 (1798), p. 166.

19 Jane Austen, *Northanger Abbey*, ed. Barbara M. Benedict and Deirdre Le Faye, in *The Cambridge Edition of the Works of Jane Austen*, Vol. I (Cambridge University Press, 2006), p. 108.

20 Jane Austen, *The Letters of Jane Austen*, ed. Deirdre Le Faye, 4th edn. (Cambridge University Press, 2011), p. 15. (Letter from Jane Austen to Cassandra Austen, October 24, 1798).

21 Joanna Baillie, "Introductory Discourse," in *A Series of Plays, in Which it is Attempted to Delineate the Stronger Passions of the Mind* (London: T. Cadell, 1798), pp. 19–20.

22 Baillie, "Introductory Discourse," p. 4.

23 Elizabeth Polack, *St. Clair of the Isles* (London: James Pattie, 1838), p. i.

24 Charlotte Dacre, *Zofloya* (1806), ed. Adriana Craciun (Ontario: Broadview, 1997), p. 39.

25 Dacre, *Zofloya*, p. 210.

26 Mary Shelley, "Introduction," in *Frankenstein*, 3rd edn. (London: Colburn and Bentley, 1831), p. ix.

27 Shelley, *Frankenstein*, p. 9.

6

ELIZABETH A. FAY

Travel writing

Travel writing (or travel literature) in the late eighteenth century came to denote a memoir-style approach to personal experience in neighboring and exotic lands. This kind of writing became an outlet for anyone happening to travel who had a curiosity about other cultures, along with literary aptitude. Because so few in England traveled, even neighboring Scotland or nearby France were seen as unknown, foreign lands. Travel writing provided the middle-class reader with an affordable, if imaginative rather than substantial, substitute for the elite experience of the Grand Tour. (The Grand Tour, a fashionable but expensive way for scions of the aristocracy to polish off their university education, typically lasted four years, with prolonged stays in European cultural centers on the continent, particularly Paris and Rome.) Readers were also avid for insights into foreign lands made only somewhat more familiar through the growing British Empire, and travel literature fed this increasing consumer appetite. The genre quickly became a mainstay of the bookseller's inventory and then of the circulating library.

Travel writing is characteristically personal in tone, predicated on the concept of the traveler as observer rather than authority, and it typically uses the author's own itinerary for structure, plot, and organization of material. Because it assumes the author as amateur – that is, neither a scholar nor an authority on the visited land, even if the author has published in other genres – travel writing was also an ideal outlet for women. And because the traveler as observer was an established narrative perspective for the genre going back to Herodotus, and turned into more of a subjective yet eyewitness account by Lady Mary Wortley Montagu in her hugely popular, posthumously published *Turkish Embassy Letters* (1762), the woman travel writer could rely on ordinary daily activities as much as extraordinary festivals or customs to satisfy the reader's desire for detail and anecdote; similarly, an informality of tone is as well suited to the conveyance of foreignness as it is to the ordinariness of the traveler's daily regimen, yet can easily escalate into ecstatic description or wonderment when the extraordinary takes over the narrative. That women traveled at all made a small opening for them in the public sphere by providing them with the necessary authority to compete in the literary marketplace; this alone helped increase women's presence in this market. Yet many more women traveled than wrote about it, so while travel literature provided a more accessible genre for the amateur writer, it cannot be dismissed as cultural flotsam; moreover, that dedicated women writers took it on indicates its value as a flexible tool for exploring intellectual, emotional, and cultural values.

Women writers such as Mary Wollstonecraft and Mary Shelley used travel writing early in their careers to hone their use of character, episode, detail, and narrative voice. Elite women such as Lady Hester Stanhope followed Montagu's lead in using her title to lend interest to her account, which was particularly useful for those women with the freedom or necessity to retire to the continent. But the British Isles and the continent generally circumscribed the terrain covered by such writers. Exotic travel writing was more typically done by men on military or political missions to the Near East and Far East, or on explorations of Africa and the more forbidding territories in North and South America. Nonetheless a few intrepid women braved public opinion to experience inhospitable regions in the Near East or to go as far away as South Africa.

Whether a writer was visiting Europe or exotic lands, the basic tenets of travel writing remained the same, meaning that readers could consume a range of travel writing in expectation that regardless of the author's gender, readerly desires would be met. But while men travelers tended to intrude certain kinds of analyses into their narratives – of the military structures, political governance, trade, and natural resources – the general coverage of classes of people, marketplaces, native dress and foods, architecture and the arts (especially music and dance), and religion and religious festivals were something a writer of either sex could provide. Indeed, such ethnographic observation became a staple of the genre. Although men included such observations along with analysis, women writers were seen as peculiarly suited to a more intimate engagement with cultural practices, as they were often constrained by propriety and custom from political, military, or trade analysis. What women writers realized was the importance of encounters to organize and personalize cultural information, to make it readable and pleasurable, turning fact into commodity. This was something the woman writer could turn to her advantage, particularly when it came to describing the customs and lives of other women who inhabited a private world closed to male travelers.

Montagu exemplified a female-oriented gaze when she used her *Turkish Embassy Letters* to contest Western perceptions of Turkish women and harem life. Initially circulated in manuscript, the letters were received unevenly, but after publication they became increasingly popular for their insights, factual descriptions, and honesty. Women travel writers used their access to the female domestic sphere where possible, and their observations of women outside the home otherwise. When this was not the case, women writers could create a relationship between the narrative voice and the object of study by posing that object as female, a trope that worked particularly well with works written about Italy. Beginning with Madame de Staël's (1776–1817) *Corinne, or Italy* (1807), and reinforced by Byron's *Childe Harold's Pilgrimage* (1812–18), Italy imagined as feminine had gained popular credence with British readers. Most importantly, women's travel writing took form in a variety of genres, illustrating the difficulty women had with locating ways to enter the public sphere: letters that could form a body of work in the manner of Montagu's *Turkish Embassy Letters*, journals such as Dorothy Wordsworth (1771–1855) kept, and landscape descriptions interwoven with normative fiction such as Ann Radcliffe (1764–1823) incorporated into her Gothic novels shared the same motivations as published travel writing. The guides that Mariana Starke (*c.* 1761–1838) innovated were memoirs that more closely resembled the travel writing of male adventurers and scientific explorers.

British men's travel writing in the Romantic era provides the context for women's contributions to this field. It included widely read accounts such as William Gilpin's (1724–1804) *Observations on the River Wye* (1782); James Bruce's (1730–94) account of his travels along the Nile river, which appeared in five volumes in 1790; Mungo Park's (1771–1806) posthumous 1815 narrative describing his legendary explorations of central Africa; James Cook's (1728–79) writings describing his famed excursions to the Pacific and both the Arctic and Antarctic during 1768–79; Captain John Ross's (1777–1856) and Sir Edward Parry's (1790–1855) writings documenting explorations of the Arctic in several expeditions (Parry's *Narrative* was published in 1843). There were also many accounts by male travelers to the Near East and to the Indian subcontinent, including Lord Macartney's (1737–1806) travelogue of his embassy to China and Sir John Barrow's (1764–1848) *Travels in China* (1806). These are just a few of the many male travelers whose scientific, political, or sheer adventuring missions proliferated during this period, generating a large public interest in travel writing as a genre. Women intervened where they could, avoiding the bravura of the men's accounts while cultivating a perspective better suited to women's socially acceptable discernment and interests.

Women competing in this market could do so through studiedly circumscribed experiences; through innovation, as did Mariana Starke with her groundbreaking travel guides; through social prestige, as Lady Elizabeth Craven (1750–1828) was able to do; or through their established reputation as literary artists, as Sydney Owenson, Lady Morgan (c. 1776–1859) did. But women of the middling classes were also able to contribute to the growing number of travel works available because of the authority gained through sheer experience in living or traveling abroad. While the men travelers who documented their heroic explorations and discoveries, or their political and trade missions to far distant countries, were widely read for the political, market, scientific, and cultural information they provided, women writers were read more for the discerning details they could provide about customs, dress, architecture, markets, music, and food. These provided would-be tourists and armchair travelers with the specifics necessary to imagine life in a foreign country, while the women's travelogues typically combined a first-person narrative with ethnographic anecdotes to create a lively sense of what it was like to be a tourist in an age when few even traveled from one district to another, let alone from England to Scotland or Ireland, or to the interiors of Wales or Cornwall, or vice versa.

But ethnography was not the sole impetus for many women travel writers. In particular those traveling on the continent during the French Revolution used their travelogues to present radical (as did Helen Maria Williams, c. 1759–1827) or conservative (as did Mariana Starke) views of foreign politics and policies. Women advocating for radical political schemes had a short period of acceptance and popularity, but a growing conservatism in Britain as a result of the execution of the French monarch and then of the Napoleonic threat meant the end of popular reception for radical views. As a result, just as demand for travel literature was increasing, the ability of women to speak publicly on political matters decreased, except when they restricted their views to a conservative perspective.

Women travel writers were able to exploit this seeming impasse by discovering they could persuade the public toward a positive reception of their work even when stepping outside allotted feminine spheres – such as history and politics – precisely by keeping to a conservative viewpoint. Mariana Starke, for instance, publishing in 1800, was able to obtain a remarkable popularity despite her focus on French politics because she espoused such an Anglocentric, Tory ideology. Women who refused this ideological protection, or in the case of elite women, thought themselves above such protection, gained notoriety for their adventures and exploits but also disapproval, discovering that once they had crossed the line of feminine acceptability English society would not welcome them home again. Such women travelers often had to go into permanent exile, and almost as often ended their days eccentric, alone, and impoverished.

Cases such as those of Lady Elizabeth Craven and Lady Hester Stanhope served to provide women contemplating travel abroad with admonitory examples; while this might not have prevented women from traveling, it did encourage them to publish their travelogues with prefatory statements proclaiming their diffidence and anxiety over publication, and other protestations of any desire for public notice. And it certainly encouraged them to adopt conservative political views and narrative styles; unfortunately this toning down of their accounts caused many travel publications to have a stiff, boring, or template-like quality that makes for tough going for today's readers. By contrast, the accounts by those women who clearly enjoyed their free range of movement in foreign lands, and who were willing to communicate this joy, are more pleasurable, if not downright exciting, to read.

Not surprisingly, the travel writing by women that reviewers chose to commemorate at the end of the Romantic period was either that of recognized authors or of unknowns who followed the rules of feminine anonymity and politeness; those women who flouted the rules were ignored. For example, Robert Chambers's *Cyclopaedia of English Literature: A Selection of the Choicest Productions of English Authors, from the Earliest to the Present Time, Connected by a ... Biographical History*, revised by Robert Carruthers, devotes a section to travel writers. The entry is focused largely on men travelers, but it does include several women travel writers, including the well-known Lady Morgan and Madame de Staël, but also the unknown "Miss Waldie" (Charlotte Anne Waldie Eaton, 1788–1859). Lady Morgan published *Italy* in 1821; the *Cyclopaedia* only comments that it "contain[s] pictures of Italian society and manners, drawn with more vivacity and point than delicacy, but characterized by Lord Byron as very faithful" (16), which is considerably more than "Miss Waldie" garners – only her name and book title are given.

The *Cyclopaedia* section on travel literature is divided into travelers to Africa, especially those who gained fame by searching for the source of the Nile; "classic travellers" or travelers to Greece and Italy, still exotic lands in the Romantic period but made fascinating by Byron's hugely popular *Childe Harold's Pilgrimage* and John Cam Hobhouse's (1786–1869) accompanying descriptive account of the actual tour behind *Childe Harold*'s composition. The *Cyclopaedia* notes that Byron's poetry also stimulated a popular interest in Italy, although Joseph Forsythe (1763–1815) had set the tone in 1812 with his scholarly publication on Italy's antiquities. Publications on travels to the Near and Far East, the Asian subcontinent, and the Arctic are also selectively reviewed. For all the writers surveyed, most receive a sentence or two, and only a few – all men – are selected for a more informational description and excerpted passages. The near occlusion of women travel writers by the *Cyclopaedia* obscures the fact that traveling women were on the rise, and were increasingly writing about their experiences.

Although men's explorations and adventures provided tough competition, women were able to contribute significantly to broader cultural understanding through their observations of women's social roles and gendered customs, and their commentary on contrasting freedoms granted to and constraints imposed on women by other societies. This socially acceptable "feminine" contribution to imperial knowledge had to compete, however, with the travelogues of those women who flouted convention, writing about their daring exploits, and even choosing to live abroad or in self-exile. However much many women writers strove to conventionalize their travel literature, they stood side by side others who promoted self-fashioned images of unconventionality, thereby gaining renown but also social unacceptability. These two aspects of women's travel literature highlight the socially dangerous aspects inherent both in women's literary publications and in women traveling abroad: however much women strove to tamp down the incendiary aspects of their travel writing, none of them were entirely safe from potential attacks on their characters and reputations stemming from their self-presentation to the public as travelers. Even a quick survey of women's travel literature of the period reveals a large variety of strategies for preempting criticism or for self-authorization; the strategies themselves suggest inherent tensions and authorial apprehensiveness. Nonetheless, the narratives clearly made for fascinating reading, and a public whose imperial curiosity was ever increasing was eager for every word, no matter how poor the writer's skill or how shocking her revelations.

Despite travel literature's enormous popularity starting in the late eighteenth century, women's contributions remain little theorized today, providing a tantalizingly nascent area in the study of travel literature. Historians of travel writing have tracked the major patterns and characteristics of the genre, but primarily for male writers. In terms of women's writing, much still remains to be done. We must define the contours of women's travel writing beyond that of social description, parsing its underlying patterns beyond obvious similarities to or differences from men's writing. That work is too large a project for this essay, but a brief survey of key figures and lesser-known travelers might provide a starting point.

Anna, Lady Miller (1741–81) was born to wealth, her grandfather serving as Privy Councillor in Ireland and in the Irish House of Commons. She married John Miller, of an impoverished Irish family, but they were able to live lavishly at first on her inheritance. She became known as a poet and later, after her husband became a baronet, as a salon hostess at their estate in Batheaston (near Bath). She was unfortunately ridiculed in fashionable society for her attempts to be an arbiter of taste; public reception also extended to her travelogue of the stay in France that she and her husband made on the continent in an attempt to retrench; they also toured in Italy to view the antiquities, an experience that provided much of the interest of her travelogue. *Letters from Italy, Describing the Manners, Customs, Antiquities, Paintings, &c., of the Country, in 1770–71* consists of a series of letters sent to a friend, which Lady Miller published anonymously as a three-volume set in 1776; it was popular enough on first appearing to require a second edition the following year, but Horace Walpole (1717–97) notably ridiculed it for its illiteracy and pretension. By the era of Rudolph Ackermann's publishing franchise, which specialized in illustrated satires and picture books of English institutions and places, Miller's *Letters from Italy* had become fodder for travesty.

Elizabeth Craven (1750–1828), born Lady Elizabeth Berkeley (her father was the fourth Earl of Berkeley), married William Craven, sixth Baron Craven; on her second marriage, not entitled to share her new husband's title, she styled herself the Margravine of Brandenburg, Ansbach, and Bayreuth; to compensate, the Holy Roman Emperor titled her Princess Berkeley. An author and playwright, she was best known for her travelogues: *A Journey through the Crimea to Constantinople ...* (1789) and *Memoirs of the Margravine of Anspach ...* (1826). She began traveling in 1783 after a failed marriage, with affairs on both sides, not stopping until 1817 when she settled in Naples. A guest at royal courts through Europe, she alternated between traveling with an entourage and traveling alone on horseback. She traveled as far as Turkey before arriving in Anspach, Bavaria, home of the Margrave of Brandenburg; after the deaths of both their spouses, the two married in 1791. The couple traveled to England, but her scandalous life meant they were socially rejected, including by the Margrave's cousin, King George III; they lived lavishly, however, until 1806 when the Margrave's death spurred her to tour again, this time through revolutionary France, until she stopped in Naples. Like many other ex-patriots, she stopped socializing, and adopted a decidedly eccentric, isolated lifestyle.

Eliza Fay (1756–1816) wrote her travel memoirs at the end of her life. They were published posthumously, probably to realize more from her modest estate. As memoir, Fay's narrative took the opposite approach of the travelogue, with its on-the-spot-reporting style of commentary and narrative, instead using her work to recount all of her voyages and experiences. Possibly her low social status accounts for the small acclaim her book garnered. Nonetheless, *Original Letters from India: Containing a Narrative of a Journey through Egypt, and the Author's Imprisonment at Calicut by Hyder Ally ...* (1817), which contains an account of three additional voyages, recounts a wealth of experiences that few women could hope to match. She recorded the voyage to India with her new husband in 1779, describing in detail their crossing the Alps and then subsequent crossing of the Egyptian desert, and the nearly disastrous attack made on them as they traveled from Cairo to Suez. In Calicut the couple was imprisoned by Hyder Ali, sultan of the Kingdom of Mysore and father of Tipu Sultan; Hyder Ali held strong anti-British sentiments and was militantly anti-colonialist. Anthony Fay served until 1784 as advocate to the Calcutta Supreme Count under Warren Hastings's government before being dismissed; once there Eliza fell in love with India and out of love with her husband. Later she returned several times to India on entrepreneurial schemes, one of which – a muslin exporting scheme – took her to America to promote her business. Although she wrote her memoirs in England, she finally returned again to Calcutta for the remainder of her life.

Mariana Starke was the author of *Letters from Italy* (1800), *The Beauties of Carlo-Maria Maggi* (1811), *Travels on the Continent* (1820), and *Travels in Europe* (1836). Starke's main contribution to travel literature was her travel guide for France and Italy, *Letters from Italy, Between the Years 1792 and 1798, Containing a View of the Revolutions in that Country, from the Capture of Nice by the French Republic to the Expulsion of Pius VI from the Ecclesiastical State: Likewise Pointing out the Matchless Works of Art which still Embellish Pisa, Florence, Siena, Rome, Naples, Bologna, Venice &c. with Instructions for the Use of Invalids and Families who may not Choose to Incur the Expense Attendant upon Traveling with Courier*. This work revolutionized the travel writing genre by creating a format for the guidebook. In her subsequent books she also developed an itinerary for the traveler, a review of all relevant literature on the place, and a rating system for the sights and objects of interest, which made her guides not only popular, but the model for the first guidebooks produced by John Murray and Karl Baedeker (1801–59).

Starke's first book, however, had a more primary focus in its substantial commentary on French politics and Italian resistance to Napoleon from a conservative, patriotic ideological perspective. What she could give readers was her eyewitness account, whether in actual fact or as a narrative style, with a running commentary much like a textual documentary. The effect was to induce trust in the reader along with a desire to see these countries for oneself, particularly her Italy of small towns and citizen resistance, but also of Mediterranean indolence, a fecund nature, old wealth, and antiquities. Starke created another layer of comfort for the reader by describing her adventures as taking place within the protection of her family with whom she made the journey; this draws a direct contrast to the pro-Jacobin

Helen Maria Williams, who reported on Paris during the initial stages of the French Revolution as an unprotected traveler, accompanied only by female family members. And in keeping with her feminine status, Starke's ethnographic interest is repeatedly drawn to the women of the land, as when she describes an encounter with a peasant girl who took the money given her by the Starkes to "immediately purchase a stock of flax; and then should the Madonna bless me with health to work hard, I may soon be able, by selling my thread, to buy decent apparel, and wait upon you, clothed with the fruits of your bounty."[1] The girl soon did. In this way, Starke portrays British charity as both a Christian duty and an embrace of the reformist attitude developing from new theories of domestic economy that were permeating British thought. These are qualities Starke kept in her subsequent travel guides, although there her established expertise on travel advice meant shedding the feminine modesty that could undermine her claims to authority. These guides frequently recycled material from the first work, but in doing so changed the informal tone and style of the *Letters from Italy*, with its anecdotal riches, to a more neutral and impersonal voice and format. This innovation would provide not just the format, but the recognizable style, of the nineteenth-century travel guidebook.

Lady Maria Nugent (1771–1834) was one of several women travelers who could rely on their elite social status to make their travelogues interesting to readers. Nugent wrote about two regions particularly interesting to an empire on the increase: the Caribbean and India. Her first work, *A Journal of a Voyage to, and Residence in the Island of Jamaica, from 1801 to 1805, and of Subsequent Events in England from 1805 to 1811* (1839), covers a substantial period and was accompanied by engravings and a colored lithograph, making it more eye-catching than cheaply printed travelogues of one-time travelers, but also more expensive. Her second work, *A Journal from the Year 1811 till the Year 1815, including a Voyage to and Residence in India …* (1839), which includes her account of visits to the northwest of the Bengal territory, was printed for private circulation only, revealing the class of readers her travel writing was intended to interest. The parameters of her journals – the west and the east of empire – obscure her real interest, which concerned keeping up elite standards while abroad. This, too, was a concern of British abroad – how to maintain home and health while elsewhere, and in that sense both of Nugent's journals could function as travel guides for women accompanying spouses or fathers engaged in trade or appointed to political missions or military posts. Indeed, her title was the result of her husband's political appointments in Jamaica and India, both the result of military successes prior to and early in their marriage.

Fig. 4 Robert Jacob Hamerton, *Lady Hester Lucy Stanhope, c.* 1830s.
© National Portrait Gallery, London

    Lady Hester Stanhope (*c.* 1776–1839; see Figure 4), higher born than Lady
Nugent as daughter of Charles, third Earl of Stanhope, was also the niece
of statesman and prime minister William Pitt, the Younger (1759–1806).
In many ways she was the most intriguing and daring of the Romantic era
women travelers who wrote about their adventures. Ignored by her father,
who refused to educate his sons and daughters, and her stepmother (her
mother died when she was four), Lady Hester learned self-reliance in solitary settings early. But when she went to live with her grandmother in 1800,
she learned to successfully negotiate the world of the London elite; when
she moved in with her bachelor uncle Pitt, she learned to negotiate the

intelligentsia; Pitt, his friends, and even George III recognized her social and political acumen. Just before that she had joined her favorite stepbrother on a Grand Tour through France, Italy, and Germany; the tour also included a mule ride through the mountain pass of Mont Cenis, a danger-filled passage that gave Lady Hester a taste for thrill seeking. It was perhaps this experience that ultimately led her to decide on a life of travel after Pitt's death in 1806, which had left her homeless and without protection.

Aided by a regular pension granted by Pitt's will, and later by contributions from the father of her lover Michael Bruce, whom she met in 1810 when she sailed to Gibraltar with another stepbrother, she began a life abroad and never returned to England. After abandoning her original and highly dangerous plan of entering France by diplomatic intervention (in order to seduce Napoleon while procuring his master plan for imperial conquest), she decided to focus on the biblical sights of Egypt and Jerusalem. Her letters reveal her ability, learned in Pitt's household, to charm powerful, arrogant men with her cosmopolitan manners, personal flair, and disregard for gender conventions. In this last trait Lady Hester was unusual, changing her dress to the native costume of elite males after her shipwreck at Rhodes in 1811. She recounts dressing in the mameluke costume (vest, short jacket, full trousers, and burnoose), or in the vividly colored pantaloons, turbans, waistcoats, and girdles of the Arabs, complete with a sword and cartridge belt. Her choice was both a practical one, making travel much easier, and a political one: unlike Lady Mary Wortley Montagu, she was horrified at women's harem life.

It was to Bruce's father, Crauford Bruce, that Stanhope faithfully corresponded, detailing her travels in the lively, fascinating letters that created the basis for the memoirs of her extraordinary travel adventures, *Memoirs of the Lady Hester Stanhope, as Related by Herself in Conversations with her Physician* (1845). Charles Lewis Meryon (1783–1877), the physician Lady Hester hired to attend her on her travels and to whom she narrated her adventures, accompanied her from 1810 to 1817. Before his departure, Meryon and she both suffered attacks of the plague that was spreading throughout the Near East, and after enduring the high fevers associated with the illness, Lady Hester became increasingly erratic in her moods, eccentric, and isolated. Debilitating illness and even death were just two of the consequences of exotic travel that had to be anticipated; others were robbery, imprisonment, poor or little food, inadequate housing, and the very real possibility of getting lost. Despite these deterrents, Lady Hester never wanted to return to England; her travels took her throughout the Near East, from the capitals and smaller cities of each country to several great cities of antiquity whose ruins were still visible: Palmyra, Baalbek, and Tyre.

Stanhope's memoirs relate the variety of ways she found to impress the rulers of nations where women were seen but not heard, or not seen except when heavily veiled; the ways she found to create safe passage for her entourage through dangerous territories; and the exploits that made her one of the most famous travelers of her day.

Mary Wollstonecraft (1759–97), more famous (and infamous) after her death for her *A Vindication of the Rights of Woman* (1792), experimented with travel writing before she began her polemical contributions to rights discourse. Her account of her travels in Scandinavia, *Letters Written in Sweden, Norway, and Denmark* (1796), is conveyed through letters that meditate on the sociology of the societies she visits as much as they philosophize about the nature of identity. The letters are best known today for their use of the sublime to examine the relation between individual and society, an exercise in which she lands squarely on the side of domestic life rather than that of the solitary wanderer. To achieve this result without resorting to the mere expectation of femininity, Wollstonecraft considers subjective experience as heightened by nature to be intrinsic to the social self. The successful blend of personal experience with sociological and economic critique made this Wollstonecraft's most popular work during her lifetime.

Some women travel writers took one journey and wrote about their experiences, without producing more than a socialite's memoirs in a different setting. Such was the case with Anne Carter, whose account of her visit to post-Napoleonic France reveals Parisian society during the critical moment of Napoleon's abdication (*Letters from a Lady to her Sister During a Tour of Paris, in the Months of April and May, 1814*, published anonymously). She was able to obtain tickets for Louis XVIII's coronation at Notre Dame, fortuitously attending the opera on the same night as Wellington. Her account is spellbinding for its historical details, but it stands in stark contrast to the astute reportage and ethnographical acumen displayed by Helen Maria Williams in her far more fascinating account of the French Revolution.

Williams's reports, published as *Letters Written in France: In the Summer 1790, to a Friend in England; Containing Various Anecdotes Relative to the French Revolution* (1791), are some of the best-known travel writing of the Romantic period for twenty-first-century scholars. Their political analysis, close descriptions of the carefully scripted but crucial revolutionary celebrations such as the Fête de la Fédération, sentimental set pieces aimed at winning the British public over to the revolutionaries' cause, and intimations of threat and excitement mark Williams's journalism as top-notch war reportage. Because she aligned herself with the moderate party, the Girondists, after the September Massacres, she and her mother and two sisters (whom she had invited to join her in 1792) were thrown into prison where she continued to write. She followed her astounding eye-witness account of the revolution with *Sketches of the State of Manners and Opinions in the French Republic* (1801) and *Letters on Events Which Have Passed in France since the Restoration in 1815* (1819). In 1798 she also published *A Tour of Switzerland*, documenting her travels with John Hurford Stone, her companion, who was still legally married to his first wife. Their improper relation, which led to her social stigmatization, more pointedly displays Williams's unconventionalism. Her Swiss travelogue also includes her political analysis of that country, as well as an intimate note in the form of a poem written among the Alps. The poem, a "hymn," helps locate this work as Romantic with its meditation on the sublime, a neces-sary experience for the true traveler on the Romantic path as originated by Goethe. That she would deliberately engage this touchstone of male travel literature only underscores her desire for experiences unconstrained by gendered notions of propriety.

Maria Graham (later Lady Callcott, 1785–1842), the daughter of a rear-admiral, married the ship's captain on her first voyage bound for India. A born sailor, she made ship voyages the center of her life, sailing with her husband when he was on leave, as when they went around the Asian sub-continent, visiting Ceylon, Cape Town, and St. Helena; and a few years later sailing to Italy. After that she accompanied him on his trip to Brazil, and then to Chile; unfortunately he caught fever on this trip and died off Cape Horn, but she went on to live in Chile for a year during which she experienced the earthquake of 1822; she then returned to Brazil en route to England, where she agreed to act as governess to the daughter of the Prince of Portugal, who ruled Brazil, on her return. In London she published her manuscripts on South America with Longman, Hurst, who had published her second book on India (her first was with the Edinburgh publisher Constable) and her book on Rome. Once back in Rio de Janeiro she began her post in the Imperial Palace, but by 1827 she had returned to London where she mar-ried the painter Sir Augustus Callcott, R.A. (1779–1844), who specialized in rural landscapes detailing peasant life. On their tour of Europe, the couple documented their travels; he painted highly detailed landscapes of ruins, particularly in Italy, while she wrote books on European art and architec-ture, which he illustrated. Unlike women travel writers who typically con-fined themselves to observations of women's lives in other cultures, Graham filled her travelogues with politics and history, more in the vein of mod-ern travel guides, earning her censure from critics. These included mem-bers of the Geological Society who pamphleteered against her description of the 1822 Great Earthquake, deriding it as the product of imagination rather than testimonial. She defended her reportage, but critical reception of her work reveals the deterrents women travel writers faced: the very facts as they experienced them were subject to question and ridicule by male experts, while history and politics were unsuitable topics for female scrutiny and commentary.

Charlotte Anne Waldie, later Charlotte Eaton, so briefly mentioned in the *Cyclopaedia*, wrote *Rome in the Nineteenth Century* (Edinburgh, 1820) in "A Series of Letters Written During a Residence at Rome, in the Years 1817 and 1818," as the work's subtitle explains (somewhat contradicting the promise of the title). She uses the same ethnographic categories that explorers of more exotic lands were using, as well as those employed by practical guides for travelers such as Anna Lady Miller's guidebooks. Waldie's title promises "A Complete Account of the Ruins of the Ancient City, the Remains of the Middle Ages, and the Monuments of Modern Times: With Remarks on the Fine Arts, on the State of Society, and on the Religious Ceremonies, Manners, and Customs, of the Modern Romans." However, even as Waldie modestly raises doubt over her "incompetency to such a task," she takes the opportunity to critique continental attitudes according to British middle-class norms.[2]

There are many more women whose travel writing provides insights into the experiences of the British abroad during the Romantic period: Anne Plumptre (1760–1818) lived in France for three years, parlaying that experience into *Narrative of a Three Years Residence in France* (1810); Fanny Lewald (1811–89) importantly documented the Italian Risorgimento or unification; Frances Jane Carey (d. 1860) recorded French customs and everyday life; Marianne Baillie (c. 1795–1831) traveled throughout the continent; Lady Anne Barnard (1750–1825) lived abroad in South Africa and wrote about her life there; and Mary Shelley's (1797–1851) novels provide travelogues and document life in other countries, as much as did her own travelogues, *History of a Six Weeks' Tour* (1817), written with Percy Bysshe Shelley, and *Rambles in Germany and Italy in 1840, 1842 and 1843*, published in 1844 toward the end of her life. Romantic period women's travel writing, like the men's, ranges from the extraordinary to the mundane, from the brilliantly written to the forgettable. But we should read these various works together, not only to discern patterns and genre conventions for women as well as men writers, but also because the very range itself replicates the experience of a subscriber to a circulating library surveying titles on the "travel" bookshelf, or indeed of the consumer looking over a bookseller's list of titles for the year. What such a perusal would have revealed is just how many of the travel titles were written by women.

NOTES

1 Mariana Starke, *Letters from Italy, Between the Years 1792 and 1798, Containing a View of the Revolutions in that Country, from the Capture of Nice by the French Republic to the Expulsion of Pius VI from the Ecclesiastical State* ... (London: R. Phillips, 1800), p. 83.
2 Charlotte Anne Waldie [Eaton], *Rome in the Nineteenth Century* (Edinburgh: Archibald Constable, 1820), p. x.

7

CRYSTAL B. LAKE

History writing and antiquarianism

The reading and writing of history changed dramatically during the Romantic period. In content and form, earlier eighteenth-century histories emphasized the march of civilization's progress. Sweeping histories of empires and nations – such as David Hume's *History of England* (1754–61), and Edward Gibbon's *History of the Decline and Fall of the Roman Empire* (1776–89) – were organized chronologically around major political, social, and religious figures and events. By the Romantic period, however, readers had become captivated by the histories of private lives, local regions, and social manners. This meant that histories took an increasingly experimental turn, focusing on topics rather than chronologies and everyday experiences rather than statecraft. Similarly, historians began to see themselves as something more than the empirical gatherers of unassailable data that they would arrange into teleological order. No longer a mere collection of facts to arrange, history functioned as an imaginative, sentimental excursion that defined the present as much as it did the past. Romantic writers mined medieval source material for inspiration, and the era's historians indulged in imagined dialogues, descriptive details of everyday lives, examinations of individual genius and revolution, and the lingering – even sometimes haunting – sentimental effects of bygone ages. All of this meant that Romantic historiography found new opportunities for expression, especially in popular culture: in the form of historical novels, poems and plays, staged historical battles, history paintings, and museum collections, for example.

These new modes of history may seem, at first glance, welcoming to women writers. Clio, the classical Muse of History, was after all a woman. As historiography shifted its feet between the Enlightenment and the Romantic period, it promised to yield new ground for women to claim. Women had long been encouraged to eschew reading romances and novels in favor of reading histories. Histories were thought to offer more suitable models of virtues to imitate and vices to avoid. Moreover, women were encouraged to capitalize on feminine sensibilities in order to empathetically engage with

88

Britain's "imagined community" as "mothers of the nation," taking to heart their responsibility for safeguarding both ancient and national virtues.[1] Not surprisingly, historical memoirs and correspondences of women were published in growing numbers at the end of the eighteenth and the beginning of the nineteenth century. These emphasized the triumphs and failings of virtues in both the public and private spheres. As Romantic histories turned their focus to social customs and manners, they offered women new opportunities to immerse themselves in history's material cultures, including the fashion, art, and artifacts that revealed the everyday lives of historical individuals.

Despite historiography's new Romantic forms, women remained marginalized in historical studies and were viewed as incapable of writing as historians themselves. Mary Astell complained in 1705 that "the Men being the Historians, they seldom condescend to record the great and good Actions of Women; and when they take notice of them, 'tis with this wise Remark. That such Women *acted above their sex*."[2] For Astell, because men dominated the public while women were relegated to the private sphere, women of the past would have found themselves with few opportunities to shape the kinds of national destinies that preoccupied early historians; thus historians inevitably omitted women from their histories. Moreover, because history writing was considered a masculine pursuit, men who researched and documented the past inevitably emphasized the actions of men. When historians accounted for exceptional women, they either idealized feminine virtues (such as a propensity to retreat to the home where feminine sensibilities left women room to do little more for history than to nurture statesmen), or they found that the most historically significant women possessed an unusual capacity for stereotypically masculine virtues.

Nearly a century after Astell, Jane Austen would have *Northanger Abbey*'s protagonist, Catherine Morland, famously voice what had become a long-standing complaint: "[H]istory, real solemn history, I cannot be interested in."[3] She admits that she "read[s] it a little as duty," but confesses that history's lingering insistence on the "quarrels of popes and kings" and "wars or pestilences" "vex[es]" her (109). There are "hardly women at all" in histories, Catherine opines in frustration (109). Even as she acknowledges the new trend toward sentimental history, the novelistic "invention[s]" that characterizes historians' attempts to imagine what individuals in the past said or thought, Catherine laments that there is little in historiographical discourse, despite its Romantic run, that will appeal to female readers (109). Although Austen, who herself wrote an experimental and satirical history of England in 1791, here satirizes Catherine's naïve taste in reading, she nevertheless reminds readers that even as the Romantic period saw a rise in the number of histories taking women into account, historiography remained a genre from which women writers were imagined to be excluded.

The historian Catharine Macaulay is an exception that proves the point. Macaulay's eight-volume *History of England from the Revolution to the Present Time* (1763–83) was the first widely read history written by a woman. Although readers complimented Macaulay's accomplishments as a historian, they almost always did so aslant. The review of Macaulay's *History* in the *Monthly Review* of July 1763, for example, quickly drifts away from assessing Macaulay's work as a historian and toward condemning her for her gender. The review begins by acknowledging that Macaulay has charted new historical territory by "collecting and digesting" "political fragments which have escaped the researches of so many learned and ingenious men" (372). The reviewer's praise for Macaulay's history is short-lived, however. Her gender consistently preoccupies him and undermines her accomplishment. Despite Macaulay's historical "ability and industry," the reviewer "wish[es] that the same degree of genius and application had been exerted in more suitable pursuits" (372). Predictably enough, then, the reviewer takes Macaulay's *History* to task. The "exuberance of zeal" that Macaulay felt justified her work as a female historian inevitably compromises her ability to "present facts in a partial view" (374). Macaulay has fallen into the trap of Romantic, sentimental history in the worst ways. Her enthusiasm for her subject consistently marks her as a woman in the throes of Romantic sensibility. In the reviewer's final estimation, the Romantic turn of Macaulay's work means that it may not even deserve to be called a "history" in the first place. Women, the reviewer states, are simply not designed for such intellectual labor. "[T]he soft and delicate texture of a female frame" is not "intended for severe study," and "[i]ntense thought spoils a lady's features" (373).

That women were encouraged to read and sympathize with a history that marginalized them in myriad ways, while they were discouraged from writing it themselves, engendered unique opportunities for women to intervene creatively in historiography. Rather than abandon writing or reading history, many women writers participated in Romantic historiography through fiction, poetry, and drama. These literary genres illustrate a wide range of historical interests and a commitment to finding new methods for imagining the past and conveying its importance to their readers. In other words, Romantic women's literature was frequently the pursuit of history by other means.

Most accounts of the rise of the historical novel continue to place Sir Walter Scott and his *Waverley* novels at the forefront of the genre, both in terms of its instigation and accomplishment. Yet women writers played an especially significant role in popularizing imagined prose accounts of the past. Romantic novelists, including Jane and Anna Maria Porter, Sydney Owenson (Lady Morgan), and Maria Edgeworth, crafted works that illustrate a deep, if sometimes eclectic, familiarity with published histories and a richly imaginative, if sometimes extravagantly sentimental, engagement with the everyday lives of historical figures, especially women. Historical novels, in other words, offered women writers a chance to introduce women into the fictional historical record, as well as to consider anew methods for history's interpretation.

This was especially the case with Gothic novels. Their medieval settings facilitated their depictions of the supernatural which, in turn, reflected both a Romantic literary sensibility and an opportunistic appropriation of the interests and uncertainty engendered by the new, shifting historiography. Clara Reeve's *The Champion of Virtue* (1777), one of the first Gothic novels, functions as a commentary on gender and historicism. Written in response to the antiquary Horace Walpole's *The Castle of Otranto* (1764), Reeve's novel takes issue with Walpole's way of depicting history. In the preface, Reeve describes her novel as the "literary offspring" of Walpole's attempt to combine the "ancient romance" with the "modern novel."[4] For Reeve, this particular generic combination offers an opportunity to critique traditional forms of history writing: "History represents human nature as it is in real life, alas, too often a melancholy retrospect!" As Austen's Catherine Morland would attest, history was a "melancholy retrospect" for women.

Yet Reeve is less interested in an optimistic historiographical project of feminist retrospection than she is in a literary experiment. Reeve finds that unlike history, fiction will "first excite the attention" and then "direct it to some useful, or at least innocent, end" (iv). If Reeve's statement here appears to dismiss history's dreary, factual certainty, she nevertheless rewrites Walpole's supernatural plot devices, claiming for herself a special ability to author new forms of realistic fiction set in the haunting, medieval past – forms that entertain as much as they instruct, without recourse to overly impassioned hyperbole. Walpole's novel disappoints, Reeve argues, specifically because its reliance on the uncanny to advance its plot calls into question its historical believability, compromising its capacity both to immerse and persuade its historically minded readers. Reeve's complaint about Walpole's irrational tropes is a subtle but certain assertion that women writers can engage empirically and rationally with the past, even when operating in the realms of sentimental fiction and historiography's rising interest in asynchronous details. That is to say, the new subjectivity of Romantic history need not mean that women have to engage with the past by capitalizing on their presumed capacity for impassioned responses to history; rather, the new historiography's affinity for forms of fiction could be redeployed by women for rational ends.

Where Reeve sought to recreate in her fiction a more believable and instructive past, the Gothic novelist Sophia Lee sought to recreate a more equitable one. Lee's *The Recess* (1783–5) reimagines the reign of Queen Elizabeth. In Lee's fictional account of the sixteenth century, Mary, Queen of Scots gives birth to twin daughters, Ellinor and Matilda, who are raised in a subterranean secret hideaway underneath a ruin. There, they fall victim to various romantic and political intrigues that are depicted in highly sentimental prose. Lee represented her novel not as fiction but as fact founded on the discovery of a mysterious manuscript in which "a wonderful coincidence of events stamps the narration at least with probability."[5] Although the appeal of Lee's novel resides largely in its sentimental account of the lost histories of fictionalized women, the novel's political implications are unmistakable. Not only does *The Recess* offer an inventive and alternative history of women; her narrative invites her readers to imagine a lost line of monarchs. When Elizabeth I died without marrying or childbearing, James I ascended to the throne, instigating a series of political calamities that continued to resonate in the late eighteenth century. Lee's novel raises the specter of a different political history, one rooted in royal daughters, rather than sons.

The reviewer for the *Gentleman's Magazine* in April of 1786 recognized at once *The Recess*'s historical ambitions, remarking that Lee's depiction of "the peculiarities of Elizabeth and James" rivaled "Hume or Robertson" in their "exactness" (327). "The imagination," the reviewer writes, "is indeed transported into other times" while reading the novel. At the same time, the reviewer worries that Lee's reconstruction of the past is so thorough and so thoroughly absorbing as to be problematic: "we cannot entirely approve the custom of interweaving fictitious incident with historic truth" (327). Robert Graves, in a brief dig at Lee's *The Recess* in the "Preamble" to *Plexippus, or The Aspiring Plebian* (1790) went so far as to suggest that Reeve's historicity had made a fool of its female readers, leading them mistakenly to take Reeve's fiction to be fact. In a casual dinner conversation, one woman indignantly chastises Mary, Queen of Scots as "an abandoned" mother of two illegitimate daughters.[6] When one of the guests remarks that he has never heard of this fact in "any history of those times," the woman insists in a comically circular way that "it is very true" because she has "just been reading an entertaining *novel*, which is *founded* entirely upon *that fact*" (xii).

Readers of Ann Radcliffe's Gothic novels would likely not have been subject to the same kinds of mistaken notions about history. Although Radcliffe deploys techniques similar to Lee's, she pays sparse attention to major political events and famous individuals. For Radcliffe, the Romantic historicity of the

Gothic functioned formally as a setting. Radcliffe's historical settings suspend her readers' belief systems and facilitate their heightened emotional experience of reading about unusual damsels in unusual distress. At the same time, by setting her novels in distant places and times, Radcliffe creates a sly opportunity to critique contemporary patriarchal models of domination. This can be seen, for example, in a work like *The Mysteries of Udolpho*.⁷ Evocative descriptions of half-perceived scenes steeped in historicity, such as the one where the heroine, Emily, believes she has found the corpse of the villain Montoni's murdered wife, transfer the terror of the supposed barbarism of past patriarchs to the present. The novel later reveals that the corpse is merely a wax effigy, a product of a bygone Catholic superstition; but it haunts readers and its heroines for hundreds of pages, inviting them to consider that, although the contexts may be different, the dangers women face in patriarchal societies remained.

The dramatist Joanna Baillie similarly used history to explore affective forms of masculinity and stage political conflict at a distance. The concluding piece of her *Miscellaneous Plays* is a tragedy, *Constantine Paleologus*, first performed in 1808. It is an unusual text, not least because it brings a Radcliffean aesthetic to bear on men and classical, rather than Gothic, history. As Baillie tells her readers, she was inspired to write *Constantine Paleologus* after reading Gibbon's *History of the Decline and Fall of the Roman Empire*, whose description of the 1453 siege of Constantinople "was a subject that pressed itself upon" her.⁸ For Baillie, the appeal of history resides in its revelation of character. She has little interest in narrating the decline and fall of an empire. Rather, the image of "a modest, affectionate, domestic man … without ambition, even without hope, rousing himself upon the approach of unavoidable ruin" compels Baillie; Constantine's "noble and dignified exertion" as the "last Roman" proved "impossible for [her] to resist" (xiv). This was so much the case that Baillie admits her preference was to exclude female characters and a stereotypical romance plot entirely from the play: "had I followed my own inclination, delineating" the "generous ties" between Constantine and his "brave imperial band" of men "would have been the principle object of the piece" (xv). But the "common audience" of playgoers demands a love interest, and so Baillie admits to inventing the figure of Valeria so as to heighten "the domestic qualities of Constantine" (xv).

Baillie has reservations about this decision; these are as historical as they are literary or protofeminist. "To alter, for the idle convenience of poetry … any characters that have been known in the world, appears to [Baillie] highly blamable" (xv). At the same time, Baillie finds that she is entitled to "[fill] up an outline given us by history" and to "[heighten] or [diminish] the general effect" (xv). Baillie's capacity for sympathetic engagement with the past and her literary sensibilities mean that in composing a play like *Constantine Paleologus* she foregoes identifying with history's women and instead speculates on the inner life of its men. Baillie admits to imagining the character of Justiniani not as "natively brave," but as "particularly punctilious in every thing that concerns a soldier" (xvi). Her dismissal of *Constantine Paleologus*'s romance plot and the fact that the play was written against the backdrop of the Napoleonic Wars suggest that history allowed Baillie to engage unconventionally with the public sphere from which women had traditionally been excluded. *Constantine Paleologus* is more than just a sentimental study of masculine character.

If, as Astell had claimed, women were frustrated to find themselves perpetually alienated from the public sphere preoccupying men's historical consciousness, Baillie would turn Romantic women's alienation from contemporary politics into a return to the past by staging political conflict at a historical distance. History allowed Baillie conceptually to occupy forms of political conflict that had long been reserved for men. Baillie worries, however, that the play's aesthetic successes won't translate onto the page, because it was staged with "magnificence and show" (xvii). That the play was an elaborately staged one in order to immerse its viewers in the past offers Baillie a chance to meditate on the relationships between history, perception, and form. She admits that the plot of the play may seem suspiciously incongruous at times.

Baillie casts this, however, as a conflict between elaborately staged static scenery and teleology, and she claims an authority over both. Advancing a romance plot would have "assigned[ed] imaginary causes to great public events" (xviii). In contrast, Baillie decided to stage "imaginary characters and circumstances of no great importance" in her play, in the same way that a "painter decorates the barrenness of some well-known ... landmark ... with brushwood, and ... a few storm-stunted oaks" (xviii). These "bring into stronger light" the scene, even as the "general form must remain unaltered" (xviii). That Baillie would compare the formal elements of her historical play to the kinds of objects painters might legitimately insert into their paintings highlights Romantic women writers' deep engagement with history as material culture and suggests that these kinds of materialist engagements with the past did, in fact, promise to refashion history's forms.

This can especially be seen in women's poetry from the period. A writer like Charlotte Smith illustrates the dexterous uses of history Romantic women writers could make across genres. Smith herself wrote Gothic novels that characteristically belie an interest in history. She would also go on to try her hand at a more traditional history of England. Although it started out as a compilation largely drawn from popular histories written by men like Oliver Goldsmith, it would go on in its third volume to be a more radical and inventive collaboration with the Romantic writer Mary Hays. Smith's poetry, however, most exemplifies a sustained and opportunistic appropriation of Romantic historiography's materialist turn. Her late, long poem *Beachy Head* (1807) provides a compelling example of the ways that women poets used history's objects for their own objectives.[9] *Beachy Head* narrates five histories simultaneously: the history of England, the histories of two local men, Smith's own personal history, and the natural prehistory of Beachy Head.

Smith's engagements with the objects of natural history allow her to position her poem as a historiographical experiment and critique. For example, after "observing" Beachy Head's "minute" geological "objects," its "fossil forms," Smith castigates proud, boasting "Science"; it "lends" "but a little light" even to its "most ardent votaries" (27). Smith is just such an ardent votary, and her diction here encourages readers to sympathize with women's limited ability to engage with the discourses traditionally reserved for men. Smith's is more than an accusation that women have been excluded from science, for the line turns to insist that the prehistorical shells and rocks at Beachy Head do not easily yield to scientific conclusions for any of their observers. The physical signs of a deep, geological past are mere "food for vague theories, or vain dispute" (27). In contrast to the men of science, a peasant at Beachy Head doesn't even consider the nature of the deep time signified by fossils. Between the vain scientist and the unaware peasant, Smith charts a different course for herself as a poet–historian.

Immediately following this passage, she implores Ambition to come to her. Ambition arrives, but Smith doesn't channel Ambition's narrative; she speaks back and insists that Ambition recognize that the minute objects at Beachy Head point to a dispiriting political history in which everything (and every thing) is rendered into "nothingness": "Behold," Smith commands, "the nothingness of all / For which you carry thro' the oppressed Earth" (29). Specifically for Smith, "War, and its train of horrors" have rendered history into a mute morass of archaeological and geological accumulation (29). Consequently, she will "turn" from the "thoughts" of specimens and nothingness "suggested" "by human crimes," to a "more attractive study [that] courts / The wanderer of the hills" (30). Smith's turn toward a "more attractive study" promises to deliver an idealized depiction of Beachy Head, yet the poem's extensive annotations drag its readers back into the scientific accounts of history that she implicitly criticizes on theoretical grounds. Consequently, Smith's use of the word "study" here to launch her own account of Beachy Head is not accidental. *Beachy Head*'s footnotes crowd the pages like buried objects. They relentlessly emphasize her own deep and eclectic study. *Beachy Head*'s annotations, therefore, exemplify Smith's capacity for poetically appropriating the myopia of the new Romantic and the inherited panopticism of Enlightenment historiography. She finds special poetic purchase in the liminal spaces of Beachy Head as a site of connect and disconnect where no thing and every thing can be turned into everything and nothing.

Comparably, Felicia Hemans found the gaps in the historical record to be ripe for filling with imagined details. In fact, Hemans's "first poems" were characterized by her early biographer, Henry Chorley, as "antique groups of sculpture, or the mailed monumental figures of the Middle Ages set in motion."[10] Chorley is referring to Hemans's *The Forest Sanctuary and Other Poems* (1825), which contained the inset of Hemans's series "Lays of Many Lands" and her *Records of Woman* (1828). Both of these collections could be characterized as historiographical experiments. Hemans's "Lays of Many Lands" shares with Smith an interest in local sites marked by their historicity. The "Lays" are a series of poems set in varying geographies and time periods. As Hemans describes in a brief introduction, each poem is "intended to be commemorative of some national recollection, popular custom, or tradition" (106). She takes her inspiration from Johann Gottfried Herder's *Stimmen der Volker in Liedern* (1773); but where Herder's poems are translations, Hemans's are imaginative excursions. Hemans illustrates a startling breadth of interests: from India to Switzerland, from the time of the ancient Greeks to the reign of Henry VIII; many of the poems focus on historical-mythical events, which comprise "national ... tradition[s]." The poems often turn on what women might have told or might tell about such histories.

Where the "Lays of Many Lands" reveal the stories about national traditions that women could have revealed, *The Records of Woman* imagines new histories of and for women. Dedicated to Baillie, this collection of poems recounts the experiences of fictional figures alongside famous women. Like the "Lays of Many Lands," *The Records of Woman* is geographically and temporally diverse in its scope. But unlike the "Lays of Many Lands," it sentimentally emphasizes the anguish of women wrenched from their loved ones. In other words, as the epigraphs from Wordsworth and Schiller underscore, the poems are concerned primarily with the "agony" of "love," which is the "lot" of the "beautiful." In the "Lays of Many Lands," women confront the impossibility of narrating the histories of men, an impossibility that proves detrimental for nationalistic legacies; in contrast, *The Records of Woman* attempts to locate permanence in a transhistorical and global construction of feminine sentimentalism. To some extent, Hemans loses ideological ground here; but in other regards, she gains a poetics of history.

In the collection's concluding poem, "The Grave of a Poetess," the narrator grieves at a picturesque tomb: not over the loss of love, as in many of the other poems, but over the presumed loss of a historic poetic voice. The poem's volta, however, insists that although the poetess's voice may not have been "loud," it is "deep" and persistently inspiring.[11] This final poem functions as a distinctively different kind of promise than the one the Valkyriur could make: that women like Hemans who rewrite the past in the present moment will be the future's history.

That the final poem is set at a gravesite is no accident. The unknown, recovered, and invented histories of women that weave through Romantic women's writings coincided with the culture of sensibility's focus on women's bodies (their tears, blushes, and nerves) and the marketplace for sentimental commodities (lockets, miniatures, and memento mori). That the culture of sensibility granted women special, although fraught, authority over material experiences and symbols of feeling meant that Romantic historiography's impulse to discover, curate, and explicate the material cultures of the past allowed women to claim new forms of authority over the significance of historical objects. The relationships between women, history, and objects must have seemed especially intuitive by the turn of the nineteenth century; this would explain in part why so much of women's literature sentimentally engaged with descriptions of historical places and artifacts.

Richard Lovell Edgeworth and Maria Edgeworth's *Practical Education* (1798) reveals how women responsible for educating their children would have found ample opportunities to use an increasingly diverse range of objects for creative historical instruction.[12] Edgeworth describes the "technical helps to the memory" for chronological and geographical details (I.219). These ranged from the singsongy ballad of the Chapter of Kings, to homemade globes, to Sarah Trimmer's small-scale prints, to Joseph Priestley's "Chart of Biography" (1765), a print that occupied six square feet of wall space (II.418). Edgeworth remarks that prints, as well as "maps and medals," were "part of the constant furniture of a room" (II.419). Like literature, these kinds of visual–material texts could also entertain. Edgeworth, for example, suggests that "[i]f any expedients are thought necessary to fix historic facts early in the mind, the entertaining display of Roman and Emperors, and British Kings and Queens, may be made ... in a magic lanthorn," a device that could project moving, flickering pictures onto a blank screen (I.349).

Women like Edgeworth were not only advocates for such devices; they increasingly became their creators. In 1815 Mary Rundall published her own innovative mnemonic system for memorizing history entitled *Symbolic Illustrations of the History of England*.[13] Rundall's text provides her readers with chapters that briefly review major periods in British history; these are organized chronologically and usually by monarchs' reigns. Each brief chapter is accompanied on the facing page with a grid, and in each grid appears a small, singular, simple drawing. These drawings feature boxed dates at the top and represent significant events. As the title suggests, the drawings are symbolic: monarchs are often stick-like figures who wear a crown with an iconographical stamp; an event like the beheading of Charles I in 1649 is represented as a black triangle with a skull at the top, an ax with a hat signifying the ascendency of Oliver Cromwell on the bottom left, and a crown on the bottom right. Explanatory guides follow the grids, where the symbolical function of each item in each box is explained in more detail.

Rundall's simple yet innovative rendering of symbolic collections of objects owed a significant debt to the rising popularity of antiquarianism, a practice that entailed finding, explicating, and arranging artifacts into collections in order to reveal previously unknown histories, especially of the everyday lives of historical individuals, often for powerful, sentimental effect. Where Enlightenment historiography excluded women from the sweeping political narratives of the rise of empires, the antiquarian branch of Romantic historiography invited imaginative speculation on the fragmented materials of history: small and evocative signs of everyday lives. Although women did not quite fit into the stereotypical mold of the antiquary as an eccentric pedant with a preference for the moldiest, dustiest ruins of the past, there is evidence to suggest that antiquarianism's focus on the discovery and recovery of unknown histories might have intrigued women. Museums such as that of Dr. Greene in Lichfield or Sir Ashton Lever in Leicester Square consistently reported in their catalogues receiving donations of coins, jewels, pottery, and historical garments from "a lady." Similarly, Don Saltero's coffeehouse in Chelsea, which featured more than a thousand artifacts, including Mary, Queen of Scott's pincushion, paste copies of famous jewels, old books, and mummified body parts, published an extensive list of benefactors that included not only the writer Tobias Smollett, the collector Sir Hans Sloane, and the artist Sir Joshua Reynolds, but also a surprising number of anonymous young women.

Women also submitted to periodicals accounts of their encounters with antiquities alongside occasional verses composed at historical sites; both exemplify the new vogue for the kinds of ruins that intrigued antiquaries. Records from the Society of Antiquaries suggest that some women found themselves increasingly comfortable with claiming expertise and ownership over their own antiquarian discoveries. In 1783, Daines Barrington read a letter written by the Countess of Moira to the Society of Antiquaries, reporting on the skeleton of a woman discovered on the countess's estate in Ireland in 1781. Countess Moira's is a lengthy, precise description of the skeleton, including its accoutrements and the elaborate narrative of its discovery. She encloses sketches, patterns of the garments, and "a sample of the stuff."[14] Although she had hoped to conduct a more thorough excavation of the site and to consult a naturalist for further information on the kinds of fur that accompanied the skeleton, the countess was unable to do so; she proceeds with her own observations in the absence of more reliable access to presumably masculine expertise. Thus, she generates her own itemized list of objects associated with the skeleton. Countess Moira demonstrates an enthusiasm for and a familiarity with established antiquarian collections and research. She describes these sources with casual expertise as "the particulars in dress of manufactures as appear to [her] to bear a degree of similitude" between the items found in the grave and the items she remembers well from "memory, either from prints, or relations" (95). The countess demonstrates a shockingly comprehensive knowledge of specialized antiquarian sources, some of them at least a century old. Importantly, she does not shy away from drawing a politicized conclusion about the remains, theorizing that the corpse was that of a woman "who had fallen ... prey to famine, in consequence of the prosecution [employed in Elizabeth's reign] to civilize the Irish." The countess confesses that she's only being "candid" in "relating [the cruelties that] the ancient Irish endured" at the hands of "the English" (92–3).

As the countess's account suggests, oscillating as it does between speculations about fashion and the history of Britain's imperialistic activity, women's engagement with history was always a complex endeavor in terms of both gender and politics. Therefore, although it is possible to trace formal lines of influence around the shifts in historiography that occurred in the Romantic period, especially around the increasing focus on subjective experiences of material objects, it remains difficult to identify a cohesive ideology governing those shifts or their effects. Women's contributions to history used historical discourses for varying purposes across diverse genres.

These experiments with historiography do not offer up a singular agenda. That is to say, not all women writers felt compelled to craft radical, feminist accounts of the past. Some recovered the histories of women that did little more than bolster prevalent stereotypes; others invented problematical fictions; where some women claimed poetic license to interpret history in feminist ways, they nevertheless justified their literary-historical aesthetics with questionable appeals to British nationalism; finally, others seemed blind to the privileges of their class status in undertaking historical research in the first place. Nevertheless, women's historiographical experiments deserve serious consideration, not least because of the diversity of their methods and politics. In fact, the sheer diversity of women writer's contributions to

Romantic history itself speaks to their ability to shape the changing field of historiography.

NOTES

1 Benedict Anderson, *Imagined Communities: Reflections on the Origin and Spread of Nationalism* (New York: Verso, 1991). Anne K. Mellor, *Mothers of the Nation: Women's Political Writing in England, 1780–1830* (Bloomington, IN: Indiana University Press, 2000).

2 Mary Astell, *The Christian Religion, as Profes'd by a Daughter of the Church of England* (London, 1705), p. 293.

3 Jane Austen, *Northanger Abbey*, ed. Barbara M. Benedict and Deirdre Le Faye, *The Cambridge Edition of the Works of Jane Austen* (Cambridge University Press, 2006), p. 109. Subsequent references cited parenthetically in the text.

4 [Clara Reeve], *The Champion of Virtue: A Gothic Story* (Colchester: W. Keymer, 1777), p. ii. Subsequent references cited parenthetically in the text.

5 Sophia Lee, *The Recess: or A Tale of Other Times*, 3 vols. (London: T. Cadell, 1783–85), Vol. I, p. i.

6 Robert Graves, *Plexippus, or The Aspiring Plebian*, 2 vols. (London: J. Dodsley, 1790), p. xi. Subsequent references cited parenthetically in the text.

7 Ann Radcliffe, *The Mysteries of Udolpho*, 4 vols. (London, 1794).

8 Joanne Baillie, *Miscellaneous Plays* (London: Longman, Hurst, Rees, and Orme, 1804), p. xiv. Subsequent references cited parenthetically in the text.

9 Charlotte Smith, *Beachy Head: With Other Poems* (London: J. Johnson, 1807). Subsequent references cited parenthetically in the text.

10 Henry F. Chorley, *Memorials of Mrs. Hemans*, 2 vols. (London: Saunders and Otley, 1836), Vol. I, p. 20.

11 Felicia Hemans, *The Forest Sanctuary: With Other Poems* (London: T. Cadell, 1825), p. 163.

12 Maria Edgeworth and Richard Lovell Edgeworth, *Practical Education*, 2 vols. (London: J. Johnson 1798). Subsequent references cited parenthetically in the text.

13 Mary Rundall, *Symbolic Illustrations of the History of England* (London: G. and W. B. Whittaker, 1815).

14 "Particulars Relative to a Human Skeleton," *Archaeologia* 7 (1785), pp. 90–110, p. 96. Subsequent references cited parenthetically in the text.

8

CATHERINE INGRASSIA

Writing in wartime

"War's least horror is the ensanguined field,"[1] writes Anna Letitia Barbauld (1743–1825) in *Eighteen Hundred and Eleven* (1812). Barbauld's poem depicts the global consequences of conflict wrought of imperial ambition; apocalyptic in its vision and vast in its scope, the poem's most affecting passages are perhaps those that intimately represent the cost of war to the domestic, the familiar, and the personal – the bereft mother and the fallen son. Her poem, like many others of this period, makes clear that war was an insistent presence in the lives and writing of female poets of the late eighteenth and early nineteenth centuries. After tumultuous eighteenth-century conflicts and the loss of the colonies in the American War, Britain entered a sustained period of war with France that lasted twenty years, with only one brief thirteen-month interruption. War had pervasive, often unimagined, effects that touched nearly all British subjects. While removed from actual military engagement, women bore the cultural and emotional weight of war: the restrictions on commerce, increasingly limiting governmental policies, and the loss of sons, husbands, or brothers.

This essay explores poems by female poets that represent the cost of war: the human price exacted during battle, the toll on women on the domestic front, and the ignored debt owed to returning veterans due to governmental indifference to their situation and to the moral consequences of war. Poems representing battle attempt to convey the loss, horror, and devastation of body and mind. That devastation, in turn, shapes the memories held by those left behind. Indeed, the domestic front was not immune from violence, unrest, and the effects of conflict. Poems of domestic wartime describe the displacement of a family, the "sacrifices" that are being required in the form of general fasts and days of prayer, or the presence of as yet undeployed soldiers in military encampments. Removed from the actual risks of military engagement, female poets examined the other kinds of sacrifices or potential fissures war engenders. The greatest price of war, however, is perhaps captured in the poems that represent its after-effects in the often shattered figure of the returning soldier. The homeless veteran, like the impoverished widow, or the compromised morality of England itself, is another victim of the war. A culture's attitudes toward war, like the demands war makes, are as varied as the women themselves. Voices range from exultation to rage to despair. Some poets celebrate the demonstration of imperial power and revel in the display of military grandeur; others critique England's role as a martial nation and reflect upon the cost to communities, families, and individual bodies. All summon the deadening effects of conflict without end.

Although this essay focuses only on poetic texts, war seeped into cultural consciousness and creative discourse across multiple genres; drama, fiction, and essays similarly grappled with the issue. The material reality of wartime made it nearly inescapable. Many writers strived to force citizens to see the effects of war, which were vast. Historians estimate that one in every four families had a direct involvement in the war as a result of adult male participation in either the voluntary or "regular" military. The "military fiscal state," John Brewer's well-known term for British government during this period, determined the direction of military policy in the service of England's colonial and economic interests, and continued largely unchecked. The demands for money, men, and material resources escalated as Great Britain, with a shifting coalition of allies, waged what are known as the French Revolutionary and Napoleonic Wars. This ongoing conflict spanned the period following the execution of Louis XVI in 1793 and ending with the defeat of Napoleon at the Battle of Waterloo in 1815. The British military required unprecedented numbers of soldiers to respond adequately to the tactical strategies and sprawling ambitions of Napoleon, who played an integral role in military planning, even prior to his ascent to power in 1799. As a result, few individuals were immune from the reach of war. After 1780, more than one million men were serving in the military. The regular army expanded from 40,000 men in 1793 to 250,000 in 1813, and the navy from 45,000 sailors in February 1793 to 145,000 in 1812. Additionally, the men serving in a professional capacity were bolstered by volunteer forces; by some estimates, there were as many as 400,000 men serving as volunteers at the turn of the nineteenth century. While many men served on the continent, the wars were truly global in nature. The centrality (and mobility) of the British navy coupled with the scope of French and British imperial power meant that battles occurred on at least three different continents: Africa, South America, and Europe. Thus a British soldier fighting the French did not necessarily die in France, but possibly Egypt, India, or somewhere in "Spanish America." As Barbauld writes in *Eighteen Hundred and Eleven*, British mothers are "Fruitful in vain"; "No son returns ... / Her fallen blossoms strew a foreign strand" (lines 23, 25–6). These "foreign" locations exacerbated the sense of unfamiliarity and distrust, and increasingly, as Barbauld's biographer William McCarthy suggests, geography no longer represented the glory of Britain's global power but rather separation, death, and loss, personal and national. Death, whether in France or a more far-flung location, did not necessarily happen on the field of battle. Disease, starvation, illness, or accidents claimed a significant number of soldiers. In "Henry and Lucy, or The Loss of the Royal George at Spithead" (1784), Ann Thomas (*fl.* 1782–95) details Henry's death (and that of his commander, Captain Kempenfelt) not in heroic battle, but when the ship sank in the harbor, becoming a "wat'ry urn."[2]

Although no battles occurred on English soil during the Romantic period, war had a physical presence on the island of Great Britain. For example, England had nine prison camps – as well as numerous decommissioned boats or "floating tombs" – that held French soldiers captured in war. Anna Seward (1742–1809) witnessed the experiences of the prisoners of war at a camp near her home in Lichfield and in *Elegy Written as from a French Lady* (1810) sympathetically imagines the feelings of a French prisoner's wife who laments the "Ruthless … foe who … / … bids thee in unransome'd bondage pine!" She asks "why are bonds for him who knows not crime? / Fierce War ordains them!–Fiend of human kind!–/ Fetters and death one murder overtake; / From thee the Guiltless no exemption find."[3] Anxiety about the "French threat" and the persistent fears of an invasion on the coast of England led to the creation of military encampments at strategic points along the English coast beginning in 1778 and continuing through the early nineteenth century. As poet Ann Thomas details, such camps provided entertainment, titillation, and, significantly, commercial opportunities for the civilians who lived in the area. Additionally, individuals were reminded daily that they lived in what the scholar Mary Favret terms "wartime" or the everyday state of war. Illuminations for military victories, returning veterans, increased taxes, published lists of the dead and wounded, food shortages, and general fast days seamlessly became part of the cultural fabric.

War also had a specific economic impact, negatively affecting trade in an already unstable market and yet also creating new commercial possibilities. The global scope of conflict impeded British merchants from continuing their business uninterrupted. Consequently, Mary Masters's (*c.* 1694–1771) *On the Peace* (1755) celebrates not only a military victory but, essentially, a commercial one: "Merchants, look round, the joyful Prospect see, / Send out your Ships, for ev'ry Port is free."[4] In *Ode on General Eliott's Return from Gibraltar* (1787) Anna Seward praises General Eliott's victory for now can

"Commerce widely sail." Mary Whateley Darwall (1738–1825) details how, with the Paris of Peace, "Commerce shall raise her languid head."[5]

War also proved commercially valuable for those selling their poems, treated, as *The Analytical Review* noted in 1793, by "every hireling scribbler."[6] It was part of daily discourse. Poets – whether publishing in newspaper, periodicals, broadsides, or volumes – found a willing audience for the topic. As such, poems complement the other commercial elements of war; as Kathleen Wilson details, mugs, plates, teapots, medals, and other tokens of military victory were desirable consumer goods whose iconographic representations helped advance the idealized qualities of the national character necessary for success.[7] While not everyone subscribed to that official message – many poets sharply critique both those ideals and the government that espouses them – it functioned as a cultural backdrop to the other representations of the war.

Indeed, sharp political divisions existed within society and resistance to the dominant discourse is an important component of much war poetry. Conservatives, often figured as "patriots," feared that ideological positions motivating the revolutionary activities in France – the desire for "Liberty" and "Freedom" – would infect the British citizens, particularly the lower classes. Mary Alcock (*c.* 1742–98), in *Instructions, Supposed to be Written in Paris, for the Mob in England* (1799), suggests that "Liberty, Reform, and Rights" (p. 48, line 1) really lead to "Liberty, Reform, and Riot" (p. 49, line 27): "The liberty to raise a mob or riot / ... The liberty to overturn the state" (p. 48, lines 11, 14).[8] Conservatives supported war efforts and British government policies almost unequivocally just as they resisted the attitudes of "Jacobins" who supported (some only initially) the revolution in France, sympathized with the pursuit of liberty, and denounced the British governmental policy of war and increasingly draconic domestic policy (e.g. the suspension of habeas corpus). Those assuming a Jacobin position were viewed as radicals and poets Mary Robinson (1756?–1800) and Helen Maria Williams (1759–1827), supporters of the revolution, even traveled to and lived in France. Yet such poets remained committed to illustrating how Britain's wartime policies were inconsistent with the nation's image of itself; they expressed concerns that the erosion of civil liberties presented a greater threat. While "Jacobin" and "anti-Jacobin" were common appellations for those who supported or opposed the French Revolution, those monolithic terms fail to adequately capture the complexity of the political allegiances held by female writers of this period. For very few writers can the terms be used unequivocally over a sustained period of time. For example, Linda Colley observes that during the wars against Revolutionary and Napoleonic France, "women were more prominently represented among the ranks of conventional patriots ... than in any of Britain's previous wars." Simultaneously, however, "women of all social levels" either believed war was "always sinful, or that these wars in particular were wrong and oppressive."[9] For others, attitudes toward the events in France shifted radically. A poet like Anna Seward, as Claudia Kairoff has sensitively detailed, long regarded as a staunch anti-Jacobin poet, displays changing attitudes toward war as it continues. [10] Personal correspondence and poems unpublished during her lifetime reveal her resistance to British intervention and her anti-magisterial views. Because of the dangers that accompanied publication following the Royal Proclamation Against Seditious Writings and Publications in May 1792, many poets withheld, revised, or withdrew poems that expressed an anti-war attitude that might be considered seditious or unpatriotic. Consequently, scholars' ability to classify poets and gauge their shifting attitudes toward war becomes more challenging.

The most obvious cost of war is the loss of human life in battle. Descriptions of the battlefield demonstrate a preoccupation with the physicality of war while simultaneously critiquing the abstract concepts used to justify the military engagement. A variety of female poets vividly present the field of battle with language of intensity: Mary Robinson details "the red scene of slaughter,"[11] filled with what Amelia Opie (1769–1853) terms "works of carnage, scenes of strife";[12] in Anne Bannerman's (1765–1829) words, a "pile of human sacrifice."[13] There, Opie writes, on "War's red shrine" "unnumber'd victims bleed."[14] The sea, too, as Charlotte Smith (1749–1806) details, is marked by the effects of war as "the waves" carry "the war-freighted ships"; "and fierce and red, / Flash their destructive fires – The mangled dead / And dying victims then pollute the flood."[15] In Ann Yearsley's (1753–1806) *Anarchy: A Sonnet* (1796) the intense language uttered by "Anarchy" captures not only the physical confusion of battle – "carnage," "mangled limbs," "ensanguined race" – but the always threatening, systemic violence that can result from such passionate pursuits. Anarchy tells the Furies to unleash the "wolves of war" and bring "daggers yet reeking," and tells the "World" to "give my monsters way!"[16] Jane Cave Winscom (1754–1813) envisages the battlefields "drench'd with human blood, / When armies after armies prostrate lie, / And brother, by his brother's hand must die."[17] These locations, typically, are distant, unknown, and unknowable; soldiers, writes Eliza Tuite (1764–1850), "while on foreign ground, / ... bleed at honor's call."[18] Yet the imaginative vision of the battlefield is so all-consuming that it colors all other associations. Although it is spring, "thy softest zephyrs breathe, / Of sorrow's soul-distracting tone," writes Amelia Opie, "To me thy most attractive wreath / Seems ting'd with human blood alone." [19]

Some poets depict the actions of specific military leaders in heroic, often uncritical, terms. Mary Whateley Darwall lauds the success of General George Eliott (1717–90), Governor of Gibraltar, who wrested control of that strategic entry point to the Mediterranean from the Spanish. His victories invoke a patriotic ardor that simultaneously transgresses and reinforces Darwall's status as a woman writing about war: "Glory fires me, / Fame inspires me, / E'en a woman's heart grows bold."[20] Darwall, shifting temporal registers, imagines Eliott leading with similar success during the Trojan War. "Had Elliott rul'd in Troy, the Greeks had fail'd" (line 30); by inference, Eliott proves a greater hero than Achilles. For Anna Seward, Eliott completes a lineage of exalted British generals whose heroics advance "Freedom's cause": "intrepid Marlborough," John Churchill, first duke of Marlborough (1650–1722) victorious at the Battle of Blenheim, or William Augustus, the Duke of Cumberland (1721–65) at Culloden, "When gaunt Rebellion grimly cower'd."[21] *Ode on General Eliott's Return from Gibraltar* (1787) describes how Eliott "lighten'd on thy Foes, / Wing'd his red bolts, that wrapp'd their Fleets in flame, / Resistless as his sword, and glowing as his fame!" He becomes "the British Lion" whose roar brings "the o'erwhelming Flood, and raging Fire!" As the *Gentleman's Magazine* notes, the publication of Seward's poem was "particularly well-timed, as the gallant veteran arrived in London" simultaneously with the poem's publication.[22]

The seductive appeal of victory, praised in the poems of those who support the war, has a sharply different effect on the young man seeking glory in battle, as presented in poems with a more critical perspective. In Fanny Holcroft's (1780–1844) "Annabella" (1797) a widowed mother curses the war that "divorced" her husband Henry "from his bride." Seduced by "roaring drums, and trumpets shrill, / More grateful to thy ear / Than notes of love," he sought "Glory," whose voice "thunders war and rage."[23] Mary Robinson describes "School-boys, smit with martial spirit, / Taking place of vet'ran merit";[24] they are led to inglorious deaths. In the ballad "Anna's Complaint, or The Miseries of War: Written in the Isle of Thanet, 1794" (1795), published in *The Universal Magazine* by "Mrs. Moody," the "lowly maid" Anna looks to "Gallia's cliffs" with "streaming eyes" and laments the death of her lover William. "Won by war's deceitful charms," the "simple youth" failed to recognize "the monster war doth falsely show": "He decks his form with pleasing art, / And hides the daggers in his heart." Thus, the metonyms of military life – "the *music* of his martial band, / The shining *halbert* in his hand; / The *feather'd helmet* on his head, / And *coat* so fine of flaming red" (emphasis mine) – lead William "the dangerous paths of war to tread." Moody critiques the abstractions that lure men into battle, discursive

constructs that serve the ends of the already powerful at the expensive of
the less fortunate:

> Fair-sounding words my love deceiv'd,
> The great ones talk'd, and he believ'd,
> That war would fame and treasure bring,
> That glory call'd to serve the king.[25]

"Glory," "fame," and "treasure" all recruit those susceptible to the rhetoric.
The result? William, "amid a savage train, / wert mingled among heaps of
slain." The word "heaps" is simultaneously non-specific and all too evocative of the cost of human life.

Military leaders and government officials are represented as also seduced
(and distracted) by visions of glory that exceed their actual capacity. In
"Written by the Desire of a Lady, on Building of Castles" (1795), which
critiques the British imperial project, Jane Cave Winscom condemns British
involvement in the American war and traces the transition from a time when
leaders defended recognizable, geographic, material fortifications to the present when they pursue abstract, unreal "castles." Previously, castles were
built "Adjacent to the Seat of war; / Where blood and slaughter did abound,
/ And drench'd with gore the thirsty ground; / Where powder, darts, and
bullets flew, / Nor one relenting passion knew; / But winging through the
smoak and fire, / Made thousands groan, bleed, and expire."[26] She celebrates
a nostalgic vision of battle, albeit bloody, when countries or rulers protected
clearly defined, existing territory and borders; though implicitly set in the
past, the graphic language of military encounters simultaneously makes it
very current. The "bullets," "powder," and "fire" allude to the technology of
modern warfare, a battle where "blood and slaughter did abound." But now
Britain attempts to defend a "castle" "fabricated in the air" by the words of
an ultimately anonymous "ministry," which creates a structure "of the mental kind" (lines 23–5):

> Our ministry this castle built,
> By which the blood of thousand's spilt;
> Fancy'd a thousand men or two
> Could all AMERICA subdue.
> But thrice ten thousand cross'd the main,
> A million's in the contest slain.
> Yet, ah! fell castle, direful ill,
> AMERICA'S unconquer'd still.

The imaginative construction of "America," solely a "construction of the
mind," proves undefendable and an extravagant cost of human life. The
poem subsequently characterizes the loss in the American War as a kind of

divine retribution, although Winscom also offers a detailed interrogation of the governmental policies and pursuits and the physical result on the battlefield.

While poets wrote vividly about imagined battles, more powerful perhaps were the descriptions of the costs of war on the home front. War disrupts the boundaries between the public and the domestic, and women had various opportunities to view the pressures of the wars. Soldiers in encampments or prisoners of war on domestic soil allowed a glimpse into war efforts. The series of defensive fortifications established along the southeast coast of England during the height of anxieties provided a (perhaps false) sense of security, as well as a revenue boost to and source of entertainment for the area. Ann Thomas describes the welcome diversion offered by the soldiers at the camps. While the threat of invasion creates anxiety (and prompts evacuation) in some, the speaker, having "no Money ... no Plate" and thus no fear of "the plund'ring Foe," chooses instead to explore the camp. "We'd such Amusements every Day; / The People from the Country tramp / To see the Manners of the Camp."[27] The "Martial Plain" (21), now domesticated, is a site of amusement and contentment (although the term underscores the pervasive fear of invasion and the risk that England could itself become a site of battle, a martial plain). In the camp, the Scottish soldiers are appealing "with Legs quite bare up to the Knee; / They look'd as we are often told / Brave Roman Warriors did of old," a comic application of the classical imagery common to poetry of another war. China broken during an evacuation from the coast is "a Loss we may regain / When India Ships come home again." The effect of the war on Britain's mercantile interests appears throughout the poetry, representing the domestic front. For some it's a marker of the morally bankrupt motivations for war. For others it solidifies the inextricable connection between Britain's military and mercantile interests. Mary Robinson similarly describes "Tradesman, leaving shops, and seeming / More of *war* than profit dreaming."[28] The postwar world always holds the promise of domestic pleasures and commercial possibilities. Robinson captures the "confusion, din, and riot" (line 47) of a camp, and the heterogeneous mix of people, commodities, and activities that illustrates the indiscriminate reach of war. These camps emerge as complicated sites where the domestic and the military meet and, at times, overlap, where "martial sound, and braying asses" create a cacophony rivaling the noise of the battlefield itself.

Other poems look on the demands made on England's citizens individually or collectively, specifically in the form of so-called "fast days" – days of general prayer and fasting designed to demonstrate the nation's piety and dedication to the collective cause. Jane Cave Winscom and Anna Seward each write poems about fast days, but with distinctly different perspectives. Winscom devoutly situates the fast within her nation's urgent need to comply with a larger morality. War, in Winscom's configuration, is the work of "Jehovah": "'Tis I make peace, and I create stern war, / And ride to battle in my flaming car, / I guide the bullet, point the glitt'ring sword / Defeat, or conquest, wait my awful word."[29] England's success or victory in military endeavors, suggests Winscom, stems directly from its worthiness as a Christian nation. She praises the fact that "a day is sanctify'd / T' implore thy aid, and humble BRITAIN'S pride" (21–2); but she warns that if everyone does not fully participate, "if all the heart be not engaged there, / Is empty shew, a poor external part" (28–9), "The whole will be offensive in His eyes" (32). Fast days provide the opportunity to participate in a form of piety, even redemption, to compensate for previous failures of faith or devotion. Seward, however, recognizes the distance between public rhetoric and personal experience and assumes an ironic tone in "Verses, Inviting Stella to Tea on the Public Fast Day" (1791). Seward, like Winscom, acknowledges the widespread effects of war but questions the degree to which the sacrifice is really shared or authentically experienced. "Our Monarch bids us" to feel "pious sorrow," just as the public is expected to feel "zeal," "penitence," and "vengeance."[30] But does this "abstinence" intensify those sentiments or produce any real effect? Does it "whet our edgeless sword," and help "cut Provincial throats at will?" In the face of forced abandonment of tea, the "pampering juices," for "that day," the speaker and her friends will "banish the ungodly Aces" and "take of food a sparing bit." However, they will still be free to "gluttonise on ... wit" and other forms of social pleasure from which they won't abstain. The "price" they pay on the fast day will be merely symbolic, an inconvenience for which social exchange (and of course a poem) provides an abundant compensation. The poem ventriloquizes the voice of the "Patriot" who scolds them for their plan and reminds them that tea is "that curs'd libation, / That cost the lives of half the nation." Seward's poem simultaneously embeds language of martial violence ("cut provincial throats") and ensuing social unrest to capture the diversity of attitudes toward enforced devotion to the military cause and daily sacrifices from citizens.

The consequences of battle and the impositions on the home front are arguably exceeded by the price of war paid by returning veterans whose sacrifice does not end with their military term of service. The demobilization of soldiers and their return to England caused a rise in the homelessness and unemployment of many veterans. The image of the homeless or displaced veteran consistently appeared in poetry of the period and his presence raised a fundamental question about the morality of a government that failed to take care of the men who, for little pay (and often against their own will), risked their lives for their country. Masculine imagination, and its capacity to deflect or compensate for governmental neglect, is an important part of poems presenting the homeless veteran. The powerful image of the "poor old" soldier, "helpless and forlorn," fed by a family which itself barely has a subsistence existence shapes Joanna Baillie's "A Winter Day" (1790).[31] After dinner, the veteran, taken in by the farmer and his family, entertains his host with narratives, his "tales of war and blood" (line 270) that recount how "oft' ... [he] stood undaunted in the battle/ Whilst thund'ring cannons shook the quaking earth, / And showering bullets hiss'd around his head" (lines 273–5). These stories contrast sharply with his physical presence: "They gaze upon him, / And almost weep to see the man so poor, / So bent and feeble, helpless and forlorn" (lines 270–2) prompting the family, and the reader, to bridge imaginatively the gap between teller and tale. Having fought for his country, the veteran now receives only this humble hospitality, a welcome but meager substitute for employment or a government pension. Yet the veteran too relies on memory to close the temporal gap between his present and his past. Surrounded by the young boys of the family, "his thoughtful mind is turn'd on other days" (line 217) when his own sons played with him; sons who, like him, have been displaced by the hardships of war and "now lie distant from their native land / In honourable, but untimely graves" (lines 219–20). The unnamed veteran's situation allows only a transient experience "with the cheerful family, / Around the plain but hospitable board" (lines 231–2). His homelessness is accentuated by his placement, however brief, within this domestic space.

In her sonnet "The Soldier" (1800) Anne Bannerman similarly relies on masculine imagination and absent domestic space. The sonnet describes how the veteran, borne home on a ship while "sick, and wounded, and opprest," is buoyed when "rush'd thy fancy on the scene of home."[32] Home, or the imagined recreation of the same, recalls its "guiltless pleasures" of a wife "who chas'd / With looks of anxious tenderness, thy woes" (lines 9–10). Yet the soldier's "fond hopes" – fond both in the sense of affectionate and foolish – are dashed when "all that met thee on thy native soil" (13) was his wife's cold grave. Although titled "The Soldier," the sonnet describes him as a "time-worn vet'ran" (2), suggesting his liminal state, his inability to define himself apart from his military existence, and Bannerman's refusal to strip him of his role as "soldier." While it is the veteran who should be angry, it is instead the "winter's sky" that expresses "keen fury" (3). The veteran, by contrast, "heaves impetuous thine indignant breast" (5). The veteran is indignant, but even his anger is displaced – his physical gesture is marked by the forcible rushing or violence of his breathing, but he himself does not act impetuously. Rather, he moves "slow" (4); his fate, to "'beg thy bitter bread,'" and his wife's grave are "all thy country gave, for years of blood and toil" (14). The use of first person in the poem makes our understanding of the veteran's plight even more immediate – not "his" but "thine."

If the lone figure of the homeless veteran makes visible the oft-ignored consequences of war, representations of personal grief at moments of national celebration make legible another cost of war. In "Lines Written at Norwich on the First News of Peace" (1802), Amelia Opie creates a complicated scene that demonstrates how, initially, news of the peace appears (falsely of course) to erase divisions of class in the face of national victory: "In one warm glow of Christian love / Forgot all proud distinctions seem; / The rich, the poor, together rove."[33] Peace, a concept as abstract and unrealized as a "glory" or "fame," will ameliorate persistent social ills: the poor will be fed "for Plenty comes with Peace along" (28); a soldier currently serving will be spared, for "Peace now shall save their precious lives" (31). However, the mourning mother, a "shrunk form" (34), "dead" (33) to "general transport" (44), scorns the news of peace: "'Talk not of Peace, ... the sound I hate,' / The mourner with a sigh replied; / 'Alas! Peace comes for me too late ... / For my brave boy in Egypt died!'" (37–40). Private pain is exacerbated not alleviated by public celebrations. Anne Bannerman explores the same dynamic in "Verses on an Illumination for a Naval Victory" (1800), likely written about the celebrations of General Howe's defeat of the French fleet in June of 1794.[34] The poem initially interweaves the language of loss with descriptions of victory: the "loud peals of triumph *rend* the startled sky" as "Conquest rides the *crimson'd* waves" (lines 5, 8). Blood and carnage cannot be ignored nor separated from victory, suggesting a celebration is almost unnatural. How can a nation "Rejoice o'er thousands in untimely graves" (7); "Is this a time for triumph and applause, / When shrinking Nature mourns her broken laws?" (8–9). Rather, what is natural is the private grief of women "hid in some dark retreat":

> ... the widow weeps
> Her heart's best treasure buried in the deeps;
> The frantic mother's cries of Heaven implore
> Some youthful warrior – she shall meet no more:
> From the first beam, that wakes the golden day,
> To ling'ring twilight's melancholy ray,
> No respite comes, their breaking hearts to cheer,
> Or, from the fount of misery, steal a tear!
>
> (13–20)

Bannerman hopes "the scenes, the poet's fancy drew" (89) will help the reader to imagine peace: "Some fairy isle ... / Where War ne'er led his victims to the grave" (77–8). By describing Peace as a "fairy isle," Bannerman reveals how unlikely that state would be. Mary Robinson similarly characterizes "hope" as a deceptive emotion, a "flatterer" of unknowing widows. Robinson describes the life of "the Soldier's Widow" who "every hour anticipates the day / (Deceiv'd, yet cherish'd by the flatt'rer hope) / When she shall meet her Hero."[35] Yet, she will never enjoy "peace domestic" (83), a term doubly directed both to her home and to her country's peace. Like his mother, her son, "the only dear and gay associate / Of her lone widowhood" (35–6), is also ignorant of the fact his father "Sleeps on the bed of death!" (78). Just as the forlorn mother in Bannerman's "Verses on an Illumination" must witness public triumph in the face of personal loss, so too the widow, unknowingly, must reconcile her husband's absence and anonymity with the celebratory tributes to the generals and ministers of state:

> ... His very name
> Is now forgotten! for no trophied tomb
> Tells of his bold exploits; such heraldry
> Befits not humble worth: For pomp and praise
> Wait in the gilded palaces of Pride
> To dress Ambition's Slaves.
>
> (86–91)

Questioning the value of the conflict and illustrating the difficulty of reconciling national gains with personal loss, these poets ultimately interrogate the morality of England itself. Eliza Tuite asserts, "Useless their triumphs o'er the main, / Our gallant soldiers, bleed in vain, / While luxury's destructive band, / Thus locust-like, pollute the land."[36] Victory is meaningless in the face of national immorality; the cost of the human life is wasted on a "polluted" nation.

The cost in terms of human life, domestic deprivation and unease, and uncared for veterans can be illustrated with specific examples visible in daily culture. It is perhaps more challenging to represent the intangible but all too powerful effects of an empire made possible only through global military conflict. The scathing representation of the imperial project in Barbauld's *Eighteen Hundred and Eleven* makes legible the moral erosion to which Britons have perhaps become inured.

> But fairest flowers expand but to decay;
> The worm is in thy core, thy glories pass away;
> Arts, arms and wealth destroy the fruits they bring;
> Commerce, like beauty, knows no second spring.
>
> (313–16)

Ultimately, if perhaps imperceptibly, the line between war and commerce blurs, situating war as another calculated national expenditure. Many of the female-authored poems of this period, like contemporaneous fiction, essays, and drama, recognize how dearly Britons experienced war, personally and culturally, and seek to account for those cultural costs that remain incalculable.

NOTES

1 Anna Letitia Barbauld, *Eighteen Hundred and Eleven, a Poem*, in *British Women Poets of the Romantic Era: An Anthology*, ed. Paula R. Feldman (Baltimore: Johns Hopkins University Press, 1997), p. 70, line 22.
2 Ann Thomas, "Henry and Lucy, or The Loss of the Royal George at Spithead," in *British Women Poets of the Long Eighteenth Century: An Anthology*, ed. Paula R. Backscheider and Catherine E. Ingrassia (Baltimore: Johns Hopkins University Press, 2009), p. 443, line 54.
3 Anna Seward, "Elegy Written as from a French Lady, Whose Husband Had Been Three Years Prisoner of War at Lichfield," in Backscheider and Ingrassia, p. 456, lines 44–6.
4 Mary Masters, "On the Peace," in Backscheider and Ingrassia, p. 436 lines 9–10.
5 Mary Whateley Darwall, "Ode on the Peace," in Backscheider and Ingrassia, p. 440, line 53.
6 *The Analytical Review*, Vol. XVII (1793), p. 148.
7 Kathleen Wilson, *The Sense of the People: Politics, Culture and Imperialism in England, 1715–1785* (Cambridge University Press, 1998), p. 147.
8 Mary Alcock, *Poems, &c. &c. by the Late Mrs. Mary Alcock* (London: C. Dilly, 1799). Individual lines quoted as above in parenthetical citations.
9 Linda Colley, *Britons: Forging the Nation 1707–1837* (New Haven and London: Yale University Press, 1992), p. 254.
10 Claudia Kairoff, *Anna Seward and the End of the Eighteenth Century* (Baltimore: Johns Hopkins University Press, 2012).
11 Mary Robinson, "Edmund's Wedding," in *Lyrical Tales* (London, 1800), p. 157, line 17.
12 Amelia Opie, "Lines on the Opening of a Spring Campaign," in *The Warrior's Return, and Other Poems* (London, 1808), p. 122, line 20.
13 Anne Bannerman, "Verses on an Illumination for a Naval Victory," in Backscheider and Ingrassia, p. 451, line 12.
14 Amelia Opie, "Ode: Written on the Opening of the Last Campaign," in Feldman, p. 530, lines 27–8.
15 Charlotte Smith, "Sonnet LXXXIII. The Sea View," in *The Poems of Charlotte Smith*, ed. Stuart Curran (Oxford University Press, 1993), p. 72, lines 11–13.
16 Ann Yearsley, "Anarchy: A Sonnet," in *British War Poetry in the Age of Romanticism 1793–1815*, ed. Betty T. Bennett and Orianne Smith. www.rc.umd.edu/editions/warpoetry/.
17 Jane Cave Winscom, "On the First General-Fast after the Commencement of the Late War," in Backscheider and Ingrassia, p. 438, lines 2–4.

18 Eliza Tuite, "Song: In the Year 1794," in Backscheider and Ingrassia, p. 448, lines 6–7.

19 Amelia Opie, "Ode: Written on the Opening of the Last Campaign," in Feldman, p. 530, lines 13–16.

20 Mary Whateley Darwall, "Ode on the Peace," in Backscheider and Ingrassia, p. 440, lines 18–20.

21 Anna Seward, *Ode on General Eliott's Return from Gibraltar* (London: 1787), p. 7, lines 59, 62.

22 "Review of New Publications" section of the *Gentleman's Magazine*, 57 (June 1787), p. 523.

23 Fanny Holcroft, "Annabella," in *Romantic Women Poets 1788–1848*, Vol. II, ed. Andrew Ashfield (Manchester University Press, 1998), pp. 89–90, lines 7, 13–16, 21–3.

24 Mary Robinson, "January, 1795," in Feldman, p. 613, lines 39–40.

25 "Mrs. Moody," "Anna's Complaint, or The Miseries of War: Written in the Isle of Thanet, 1794," in *British War Poetry in the Age of Romanticism 1793–1815*. www.rc.umd.edu/editions/warpoetry.

26 Jane Cave Winscom, "Written by the Desire of a Lady, on Building of Castles," in *Poems on Various Subjects, Entertaining, Elegiac, and Religious* (Bristol: 1786), pp. 56–7, lines 4–11.

27 Ann Thomas, "To Laura, on the French Fleet Parading before Plymouth in August 1779," in Backscheider and Ingrassia, pp. 437–8, lines 33, 32, 44–6.

28 Mary Robinson, "The Camp," in Feldman, pp. 635–6, lines 43–4.

29 Jane Cave Winscom, "On the First General Fast," in Backscheider and Ingrassia, p. 438, lines 11–14.

30 Anna Seward, "Verses, Inviting Stella to Teach on the Public Fast-Day," in Backscheider and Ingrassia, p. 285, 2, 1, 9–11.

31 Joanna Baillie, "A Winter Day," in Backscheider and Ingrassia, pp. 58–9, lines 206, 221.

32 Anne Bannerman, "The Soldier," in Backscheider and Ingrassia, p. 450, lines 7–8.

33 Amelia Opie, "Lines Written at Norwich on the First News of Peace," in *British War Poetry in the Age of Romanticism 1793–1815*, ed. Betty T. Bennett and Orianne Smith, *Romantic Circles*. www.rc.umd.edu/editions/warpoetry, lines 9–11.

34 Anne Bannerman, "Verses on an Illumination," in Backscheider and Ingrassia, p. 451.

35 Mary Robinson, "The Widow's Home," in *Lyrical Tales* (London: 1800), p. 50, lines 23, 25–8.

36 Eliza Tuite, "Written at the Close of the Year 1794," in Backscheider and Ingrassia, p. 447, lines 55–8.

9

CAROLINE FRANKLIN

Enlightenment feminism and the bluestocking legacy

Sir Richard Bluebottle:
What with learning and teaching and scribbling and shining,
In science and art, I'll be cursed if I know
Myself from my wife, for although we are two,
Yet she somehow contrives that all things shall be done
In a style which proclaims us eternally one.
But the thing of all things which distresses me more
Than the bills of the week (though they trouble me sore)
Is the numerous, humorous backbiting crew
Of scribblers, wits, lecturers, white, black and blue
Who are brought to my house as an inn ...
                    [Lord Byron], "The Blues: A Literary Eclogue" (1820)

Emma: "I think them [*bas bleus*] very harmless and even commendable persons; for their greatest crime seems to be preferring having full to having empty minds; literary conversation to gossip, scandal and cards; nor do they do anything which you and I ... do not do every day."

"Perhaps not," replied Mrs Castlemain, "still there is such a prejudice against blue stockings that I should be very sorry to hear you called by the name."

Amelia Opie, *Temper, or Domestic Scenes: A Tale in Three Volumes* (1812)[1]

Sir Richard Bluebottle resents his bluestocking wife's assumption that they will participate together in scholarly pursuits and that she considers herself free to invite intellectuals including blacks (probably fellow abolitionists) to the home *he* owns and pays for. Byron's satire shows that "the blues" persisted as a label for intellectual women even at the close of the Romantic period. Wearing blue woollen stockings at a party in the eighteenth century – like blue jeans now – was a rejection of sartorial etiquette and symbolized a loosening of social stratification. Originally applied to scholar Benjamin Stillingfleet (1702–71), the nickname "bluestocking" became transferred to wealthy hostesses such as Elizabeth Montagu (1718–1800), Elizabeth

Vesey (1715–91), and Frances Boscawen (1719–1805), who invited a social mix to breakfast, teatime gatherings, or salons. In these gatherings, witty conversation between men and women on intellectual topics replaced the male-dominated pleasures of hunting, playing cards, and drinking. Female intellectuals became celebrated in the press at this time, but by the early nineteenth century, the tide had turned against them.

Byron complained that bluestockings did not make submissive wives: "But – Oh! Ye lords of ladies intellectual / Inform us truly, have they not hen-pecked you all?" (*Don Juan*, 1, 22). His own wife, Annabella Milbanke (1792–1860), was an aristocratic bluestocking: a mathematician and progressive educationalist whose closest friends the art historian Anna Jameson (1794–1860), sociologist Harriet Martineau (1802–76), and penal reformer Mary Carpenter (1807–77) continued to pursue the Enlightenment quest for rational knowledge with a moral or social purpose. All, apart from Jameson, were from Unitarian intellectual circles (as had been the champion of women's rights, Mary Wollstonecraft). These Romantic-era women were heirs – not of the original *salonnières* – but of second-generation Unitarian bluestockings, such as the poets Anna Barbauld (1743–1825) and Helen Maria Williams (1759–1827). Unitarian women were exposed to unorthodox religious philosophy, which enabled them to participate in cutting-edge scientific thinking. They had become politicized by the Dissenters' 1780s campaign to repeal the Test and Corporation Acts, eventually achieved in 1828. As nonconformists were often business people, they were not prejudiced about participating in the print trade and more readily became professional women of letters. It would be out of Unitarian circles that Victorian feminism eventually emerged.

Nineteenth-century female social reformers like Annabella Milbanke developed bluestocking philanthropy so effectively that so-called women's issues of education and welfare eventually became policy matters. However, they found that acting independently of men – even in a good cause – could bring them savage treatment in the press. Opie's Emma cannot understand how harmless scholarly and charitable pursuits can be a threat to her good name or respectability. But Mrs. Castlemain knows that society's prejudices against women intellectuals should not be treated lightly. It was not merely that a modern bluestocking might be tainted by association with Wollstonecraft's unconventional sex life, as disclosed by her husband William Godwin's *Memoirs of the Author of 'A Vindication of the Rights of Woman'* (1798). Even Wollstonecraft's most conservative bluestocking opponent, the Evangelical Hannah More (1745–1833) (author of "The Bas-Bleu" and one of the "Nine Living Muses of Great Britain" depicted in Richard Samuel's 1778 painting by that name), was not immune. During the

Blagdon controversy, a Sunday school that More founded in the Mendips was criticized as being too Methodist. A pamphlet war raged from 1800 to 1803 and More, who had been the scourge of radicals like Thomas Paine, herself became the favorite target of the *Anti-Jacobin Review*.

National pride at the achievements of the original Bluestocking Circle had morphed into outright hostility within a generation. This was part of a general backlash against any socially progressive ideas – now tainted by association with the French Revolution. During the wars against the French Republic, re-masculinizing the public sphere became a patriotic duty in Britain. Yet we can see by Byron's satire that bluestockings were not extinct by the nineteenth century. Rather, they evolved into philanthropic activists. I suggest that the ideology of the bluestockings had never been especially conducive to the rise of feminism but directed female energy into bourgeois paternalism.

Enlightenment philosophers of Europe and America had all called for improved education of women, but it was the Protestant stress on the religious duty of mothers to teach children and dependents to read the Bible that gave British women the opportunity to extend this role into education and authorship in the public domain. Female literacy rates greatly improved, though women had not caught up with men by the end of the Romantic period. Many Anglican and Dissenting clergymen educated their daughters and nieces at home, and male mentors such as Dr. Johnson and publishers Samuel Richardson, Edward Cave, and Joseph Johnson encouraged bluestocking intellectuals such as classicist Elizabeth Carter (1717–1806) and poet Mary Scott (1751?–93), author of *The Female Advocate* (1774), to publish their work. Female genius inspired Thomas Seward's poetic epistle "On the Female Right to Literature" (1746), George Ballard's *Memoirs of Several Ladies of Great Britain who Have Been Celebrated for their Writings or Skill in the Learned Languages, Arts and Sciences* (1752), and John Duncombe's *The Feminiad* (1754).

Wealthy bluestockings eagerly adapted the role of patron – accepting dedications and paying pensions to poor scholars or finding them positions, such as when the Duchess of Portland (1715–85) employed the pioneering Anglo-Saxon scholar Elizabeth Elstob (1683–1756) as a governess. Women came together in friendship groups in the provinces, too, exchanging occasional verse, correspondence, and visits. The quasi-domestic space of salons enabled contact with the commercial and public world of letters. Bluestockings helped proto-Romantic male poets such as James Beattie and laboring-class antiquarians such as Iolo Morganwg to negotiate with the print trade. They used their group identity to good advantage by minimizing the risk of a publishing venture, through collecting subscriptions from enough readers to cover costs and pay the author. Bluestockings enabled extraordinarily gifted laboring-class servants such as Mary Leapor (1722–46), Mary Collier (1688–1762), and Elizabeth Hands (1746–1815) to become published poets. However, geniuses were expected to demonstrate gratitude to their female patrons for publication – seen as a predominantly philanthropic gesture. The Bristol milkwoman Ann Yearsley (1753–1806) was severely criticized when she objected to patron Hannah More controlling access to her subscription money.

Romanticism inflated the concept of authorial genius with theories of sublime inspiration. Critics despised mere craftsmanship, popular fiction or writing with a utilitarian purpose. It is no coincidence that this occurred just as women had begun to dominate the market as readers and authors, commanding the new genre of children's literature and inflecting the novel and poetry with women's experience and concerns. Whereas male-authored novels outnumbered those by women by two to one in the 1770s, females outperformed their male peers by the 1790s. Ann Radcliffe and Frances Burney commanded record advances as well as critical plaudits. Women poets Anna Seward, Anna Letitia Barbauld, Helen Maria Williams, Charlotte Smith, and Mary Robinson and dramatists Hannah More, Hannah Cowley, Elizabeth Inchbald, and Joanna Baillie were the most important poets dominating the literary scene from 1770 to 1800. The re-masculinization of literature in the nineteenth century involved replacing the patronage of salons with conducting literary business in publishers' premises. Instead of treating women's books with condescending gallantry, nineteenth-century critics such as John Wilson Croker wielded the lash against Anna Barbauld and Lady Morgan for encroaching on the masculine subject of politics. Meanwhile, female writers who themselves extolled Romantic genius – such as Madame de Staël – preferred to be considered exceptional than to make common cause with their own sex.

Bluestockings had not merely sought authorship for themselves or others. Seeing vernacular literature as their particular domain, they had become women of letters – taking a prominent role in patriotic canon formation after perpetual copyright ended in 1773. During the Romantic period they were producing critical editions of selected works of the eighteenth century. Anna Barbauld edited the correspondence of novelist Samuel Richardson, wrote critical prefaces to editions of poetry by Mark Akenside and William Collins, and published a monumental fifty-volume reprint series *The British Novelists* (1810); while Elizabeth Inchbald produced an ambitious twenty-five-volume selection of plays, *The British Theatre* (1806–9). Each reprint was introduced with a literary essay.

Bluestocking literary critics had contributed to the renewed appreciation of Shakespeare, which would help inspire Romanticism. For example,

Charlotte Lennox published *Shakepear Illustrated, or The Novels and Histories on which the Plays of Shakespear are Founded* (1753–4); Elizabeth Montagu defended Shakespeare against the criticism of Voltaire in her *Essay on the Writings and Genius of Shakespear* (1769); and Elizabeth Griffith followed with *The Morality of Shakespeare's Drama Illustrated* (1775). Women were also associated with modern romance. Romantic Gothic was a female-dominated genre, theorized by its practitioners. Clara Reeve argued for the revaluation of the romance form in *The Progress of Romance, Through Times, Countries, and Manners* (1785), while Ann Radcliffe's 1826 essay justified the use of the supernatural in poetry.[2] Joanna Baillie's "Introductory Discourse" to her *Plays on the Passions* (1798) can be compared to Wordsworth's 1800 "Preface" to the second edition of *Lyrical Ballads*: arguing that drama and fiction need not be merely sensationalist but could evoke emotion for a moral purpose.

The bluestockings created a precedent for nineteenth-century women writers not merely to become intellectuals but to regard culture as an arena where they could take leading roles. We need to consider now whether this was at the price of accepting governance by men in the nation, church, and family. Proto-feminist writing had appeared early in the Enlightenment, arguing that Protestantism denied single women and widows an intellectual or religious vocation, for monasticism and female preaching were proscribed by the Anglican Church and universities were male-only until 1878. Mary Astell proposed a secular convent for single women in *A Serious Proposal to the Ladies* as early as 1694. The novelist Sarah Scott (sister of Elizabeth Montagu, the "Queen of the Bluestockings") developed this notion further in her successful utopian novel, *A Description of Millenium Hall and the Country Adjacent* (1762), describing a self-supporting female commune devoted to bluestocking intellectual pursuits and philanthropy. Scott's idea was revived by Robert Southey's *Colloquies* as late as 1829 – to provide for single women and harness their abilities. Tories such as Astell had been particularly torn over the royalist credo of patriarchy and the absolute obedience owed to both king and the head of a family, whether father or husband. Her *Reflections upon Marriage* (1700) debated whether a Protestant marriage was a contract, which could be revocable, or a sacrament, as in medieval times. The legal position of wives was taken up trenchantly in *The Hardship of the English Laws in Relation to Wives, with an explanation of the original curse of subjection passed upon the woman. In an humble address to the legislature* (1735), anonymously published but probably written by Sarah Chapone (1699–1764). This pamphlet likens the British married woman's lot to slavery, and argues that – though God cursed women with subjugation to man because of Eve's disobedience – English law was not justified in interpreting this as absolute power of a husband over his wife, her person, property and children.

Sarah's daughter-in-law, Hester Mulso Chapone (1727–1801), in her 1753 "Story of Fidelia" used the framing device of the repentant sinner's confession to portray a woman who espouses deist philosophy being free to make her own choices about sexuality. She refuses an arranged marriage to a man she is not in love with – instead living independently and choosing free love – before being persuaded by a priest that Christian stoicism and social conventions are necessary to help sexually active women cope with desertion and emotional traumas connected with rearing children. Chapone's much-reprinted conduct book *Letters on the Improvement of the Mind* (1773), which argued for balancing bluestocking intellectuality with the pleasures of companionate marriage, received an honorable mention in Wollstonecraft's *A Vindication of the Rights of Woman* (1792). Chapone's posthumously published *Letters on Filial Obedience* (1807), which argued for a daughter's right to refuse the suitor selected by her father, by then seemed quaint: fathers in Jane Austen's courtship novels are weak and silly, and all the interest lies in the heroine's own ability to choose her life companion wisely.

Bluestocking salons such as those hosted by Montagu, Vesey, and Boscawen did not directly contribute to these arguments on women's roles and rights but had a dialectical relationship with them. Like the French *salonnières*, bluestockings took on the pseudo-authority appertaining to ruling-class women, as courtly ideology still paid lip service to chivalry. They attempted to exemplify the theory of male conjectural historians that women were a civilizing influence on male barbarity: bringing into being a society based on law and commerce instead of violence. John Millar's *The Origin of the Distinction of Ranks* – an important forebear of Karl Marx and Friedrich Engels – argued that gender predated rank as the primary category of oppression, originating in the strong oppressing the weak rather than the rule of law.[3] Millar saw respect for women as an index of the degree of civic progress:

> When men begin to disuse their ancient barbarous practices, when their attention is not wholly engrossed by the pursuit of military reputation, when they have made some progress in arts, and have attained to a proportional degree of refinement, they are necessarily led to set a value upon these female accomplishments and virtues which have so much influence upon every species of improvement, and which contribute in so many different ways to multiply the comforts of life. In this situation, the women become neither the slaves not the idols of the other sex but the friends and companions.

(pp. 89–90)

Millar's thesis inspired stadial histories wholly devoted to women but always written by men: Antoine Leonard Thomas's *An Essay on the Character, the Manners and the Understanding of Women in Different Ages* (1772); William Alexander's *The History of Women From the Earliest Antiquity to the Present Time, Giving Some Account of Almost Every Interesting Particular Concerning that Sex, among All Nations, Ancient and Modern* (1779); Joseph Alexandre Ségur's *Women: Their Condition and Influence in Society* (1803); and Christoph Meiners's *History of the Female Sex: A View of the Habits, Manners and Influences of Women, among All Nations, from the Earliest Ages to the Present Time* (1788–1800).

The achievements of the most renowned bluestockings had been celebrated in poems and paintings because the high cultural status of its women displayed Britain's modernity, especially in comparison with the East. However, stadial theory was inherently unstable, as effeminization might be taken too far and lead to degeneration of male martial virtues. The bluestockings' critique of aristocratic libertinism and adoption of the bourgeois values of patriotism and piety helped assuage fears that the British Empire was becoming degenerate through luxury like that of ancient Rome. On this, even Wollstonecraft and More could agree. The fear that the effeminization of France had gone too far and was responsible for the excesses of the French Revolution dominated the later histories by Ségur and Meiners, who blamed *salonnières* for encouraging radical philosophers and for politicking. They explicitly called for women to vacate the public sphere and to instigate the separation of male civic duty from domestic life associated with the Roman republic of classical times.

The Enlightenment sociability of the bluestockings was largely lost to the age of Romantic individualism. It had temporarily brought together those of different classes and opposing religious denominations and shown that women could act together. Elizabeth Carter, Elizabeth Montagu, Frances Burney, and Hannah More were staunch Anglicans inclining to Christian Stoicism, politically conservative and implicitly endorsing aristocratic ideology. Clara Reeve and Anna Seward were "Old Whigs," while Dissenters Anna Barbauld and Helen Maria Williams were politically radical, yet accepted conventional gender distinctions. When in 1774 Barbauld was invited to become principal of a women's college, she declined, arguing:

> A kind of Literary Academy for ladies ... where they are to be taught in a regular systematic manner the various branches of science, appears to me better calculated to form such characters as the "*precieux*" or the "*femmes savantes*"of Molière, than good wives or agreeable companions. ... [Y]oung ladies who ought only to have such a general tincture of knowledge as to make them agreeable companions to a man of sense, and to enable them to find

rational entertainment for a solitary hour, should gain these accomplishments in a more quiet and unobserved manner.[4]

This indicates to me that Barbauld accepted Jean-Jacques Rousseau's argument that men and women's roles were now complementary, not equal as they had originally been before settled society, and that she even accepted his assertion in Chapter 5 of *Émile, or On Education* (1762) that women should be socialized to please men on whom they were dependent. In 1804, Barbauld refused Maria Edgeworth's invitation to discuss the setting up of "a periodical paper, to be written entirely by ladies," stating:

> There is no bond of union among literary women, any more than among literary men; different sentiments and different connections separate them much more than the joint interest of their sex would unite them ... To write professedly as a female junto seems in some measure to suggest a certain cast of sentiment and you would write in trammels.
>
> (*The Works of Anna Laetitia Barbauld*, Vol. 1, p. xv)

Barbauld's allusion to "a certain cast of sentiment" refers to the first stirrings of feminist political consciousness in those arguing during the revolutionary period for an extension of woman's role in society. Female intellectuals of the 1790s had begun to question the way that, despite its apparent universalism, the discourse of civic humanism excluded women (alongside children and landless labourers) from civil rights, citizenship, and the professions. The republican historian Catharine Macaulay was the first person to argue that the perceived inferiority of women, "their peculiar foibles and vices," did not result from differences ordained by God but "originate in situation and education only." Letter 22 of her *Letters on Education* (1790) entitled "No Characteristic Difference in Sex" advocated co-education and inspired Mary Wollstonecraft to develop the implications of the theory that gender difference is cultural not natural. *Vindication of the Rights of Woman* (1792) was a revolutionary text that argued that a common moral standard based on reason should apply equally to men and women and to all classes, and it was translated into French and German. In France, Olympe de Gouges and the male *philosophe* the Marquis de Condorcet had already put women on the revolutionary agenda, while in Germany Theodor Gottlieb von Hippel now published *On Improving the Status of Women* (1792).

However, Wollstonecraft's originality consisted not so much in specifying how women's rights and roles in society should be extended (though there was some of that) as in a radical critique of femininity itself. She specifically attacked aristocratic women's illicit power in a move perhaps implying dissatisfaction with bluestocking patronage. She was particularly scornful of Rousseau for not applying his admirable progressive educational theories to both sexes alike. Like an Enlightenment Judith Butler, Wollstonecraft pointed to the performativity of gender. The outwardly docile but scheming behavior of conventional femininity is characteristic of all subordinates who study a master to gain favor:

> Women are told from their infancy, and taught by the example of their mothers, that a little knowledge of human weakness, justly called cunning, softness of temper, *outward* obedience and a scrupulous attention to a puerile kind of propriety will obtain for them the protection of man, and should they be beautiful everything else is needless for at least twenty years of their lives.[5]

Wollstonecraft's call for "a revolution in female manners" asked women to abandon their fear of being judged unfeminine by men and urged men, "Let women share the rights and she will emulate the virtues of man." Setting "masculine" rationality as the standard to aim at seemed misogynistic to second-wave 1980s feminists, who extolled "feminine" irrationality and sensuality and reclaimed difference as not necessarily unequal. Anticipating Engels, Wollstonecraft demanded the work that women did at home be valued equally by the state as public service, declaring that in a new egalitarian society, women would attain full citizenship through republican motherhood as men bore arms. Elizabeth Carter was apparently impressed, and Anna Seward wrote excitedly to a friend, "Have you read that wonderful book, 'The Rights of Women'?"[6]

Paradoxically, the new generation of radical female intellectuals were much less of a cohesive group than their bluestocking forebears. Mary Wollstonecraft, Mary Robinson, and Mary Hays – although personal friends – were perceived not as a coterie but as avant-garde individuals. They were treated as scandalous aberrations of their sex by the hostile press. After her death in 1797, public admiration of Wollstonecraft turned to hostility. Yet when the bluestocking Mary Berry was reading Hannah More's answer to Wollstonecraft, *Strictures on the Modern System of Female Education* (1799), she averred that actually they "agree on all the great points." There were certainly similarities: both were puritan professionals attacking their own sex in arguing that the feminization of modern society drove consumer desire for luxuries, and criticizing female aristocrats' power operating through dynastic networks or illicitly through the mistress system. Both threw out the bluestocking baby with the bathwater through class-conscious repudiation of the *ancien régime*, which all agreed needed reform.

That they actually concurred on all the great points of female education, however, is palpably untrue. More stresses the social usefulness of religion and education in curbing children, who are not viewed as innocent but "beings who bring into the world a corrupt nature and evil dispositions"[7] – especially girls:

> An early habitual restraint is peculiarly important to the future character and happiness of women … [They] should be led to distrust their own judgment … it is a lesson with which the world will not fail to furnish them; and they will not practise it the worse for having learnt it the sooner. It is of the last importance to their happiness that they should early acquire a submissive temper and a forbearing spirit.
>
> (Vol. 1, p. 142–3)

Wollstonecraft, however, wants education to "strengthen the female mind by enlarging it and there will be an end to blind obedience … ever sought for by power" (*Vindication of the Rights of Woman*, p. 45). Women should learn to exercise independent individual judgment: "the grand end of their exertions should be to unfold their own faculties and acquire the dignity of conscious virtue" (p. 48).

More's fellow conservative Jane West debated Wollstonecraft's ideas in her novel *The Advantages of Education, or The History of Maria Williams* (1793). While West's old maid narrator Prudentia Homespun agreed with More that education should equip girls for life and marriage rather than for pleasing men, utopian radicalism was portrayed as dangerous romantic fantasy. Her later fiction, *A Gossip's Story* (1796) – recommended by Wollstonecraft to Mary Hays – contrasted a stoical with a romantic protagonist and inspired Austen's *Sense and Sensibility* (1811). Like Carter and Montagu of the Bluestocking Circle, West and More were fortified by a stoical Anglicanism, which sanctioned social usefulness. Their bleak realism in considering women's lives could be compared to Wollstonecraft's earliest writings, such as her children's book *Original Stories* (1788).

The Quaker writer Priscilla Wakefield (1751–1832) in her *Reflections of the Present Condition of the Female Sex with Suggestions for its Improvement* (1798) looked at the question of women's role through an economic lens. Taking Adam Smith's ideas as her starting point, she proposed woman should have many more opportunities opened to them for employment. Her argument did not rest on abstract rights but on social obligations, which females could fulfill through useful participation in trades and commerce. Even the Anglican educationalist Sarah Trimmer (1741–1810) in her *The Oeconomy of Charity* (1786, rev. 1801) reflected a comparable turn toward political economy in setting out practical proposals as to how women of means could become activists in implementing paternalistic charitable schemes for the relief of the poor. Trimmer edited the *Guardian of Education* (1802–6), which reviewed educational publications and schemes dominated by female experts, such as Maria Edgeworth and Barbauld. It was apparent that, despite their conservative views on gender roles, surviving bluestockings and Evangelicals had amassed and retained considerable cultural capital in national debates on education and welfare. Early nineteenth-century economists such as Jane Marcet and Harriet Martineau would build on these beginnings to popularize utilitarianism.

However, the notion of sexual equality was too dangerous to be aired. A rash of anti-Jacobin comic novels mocked the utopian ideas of radicals Wollstonecraft, Mary Robinson, and Mary Hays, for example Amelia Opie's *Adelina Mowbray, or Mother and Daughter* (1804). Caricatures of female philosophers included Harriet Freke in Edgeworth's *Belinda* (1801) and Bridgetina Botherim in Elizabeth Hamilton's *Memoirs of Modern Philosophers* (1800). Satirical poetry flourished at the turn of the century, and women intellectuals were now targeted. Popeian and Juvenalian poets also lampooned poetry of humanitarian concern by Romantic poets such as Samuel Taylor Coleridge and Robert Southey, alongside the writings of their friends William Godwin and Mary Wollstonecraft who had criticized the institution of marriage.

The Tory polemicist William Gifford (Byron's literary adviser) was editor of various government-sponsored periodicals throughout the Romantic period, *The Anti-Jacobin* (1798), *The Anti-Jacobin Review* (1798–1821), and *The Quarterly Review* (founded 1809), whose mission was to combat French sympathizers during the Napoleonic Wars. Gifford made a point of singling out women voicing liberal views in literature, targeting the popular Della Cruscan poets Mary Robinson and Hester Thrale Piozzi in *The Baviad* as early as 1791 for support for the French Revolution (Robinson) and voicing anti-Hapsburg sentiment in support of Italian cultural nationalism (Piozzi). "The New Morality" from Gifford's *The Anti-Jacobin* (1798) casually cast doubt on the gender of Madame de Staël, the leading female intellectual of France, dubbing her "Staël the epicene." The periodical proclaimed Wollstonecraft to be a prostitute, following William Godwin's revelation in *Memoirs of the Author of A Vindication of the Rights of Woman* (1798) that she had given birth to an illegitimate child.

T. J. Mathias's *Pursuits of Literature* (1794–7) had contained onslaughts on novelist and poet Charlotte Smith, novelist and dramatist Elizabeth Inchbald, and novelist and poet Mary Robinson. The fact that they all wrote for a living and also made use of sentimental literature for social protest stripped them of their femininity, making them "unsexed female writers." Now Mathias's admirer, the Anglican clergyman and *Anti-Jacobin* contributor Richard Polwhele, saw his opportunity to make women writers the subject of an entire Juvenalian satire entitled *The Unsex'd Females* (1798).

Interestingly, however, Polwhele's purpose was not only to mount a savage attack on the recently deceased Mary Wollstonecraft, whom he declared had been punished for impiety by God for writing *Vindication of the Rights of Woman* through the particular manner of her death (blood poisoning following childbirth). He attempted to create a distinction between the original Bluestocking Circle, many of whom had been mentored by Anglican clergymen fathers, and those of the next generation who were challenging the distinctions of class, gender, and race that he held as God-given. Polwhele damned Wollstonecraft, her friend the republican Helen Maria Williams, and her followers Mary Robinson (author of the pseudonymous *Letter to the Women of England on the Injustice of Mental Subordination*, 1799) and Mary Hays (author of the anonymous *An Appeal to the Men of Great Britain on Behalf of Women*, 1798); Anna Letitia Barbauld and Catharine Macaulay, who were both Dissenters and "True Whigs"; the reformer Ann Jebb; liberal-leaning Charlotte Smith and Ann Yearsley; and the artists Angelica Kauffmann and Emma Crewe. However, he paid compliments to Elizabeth Montagu, Anna Seward and Hester Thrale Piozzi, Elizabeth Carter, Frances Burney and Ann Radcliffe, Hester Chapone and Hannah More, and the artist Diana Beauclerk. All with the possible exception of Radcliffe were devout Anglicans, and Polwhele selected the Evangelical campaigner Hannah More as a worthy role model for the younger generation, to replace Wollstonecraft.

Twentieth-century feminists reversed Polwhele's judgments while retaining his binary oppositions: identifying Wollstonecraft as their forebear and criticizing More as hypocritical, as she lived an independent life as a professional writer despite urging other women to accept the separate gendered spheres of the domestic ideology so beloved of the Victorians. More recently, however, More's anti-Jacobin propaganda has been credited with ensuring that violent revolution never happened in nineteenth-century Britain. She and other conservatives paradoxically helped lay the foundations for the future feminist movement by giving women roles to play within Anglicanism. By accepting that femininity was secondary in the social hierarchy (because that was ordained by God), More was able to stress instead women's potential moral superiority. This sleight of hand allowed many, while theoretically accepting that women were not equal to men, to become philanthropic activists in their hometowns and to gain experience in organizing reform. However, More had scaled back the bluestockings' civilizing mission to the domains of kitchen and the church.

Polwhele tactically conceded the cultural achievements of the bluestockings. This was not surprising as most of even the first generation were still alive and some still publishing when he wrote. Historian Catharine Macaulay and *salonnière* Elizabeth Vesey had died in 1791, but Elizabeth

Robinson Montagu lived until 1800, Hester Chapone until 1801, Frances Boscawen to 1805, Elizabeth Carter to 1806, Clara Reeve to 1807, and Hester Thrale Piozzi until 1821. Anna Letitia Barbauld wrote little after being savaged in the *Quarterly Review* in 1812 but lived on until 1825, as did the redoubtable Hannah More, until 1833.

The Romantic period commemorated the achievements of the bluestockings even as Wollstonecraft's name was obliterated. Memoirs of Elizabeth Carter were edited by her Anglican clergyman nephew Montagu Pennington in 1807, who also brought out the works of Catherine Talbot (1809), and (against his aunt's wishes) the correspondence between Carter, Talbot, and Elizabeth Montagu (1808, 1817). The influential woman of letters Anna Seward had prepared her own correspondence for the press and consigned the publication of her collected works to a literary executor (Walter Scott). Mary Robinson and Anna Barbauld, who had been battered by the press, each entrusted posthumous publication and championship to a female literary descendant who would carry their torch: daughter Mary E. Robinson and niece Lucy Aikin, respectively. During the revolutionary and Napoleonic period, it was only the most cosmopolitan of female Romantic writers who perpetuated the "frenchified" role of the political *salonnière*: Helen Maria Williams in republican France and Madam de Staël, in Switzerland, while the Irish woman of letters Sydney Owenson, Lady Morgan was a literary hostess in Dublin well into the nineteenth century.

Insofar as the original bluestocking hostesses had assumed the power of aristocratic and courtly women, that authority had undoubtedly been lost in the age of the French Revolution. But several British female intellectuals, such as Elizabeth Elstob and Elizabeth Carter, had come from backgrounds as modest as those of the second-generation Wollstonecraft and More. Bluestocking culture helped make ubiquitous the presence of such women as cultural leaders, authors, editors, and critics – indeed, that is why the "masculine" realm of politics had to be ringfenced by Gifford's reviewers, in case another Wollstonecraft should appear to put the case for equal civil rights. It is true that nineteenth-century female intellectuals continued to be figures of fun for Whig wits as well as Tory moralists. Byron's friend Thomas Moore wrote a successful comic opera *M. P., or The Blue-Stocking* (1811), whose ridiculous lady scientist Lady Bab Blue composes a poem on the lines of Erasmus Darwin's *The Botanic Garden* (1791). She personifies the chemical elements and allegorizes their reactions to one another as sexual attraction. This idea shockingly implied that the behavior of human reproduction itself might be governed merely by the laws of biology. However, such weak squibs tell us more about masculine fear of intellectual rivals than the diminishing of women's

cultural capital. In fact, the bluestockings' notion of women's special civilizing role lived on in a more moralizing form into the Victorian age. Its
success was arguably more of a hindrance to the evolution of the feminist
movement than the extinguishing of Wollstonecraft's reputation.

NOTES

1 George Gordon, Lord Byron, "The Blues: A Literary Eclogue," in *Lord
Byron: The Complete Poetical Works,* ed. Jerome J. McGann, 7 vols.
(Oxford: Clarendon Press, 1980–93), Vol. VI, pp. 296–308; Amelia Opie,
Temper, or Domestic Scenes: A Tale in Three Volumes (London: Longman,
Hurst, Rees, Orme and Brown, 1812), Vol. II, p. 9.

2 "On the Supernatural in Poetry," *New Monthly Magazine,* 16 (1826),
pp. 145–52.

3 John Millar, *The Origin of the Distinction of Ranks, or An Inquiry into the
Circumstances Which Give Rise to Influence and Authority in the Different
Members of Society* (London: John Murray, 1771, repr. 1793), p. 109.
Subsequent references from the 1793 edition cited parenthetically in the text.

4 Anna Letitia Barbauld, *The Works of Anna Laetitia Barbauld with a Memoir
by Lucy Aikin,* intro. Caroline Franklin, 2 vols. (London: Longman, Hurst,
Rees, Orme, Brown and Green, 1825, repr. London: Routledge/Thoemmes
Press, 1996), Vol. I, p. xiii. Subsequent references cited parenthetically in the
text.

5 Mary Wollstonecraft, *A Vindication of the Rights of Woman,* 3rd edn.
(London: Joseph Johnson, 1796), p. 33.

6 Anna Seward, *Letters of Anna Seward Written between the Years of 1784 and
1807,* 6 vols. (Edinburgh: Constable, 1811), Vol. III, p. 117.

7 Hannah More, *Strictures on the Modern System of Female Education,* 2 vols.
(London: Cadell, Jun. & W. Davies, 1799), Vol. I, p. 57. Subsequent references
cited parenthetically in the text.

10

DEIRDRE COLEMAN

The global context

In her essay "On Ghosts" (1824) Mary Shelley mourned the loss of an older, antediluvian earth across which the "eagle-winged" imaginations of our ancestors "dived and flew, and brought home strange tales to their believing auditors. Deep caverns harboured giants; cloud-like birds cast their shadows upon the plains; while far out at sea lay islands of bliss, the fair paradise of Atlantis or El Dorado sparkling with untold jewels." Compared to this dreamlike and mythical golden age, the present seemed devoid of mystery: "Our only riddle is the rise of the Niger; the interior of New Holland, our only terra incognita; and our sole mare incognitum, the north-west passage"; and even these, Shelley mused, are "tame wonders, lions in leash." The forlorn suspicion that the globe's furthest reaches were now a humdrum affair made it sometimes feel as though the very "empire of the imagination" had shrunk,[1] a sensation exacerbated by the politically reactionary period that followed France's failure to produce an enduring republic.

In this chapter, which can open only a small window on the international dimensions of British women's writing in what is now dubbed "the age of imperial revolutions,"[2] I focus primarily on those women writers for whom travel and the discourse of a highly politicized public sphere led to new insights into the complex interactions between local practices and a transnational discourse of universal rights and equality. The centrality of colonial slavery in the far-distant West Indies to British women's demands for greater equality at home is an obvious example of the "glocal" perspective which came to prevail in "the new order of the ages" – *Novus ordo seclorum*, the Latin inscription on the Great Seal of the United States, first designed in 1782 – ushered in by the American Revolution.

Mary Shelley was only four years old during the Peace of Amiens, that brief window when, in Anna Letitia Barbauld's words, the huge lodestone of France drew "every mother's child" to its coast.[3] Mindful, perhaps, of her mother's adage that "The art of travelling is only a branch of the art of thinking,"[4] Shelley was among the first to escape across the Channel when the continent reopened in May 1814. Journeying by foot and by boat in July–August through France, Switzerland, Germany, and Holland, in company with her stepsister and Percy Bysshe Shelley, the sixteen year old described in spare and sobering prose the sufferings of the French citizenry, their countryside laid waste by revengeful Cossack "barbarians." Her theoretical "detestation of war" was stung into life by the horrors she saw around her: the citizens' houses burned, "their cattle killed, and all their wealth destroyed ... a country pillaged and wasted."[5] Two years later, when the three young travelers returned to Paris, Shelley accepted the ire directed at them and other English visitors. After all, she comments, the British government "fills their country with hostile garrisons, and sustains a detested dynasty on the throne." Instead of being resented, the hostility shown to them was "honourable ... and encouraging to all those of every nation in Europe who have fellow feeling with the oppressed, and who cherish an unconquerable hope that the cause of liberty must prevail."[6]

Shelley's belief that the principles underpinning the French Revolution marked a turning point not just in French but in world history continues the theme of the Francophile foreign correspondent Helen Maria Williams. In 1790, with the fame of the French legislators extending through "every civilized region of the globe," Williams rejoiced in letters home to England that "the reign of reason, virtue, and science" was imminent.[7] It is a measure, perhaps, of the fourteen years between Williams's euphoria at "treading on the territory of History"[8] and Shelley's more jaundiced outlook on the world, that the striking "equality of classes" achieved by Swiss republicanism did not exempt the natives from appearing (in Shelley's words) "slow of comprehension and of action." As for the lower order of "smoking, drinking Germans," they were "horribly disgusting," and the Dutch "timorous."[9]

Although Shelley did not share Williams's cosmopolitan outlook, she attempted to call on her in Paris in July 1814, but she had left town for the summer. Famous for her eyewitness *Letters Written in France* (1796), Williams would have endorsed two of Wollstonecraft's key observations about travel: that travelers "who require that every nation should resemble their native country, had better stay at home," and that the best travel writer avoids "those dogmatical assertions which only appear calculated to gird the human mind round with imaginary circles, like the paper globe which represents the one he inhabits" (p. 266). In the final volume of her *Letters Written in France*, Williams takes a decidedly critical view of her native country, warning her compatriots against a narrow-minded, partial morality "which measures right and wrong by geographical divisions," with the skewed result that human crimes denounced in France are sanctioned in Africa. Such national distinctions would soon disappear, Williams believed, since "it required but the common feelings of humanity to become ... a citizen of the world." The boldness of her claim that a feeling heart would unlock universal citizenship, normally denied to both women and the poor, was accompanied by a playfully coy appeal to her fictitious correspondent – "you are not one of those who will suspect that I am not all the while a good Englishwoman" – a disclaimer that did not of course prevent her from being demonized as a "democrat" and "professed jacobine."[10]

Two collections of women's travel writings accompanied Mary Shelley in 1814: Lady Mary Wortley Montagu's *Turkish Embassy Letters* (1763) and her mother's *Letters Written during a Short Residence in Sweden, Norway, and Denmark* (1796). The beauty of Wollstonecraft's book about remote and little-known Scandinavia, published before the definitive defeat of France's ideals, lay, in her daughter's words, in its narrative "*I*, this sensitive, imaginative, native, suffering, enthusiastic pronoun [which] spreads an inexpressible charm" over the text.[11] Although described by its author as "a simple record of Scandinavian morals and manners," the text ambitiously pursues its twin aims of tracing "a just idea of the nature of man" and "the progress of the world's improvement."[12] Refusing to indulge in painting "national characters," Wollstonecraft's methodology is quasi-scientific, based on stadial theorizing as to the rise of civilization in different countries. She observes the effects of climate on character, is careful to distinguish the natural from the cultural, and argues that traveling on a rational plan, i.e. visiting the far north of Europe before its "more polished parts," marks "the completion of a liberal education" (p. 327). But because she wanted her remarks and reflections to "flow unrestrained," the *Short Residence* deserts political philosophy for some strikingly lyrical passages. Indeed, at one point in her travels Wollstonecraft sets out to explore the northern reaches of Norway because the glowing reports of that region's farmers carry her back to "the fables of the golden age" – to an "asylum" of "independence and virtue; affluence without vice; cultivation of mind, without depravity of heart; with 'ever-smiling liberty'; the nymph of the mountain" (p. 308). Impatient at the thought of being "bastilled," and believing in the twinning of intellectual and physical exertion, Wollstonecraft equates exercise and the mountainous landscape with liberty. She walks for the pure pleasure of walking; she also goes horse riding, boating, and swimming, all activities that take her out into the open air where she can either clarify her observations on the gap between profit and labor, consider the inscrutable workings of the universe, or turn over a new page in the history of her heart (pp. 287, 289).

The book's ability "to make a man in love with its author" (as William Godwin so famously put it) can be seen in the narrative's shuttling between careful observation of facts and the "poetical fictions" generated by an imagination that "bodies forth its conceptions unrestrained, and stops enraptured to adore the beings of its own creation" (p. 286). Reason vies with imagination, expansion with contraction. Likening herself to a quivering Aeolian harp "agitated by the changing wind" (p. 271), Wollstonecraft oscillates between sinking into melancholy and rising into ecstasy, at one moment projecting an expansive interior life with intimations of immortality, at another bleakly conceding that the Deity's design is clearly "the preservation of the species, not of individuals ... what a large proportion of the human race are born merely to be swept prematurely away" (p. 336). Nevertheless, determined to arrive at a revolutionary politics that "enlarges the heart by opening the understanding" (p. 274), Wollstonecraft's imagination is tempted to dip "her brush in the rainbow of fancy, and sketch futurity in glowing colours" (p. 310). At other times utopian imaginings about the planet trail off into bleakness. Traveling along the rocky coast of Norway Wollstonecraft projects her imagination a millennium or two hence, when the world's population will fill even these "bleak shores." Time-traveling even further into futurity she then pictures "universal famine" in a distressingly overpopulated world, which has suddenly turned into "a vast prison" (p. 295).

Wollstonecraft's ability to think globally and across vast timescales was evident in *Vindication of the Rights of Men* (1790), her lightning-fast response to Edmund Burke's *Reflections on the Revolution in France* (1790). Pouring contempt on Burke's "rhetorical flourishes and infantine sensibility," she scoffed at his narrow focus on a single unpleasant day for the king and the royal family when he ought to consider the "continual miseries" of the degraded poor, and the "tremendous mountain of woe that thus defaces our globe! ... You mourn for the empty pageant of a name, when slavery flaps her wing, and the sick heart retires to die in lonely wilds, far from the abodes of men ... Hell stalks abroad."[13] The journey to Scandinavia concludes with a full-scale critique of the evils of commerce (pp. 330, 309). For all her detestation of war, she concludes that the sword "has been merciful" compared with men of commerce, a "swarm of locusts who have battened on the pestilence they spread abroad." From locusts and universal plague she moves, in the book's final paragraph, to the lucrative business of slavery, an iniquity in which Britain was leading the world in 1796. Here she argues that businessmen, "like the owners of negro ships, never smell on their money the blood by which it has been gained, but sleep quietly in their beds, terming such occupations *lawful callings*" (p. 344).

The international movement for the abolition of the slave trade was one of several new opportunities for women of widely differing social and religious backgrounds to be politically active and vocal. For instance, in joining the abolitionist campaign, the conservative Hannah More collaborated not just with fellow-Evangelicals but with pro-revolutionary sympathizers as well, women such as Anna Letitia Barbauld, Wollstonecraft, and Ann Yearsley. All adopted different tactics. Some confined their focus to Africa and the distant West Indian islands; others brought the sufferings of black slaves into conjunction with "home" issues such as the plight of the laboring poor, evicted Irish peasants, the evils of commercialism, and the sufferings of white women in marriage and under patriarchy. In considering the voices of women in the abolitionist movement, many scholars have concluded that modern Western feminism developed in Britain in the context of imperialism and anti-colonialism. But chattel slavery was only one of several complex global issues and conversations to which British women contributed during this period. As we will see later in this essay, the ritual of sati, or widow burning in India, became another focus for teasing out cross-cultural analogies concerning the ways in which women were subordinated around the globe – culturally, economically, and religiously.

Jane Austen can also be counted in the body of women writers engaged with war, slavery, colonialism, exile, travel, and alternative imagined communities. In 1792, just as the vote went in favor of William Wilberforce's amended bill for abolition of the slave trade, the seventeen-year-old Austen started writing a novel she would never finish, *Catharine, or The Bower*. From the fate of the destitute orphan Cecilia Wynne it is clear that the sharp-eyed Austen was alert to the marriage market as yet another form of body trade. Penniless Cecilia is shipped out (according to one heartless character) to "Bengal or Barbadoes or wherever" for a husband and a "maintenance," a fate "so opposite to all her ideas of Propriety, so contrary to her wishes, so repugnant to her feelings, that she would almost have preferred Servitude to it, had Choice been allowed her."[14] There is no choice, of course. In fact, the suggestion of choice implied syntactically by "Bengal or Barbadoes or wherever" only deepens the irony, with both named destinations synonymous with servitude for vulnerable women. In the women's rights literature of the 1790s, Bengal often features as a trope for oriental despotism, Barbados for black slavery. Other instances of geographical imprecision are sketched in more lightly, such as the conversation between the well-traveled admiral's wife, Mrs. Croft, and the stay-at-home Mrs. Musgrove. When Mrs. Croft admits that she has never travelled in the West Indies, she explains: "We do not call Bermuda or Bahama, you know, the West Indies," to which the narrator adds: "Mrs Musgrove had not a word to say in dissent; she could not accuse herself of having called them any thing in the whole course of her life." Given that her son Richard had died abroad, Mrs. Musgrove's geographical ignorance only adds to the falsity of her "fat sighings" over his fate.[15] More sympathetic is the ignorance of young Fanny Price. As her more privileged cousins point out, Fanny is unable to "put the map of Europe together" or give an account of the principal rivers in Russia. In time, though, Fanny redeems herself with a new curiosity about the world, as can be seen in her reading of Lord Macartney's 1792–4 embassy to China, and her question to her uncle, recently returned from his plantations in Antigua, about the slave trade.[16] Both episodes signal Fanny Price's developing grasp on the wider world and her growing sense of the implications of imperialism.

Austen may have domesticated the exotic by her faux-modest description of "the little bit (two inches wide) of ivory" on which she delineated her social world but her exposure to the revolutionary upheavals and imperial expansion of her age can be seen in her firm grasp of geography, unsurprising when we consider the activities of her immediate family.[17] Her brother Frank served in the West Indies in the mid 1790s during a period of widespread uprising and revolution in the region, and her sister Cassandra lost her fiancé to yellow fever in 1797 in St. Domingo, the colonial crucible of interracial strife which would later give birth, in 1804, to the independent black republic of Haiti. India also featured prominently in Austen's life. Her aunt Philadelphia sailed to the subcontinent in search of a husband, whom she promptly found, then also (it is believed) took a lover, Warren Hastings, with whom she had a daughter, Eliza. A favorite of Austen's, Eliza would grow up to marry a French count who, when he returned to France to reclaim his estates, was guillotined in 1794. The lure as well as the threat of Britain's growing empire in the East are frequently registered in the novels: the exquisite and costly cashmere shawls, to be procured by Fanny's naval brother William, and Colonel Brandon's military career in a corrupt Orient of "nabobs, gold mohrs, and palanquins." This shallow characterization of the East by Willoughby, together with his sneer at Brandon, prompt Elinor to defend her friend as a mine of valuable information. Brandon had seen "a great deal of the world," she argues, an experience which is further enriched by his extensive reading and his possession of "a thinking mind." To this her younger sister Marianne can only contemptuously respond with yet another cliché about the East, namely that the sum total of Brandon's information is that "the climate is hot, and the mosquitoes are troublesome."[18]

The worlds of the East and the West Indies can be found in many women's novels of the late eighteenth century, from Elizabeth Inchbald's *A Simple*

Story (1791) and Mary Hays's *Memoirs of Emma Courtney* (1796), to less well-known works, such as Elizabeth Helme's *The Farmer of Inglewood Forest, or An Affecting Portrait* (1796) and Helena Wells's *Constantia Neville, or The West Indian* (1800). The mixed-race or "brown women" of these last two novels make a fleeting appearance in Austen's last, unfinished work, *Sanditon* (1817), in which a wealthy West Indian heiress, Miss Lambe, is referred to as a "half mulatto," and the West Indians imprecisely described by the grasping Lady Denham as the "West injines" or the "West Indy family." Notably, while Austen did not represent an interracial marriage directly in her fiction, as did Maria Edgeworth in her novel *Belinda* (1801), she did not hesitate to list this work amongst three woman-authored novels "in which the greatest powers of the mind are displayed, in which the most thorough knowledge of human nature, the happiest delineation of its varieties, the liveliest effusions of wit and humour are conveyed to the world in the best chosen language."[19] Clearly the marriage of Juba, the former African slave, to the English farm girl Lucy presented the welcome prospect of human "varieties," a phrase suggestive of the new pressures to taxonomize and tabulate racial distinctions.

Edgeworth's interracial marriage of Juba and Lucy did not, however, enjoy universal approval, with Richard Lovell Edgeworth warning his daughter that "gentlemen have horrors upon this subject, and would draw conclusions very unfavourable to a female writer who appeared to recommend such unions." Despite being an abolitionist like his daughter, Edgeworth had "great delicacies and scruples of conscience" on the topic of mixed-race marriage.[20] Reluctantly bowing to pressure, Edgeworth dropped "poor Juba" and his wedding from the novel's third edition in 1810. We might even say that she dropped a second mixed-race marriage when she distanced her heroine Belinda from the wealthy white West Indian Augustus Vincent, a suitor who had presented a strong marriage prospect in the first edition.

From the 1770s onwards, British women began traveling and publishing in ever greater numbers, with approximately fifty travel narratives appearing between 1770 and 1830 to destinations as diverse as Egypt, India, Tripoli, Africa, and Chile. Such accounts even included the "rare circumstance," as the *Monthly Review* of May–August 1796 put it, of seeing "a female name in the list of circumnavigators," namely Mary Ann Parker, who sailed to and from Botany Bay in the early 1790s. The Romantic period was also rich in translations and adaptations of contemporary European literature and drama. Female translators acted as cultural mediators in the Romantic era, introducing and diffusing European literature throughout Britain and Ireland; in the process they confirmed the central role of foreign literature in their own self-definition as woman writers.[21] Perhaps the most well-known example of this phenomenon is Elizabeth Inchbald's translation of Kotzebue's *Lovers' Vows*, a bold, ideological appropriation of a foreign work which strictly subordinated her respect for the German author to her even more profound respect "for the judgment of a British audience." The intellectual curiosity and taste for experimentation which motivated so many of these women's translations may have led (in Susan J. Wolfson's words) to the "happy Englishing of world literature," but the circulation of so many Anglicized versions of foreign literature also exposed writing in English to new and different generic and thematic traditions.[22]

At the early age of fourteen Felicia Dorothea Browne (later Hemans) began publishing verse and translations from the many languages in which she was fluent: Spanish, German, French, Italian, and Latin. While she never traveled further from home than Dublin, her wide reading and gift for languages, plus the fact that she had two brothers in the army and a sister in Europe, meant that her imagination ranged far and wide across the globe. Her themes were popular ones, addressing a broad range of local and international subjects and drawing on both English and European literature, past and present. In many ways her reading stands in for travel abroad, as can be seen in the playful verse she addressed to her sister in Rome, laid low by a fever. Hemans imagines that high temperatures have led to a poetical voyage to China via the islands of Loo Choo, performed in a cocoa-nut shell with John Evelyn.

Other literary texts open up different forms of imaginary travel such as "that wonderful frigate (see Curse of Kehama) / Which wafted fair Kailyal to regions of Brama ... / Or the Vale of Cashmere, as described in a book, / Full of musk, gems and roses, and called 'Lalla Rookh.'" Even in her thinking about her globetrotting contemporaries Hemans writes as though she herself were just as well-traveled. Reading about Lord Byron in the *Quarterly Review* she muses that his character reminded her "of some of those old Eastern cities, where travellers constantly find a squalid mud hovel built against the ruins of a gorgeous temple; for alas! The best part of that fearfully mingled character is but ruin – the wreck of what might have been."[23] In one of her earliest poems, *England and Spain, or Valour and Patriotism* (1808), we see her honing her skills at literary metonymy in order to conjure up a world beyond England's shores. In this intensely patriotic poem, inspired by her brother's service in Spain under Sir John Moore, Hemans defines England entirely in negatives, as a country devoid of the blessings bestowed on other countries:

> Hail, Albion, hail! To thee has fate denied
> Peruvian mines and rich Hindostan's pride;

> The gems that Ormuz and Golconda boast,
> And all the wealth of Montezuma's coast:
> For thee no Parian marbles brightly shine;
> No glowing suns mature the blushing vine;
> No light Arabian gales their wings expand,
> To waft Sabaean incense o'er the land;
> No graceful cedars crown thy lofty hills,
> No trickling myrrh for thee its balm distils;
> Not from thy trees the lucid amber flows,
> And far from thee the scented cassia blows!
> Yet fearless Commerce, pillar of thy throne,
> Makes all the wealth of foreign climes thy own;
> From Lapland's shore to Afric's fervid reign,
> She bids thy ensigns float above the main ...[24]

The poetically named Albion may be the land of freedom's birth, a second Rome, but commercial England has a lot of work to do in counterbalancing and stemming the tide of all those exotic items it lacks. A similar ambivalence can be felt in one of Hemans's most curious and haunting poems, *England's Dead*:

> Go, stranger! track the deep –
> Free, free the white sail spread!
> Wave may not foam, nor wild wind sweep,
> Where rest not England's dead.[25]

While some read this short poem as glorying in the worldwide expansion of English dominion, others read it as a dirge for the unnumbered dead of Britain's imperial wars. Egypt, India, the Americas, and Spain are all invoked, as are the failed voyages in search of a northwest passage through the Arctic Ocean to Asia. Hemans's most recent editor believes that *England's Dead* asks us to "ponder the empire, not as a realm on which the sun never sets, but as a global graveyard," a reading supported by the invocation "Go, stranger!," a common epitaph on tombstones.[26] No land, no ocean, it appears, is free of England's dead. That the conqueror's repeated "Free, free the white sail spread" is designed to contrast abruptly with the immobility of the dead can be seen in another poem by Hemans, "I dream of all things free" (1833), where a host of swift-moving natural and man-made objects lead to the final surprising lines: "My heart in chains is bleeding, / And I dream of all things free."[27]

If Hemans's patriotism is troubled by her cultural ambivalence about war and imperialism, then the same might be said of Anna Letitia Barbauld's *Eighteen Hundred and Eleven, a Poem* (1812), a work that opens with a chilling invocation of Europe's marauding armies and their generation of

famine, rapine, and disease, meaning that "war's least horror is the ensanguined field." Designed to shake readers out of their insular smugness,
Barbauld envisions the collapse of commerce and a Britain in ruins, visited
in the future by curious New World tourists "From the Blue Mountains, or
Ontario's lake."[28] The mighty city of London, hub of global trade and commerce, is now a ghost town, whereas once its streets were places

> ... where the turban'd Moslem, bearded Jew,
> And woolly Afric, met the brown Hindu;
> Where through each vein spontaneous plenty flowed,
> Where Wealth enjoyed, and Charity bestowed.[29]

Like Carthage and other once-mighty cities, Barbauld prophesies that
London too will, in the end, be nothing but ruins: "the fractured arch, the
ruined tower, / Those limbs disjointed of gigantic power" (p. 253). The
Thames itself, once thronged with fleets, is now choked with reeds and
sedge instead. Nor is it only "England, the seat of arts" that will be known
by "the grey ruin and the mouldering stone." Europe too will "sit in dust,
as Asia now." A feminized Fancy is the faculty that permits Barbauld to
move freely backwards and forwards in time, as well as across the planet,
a form of time and space-travel that challenged nineteenth-century restrictions on the female body and mind. But while the Genius of commerce may
depart west to the Latin American countries of Ecuador, Argentina, and
Bolivia, Barbauld takes comfort in the fact that British settlers, the English
language, and all the "stores of knowledge" derived from her nation's great
poets, philosophers, and playwrights will people and colonize the world
from "Ganges to the pole."

India was certainly a key target for the civilizing mission envisaged by
Barbauld, with sati (widow sacrifice) an obvious cross-cultural focus for
British women. Views on this ritual changed considerably from the 1760s
onwards, as the non-interventionist policy of the British gave way, under
the pressure of the missionary movement after 1813, to the outlawing
of the ritual in 1829. One of the key features of sati is its paradoxical
representation as both illustrious female heroism and miserable female vic-
timhood. In the eighteenth century it is often the heroism of the widow that
is emphasized. In 1767 John Zephaniah Holwell, a surgeon with the East
India Company and witness to many acts of sati, took an Enlightenment,
culturally relativist view of "this seeming cruel custom," inviting his "fair
countrywomen" to view the act "without prejudice, and without keeping
always in sight our own tenets and customs ... to the injury of others."[30] In
her *Letters on India; with Etchings and a Map* (1814), Maria Graham did
precisely this, paraphrasing the findings of Henry T. Colebrooke's learned

essay "On the Duties of a Faithful Hindu Widow" (1795) concerning the authenticity and meaning of the rite's ancient Sanskrit instructions.[31] Sophia Goldborne, the heroine of Phebe Gibbes's comic novel *Hartly House, Calcutta* (1789), is more enthusiastic. Revelling in the pageantry of "Eastern pomp, splendour, and magnificence," half in love with her young Bramin tutor, and filling her letters with splendid snapshots of Indian history and culture, Sophia adopts the orientalized pose of "we Asiatics." A champion of Hinduism, she praises sati as the widow's "affectionate and voluntary sacrifice," adding that, while there have been instances of seeming reluctance, these "seldom occur." For Sophia the only negatives about India are the high mortality rates and a hot climate.[32] In Sydney Owenson's *The Missionary* (1811), sati is also presented as a "voluntary immolation," the heroine Luxima mistaking the fires of the Inquisition's auto-da-fé for the pyre upon which she will be reunited with her beloved Hilarion, the Portuguese missionary to India.[33] Here Luxima is a figure of both martyrdom and transcendence, her desire for death identified as the very pinnacle of eroticism – a longing for both sexual consummation and a resolution of theological difference in the indivisible flames of the Christian and Hindu religions.

Inevitably a comparative view of the sad lot of both Indian and English wives emerged, each bound within marriage as a system of exploitation and oppression. Fanny Parkes, resident in India from 1822 to 1846, was convinced that women everywhere in the world "are considered such dust in the balance when their interests are pitted against those of men." Sati had been tolerated in British India because the government only acted on matters "where rupees are in question." Describing in detail a botched sati where the widow willingly mounted the pyre but then, in agony, tried to escape from the flames, Parkes believed that the main motive for the ritual was the greed of male relatives.[34] Later in her narrative, wandering around a sati ground near Ghazipur by moonlight, and depressed by the surprisingly large number of sati mounds, Parkes reflects on how "very horrible" it was

> to see how the weaker are imposed upon; and it is the same all over the world, civilized or uncivilized – perhaps some of these young married women, from eleven to twenty years of age, were burnt alive, in all the freshness of youth; it may be with the corpse of some decrepit sickly old wretch to whom their parents had given them in marriage.

These reflections on the cultural aspects of actual sati, designed to arouse the reader's compassion for the young bartered brides, immediately pass over into metaphorical sati in order to spotlight (and to magnify) the sufferings of her own countrywomen: "The laws of England relative to married women, and the state of slavery to which those laws degrade them, render the lives of some few in the higher, and of thousands in the lower ranks of life, one perpetual sati, or burning of the heart, from which they have no refuge."[35] While Parkes's pity for the young Indian widow-brides is palpable, her equation of the rite with metaphorical heart-burning lends support to Gayatri Spivak's claim that white women never produced "an alternative understanding" of sati.

Spivak also described the outlawing of sati in 1829 as an enterprise in which white men saw themselves as saving brown women from brown men.[36] The chivalric mission is certainly uppermost in many male-authored accounts, with the suffering widow a very marginal figure. Possessing no voice, the widow has no individual will or agency, her consent or otherwise proving to be the only point of interest for British commentators. Emma Roberts's poem "The Rajah's Obsequies" (1832) is unusual in giving voice to an older and a younger widow, and in collapsing the two mutually exclusive representations of the sati: the unflinching heroine withstanding the rage of the fires, or the pathetic, coerced victim. In constructing her poem in this way, Roberts revisits the scene of double sati that opens Robert Southey's *Curse of Kehama* (1810), where the two young wives of the dead Arvalan are burnt on the funeral pyre, one calmly and willingly, the other terrified and tied down. Since both of Southey's widows are silent it is as though Roberts has been provoked to imagine their voices. Accordingly, the younger, compliant bride, blushing and retiring, sings "with a voice divine":

> Lord of my soul! I yield my breath
> To snatch thee from the chains of death;
> I claim the privilege divine,
> Which makes thee more than ever mine! ...
> And with a sweet seraphic smile
> She gently droops her radiant head
> Beside the ghastly corse – so calm,
> So saint-like are those placid eyes,
> So softly breathes the lip's rich balm,
> So faint and indistinct her sighs,
> In some blest trance she seems to be,
> Or day's delicious reverie.[37]

Roberts is clearly familiar with some of the theological underpinnings of the rite, such as the guaranteed immortality for the couple, but this young widow is dreamily enacting a cruel tradition. Despite having a voice, she is no more substantial than the beautiful sati of Letitia Elizabeth Landon's "A Suttee" (1839) who, bejeweled and perfumed, with a garland of flowers in her hair and a white veil flung around her, is described as "a bride ... The bride of Death."[38] Roberts joins Landon in toying with the idea of the possibility of the consenting, "legitimate" sati, but allusion to a "best trance" suggests something more sinister: that the young bride may be "infatuated," i.e. drugged by her relatives.

The older widow, Mitala, voices her predicament very differently. "Revolting at the sacrifice" with a "troubled spirit nearly wrought / To madness," she proudly flings down her costly gems and throws a "scornful glance on all":

> Think not, accursed priests, that I will lend
> My sanction to these most unholy rites;
> And though yon funeral pile I may ascend,
> It is not that your stern command affrights
> My lofty soul – it is because these hands
> Are all too weak to break my sex's bands.
> I, from my earliest infancy, have bowed
> A helpless slave to lordly man's control,
> No hope of liberty, no choice allowed,
> Unheeded all the struggles of my soul:
> Compelled by brutal force to link my fate
> With one who best deserved my scorn and hate ...
> The tyrant sleeps death's last and endless sleep,
> Yet does his power beyond the grave extend,
> And I this most unholy law must keep,
> And to the priest's unrighteous mandate bend,
> Or live an outcast – reft of queenly state –
> A beggar lost, despised, and desolate ...
> But could these weak arms wield a soldier's brand,
> Could these too fragile limbs sustain the fight,
> Even to the death, Mitala would withstand
> This cruel custom, and uphold the right
> Of woman to her share of gold and gems,
> Sceptres and sway, and regal diadems.[39]

Mitala's speech focuses on the greed of the Brahmins and her male relatives to secure her wealth and inheritance, an economic explanation for sati that no doubt reflected current concerns in Britain around legal changes to married women's property rights. Nevertheless, as we see in Mitala's final oracular prophecies, the setting is safely in the distant past, well before the British, the "west's pale warriors," came to rule over India.

As the examples of slavery and sati show, the global context of Romantic women's writings can be seen in their attention to actual worldwide crossings, involving the movements of commerce and human and non-human cargos, as well as the metaphorical circuitries of their self-identity with subject groups such as African slaves and Indian widows. As their curiosity about the larger world increased, and the French Revolution appeared to open a space for the fraternity and sorority of the human race, some (like Williams) even ventured to shake off notions of nation-based citizenship. The irony, of course, was that women were not citizens; and despite their ability to think transnationally and transculturally even the most radical (like Barbauld) could only countenance the ruin of England by imagining the triumphal progress of English colonization across the globe.

NOTES

1 Mary Shelley, "On Ghosts," *The London Magazine*, 9 (1824), pp. 253–6; reproduced in *The Mary Shelley Reader*, ed. Betty T. Bennett and Charles E. Robinson (New York: Oxford University Press, 1990), pp. 334–40.
2 S. Desan, Lynn Hunt, and W. M. Nelson, eds., *The French Revolution in Global Perspective* (Ithaca: Cornell University Press, 2013), p. 3.
3 Anna Letitia Barbauld, "Letter to Mrs Carr," October 1801, in *The Works of Anna Letitia Barbauld, with a Memoir by Lucy Aikin*, 2 vols. (London: Longman, 1825), Vol. II, p. 119.
4 Janet Todd and Marilyn Butler, *The Works of Mary Wollstonecraft* (London: Pickering & Chatto, 1989), Vol. VII, p. 277.
5 Mary Shelley, *History of a Six Weeks' Tour through a Part of France, Switzerland, Germany, and Holland* (London: T. Hookham, 1817), p. 19.
6 Shelley, *History of a Six Weeks' Tour*, pp. 86–7.
7 Helen Maria Williams, *Letters Written in France, in the Summer 1790* (Peterborough, Ontario: Broadview Press, 2001), p. 82.
8 Helen Maria Williams, "Introduction," in *Poems on Various Subjects* (London: Whittaker, 1823), p. x.
9 Shelley, *History of a Six Weeks' Tour*, pp. 103, 50, 68, 79.
10 Helen Maria Williams, *Letters Written in France*, pp. 189, 69, 91, 222.
11 Shelley, *The Mary Shelley Reader*, pp. 331–2.
12 Mary Wollstonecraft, *Letters Written in Sweden, Norway and Denmark*, ed. Janet Todd and Marilyn Butler, in *The Works of Mary Wollstonecraft*, 7 vols. (London: Pickering & Chatto, 1989), Vol. VI, p. 354. Subsequent references cited parenthetically in the text.
13 Mary Wollstonecraft, *Vindication of the Rights of Men*, ed. Janet Todd and Marilyn Butler, in *The Works of Mary Wollstonecraft*, 7 vols. (London: Pickering & Chatto, 1989), Vol. V, p. 58.
14 Jane Austen, *Catharine, or The Bower*, in *Juvenilia*, ed. Peter Sabor, *The Cambridge Edition of the Works of Jane Austen* (Cambridge University Press, 2006), p. 244.
15 Jane Austen, *Persuasion*, ed. Janet M. Todd and Antje Blank, *The Cambridge Edition of the Works of Jane Austen* (Cambridge University Press, 2006), p. 73.

16 Jane Austen, *Mansfield Park*, ed. John Wiltshire, *The Cambridge Edition of the Works of Jane Austen* (Cambridge University Press, 2005), pp. 230–1.

17 Jane Austen, *The Letters of Jane Austen*, ed. Deirdre Le Faye, 4th edn. (Cambridge University Press, 2011), p. 337.

18 Jane Austen, *Sense and Sensibility*, ed. Edward Copeland, *The Cambridge Edition of the Works of Jane Austen* (Cambridge University Press, 2006), p. 61.

19 Jane Austen, *Northanger Abbey*, ed. Barbara M. Benedict and Deirdre Le Faye, *The Cambridge Edition of the Works of Jane Austen* (Cambridge University Press, 2006), p. 31. This famous defense of the novel was probably added in 1803, when *Belinda* (1801) was still fresh in Austen's mind.

20 Maria Edgeworth, *Belinda*, ed. Siobhan Kilfeather, *The Novels and Selected Works of Maria Edgeworth*, 12 vols. (London: Pickering & Chatto, 1999–2003), Vol. II, pp. xxxii, xlii.

21 Diego Saglia, "National Internationalism: Women's Writing and European Literature, 1800–1830," in *The History of British Women's Writing, 1750–1830*, ed. Jacqueline M. Labbe (London: Palgrave Macmillan, 2010), pp. 268–87.

22 Saglia, "National Internationalism," pp. 277–8.

23 Felicia Hemans, *The Works of Mrs. Hemans, with a Memoir by Her Sister*, 7 vols. (Philadelphia: Lea & Blanchard, 1840), Vol. I, pp. 46, 227.

24 Felicia Hemans, *Selected Poems, Prose, and Letters*, ed. Gary Kelly (Peterborough, Ontario: Broadview Press, 2002), p. 98.

25 Hemans, *Selected Poems*, pp. 213–15.

26 Susan J. Wolfson, *Felicia Hemans: Selected Poems, Letters, Reception Materials* (Princeton University Press, 2000). http://press.princeton.edu/chapters/i6994.html.

27 Paula R. Feldman, ed., *British Women Poets of the Romantic Era: An Anthology* (Baltimore: Johns Hopkins University Press, 1997), pp. 323–4.

28 Feldman, *British Women Poets*, p. 130.

29 Feldman, *British Women Poets*, p. 75.

30 Andrea Major, ed., *Sati: A Historical Anthology* (Oxford University Press, 2007), pp. 44–51.

31 Maria Graham, *Letters on India; with Etchings and a Map* (London: Longman, Hurst, Rees, Orme & Brown, 1814), pp. 303–6. Colebrooke's essay was published in *Asiatick Researches*, 4 (1795), pp. 215–25.

32 Phebe Gibbes, *Hartly House, Calcutta* (1789), ed. Michael J. Franklin (New Delhi: Oxford University Press, 2007), pp. 100, 13, 86.

33 Sydney Owenson, *The Missionary* (1811), ed. Julia M. Wright (Peterborough, Ontario: Broadview Press, 2002), pp. 248–52.

34 Fanny Parkes, *Wanderings of a Pilgrim, in Search of the Picturesque: During Four-and-Twenty Years in the East, with Revelations of Life in the Zenana*, 2 vols. (London: Pelham Richardson, 1850), Vol. I, p. 162.

35 Parkes, *Wanderings of a Pilgrim*, Vol. II, p. 420.

36 Gayatri Spivak, "Can the Subaltern Speak?," in *Marxism and the Interpretation of Culture*, eds. C. Nelson and L. Grossberg (Champaign: University of Illinois Press, 1988), p. 296.

37 Emma Roberts, *Oriental Scenes, Sketches, and Tales* (London: Edward Bull, 1832), pp. 55–7.
38 Letitia Elizabeth Landon, "A Suttee," in *The Zenana and Minor Poems of L.E.L., with a Memoir by Emma Roberts* (London and Paris: Fisher, Son & Co., 1839), pp. 175–7.
39 Roberts, *Oriental Scenes*, pp. 575–9.

II

JULIE A. CARLSON

Social, familial, and literary networks

If we call to mind the two women who have become the most famous writers of the British Romantic era, we confront immediately the dangers of generalizing about the relation between strong networks and successful authorship in the case of women. Jane Austen (1775–1817) was not positioned within a vibrant literary network either within the household or outside of it, but her novels provide the most incisive treatment ever of the interplay between social and marital networks. Nor did Austen pursue marriage for herself even as her female protagonists seem to pursue nothing but. Mary Shelley (1797–1851) grew up in a household so bookish and networked that it took years of her writing before a female protagonist could breathe easily on her own, and her novels make peace with marriage and family life only after she is widowed and has watched three children out of four die. Critical warnings against extrapolating from a writer's biography to his or her fiction remain valid for women writers, even if the correlation used to work in the opposite direction, where their novels were valued primarily for the insights they provided into the lives and literary productions of the men around them. Several decades of recovery work allow us to view their writings as imaginative creations in their own right and thus to consider more disinterestedly what effect relationships had on women's creativity.

Foregrounding gender in discussions of literary networks also raises the question of how well current emphases on Romantic-era circles and sociability serve comprehension and appreciation of the less canonical women writers on whom criticism only recently has begun to focus. Critical editions and authoritative biographies of many of these writers are yet to be produced, leaving us with at best cursory knowledge of their creative efforts and efficacy. If the notion of the solitary genius has been largely debunked, and the Romantic-era "cult of genius" is construed now as emphasizing the socio-literary cultures that produced it, then where does woman's subordinate positioning in society as well as her alleged group-nurturing proclivities leave her aspirations within those writing spheres? Does focus on the networks of women writers accentuate what they first had to surmount in order to achieve their singular accomplishments? Does it intensify women's desires for imaginative transport?

Michelle Levy has made the case that family authorship "came into its own" in the Romantic period.[1] She explores how the quantitative rise in printed works by family authors produced qualitative changes in both conditions and notions of authorship – effecting a shift from isolated genius to congeniality, whose defining trait is no longer "inner vision" but "ability to identify with the feelings of others."[2] Less family-centered group theorists detail other spheres and sociable spaces out of which authors emerge (bookstores, reading clubs, lecture halls, public houses), also by way of challenging the putative isolation, inwardness, and maleness of genius. Widening the conjunction to include less exclusively print-based literary productions grants an even fuller view of the popularizing of genius and lateralizing of vision. Theater in the period accentuates family authorship (Sheridans, Colmans, Dibdins) and acting families (Kemble-Siddons, Kellys, Grimaldis), sometimes as overlapping categories (Dibdins), at the same time that both domains are altering the dynastic qualities of family. Reconsidering Levy's assessment from within both print and performance contexts accentuates the importance of familial networks to Romantic-era authorship but also complicates the alleged shift from genius to congeniality, especially as it pertains to female authors and performers. Given the longstanding association of femininity with nurturance and embodiment, interventions by women writers exert special pressure on the founding distinctions of familial and media cultures, especially public/private, mind/body, legitimate/illegitimate, inner/outer. This pressure affects these women's vision, both the concept and its objects, including the line separating visionary from experiential.

Text-bound families

Consider the most widely published women who emerged out of the best-known family writing networks of the period: Maria Edgeworth (1768–1849), Anna Letitia Aikin Barbauld (1743–1825), and Mary Wollstonecraft Shelley (1797–1851). What their girlhood households shared is a family life difficult to distinguish from a literary life, home lives difficult to distinguish from social networks, networks difficult to distinguish from oppositional parties, and politics difficult to distinguish from childrearing and children's book production. Important differences notwithstanding, even basic details regarding their domestic situations and turns toward authorship reveal the intricacy of these interconnections.

The third of Richard Edgeworth's twenty-two children by four wives, Maria Edgeworth devoted a lifetime to ensuring that rising generations have the wherewithal to rise. At Edgeworthstown, the paternal estate in Ireland, she home-schooled an impressive cadre of younger siblings and, by the age of fourteen, began collaborating with her father on various educational treatises. Largely grounded in the empirical methods of the Lunar Society, Edgeworth family theory and practice culminated in the coauthored *Practical Education* (1797), in which Maria Edgeworth took the lead, and lessons from which she then transported into fiction aiming to improve rational conditions for women and the Irish. Her most famous novel, *Belinda* (1801), portrays the Percival home science lab as instrumental in effecting the re-education of Belinda and her mentor Lady Delacour by modeling the application of reason to passion and caprice, a practice that later novels apply to solving the Irish question.

Interconnections go even deeper in the case of Mary Wollstonecraft Shelley, who depicts her own turn to writing as preordained by her parents and their textual assaults on marriage and family life. Moreover, her origins were enmeshed in various aborted projects aiming at familial reform. These include her author–mother Mary Wollstonecraft's reading primer "Lessons," written to inculcate daughters more effectively into language, left unfinished by her death from complications of childbirth, and her author–father William Godwin's loving tribute in *Memoirs of the Author of A Vindication of the Rights of Woman*, which would ruin Wollstonecraft's reputation for years. Shelley's new stepmother Mary Jane Clairmont brought into the household not only more illegitimate progeny but also the bright idea to transform the house into a Juvenile Library and bookstore serving all ages of reader. The idea had legs also because of the substantial personal literary radical connections of Godwin, who was at this point the chief node in London radical networks, and his conviction that the richest seedbed for political reform was the minds of the rising generation. The rest is history. Or, Mary Shelley's fateful romance – meaning the arrival both of Percy Shelley, her father's most ardent coworker in the redesign of extra/marital familial life; and of her novel *Frankenstein* (1818), the most haunting investigation to date of how such a new species looks.

Striking about Anna Aikin Barbauld's family authorship is the way that her life as a mother, not just a writer, was indebted to brother John Aikin, and how both roles identify her distinctiveness within networks of Dissent. Only a year into her marriage to Rochemont Barbauld, Anna Barbauld asked to adopt one of her brother's children and began composing her highly influential *Lessons for Children* (1778–9) for the arrival of two-year-old Charles. A subsequent coauthored book (with Aikin), *Evenings at Home*

(1793), subtitled "A Juvenile Budget" and composed of a miscellany of genres geared for "Young Persons" aged eight to twelve, speaks at once to Charles's progress and to his father and surrogate mother's Dissent-based conviction that a nation's progress depends on having homes suffused with topical debate on pressing national issues. This belief reached its summit in Barbauld's magisterial *Eighteen Hundred and Eleven* (1812), a stunning jeremiad against England's misguided war effort and its interconnections with British mental and fiscal decline. Interestingly, she authored this work alone, while speaking on behalf of a circle of male Dissenters disheartened by their inability to reshape national policy – suggesting that gender bias sometimes aids women who qualify as mothers of the nation to venture where overtly politicized men have demonstrable reason to fear to tread.

Similarities among how these three writers opened out conventional boundaries of family and of writing make visible other points of convergence that are applicable also to women writers less intricately situated. One concerns the "experimental ethos" that informs Edgeworth's fiction and helps better to explain what her style of fiction, generally perceived as "too didactic" and insufficiently literary, is after: observation of and experimentation on moral character.[3] This more clinical approach to fiction-writing has been overshadowed by a history of the novel that values the subtleties of Austen's novels and the grandiosities of Sir Walter Scott's. But lost through this narrative is the more direct commerce that Edgeworth's narratives posit between fiction and life experiences and what learning from fictional experience offers and accomplishes. Exactly this perception reveals a kinship between Edgeworth's "moral tales" and the "new philosophical" fiction of Thomas Holcroft, Godwin, Wollstonecraft, Mary Hays, and Robert Bage, a mode similarly devalued in dominant histories of the novel. New philosophical fiction's more frequent designation as "the Jacobin novel" suggests why Edgeworth might have left the kinship unclaimed. But similarities abound, especially their inclusion of fancy into the workings of philosophy and comprehension of fiction as producing a science of man.

Also lost in dismissal of this fiction as too didactic is how differently female new philosophers depicted the interplay between fictional and actual experience from their male counterparts. Both genders inserted biographical and autobiographical episodes into their fiction in an effort to display not only the close proximity between these two spheres of existence but also the necessity for both to be reformed, often by means of each other. But female new philosophers, as well as Maria Edgeworth, used their own experience of gender to document how literature as well as life hampered prospects for women, especially when they were trying

148

in both arenas to redesign their own desires and desirability. To a sizeable degree, this project declared gender warfare on Jean-Jacques Rousseau, with whose views on the efficacy of imaginative life otherwise they were half in love, owing to his intentional restrictions on female mental life and the havoc that they witnessed such pedagogical inequities to have wrought. Not only do their fictional works seek to correct these inequities by expanding women's cognitive and affective possibilities but also they analyze failures in other fictional and personal experimentations. Edgeworth's *Belinda* famously critiques Thomas Day's actual efforts to mold his female wards into ideal wives for himself as a way of exposing the perils for women of insufficient exposure to a diverse array of real and fictional life possibilities. Lucy Aikin characterized her aunt's marriage as "the illusion of a romantic fancy – not of a tender heart" that her father "ascribed ... to the baleful influence of 'Nouvelle Heloise,' Mr. B[arbauld] impersonating St. Preux."[4]

Wollstonecraft's and Hays's texts are even more complexly fictionally self-involved. In a word, *Mary: A Fiction*. Or a set of texts (Wollstonecraft's *A Short Residence* and Hays's *Memoirs of Emma Courtney*) composed out of actual love letters that failed to win over their addressee and so were redeployed for other purposes. This suggests another gender difference in the fictional use of lived experience. In his writings, Godwin ruined other people's lives or reputations, whereas Wollstonecraft and Hays risked ruining their own. Undaunted, they narrated personal difficulties as a way to exercise the minds of their daughters, rather than dictate to them cautionary tales meant to forestall experimentation.

These women's shared approach to fiction as life experimentation also set no discernible limits to what their mode of didacticism envisioned. One notes a surprising generic kinship between Barbauld and Shelley, whose most famous texts, *Eighteen Hundred and Eleven* and *Frankenstein*, are truly epic and visionary. The cataclysms set in motion in Shelley's *Frankenstein* that culminated in her later novel, *The Last Man* (1826), are anticipated in the tone and analysis of Barbauld's *Eighteen Hundred and Eleven*, equally angry over the unwillingness of dominant parties to read and heed the signs of their decline. Distinctive about Barbauld's vision is a lack of opposition between topical and visionary, her poem arguably providing the most detailed assessment in existence of Britain's fiscal and taxation policies as they affected the war effort in 1811–12. What this alliance also makes visible is why the political activity undertaken by middle-class women writers during this period was not as oppositional or as oscillatory as that of male radicals. By this I mean less that they were more timid or consistent, though sometimes this was the case, than that, owing to their being ensconced in the home, charges that domestic settings represented a retreat from active public or political life do not exactly apply. They generally launched their attacks from the home and practiced their best modes of attack in there.

Incorporating the visionary into the quotidian defines the method and aims of their children's book-writing activity and its attempts to reform ideas about children's minds as well as the ideas that should go into them. With their large type and wide margins, Barbauld's *Lessons for Children* are considered the first children's books to discern the needs of a child reader, where instruction is conveyed through chatty dialogues between mother and child as the two experience their surroundings and experiment on them together. Barbauld's staging of a developmental approach ("lessons for children of two to three years," "of three years") influenced writers like Edgeworth, Hannah More, and Jane and Ann Taylor, also concerned to better coordinate their pedagogical approaches to a young child's quotidian experience. This coordination often entailed disrupting the circular logic governing the proper instruction of girls, designed to produce the small-mindedness that was then decried as female nature and which writers like Wollstonecraft exposed as the fault line of patriarchy. The efforts by canonical male Romantics to discredit these women's approaches as both unimaginative and inimical to fantasy were largely successful. But these efforts misconstrued what the women writers' engagements with the mind sought to actualize: fantasy lives that do not undermine a girl's current or future prospects. That domesticity only domesticates is a bubble wondrously burst at the end of Barbauld's poem, "Washing Day," where children's soap bubbles harbinge Montgolfier's hot-air balloon, the latest technological innovation in transport. No attempted shaping of girls' minds so convolutes a separate spheres mentality as does Wollstonecraft's *Original Stories from Real Life*, where "mother" is replaced by female friend and mentor "Mrs. Mason" who, at the end of the story, re-presents herself in the form of a book.

Family play book

Family authorship as it relates to theater amplifies the importance of the networks and relationships on which the expression of women's creativity relies and that it reflects and often attempts to reform. It accentuates the performative as well as collaborative dimensions of authorship, makes the publicity accorded to female experimentation a greater source of opportunity and of threat, renders didacticism spectacular, and construes vision, whether individual or collective, as multi-mediated. The domains of theater and family disrupt each other but also often as a means of consolidating each. Theater takes middle-class women out of the house, expands lower- and middle-class women's possibilities for earning a living, and heightens the marketability of female attractions. At the same time, the happy endings and generic over-simplifications of drama favor family values and display melodrama as an emergent attraction of family life.

A useful way to highlight the complexity of these interactions is by recalling heated discussions over the legitimacy of theater in this period. Legitimate vs. illegitimate structured the London theatrical scene, meaning that only those theaters that held royal patents (Drury Lane, Covent Garden, and the summer Haymarket) were licensed to perform spoken drama, a monopoly that was officially overturned in 1843 but was gradually eroding throughout this era. Embedded in the legal opposition are media-based distinctions that attempt to demarcate poetry from dumbshow. These familiar debates, which pitted imagination against the senses in ways that echoed attacks on children's books written by women, have interesting under-explored consequences on the women and children increasingly deemed il/legitimate also for finding their voices and livelihood in theater. Especially as the abolition of the patent monopoly increased possibilities for less-legitimated acting families, this broadening of opportunity intensified the need for theatrical networks to train and protect the women and children who, owing to the popularity of pantomime and stage extravaganzas, audience taste increasingly demanded.

The life and career of Joanna Baillie (1762–1851) represent the fullest exemplification of the legitimacy of theater's appeals. A playwright of tragedy and comedy; singular in her genius and favorably compared to Shakespeare; highly respected by her male poetic peers: Baillie was as chaste and avowedly middle class in her personal life as in her exemplary female character profiles. Yet, her ambitious *Series of Plays on the Passions*, which devote a comedy and a tragedy apiece to analysis of the individual passions of love, hate, jealousy, fear, and remorse, not only seek to remove impediments to healthy human relationships but also portray strong passion itself as radically isolating, a view that Baillie's plays, dramaturgy, and attitude toward theater all work to convey and amend. As her Introductory Discourse affirms, the chief goal is to render invisible processes visible and comprehensible by detailing both the early warning signs of a developing passion and how viewers can learn to detect these signs before a passion has grown to such magnitude that the individual no longer can retreat from it. Achieving this goal requires careful dramaturgical staging of the physical and physiognomic signs of passion (the sudden starts, involuntary gestures and glances) that provide a reading of character that, importantly, is legible on the surface.

Asserting that human curiosity into character would be best satisfied if we could follow a condemned man into his closet to watch how he comports himself out of view of any audience, Baillie strove to bring this view to theater audiences rather than reserving it for closet reading. Thus her pedagogical aims required the sensational features of theater, so long as the physical properties of theater auditoria did not wholly obliterate the ability to see or hear what was being manifested on the surface as character. Moreover, Baillie recognized that delight in spectacle, in the sounds and sights of our surroundings, is a baby's earliest pleasure, one that precedes cognition and therefore prepares the way for it.

Baillie's receptivity to the cognitive *and* imaginative yield of theater's externalizing properties distinguished her attitude from fellow canonical male poet–playwrights who contended that their plays were never intended for the stage. She viewed the failure of most of her plays to be staged *as* a failure, one that motivated her to envision revised theater spaces but not to browbeat theater audiences about their poor taste or benighted sensibilities. Those tragedies that were staged, for example *De Monfort* (1800, Theatre Royal, Drury Lane) and *The Family Legend* (1810, Theatre Royal, Edinburgh), are remarkably sensitive to the bloodshed mandated by family loyalty.

Both insights, I wish to suggest, were influenced significantly by Baillie's closeness to brother Matthew Baillie who, in his professional life as physician, intensified her knowledge of the body's centrality to mental and affective functioning and, as brother–friend and domestic partner until his marriage in 1790, helped shape her vision of alternate family structures and satisfactions within them. Her dedication to the second series of *Plays on the Passions* (1802) acknowledges "the unwearied zeal and brotherly partiality which have supported me in the course of this work."[5] Theater's coordination of family and anatomy merits fuller investigation as constituent benefits of Romantic-era theater. Baillie was "uniquely well-positioned" to grasp the centrality of mind–body interactions by virtue of being part of the "'most famous medical family' of the age."[6]

But other women playwrights and performers might be similarly predisposed as, for example, Edgeworth's proximity to physician–playwright Thomas Beddoes through his physician father's marriage into the family. Baillie was less well positioned to be an authority on daily theater–family life, given her residence in Hampstead as a single and childless woman. However, some of her writings (*Orra*, "A Mother to Her Waking Infant") depict the perversity of a "legitimacy" over-reliant on blood children, views strengthened when the Barbauld family moved into the neighborhood and the two women became close friends. This meeting of minds deeply attuned to mind–body interactions literally made their futures more bearable, given the catastrophes that Barbauld faced as poet–seer and spouse of a seriously deranged husband.

Women on the stage have always had to walk very fine lines, as the sensational stage careers of Sarah Siddons (1755–1831) and Dorothea Jordan (1761–1816) differentially show. "Mrs. Siddons" compensated for captivating audiences by repeatedly making a spectacle out of maternal feeling, justifying her move from Bath to Drury Lane in 1782 by parading her children on stage as the three reasons behind it and then consolidating her reign through monumental scenes of maternal pathos. "Mrs. Jordan" flaunted her charms in her breeches roles and highly publicized twenty-year relationship with the Duke of Clarence, soon to become King William IV, with whom she had ten illegitimate children. Both careers underscore the importance of patronage to securing women's opportunities in theater and the complexities of negotiating their dependence on influential men in order to attain independence and fame. Given the connections between box-office success and sexual allure, having a patron was often vital to an actress's prospects, a dynamic evident in Elizabeth Inchbald's early career, when she married an older member of the company in order to better manage conflicting propositions. Historically relevant is how this largely superannuated social and literary relationship persisted in the arena of theater and was being both intensified and deindividuated as the legitimacy of patent theaters was overturned. That is, need for patronage was intensified by the correlation between deregulation and exploitation but also diffused into networks that substituted for individualized care, often because a parent, manager, or benefactor was the chief abuser.

These changes and challenges are particularly visible in the career of actress and theater proprietor Frances Maria (Fanny) Kelly (1790–1882). Born into a theater family and making her Drury Lane debut at age seven in the chorus of *Bluebeard* and at age ten in her first speaking role, playing the Duke of York to John Kemble's Richard III, Kelly's thirty-six years of success on the stage, largely though not exclusively in patent houses, was indebted to conventional forms of theater patronage, as her own *Dramatic Recollections* and Gilli Bush-Bailey's analysis of them attest. That the author of *Bluebeard* was her uncle, the famous composer and singer Michael Kelly, suggests that her start shared advantages with other progeny born to act by virtue of blood ties (her father also was a minor actor). But *Dramatic Recollections* credits stage parents with her illustrious start, rhapsodizing that "John Kemble – the great – the inimitable" was "the first to praise me" and to augur that "'some of these days you'll be an actress'" and recounting how she became one through remaining appropriately "awe-struck" and

"enchanted" by Siddons and Jordan.[7] Other influential men backed her acting as an adult, especially Samuel Arnold, the "only manager with whom she
seems to have had entirely cordial relations," the sixth Duke of Devonshire,
instrumental in financing and legitimizing various projects, and the set of
male writers, including John Hamilton Reynolds, John Poole, and Charles
Matthews, who appear to have coauthored, not simply co-signed, her recollections (Bush-Bailey, *Performing Herself*, pp. 47, 52–3).

The context and content of *Dramatic Recollections*, composed of character sketches and songs based on her theater experiences and first performed
in 1832, is where Kelly's avowedly old-school approaches to acting and
modes of theater patronage become inextricable from her new-school versions of both. Bush-Bailey stresses the truly pioneering nature of *Dramatic
Recollections* as being the "earliest complete work performed alone by a
woman," "probably the earliest piece of auto/biographical performance
material available to us," and "a very personal theatre history written and
performed when theatre histories were being established" (Bush-Bailey,
Performing Herself, p. 100). *Dramatic Recollections* is as feminist as it is
reactionary, reviewed in the *Athenaeum* as "one of the most extraordinary
efforts of female power we have ever witnessed" while making a sustained
attack on the debased state and audiences of contemporary theater – whose
sensationalism is critiqued, however, also for forcing into early retirement
women performers of a certain age (Bush-Bailey, *Performing Herself*, p. 58).
This solo performance, moreover, was timed to support parliamentary
inquiries in 1832 into the future of the drama as well as to advertise and
raise funds for her two-pronged effort to reform the stage by building her
own theater on her household premises at 73 Dean Street and establishing a
Royal Dramatic School in which to "raise a little troop of my own" who will
learn to act more appropriately (Bush-Bailey, *Performing Herself*, pp. 20–1).

Like Baillie in this respect, Kelly's efforts to foster proper dramatic passion required having more intimate theater settings and female direction of
"At Homes," instituted by Kelly's (half) brother-in-law, Charles Matthews.
Like Siddons, Kelly's propriety was connected to her remarkable success at keeping her own affairs private, especially regarding her adopted
daughter, Mary Ellen Gerbini, who Bush-Bailey surmises is her blood child
(Bush-Bailey, *Performing Herself*, pp. 42–3). In both arenas, Kelly intended
to safeguard legitimacy by transmitting what she had learned from experience to the rising generation and to "the Drama" itself, presenting herself
as "the first – rude – Mr Bell or Mr Lancaster of the Drama" (Bush-Bailey,
Performing Herself, p. 155). Her style of reform looked ahead through its
backward glances, recollecting those "Spirits of the drama – Nay, the like of
whom I shall never see again!" who perceived the actor's group identity as

essential and thus already bemoaning the individuating features of a celebrity culture that the delegitimizing of patent houses soon bring into harsher focus (Bush-Bailey, *Performing Herself*, p. 165).

Coda: adapters

My final reflection encompasses women writers whose literary lives were happily devoted to fostering a male family member's literary productions and afterlife. Despite periodic flare-ups of feminist skepticism, evidence suggests that writers like Dorothy Wordsworth, Sara Coleridge, and Sarah Hazlitt found their largely facilitating roles rewarding. In my view, no dutiful daughter exemplifies these pleasures and pressures better than Frances (Fanny) Holcroft (*c*. 1780–1844), third child born to Thomas Holcroft (first to his third wife, Diana) and his most important literary collaborator, especially after he felt deserted by the friends and audiences who sustained his theatrical and political activity and moved his family to the continent where they lived from 1799 to 1802. Fanny Holcroft's involvement is remarkable in scope and dedication, as her father's letters from Europe and various printed dedications affirm. The merger that he effected between print and theater cultures, evident in the short-lived but ambitious *Theatrical Recorder* (1805), was indebted to her talents at translation and adaptation. Indeed, capacity to adapt is often alleged to be Thomas Holcroft's chief character failing and Fanny Holcroft's primary accomplishment.

The validity of this allegation might be questioned for either writer, but it prompts re-evaluation of the pluses and minuses for women whose writing emerged out of tight familial contexts, especially family contexts whose textual politics involved challenging the priority of blood ties over friends. The best illustration of Fanny Holcroft caught in these cross-fires involves her abrupt firing as governess to Lady Mountcashel's daughters while they were living in Paris. Her dismissal was motivated by charges printed in *The Times* (February 1802) that Thomas Holcroft was a spy and was wholly intertwined with the tempestuous friendship between Godwin and her father. Godwin had facilitated Fanny Holcroft's employment in the Mountcashel household, owing to Wollstonecraft having once been the governess of the (then future) Lady Mountcashel and Godwin having published her children's books in his Juvenile Library. Fanny Holcroft seems entirely a victim in this scenario, also in the sense that, thus far, literary history has recounted the story for its share in fracturing the Godwin–Holcroft friendship, leaving her own reactions out of the picture. What we do know is that Fanny Holcroft adapted. She moved back permanently into her father's various households and shared in his financial difficulties and literary endeavors until his death in 1809. How she adapted is a different matter. One possibility lies in, and within, the two novels that she wrote and published after her father's death, *The Wife and the Lover, A Novel* (1813) and *Fortitude and Frailty* (1817). Both novels center on the difficulties that spirited daughters face in discerning where good advice resides when seeking to disentangle filial from erotic attachments.

Now that critical trends stress interdependence over autonomy, dependence, and co-dependence, we might find new ways to assess what such adaptability cost these Romantic-era daughter–writers. One avenue is to consider the tangible effects of mourning on literary memorialization, how posthumous editing often softens critique that was far more nuanced when both writing parties were living, especially if they were living together, and where the editorial role in part consists in publicizing the depth of one's love. The span of time between the date of death and of publication might prove important in evaluating by which scales of fidelity the re/collection is to be assessed. Waning of grief may help daughters resume psycho-textual explorations of their felt reactions to existing as a radical experiment in the eyes of their parent or other domestic partner. Fortitude or frailty? A related question is how loyalty to a dead author–parent hampers forming close friendships between literary daughters or even a sense of common cause between them. It is largely from Mary Shelley that we inherit the view that Thomas Holcroft's irascibility as father as well as friend caused the rupture with her father, Shelley being "certain that Holcroft carried further than Godwin a certain unmitigated severity."[8] Seriously? Does such loyalty influence Shelley's disregard of Fanny and admiring notice of Louisa as "a graceful and amiable creature" when she visits the Holcroft (now Kenney) family on her return from Italy through Paris in August 1823?[9]

There are several deep, lasting friendships between women writers in this period, like that between Baillie and Barbauld, Wollstonecraft and Eliza Fenwick, Hester Thrale and Frances Burney, Felicia Hemans and Maria Jane Jewsbury. To what degree these friendships flourished because the women writers emerged out of looser literary–familial networks is a question that Samuel Taylor Coleridge's long narrative poem, *Christabel* (1797–1800), is brilliant at posing. Assessing these relations can be a generative way to rethink the generational dynamics that structure Romantic-era literary and familial relations.

NOTES

1 Michelle Levy, *Family Authorship and Romantic Print Culture* (New York and London: Palgrave Macmillan, 2008), p. 3.
2 Levy, *Family Authorship*, p. 10.

3 James Chandler, "Edgeworth and the Lunar Enlightenment," *Eighteenth-Century Studies,* 45:1 (Fall 2011), p. 88.
4 Quoted in Anna Letitia LeBreton, *Memoir of Mrs. Barbauld, Including Letters and Notices of Her Family and Friends. By Her Great Niece* (London: George Bell and Sons, 1874), pp. 42–3.
5 Quoted in Frederick Burwick, "Joanna Baillie, Matthew Baillie, and the Pathology of the Passions," in *Joanna Baillie, Romantic Dramatist: Critical Essays,* ed. Thomas C. Crochunis (London: Routledge, 2004), pp. 48–69 (49).
6 Alan Richardson, "A Neural Theatre: Joanna Baillie's 'Plays on the Passions,'" in *Joanna Baillie, Romantic Dramatist,* pp. 130–45 (132).
7 Gilli Bush-Bailey, *Performing Herself: AutoBiography & Fanny Kelly's "Dramatic Recollections"* (Manchester University Press, 2011), pp. 133, 134, 141, 165. Subsequent references cited parenthetically in the text.
8 Charles Kegan Paul, *William Godwin: His Friends and Contemporaries,* 2 vols. (London: Henry S. King, 1876), Vol. I, pp. 25–6.
9 *The Letters of Mary Wollstonecraft Shelley,* 2 vols., ed. Frederick. L. Jones (Norman: University of Oklahoma Press, 1944), Vol. I, p. 373.

12

JACQUELINE M. LABBE

The economics of female authorship

Although we are well past arguing, with William Wordsworth, that women writers wrote "little, and that little unambitiously" (as he reflects of Charlotte Smith), we have not yet fully uncovered the economics of female authorship. Critics have sought to understand the ramifications of depicting the writing woman as a working woman, and have revealed earnings and the relationship between incomes and outcomes. But was writing a job worth doing? What did it cost women to write, and to write to others about their writing, in particular publishers and printers? In terms of economics, the basic supply/demand curve would seem to benefit the woman writing popular fiction. Her products attract a market, the market demands more, and she supplies it: mutual benefit. However, this scenario also relies on the supplier being able to control demand, either through a direct engagement with the market, manipulation of the market's desires (and desired timelines), or an ability to command her due worth in that market.

For the woman writing, in a period that found it challenging to accept female market autonomy, direct engagement existed mainly in the form of subscription publishing, which Smith was not alone in finding "humbling."[1] Subscription entailed hawking one's wares ahead of publication for a promised payment upon its appearance. Other forms of publication included selling the copyright outright, profit-sharing, and commission. Manipulating the market depended on the supplier being less in need than the demander. Commanding one's due worth was a function of a general agreement about worth: and in the Romantic period, a woman was understood to be inherently worth less than a man. Indeed, for many women writers, supplying demand was precisely what made the act of writing laborious, since writing was work even if the pay was inadequate. This is the nub of it: as demand increases due to the attractiveness, hence success, of what is supplied (readers want more), so that supply must be continually increased. In terms of writing, there is an unending pressure to supply more and more to meet the demand: the supplier can never actually cease the supply, while at the same time the consumer will only pay to a certain level since the supply is forthcoming.

A writer, therefore, who must write constantly in order to meet her needs is caught up in a struggle with supply-side economics. Whether writing is worth the time is less about what one's time is worth, and more about whether writing repays the effort. Indeed, while the *Oxford English Dictionary* does not recognize a meaning of subsistence as "bare minimum" before the 1830s, the connotation is certainly there in Charlotte Smith. For instance, Smith in the Preface to *Marchmont* (1796) says "to the pecuniary advantages I have derived from [writing] I owe my family's subsistence and my own."[2] It is true that male writers suffered under this model as well – one thinks of William Wordsworth's notorious succumbing to paid employment and the discomfort shown by critics and readers who suspected he had "sold out." But this in itself highlights the contrast: men had access to the labor market in ways women simply did not. They (men) could supplement their income from writing without compromising their social identity.

In this essay, I will explore a group of what we might see as the more viable of Romantic-period women writers and their interactions with their publishers, the immediate purchasers of their work and the group whose demand must be solicited. The tiered nature of the demand group for writers exacerbates the issue of economics: the publisher is simultaneously middleman and initial purchaser. For the female writer, her economic viability depends on this relationship. Mary Wollstonecraft, Mary Robinson, Jane Austen, and Felicia Hemans construct carefully balanced relationships that skirt a fully realized self-presentation as vendor, preferring to reside within the interstices of supplication and benediction. Charlotte Smith's epistolary record presents a different picture, however, and by drawing on letters to her publishers Thomas Cadell, Jr. and William Davies in the early 1790s, I will demonstrate that, in terms of viability, Smith exemplifies the economic entrapment of demand management.

The market, of course, was guarded in terms of its evaluation of female output. Paternalism, not to mention legal definitions of selfhood, situated women as inherently lesser and, if married, scarcely visible. The feminist scholarship of the past thirty years does not need rehearsing unless it is to emphasize that the ideology Mary Poovey described – that which "*enables* ideas and actions" and "*delimits* responses, not just in the sense of establishing boundaries but in terms of defining territories"[3] – affected both the women who wrote and read, and the men who bought and sold. Most readers would be unable to evaluate writing by women as anything other than *by women*: as a product kitemarked by gender.

And yet women who wrote saw the resulting text as their property, to be sold for a price. Letters to publishers bear this out: women present their work as valuable and as deserving a fair price (whether they get this is another matter). They create and maintain their proprietary interest in their work at least partly through the representation of writing as employment and as income generating. This not only associates them with the act of writing, but also with the product itself: a claiming of intellectual property through sheer presence.

The experience of many female writers when they place their work on the open market, however, suggests that work, ownership, and value are not terms with an automatic register of meaning. Mary Robinson, whose personal product – the persona Perdita – was a bestseller for decades, had little control over its dissemination, which was copied and counterfeited to the financial benefit of many market parasites. Even after her death, Samuel Taylor Coleridge (himself an admirer) lamented the lack of a responsible agent to safeguard her concerns: "that that Woman had but been married to a noble Being, what a noble Being she herself would have been. Latterly, she felt this with a poignant anguish. – Well! –."[4] Robinson had been overseeing her own affairs for more than two decades, but as her correspondence reveals, she was well aware of her lack of bargaining power – or rather, her lack of bargaining visibility. On October 4, 1794 she writes that her "mental labours have failed through the dishonest conduct of my publishers. My works have sold handsomely but the profit have been theirs."[5] Only three years later, she moved publishers from Hookham to Longman, where "she simply accepted the copyright money and let Longman take care of the rest" (Fergus and Farrar Thaddeus, p. 197). Robinson's correspondence record is patchy, but nonetheless revealing: although on October 4 she refers to sales, the very next day she packages her losses in different terms: her "vain expectation that fame would attend my labours, and my country be my pride ... I regret the many *fruitless* hours I have employed" (*Works*, p. 303, emphasis added). And while she "wish[es] to employ my pen for the advantage of my finances" (p. 310), her letters show that she is much more concerned with the market value of herself than of her works. Robinson seems resigned that the market would not be sufficient to allow actual advantage to accrue, however. What Coleridge had noted as her lack of a champion may also provide the explanation for why, as her daughter Maria Elizabeth commented to Cadell and Davies when she offered them her mother's posthumous works, "my Mother has not Experienced any great share [of fairness] from those of the Trade with whom she had any transactions!" (p. 331).

Mary Wollstonecraft's desire for autonomy ("I must be independant [sic] and earn my own subsistence, or be very uncomfortable") and her frequent references to her debts and her desire to pay them suggests that for her, independence was derived from competence: work and income were intimately related.[6] Her relationship with her publisher Joseph Johnson seems based on an understanding that he will indeed pay a market rate for services rendered, and that, moreover, the business relationship will allow her independence: Johnson "assures me that if I exert my talents in writing I may support myself in a comfortable way" (*Collected Letters*, p. 139). Only six months later she writes to George Blood of success "beyond my most sanguine hopes," of her "very advantageous contract," and that "I daily earn more money with less trouble," while reiterating a few months later to Johnson that "I must exert my understanding to procure an independence, and render myself useful" (pp. 139–40, 159). She is clearly of the opinion that her work is being valued at a sufficient price – and even occasionally that she is approaching subsistence. Her characterization of her relationship with Johnson, however, veers from manifestly unbusinesslike to formal and almost cold. To others, she writes that Johnson has "uncommon kindness," has "saved [her] from despair," has displayed "*tenderness and humanity*"; he is "*very* friendly" to her daughter; he deserves more from her; he is her "dear and worthy friend" (pp. 139, 154, 171, 212). To Johnson himself, Wollstonecraft calls him "*a man* before you were a bookseller," thanks him for his "humane and *delicate* assistance," and notes she is his "sincere friend" (pp. 148, 159). She takes some pride in interacting with him as a professional, adopting an imperative tone: "remember you are to settle *my account*, as I want to know how much I am in your debt"; "Send me the Speaker – and *Mary*, I want one – and I shall soon want some paper – you may as well send it at the same time"; "You forgot you were to make out my account"; "I really want a German grammar" (pp. 147, 157, 159, 159). But Johnson's function as a banker also costs her some anxiety: "how can I apply to J[ohnson] continually you will readily guess my vexation & reluctance," and she takes refuge in curt letters of instruction: "On demand pay to Mess^r Turnbull, Forbes and C^o Thirty pounds Sterling for the value which I have received here of M^r. Christie and place it to my account, provided you have not already paid a similar order of the same date as this one"; "Please pay to M^r. Christie, on order, twenty pounds for value received by me" (pp. 218, 222, 227).

Wollstonecraft's epistolary relationship with Johnson is telling. Unlike Robinson, she does not see him in terms of his trade, as her publisher; she addresses him familiarly, as a friend to whom she feels an obligation that does not burden her. Her descriptions of him may well be accurate as to the relationship, but it is not based on business transactions. It is personalized, to the point that she can write him reproachfully when he has apparently advised her to be less personally or emotionally invested in indebtedness: "I thought you *very* unkind, nay, very unfeeling, last night" (p. 172). Her tone suggests less the marketplace than the fireside: the transactions are intimate, familial. Wollstonecraft elevates her debts to debts of honor, writing to Johnson as if he is a loved part of the circle of honor. This does not sell books, but it sells a cozy picture of the supplier/demander and allows for a sense that ownership is trumped by friendship. Wollstonecraft sells her work to Johnson, and in some letters seems to revel in their business relationship ("As I am become a reviewer, I think it right, in the way of business, to consider the subject" [p. 157]), but she does not project a market-based, transactional atmosphere. For her, the proprietary, the responsibility of ownership, the business of buying and selling, is subsumed to an abstract representation of debt and income.

Robinson and Wollstonecraft seem to have communicated with publishers as buyers of their wares directly, but for many women writers income was contingent on having the right agent negotiate on their behalf. Jane Austen's father and brother acted as her broker and, as is well documented, consistently undervalued her work, asking for too little from publishers. Austen's correspondence with publishers carries a clear class varnish as well: letters are characterized by politeness, condescension, and good breeding, and distinctly lack the personal relationship-building that Wollstonecraft sought. Austen tends toward the passive. Her publisher "Egerton advises" a second edition of *Sense and Sensibility*; a second edition of *Mansfield Park* will be "determined" at – and by? – Egerton's; the "terms on which the Trade should be supplied with" *Emma* are left "entirely to [Murray's] Judgement."[7] When Austen attempts to be professional – that is, call her own terms or assert her own wishes – she retreats almost by return: "I feel happy in having a friend to save me from the ill effect of my own blunder"; "Whatever [the Prince Regent] may think of *my* share of the Work, *Yours* seems to have been quite right"; and, rather humiliatingly, "I *did* mention the P.R- in my note to Mr Murray, it brought me a fine compliment in return; whether it has done any other good I don't know" (*Letters*, pp. 318, 327, 313). Murray returns Austen's class-based interactive style with what seems to be his own gender-based one: ladies get compliments but not his full attention. Austen's professionalism, nascent at best if measured in market terms, itself fails to find a buyer, but then Austen, who "must keep to my own style & go on in my own Way," shows a distinct disinterest: demand holds little meaning, time is not money, and while higher offers for her product would be desirable, the publisher who starts low "is a Rogue of course, but a civil one" (pp. 326, 303). In other words, exchange as play trumps economics.

Austen approaches her publishers not as a professional but as a lady: that is, she expects respect and delivers not just a product but also politeness. Felicia Hemans also utilizes politeness, moderated by deference, but she is clear in her financial expectations, and demonstrates skill in playing publishers off of one another to get better terms. Hemans also approaches the market as demand-driven, requesting that her publisher John Murray "sugges[t] to me any subject, or style or writing, likely to be ... popular."[8] Hemans wants not only to be read, but to be popular, by which she means that her books are in demand: "I have now seen how little any work of mere sentiment or description is likely to obtain popularity" (*Felicia Hemans*, p. 481). Her model is Lord Byron, or at least Murray is to understand that she has noticed how much Byron receives for his popular works: "the sum you have given [for Byron's poems] really seems immense," she remarks in the same letter (p. 481). Hemans shows her awareness of the need to find an audience and to sell to it actively: in one letter she notes that her well-placed friends in Oxford and Cambridge would ensure sales, in another she notes "the present season of the year" as "being considered the most favourable for publication," in a third she rejects the idea of reissuing her juvenile works as "its accidental coincidence of title with the Volume just published ... would make it interfere very disadvantageously with the sale of the latter ... I should indeed think such a measure seriously detrimental to the interest of my late Works as well as their Publisher" (pp. 481, 489, 508). Another thanks William Jerdan for favorable publicity "which cannot fail to be serviceable to her publications" (p. 485). Hemans understands a market wherein goods are circulated and sold as long as they attract interest: she seems content to supply this market with what it demands. In return she expects, and asks for, appropriate remuneration for her efforts: "I should like to have the volume published by you," she informs Blackwood, "provided we can come to an agreement respecting the terms" (p. 495). And once their business relationship is established, she does not hesitate to bargain: "Mr. Colburn has lately raised the terms on which I sometimes wrote for him, to two guineas a page – if I should not hear from you to the contrary, I shall conclude that you will not be less liberal," to which her publisher Blackwood replies "Though 2 guineas a page is so much higher than what I pay to even my most gifted friend, I will not grudge it to you, as I look forward to bringing out another volume in which these can be inserted" (p. 515). In other words, their relationship is built on a business understanding: she asks for a raise based on her market value, he grants it (as he would not to a "friend") as long as he can count on a return once the poems are collected: another way of representing to Hemans that he has bought and now owns her work. She does not dispute this; her letters do not indicate a discomfort with selling (and therefore losing control over) her intellectual property. She seems to understand it *as* property and willingly trades it. Of the authors discussed so far, Hemans seems most at ease with her economic relationship to literary output. Whatever her personal assessment of her own talents, she does not carry this to the marketplace in any other than financial terms.

These snapshots have suggested a complex gendering of professional correspondence and the picture they paint of the text/author as commodity. A key question underlies their variety: who owns the work if it has been sold? In other words, despite all efforts to engage with a market where intellectual property is as valid as any other more tangible product; where the author is professionalized by her exchanges with buyers and her willingness to confront market forces; where evidence of work is also evidence of value; and where the demand exists and the supply is forthcoming – can the woman author become economically viable? Can she trade her work at market value: does it *have* a stable market value? Can there be pay equal to the work?

A Romantic-period author for whom the work of writing, selling, publishing, and owning is keenly pursued is Charlotte Smith. Her notion of her work encompasses the entire act of production, from conception through to income. For Smith, writing is work to the point of exhaustion, but it is also her mode of self-visualization for public consumption. Smith is consistent in writing about writing as a labor, a chore, a necessity, and even a trauma. She fully depicts her version of the writing woman in *The Banished Man* (1794).[9] In the "Avis au Lecteur" that opens Volume 2 she constructs the act of writing in economic terms: "seek[ing] wherewithal" to "raise another" venerable castle in her pages, "borrowing" plotlines, discussing "the business of novel writing" and remarking on "the necessity [that] has hitherto made me produce so much" (pp. 194, 193, 195, 196). Her character Mrs. Denzil is "employed in" her writing but also employed by booksellers/publishers for the money such work will "procure"; meanwhile, the same booksellers dun her for the work they have "purchased" and for which she has "had money thereon" (pp. 277, 275). For Mrs. Denzil, writing drains her imagination and is hard physical work. Her publisher sees her only as a producer of a commodity for which there has been a market transaction: but what is lacking is the mutuality that would mark a professional relationship. For this publisher, a writer is a generating machine. Economically, as Mrs. Denzil demonstrates, the work of writing does not pay: she must write in order to "procure from her bookseller part of the money she has been compelled to promise to [her creditors'] peremptory demands" (p. 275). She never receives a full return on her invested time and work.

Smith's private correspondence contains voluminous records of her interactions with her publishers, which show a consistent approach to the relationship that presents her work as 1) *her* work, 2) *work*, 3) to be valued
as such, 4) vendible because worthy of notice, 5) reflecting honor on the
vendor – in this case, the publisher. Diane Boyd suggests that Smith's "choice
of publishers (working with the Cadell dynasty, for instance) shows that in
an arena where the author is so often stripped of agency by submitting to
whatever terms of payment she could scramble for, Smith proves more of
a professional businesswoman than was previously thought."[10] Certainly,
Smith's correspondence with Thomas Cadell, Sr. intimates that he was more
or less in agreement with her own evaluation of her professional standing. As
does Wollstonecraft, Smith draws on her publisher regularly for advances,
assuring her creditor that she is "good for it" because of the vendibility of
her books: for instance, she writes that in asking for an advance, she was
making a "proposal that if it was likely to answer in point of profit, I would
give up more time to encrease the quantity of Poetry than it would otherwise
be in my power to do."[11] In drawing on her publisher for an unauthorized
sum she considered her poetry to be security, or a kind of complementary
currency: "I was fully persuaded that I would be able to deliver you the
MMS ... If you still continue your intention of purchasing it on the terms
you propos'd to Mr. Hayley."[12] Smith's tone veers from proud to humble,
but underlying her words is the conviction that her work makes her worth
the outlay. "I am infinitely oblig'd to you for the accommodation you have
afforded me" is balanced by reassurances that "The 2nd part is in such for-
wardness, (as I have hardly one hundred lines to write,) that I believe you
will have it in less than ten days – which I hope will be in very good time
for the season," which itself swiftly follows another transgression on professional goodwill: "I write to repeat my thanks for your kindness & to
apologize for the drafts of which I find you complain, & with reason – But
Alas Sir, they were drawn in the hope that I should deliver the Poem before
they are [?] become due."[13]

Smith occasionally refers to a male mediator (e.g. William Hayley) who
acts on her behalf with her publishers, but her main agent is herself, and the
very repetitiveness of her expectation that her publishers will act as bankers
shows her autonomy in relying on her professional standing as author to
increase her income. She is not stopped by the unwillingness of her correspondent to engage in business talk. A telling exchange around the publication of *The Emigrants* (1793) concerns Smith's desire to know when it will
be published and how much she will make from it. On May 19, 1793 she
requests an "answer [to] the question I troubled you with": how much? "Let
me beg that you will direct some person to give me by the Post of Tuesday

[sic], the information I desire."[14] The response, from William Davies, neatly ducks the issue:

Madam

Mr. Cadell being at present at Bristol (from where we expect him to return in about ten days) I am totally unable to state the Account of the Poem with accuracy sufficient to afford the Information you wish.

This seems to be written on the paper of Smith's own letter, by return. Smith persists and writes, on May 21, "I must quit this place in a very short time & I do not know what I shall do if I am not certain abt. the Sum."[15] This time a rendering arrives, again (it seems) written on Smith's letter, which reveals that after all Davies is able to "state the Account of the Poem," but not, apparently, with accuracy; in response to his figures, Smith writes:

I think you are in a little error in regard to the profit: perhaps you may not know that Mr. Cadell proposes to print 1500 copies; and at 3. [sic] (that I see the Poem is advertis'd for) amounts to two hundred & twenty five pounds. The expence of Printing two volumes 1000 copies the size of my Novels of 12 sheets each is only 72£. Of course, the expence this Poem cannot I should think exceed fifty pounds allowing for Advertisements even in the liberal way in which Mr. Cadell advertises – As soon as a correct statement of this matter can be had I shall be very much oblig'd to you for it.[16]

Presented with an account with which she disagrees, Smith puts this disagreement on the record and, far from relying on pathos or deference, requires a "correct" – not *corrected* – statement. The inference is that Smith well knows the market value of her work and what she is owed. There is no record of Davies' response, but the exchange highlights that for Smith, hard financial facts are her expectation. Davies' casual "errors" are not allowed to pass: Smith's business acumen is apparent, as is her ability to see her work in economic terms divorced from her common tactic of justifying her monetary demands via her personal difficulties. She will not be sold short. This contrasts with, for instance, Austen's remark that "P. & P. is sold. – Egerton gives £110 for it. – I would rather have had £150, but we could not both be pleased, & I am not at all surprised that he should not chuse to hazard so much" (*Letters*, p. 205).

Insisting that writing was work and one's *own* work, Smith's letters to her publishers never lose sight of the paradox that her own work was also someone else's and at their disposal. Her compatriots also faced the alchemy that turned their words into gold, although seldom for their enrichment. The idea of property, of something tangible that could be sold, bought, and sold again, fought with the idea that female identity was property-less, and that the products of women lacked market value. Women who wrote and who did so as their profession offered their intellectual property in an atmosphere of suspicion that women had neither intellect nor property. Supply-side economics could put the work of women in demand, but there was no corresponding sinecure. Instead, the female producer was expected to submit to the market.

Many female writers were heavily burdened by their debts and their lack of options to reduce them. For most women, writing, as a genteel occupation, paid at the rate that a leisure activity would attract. As the record shows, even Charlotte Smith, prolific and popular (until she was not – another market risk), could never achieve economic viability. In this way, her position as one of the most important writers of the period did not prevent her from being, in economic terms, also one of the least financially viable. Of the writers under discussion in this essay, even Mary Wollstonecraft could at times make herself easy through her earnings, while Robinson was laissez-faire about her debts, Austen was safeguarded from them, and Hemans perhaps the most successful. But Smith never reached the point of economic success. For her, the work of writing never resulted in anything more than subsistence, and her much quoted phrase "writing only to live, and living only to write" becomes, in its absolute veracity, the motto for the economics of Romantic-period female authorship.

NOTES

1 Charlotte Smith, *The Collected Letters of Charlotte Smith*, ed. Judith Stanton (Bloomington: Indiana University Press, 2003), p. 720. Subsequent references cited parenthetically in the text.

2 *Marchmont*, ed. Kate Davies and Harriet Guest, Vol. IX of *The Works of Charlotte Smith* (London: Pickering & Chatto, 2006), p. 3.

3 Mary Poovey, *The Proper Lady and the Woman Writer* (University of Chicago Press, 1984), p. xiv.

4 Quoted in Mary Robinson, *The Works of Mary Robinson*, Vol. VII, ed. Hester Davenport (London: Pickering & Chatto, 2010), p. 330. Subsequent references cited parenthetically in the text.

5 In Jan Fergus and Janice Farrar Thaddeus, "Women, Publishers, and Money, 1790–1820," *Studies in Eighteenth-Century Culture*, 17 (1987), pp. 191–207. Subsequent references cited parenthetically in the text.

6 Mary Wollstonecraft, *The Collected Letters of Mary Wollstonecraft*, ed. Janet Todd (London: Allan Lane, 2003), p. 71. Subsequent references cited parenthetically in the text.

7 Jane Austen, *Jane Austen's Letters*, ed. Deirdre Le Faye, 4th edn. (Oxford University Press, 2011), pp. 242, 299, 310. Subsequent references cited parenthetically in the text.

8 *Felicia Hemans: Selected Poems, Letters, Reception Materials*, ed. Susan J. Wolfson (Princeton University Press, 2000), p. 481. Subsequent references cited parenthetically in the text.

9 See *The Banished Man*, ed. M. O. Grenby, Vol. VII of *The Works of Charlotte Smith* (London: Pickering & Chatto, 2006).

10 Diane Boyd, "'Professing Drudge': Charlotte Smith's Negotiation of the Mother–Writer Author Function," *South Atlantic Review* 66:1 (2001), p. 152.

11 Charlotte Smith to Thomas Cadell, Jr., April 6, 1792, p. 195. Letters are reproduced by the kind permission of Keeper of the Royal Pavilion, Brighton, reference BH/P/L/AE/1–99. Letters are held at the Keep (www.thekeep.info) by East Sussex Record Office on behalf of Brighton & Hove City. Numbers indicate handwritten page numbers on individual sheets.

12 Charlotte Smith to [Thomas Cadell?], October 3, 1792, pp. 201–2, East Sussex Record Office.

13 Charlotte Smith to [Thomas Cadell?], April 14, 1793, p. 206; April 18, 1793, p. 210; April 18, 1793, p. 209, East Sussex Record Office.

14 Charlotte Smith to Thomas Cadell, Jr., May 19, 1793, pp. 213–14, East Sussex Record Office.

15 Charlotte Smith to William Davies, May 19, 1793, p. 215, East Sussex Record Office.

16 Charlotte Smith to William Davies, May 26, 1793, pp. 217–18, East Sussex Record Office.

13

DEVONEY LOOSER

Age and aging

On January 7, 1845, Elizabeth Barrett Browning (1806–61) wrote a long, impassioned letter to the journalist and critic Henry Fothergill Chorley (1808–72), discussing the history of British women poets. Barrett Browning complained, "England has had many learned women... and yet where were the poetesses? ... I look everywhere for Grandmothers and see none. It is not in the filial spirit I am deficient, I do assure you – witness my reverent love of the grandfathers!"[1] In this and her other letters, Barrett Browning acknowledges that Letitia Elizabeth Landon (1802–38), Felicia Hemans (1793–1835), and especially Joanna Baillie (1772–1861) were gifted versifiers. But Barrett Browning will not grant that they rise to the level of her divine category of "poet," nor are they perhaps actually old enough to be her grandmother. Barrett Browning claims to have wanted exemplary, older women writers to love and revere. The problem is that she cannot see them.

Barrett Browning's invoking the phrase "grandmothers" as she tries to imagine the history of British women's poetry is significant. It is clear that she was not actually looking for *old* women writers of the past or present but merely seeking poets who had preceded her. This was done regardless of whether they were still alive and with an apparent lack of interest in the age to which they lived. Nevertheless, her use of the term "grandmothers" – in addition to demonstrating that mainstream literary histories had not successfully handed down the names of many talented and renowned poets – suggests that she envisioned accomplished older writers ("literary grandfathers" one could "revere") as males. Barrett Browning's complaint points to something that was, in the Romantic period, a larger cultural problem. Elderly female writers of the time risked becoming invisible in late life, even when they continued to write or publish. Barrett Browning at least claimed to be fruitlessly looking "everywhere" for literary grandmothers. Today, when we ignore Romantic-era women writers in late life, we do not have the same excuse. Most of us continue to do so without a backward glance. In this essay, I demonstrate that we have much to gain by exploring how women's writings take on new meanings when seen through the lens of age and aging. In order to construct more nuanced histories of British literature in the Romantic period, we must attend to women writers' efforts across the life course.

Paying attention to age and aging means considering female authorship from cradle to grave. Although it is true that some Romantic-era women's writings penned or published in young adulthood or middle age have attracted significant critical attention, rarely have they been studied in a framework that deliberately scrutinizes age. We must examine how lives in the past were imagined, assessed, and valued from youth to old age, in order to learn how such patterns may have had an impact on an individual author's career. We ought to investigate how age intersects with other identity categories that have come to the fore, including gender, class, race, sexuality, and nationality. Using the emerging insights of feminist age studies, we can begin to see how received notions of age and aging in the late eighteenth and early nineteenth centuries affected the first generations of professional women writers in Great Britain.

To begin, it is important to correct the mistaken idea that, prior to the twentieth century, few people lived long lives because life expectancy was so low. Thanks to the ongoing work of population historians, we know that when we factor out deaths in infancy and childhood, eighteenth- or nineteenth-century British men and women stood a fair chance of living to what was then considered old age. When marked by a number, old age was understood to begin around age sixty. Of course, understandings about what parts made up the life course have changed over time. A once-popular way to represent a life was in "ages and stages," rendered visually in illustrations and paintings. These images represented lives as consisting of as few as three to as many as twelve separate stages, drawing on biblical sources and classical authors, who frequently defined life stages as consisting of periods of seven or nine years. William Shakespeare popularized the idea of seven distinct ages of man in Jacques's "All the world's a stage" speech in *As You Like It*. In the medieval period, ages and stages were frequently represented in a "wheel of life." This format emphasizes what Philippe Ariès calls the "cyclical, sometimes amusing and sometimes sad continuity of the ages of life."[2]

Wheel of life representations never completely dropped out of the iconography of the life course, but a new kind of depiction became popular starting in the sixteenth century: the "steps of life" or the "steps of the ages" (*Centuries*, p. 24). Imagining life as a ladder of ascent and descent, depictions of the "steps of life" would have been well known across Europe and the Americas throughout the eighteenth and nineteenth centuries, when hundreds of these images circulated. Typical were those that showed both men and women traveling up and down through the steps in tandem, featuring nine or ten stages. Instead of using periods of seven or nine years, they increasingly began to depict stages of ten years each. Such illustrations might have been "pinned to the wall next to the calendar and in the midst of everyday objects," writes Ariès, and "fostered the idea of a life cut into clearly defined sections corresponding to certain modes of activity, physical types, social functions, and styles of dress" (p. 25). There were also many "steps of life" illustrations that depicted women alone or men alone, particularly from the early to mid nineteenth century forward. An American Currier and Ives print, "The Life and Age of Woman" (1850), derivative of many of its predecessors, became immensely popular. The woman it depicts is shown as an infant, followed by figures labeled with the ages 5, 15, 20, 30, 50, 60, 70, 80, 90, and 100. Its many distinctions among the stages of old age are intriguing and surprising.

A much earlier entrant into the field is Johann Comenius's, from his book *Orbis Sensualium Pictus*, a seventeenth-century work for Latin students, in Dutch and Latin. Translated into English in the early eighteenth century as *Visible World* (1705), it was reprinted dozens of times across the eighteenth and nineteenth centuries, providing a documentable British circulation. Comenius's work included fascinating copper cuts that indicate men and women were understood to experience stages of life differently (Figure 5).[3]

Comenius's males have seven stages – labeled infant, boy, youth, young man, man, elderly man, and decrepid old man. His female's six stages (which seem to skip infancy) are described as girl, damsel, maid, woman, elderly woman, and decrepit old woman. Notably, the female is given visual centrality in the image at the moment that she marries, as a "maid," when her position on the stairs shifts from the left to the right side, something it does once again in old age. Those who have studied such images note that from century to century, nation to nation, small changes in representations and descriptions occur – changes that deserve to be investigated further. For the purpose of this essay, these images offer tangible evidence that a strong sense of the life course had evolved in the West by the Romantic period, both as parsed out in distinct periods and as sex differentiated. They are understandings that must have had an impact on many women writers and their many readers.

The life stage we have paid the most considered attention to thus far in British women's literary history is childhood. There is now a substantial body of work considering writing *for* children, often relegated to its own separate category: children's literature. Although we expect women's literature to consist of writings by women, the term children's literature does not necessarily mean literature by children but instead indicates literature for children. This is an odd critical situation, and it speaks to the fact that child

XXXIX.
The Seven Ages of Man.

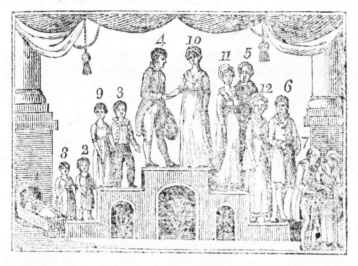

Septem Ætates Hominis.

A Man is first an Infant, 1. | *Homo* est primum *Infans,* 1.

Fig. 5 "XXXIX: The Seven Ages of Man," *Joh. Amos Comenii Orbis sensualium pictus* (New York, 1810), p. 61.
Reprinted by permission of Library Special Collections, Charles E. Young Research Library, UCLA

writers remain relatively understudied. We do employ a separate label for writing by the young: juvenilia. To date, however, most studies of eighteenth- and nineteenth-century juvenilia have focused on the *individual* child writer, looking into her unpublished writings for signs of her future greatness. No figures have loomed larger in this body of work than Jane Austen or Charlotte Brontë.

Critical, biographical, and creative works considering the childhoods of British female authors who went on to acclaim as adults have been part of our critical tradition. Two such books were published decades ago on Frances Burney, a study titled *The Young Fanny Burney* and a novel called *Young Miss Burney*.[4] More recently, the work of the Juvenilia Press has brought the study of the child writer forward enormously, by republishing newly edited writings and attending to child authors such as Lady Mary Wortley Montagu and Iris Vaughn, as well as Austen and the Brontës. Adding to the problem of learning about child writers as a group, however, is our pinning down what eighteenth- and nineteenth-century audiences considered "juvenilia," "child," "adolescent," or "youth" to mean.

Early nineteenth-century sources seem to define juvenile productions as writings undertaken well into one's twenties. Anna Seward (1747–1809), who in late life prepared her poems for a planned posthumous publication, marked with a "j" anything she wrote between the ages of seventeen and twenty-three.[5] This would seem a more capacious understanding than our own of what constitutes juvenile writing. But if we use a narrower, modern-day (and anachronistic boundary) for the transition from youth to adult, age eighteen, even that body of age-identified writings has rarely been looked at for potential age-based features. Until recently, it was believed that children's writing began in the 1850s, alongside what was thought to be the developing Victorian consciousness of childhood as a particular stage. We know now that this is far too late a date to begin a history of the child writer. Emerging scholarship indicates that the Romantic period was an important and formative moment in the emergence and popularity of – although not the origin of – the publishing of juvenile writings.

One place to begin in documenting that emergence is *Cambridge Orlando: Women's Writing in the British Isles*, a by-subscription, searchable electronic database of 1,300 writers. It tags eighty-seven of its entries with the keyword "juvenilia."[6] The first woman writer highlighted there as having written extensive juvenilia is the seventeenth-century author Margaret Cavendish, Duchess of Newcastle. Cavendish reports that she wrote sixteen early volumes of work and compares them to "Baby-books," written in her "Baby-years."[7] She describes these books as remnants, bits and ends, not fit for use, as a "mingling together" of "sense and no sense," "knowledge and ignorance" and unknown and un-legible letters (*Sociable Letters*, pp. 267–8). *Cambridge Orlando* then documents a flood of mid to late eighteenth-century writing by girls who later went on to literary acclaim, although most of their childhood writings remained unpublished in their lifetimes. One, Ann Taylor, published a verse solution to a riddle under the name "Juvenilia" in 1798 in her sixteenth year and won a prize.[8] In this era, cultural interest in child prodigies also seems to have grown, evidenced by works including the anthology *Early Blossoms of Genius and Virtue* (1797) and a biographical work, *The Blossoms of Early Genius and Virtue* (1800).[9] These books notably predate the famous poetic conceptions of the child by William Wordsworth and others. In the late eighteenth and early nineteenth centuries, a growing number of child writers saw their works reach print.

Marketing oneself as a young writer, even without signing one's name, was also becoming more common. There were many anonymously authored works from this period described as written by "A Young Author," or merely "A Youth." There was an explosion of late eighteenth-century publications that dubbed themselves, perhaps following the work of early eighteenth-century author Alexander Pope, "juvenile poems." Many anonymous late eighteenth-century works were published as by a "young lady." Rarely have we investigated what the term "youth" or "young" signifies or why it came to prominence. One such novel, *The Sorrows of Matilda* (1798), includes the term "juvenile" on its title page and in its dedication, mentioning the author's "infant pen."[10] Writers began more often to advertise their youth as a marketing tool, as in *The Rock, or Alfred and Anna* (1798), brought out by the same publisher as *The Sorrows of Matilda*, which indicates authorship "By A Young Lady. Her First Literary Attempt!"[11] This kind of self-fashioning makes a two-pronged attack on the reader, encouraging lenience due to immaturity and sex and trying impress with double precocity. It is impossible to know whether these claims of youth (or gender) were accurate or fictional.

My initial research suggests that even girls who were verifiably child authors may regularly have exaggerated their youthfulness for purposes of publication. As a teenager, Anna Maria Porter published two different works of fiction, both titled *Artless Tales* – one in 1793 and one in 1796. In the preface to the 1793 edition, she claims that the work was written when she was thirteen, but she doesn't indicate how that age coincides with the date of her book's publication.[12] In her 1796 volume, her prefatory material is dated December 1794, and she claims there that she has "just completed" her "sixteenth year."[13] Does this mean she is sixteen or seventeen years old, and how old was she when the work was published? There has long been confusion in the historical record as to whether Anna Maria Porter was born in 1778 or in 1780, a muddle that she herself seems to have done much to establish – and little to rectify – later on in her life. Similarly, Elizabeth Benger was imprecise about her age when she published her *Female Geniad* (1791), a long poem to female genius, under her own name. The title page describes the work as by "Elizabeth Ogilvy Benger of Portsmouth; Written at the Age of Thirteen." Benger was baptized in 1775, making her at least fifteen years old when this work was published and perhaps older. Her poem is advertised as "by the pen of a young author" who is "yet in a state of childhood."[14] In the prefatory material, she apologizes for her "youth and ignorance" and "immaturity" (n.p.). Attempts to highlight – we might even say distort – youthfulness seem to be at work in both Porter's and Benger's first publications.

Some chose to publish their juvenilia in adulthood. Jane West published *Miscellaneous Poetry* (1786) in her late twenties as "Mrs. West," but indicates the verses were "written at an early period of life."[15] It is difficult to estimate just how many child writers there were. Early estimates suggest there were between fifty and one hundred, but that dataset is primarily made up of child writers who became (or remained) famous as adults. A few wrote only as children and became briefly famous for it. Of that group, fewer still first became known posthumously.

One of those rare girls was Marjory Fleming (1803–11), whose three manuscript journals were written from age six to her death, just before her ninth birthday. Fleming was dubbed "Pet Marjorie" by the Victorian critic who brought her and her writings to public attention, fifty years after she died. The story of her friendship with Sir Walter Scott appears to have been fabricated by her first editor, although Fleming and Scott were distant relatives. Fleming came to be celebrated by literary lions including Mark Twain and Robert Louis Stevenson. She also became the youngest subject in the *Dictionary of National Biography*, which misidentified her as Margaret, not Marjory, although noting, "No more fascinating infantile author has ever appeared."[16] Fleming deserves to be understood as a child writer who was but one – albeit, for a time, the most visible one – among many.

Even when we have studied child writers, our scholarly focus has not necessarily been trained on the angle of the *child*. Little of the growing body of work on Phillis Wheatley or Felicia Hemans considers them in the framework of the child writer or alongside the juvenilia of their contemporaries. Felicia Dorothea Browne, later Hemans, published her first book of poems in her late teens. In her Advertisement, she claims that she reveals her age not to seek leniency but because her youth may attract to the poems the "additional interest" to which they are "truly intitled." Her *Poems* enjoyed robust sales by subscription, marketed as the production of "a young lady, written between the age of eight and thirteen years."[17] Her poems are arranged chronologically, marking the early ages at which they were composed. Hemans and other child writers arguably made possible the early careers of Elizabeth Barrett Browning, Christina Rossetti (1830–94), and Vernon Lee (1856–1935).

We refer to what comes after an author's juvenilia or early writings as mature writings, making little further differentiation. This is a lost opportunity, as a concept similar to our own of a middle-aged person dates back at least to the early modern era. One seventeenth-century source, cited by the *Oxford English Dictionary*, describes a middle-aged man as "about forty years old" ("middle-aged," *OED*, 1a.). We understand little about the historical contours of middle age, particularly about how gender made a difference in its perceived chronology or onset. Few have sought to identify whether common self-fashioning features, thematic concerns, or shared

patterns of reception coincided with the popularly conceived duties or supposed characteristics of women at that time of life. There is very little scholarship investigating age-based differentiations in authors' texts in this life
stage. There is, however, much commentary. One early nineteenth-century
source suggests that middle age was a time of fulfilling duty but of mental stagnation, concluding, "they that were wise at thirty-three are very
little wiser at forty-five."[18] We often imagine the Romantic era as defined
by youthful genius, but this notion leads us to ignore or dismiss writings
produced in middle and late life, as we have long seen in the study of
early-achieving and long-lived canonical male authors, such as William
Wordsworth (1770–1850). Using the insights of age studies, we may discover shared patterns of reception (that is, commonalities in response from
readers and critics) and possibly shared features of writing that hinged on
distinctions of sex and age.

Some then believed that a writer's age led to writing about certain topics, an idea inherited from classical authors. In a fictional letter, writer John
Stedman suggests that a poet's choice of subject in verse is determined by his
age. A youthful poet considered love. Those in a middle period had an intimacy with nature and a propensity for refined language in verse, and those in
old age choose religious subjects for their poetry.[19] Stedman is describing a
masculine tradition, but Romantic-era women poets may have understood
themselves as following with or as reacting against such stereotypes. Did
readers and critics, too, judge poets according to these expectations? We
have not yet systematically considered it. But just as readers expected certain topics and themes to be more appropriately taken up by male versus
female authors, some authors expected certain subjects to be more suited to
youth, middle or old age.

How often – and for what reasons – did Romantic-era authors directly
address readers by age? Initial research suggests it was common to separate
the middle aged from the old, who were imagined to have different responses
to texts. Both George Jerment's *Religion: A Monitor to the Middle-Aged,
and The Glory of Old Men* (1796) and John Townsend's *Three Sermons,
Addressed to Old, Middle-Aged, and Young People* (1797) conceived of
their readers in age-based categories.[20] Thomas Gisborne's *Enquiry into the
Duties of the Female Sex* (1797) devotes one chapter to women in "the middle period." That chapter focuses on the duties of wives and mothers, but it
also includes a section for middle-period "unmarried ladies," encouraging
them to accept that when "youth and beauty wear away," the "homage"
they have received will be "gradually withdrawn."[21] Such women are repeatedly admonished not to disgrace themselves and disgust others by seeking

honors, laying traps for compliments, vying with younger women for attention, or showing envy of youth (*Enquiry*, p. 399).

Recent criticism has identified the Victorian period as the time in which the concept of midlife was invented, but stories warning British women of the dangers of not recognizing a middle-age decline in sexual attractiveness appear much earlier. Rather than being labeled "midlife," however, the stage is called "the middle period," a phrase with great currency in late eighteenth-century medical and literary texts. Romantic-era women's writings describe not only the difficulties but also the advantages of this life stage. Jane Austen, for one, wrote privately of the pleasures of the middle period in a letter from 1813: "By the bye, as I must leave off being young, I find many Douceurs in being a sort of Chaperon, for I am put on the Sofa near the Fire & can drink as much wine as I like."[22] The ideals and the realities for women and women writers across the middle period suggest a rich and varied set of concerns, many focused on waning beauty, expected duties, and proper pleasures.

The end of middle age is also difficult to define in this period. Even so, a numerical concept well known in the late eighteenth and into the nineteenth century offers us ways to understand that threshold. We have seen that periods of seven and nine years were then imagined as meaningful transitions or life stages. Seven times nine – one's sixty-third year – was viewed as a highly significant moment of life, known as the great or "grand climacteric." Eighteenth-century men and women were thought to experience the grand climacteric, the moment at which a person was said to either change or die. If you managed to pass age sixty, it was believed, you would make it into extreme old age. As one early nineteenth-century medical dictionary put it, "so general" is the belief in the importance of the grand climacteric that "the passing of 60 generally gives much anxiety to most people."[23] If you lived beyond the dangerous age of sixty-three, your life span could "be protracted to 90" (*Lexicon*, p. 283). The phrase "grand climacteric" remained in use throughout the nineteenth century, although employed in increasingly medicalized ways, rather than as superstitious numerology.

Despite the numerical specificity of the grand climacteric, old age could be a slippery category. Most sources suggest that it was imagined in stages, including "green" old age and "feeble" old age. Being deemed old had more to do with physical condition than a precise number. For women, old age often had an earlier onset than age sixty, as reproductive capacity was factored in. A woman's old age could be imagined as starting ten or even twenty years before a man's. For both, old age was seen as a time that could be rewarding and happy. But old age was also envisioned as a time of pitfalls and problems. Old men were believed to be inclined to avarice. Old women were said to be prone to vanity and garrulity, querulousness and peevishness, attraction to frivolity, and an excess of affection. Did these stereotypes have an effect on a woman writer's ability to continue active authorship or to reach a public audience?

I compiled information about age and publishing for a small cohort of the first generations of professional British women writers, looking at the publishing careers in aggregate of twenty-four authors, including those born before 1770, who lived to at least seventy years old and to the turn of the century. From this data, some fascinating trends emerged. The two dozen well-known female authors were publishing as a group most prolifically in their fifties. They experienced a slightly less productive period of publication in their thirties. But in their eighties, as a group, these long-lived women were publishing at a rate similar to what they had done in their twenties. This is a surprising result, suggesting far more publication in old age, or perhaps far less in youth, than we might have expected to find. Mine was admittedly a small sample, and it focused only on known book-length publications, which may or may not be equivalent to productivity as a writer, but it offers emerging patterns to mull over. As attention to age and aging in women's writings continues, we will no doubt accumulate further data that allows us to reach new insights about authorship across the life course in the Romantic period.

We must also continue to scrutinize writings and careers at the level of the individual. We need look no further than the once-famous but today little-studied or read Jane West (1758–1852) to understand the kinds of challenges that Romantic women writers faced in late life. West struggled with whether to seek – and how to attract – a readership in late life. In youth and middle age, she established herself as a prolific author of novels, poems, and non-fiction prose works called conduct books, which were a kind of precursor to today's self-help literature. West's last novel, *Ringrove* (1827), appeared in her sixty-ninth year, after a dozen-year hiatus from publishing. West gave her book the subtitle "Old-Fashioned Notions," almost as if in anticipation of her readers' hesitancy about embracing a new work of fiction from her. Her preface reminds young readers of her literary credentials. She informs them that she was once popular with the young. She calls herself "An old, and it may without presumption be said, a favoured Mentor of youth."[24] Referring to herself in the third person, she claims that "after ten years' silence, [she] steals from her recess to say, that she has, during her retirement, endured affliction, and experienced its benefits" (p. 1). She emphasizes that she has been admirably performing old age, not becoming querulous, then considered a stereotypical character flaw of the aged. West also indicates a continued willingness to continue to appear before the public in the guise of her novel's narrator, whom she calls "the Old Woman":

> If favourably received, "the Old Woman" may make another visit to the press; but if she be judged to have turned "driveller," and the marks of fatuity be found upon her, the public will commend the decent resolution of preventing her from continuing to be "a show." Yet before she dismisses this, possibly her last appeal to the literary world, she begs to say, that she does not aspire to the distinction of being a fashionable novelist.
>
> (p. 2)

West, while encouraging readers to see the "Old Woman" as an exemplary fount of wisdom, expresses worry that the negative stereotypes associated with the aged will be ascribed to her narrator (and perhaps to the author herself). These stereotypes included garrulousness (turning "driveller"), being trifling ("fatuity"), or engaging in youthful amusements ("show"). West's attempts to stave off negative assessments by naming and then distancing herself from the supposed faults of old age, including being out of fashion, invokes what I have called elsewhere the "infirmity of age" topos. This was a formulaic apology – which may or may not have been seriously meant – found in many old women writers' books in the Romantic period. West is perceptive in recognizing that reviewers of the time scrutinized the works of elderly women writers for a falling off of powers.

She tries to forestall that kind of criticism by acknowledging that her literary skills have deteriorated, thus attempting to set her reader's expectations very low. There is no need to seek a falling off of powers, West suggests, because she freely admits them. Few of her aged female contemporaries risked such claims in their prefatory apologies. Many asked for kinder treatment based on old age, but few claimed that their work had actually worsened. Unfortunately, West's preemptive self-criticisms did not produce the result she apparently sought: the public's kind embracing of her "old-fashioned" book. *Ringrove* was neither much noticed nor oft-purchased. When it wasn't "favorably received," West was true to her word. She didn't publish another work narrated by "the Old Woman," nor did she again publish anything under her own name, though she would live for another twenty-five years.

West's *Ringrove* episode ought to be especially interesting to us because, two decades earlier, her own published statements suggest that she ought not have undertaken publication in old age at all. In West's conduct book, *Letters to a Young Lady* (1806), published when she was nearing fifty, she writes that writers in old age "seldom fail to diminish their reputation."[25] She recommends "the timely destruction of all manuscripts which unclouded judgment determines to be unworthy of publication" and the cessation of writing in old age. The only writing that West recommends undertaking in old age involves correcting the errors of works published in youth, in order to prepare for the next world (III: p. 393). In publishing *Ringrove*, then, West deviated from her own earlier advice, changing her stance on the advisability of writing in old age. She did not give up writing for the public or relinquish the possibility of attracting new audiences in old age. It is unfortunate that her seeming change of position was not better rewarded by critics or the reading public.

Some of West's contemporaries were more sanguine about the possibility that old women and older women writers could be heard and appreciated by the public. As author Anne MacVicar Grant (1755–1838) wrote in a private letter in 1822, "I think we – old women I mean – begin to be more appreciated since the spread of knowledge has made us all a *thinking* people … we grow old without growing mouldly, and the young mingle our knowledge with their own acquirements."[26] Which response, West's or Grant's, was the more typical – or the more accurate – about how old women and their writings were coming to be valued, remains difficult to judge. Perhaps both of them got at some truths of their era. As the first generations of professional women writers in Great Britain reached old age, many remained in the public eye. The reading public could, for the first time, grow accustomed to perusing many new works by old women. As we have seen, however, readers did not always greet these writers or their works with enthusiasm. Fortunately, such skepticism – and, occasionally, hostility – from readers and critics did not prevent Romantic women from writing works of significance, importance, and excellence across the life course.

NOTES

1 Letter from Elizabeth Barrett Browning to Henry Fothergill Chorley, January 7, 1845, in *The Browning Letters*, Waco, TX: Armstrong Browning Library, Baylor University. http://digitalcollections.baylor.edu/cdm/ref/collection/ab-letters/id/8863.

2 Philippe Ariès, *Centuries of Childhood: A Social History of Family Life*, trans. Robert Baldick (New York: Knopf, 1962), p. 23. Subsequent references cited parenthetically in the text.

3 Johann Amos Comenius, *Joh. Amos Comenius's Visible World, or, A Nomenclature, and Pictures, of all the Chief Things that are in the World, and of Men's Employments Therein*, 11th edn. (London: Aaron Ward, 1729).

4 Winifred Gérin, *The Young Fanny Burney* (London: T. Nelson, 1961); Anna Bird Stewart, *Young Miss Burney* (New York: Lippincott, 1947).

5 Anna Seward, *The Poetical Works of Anna Seward; with Extracts from Her Literary Correspondence*, ed. Walter Scott, 3 vols. (Edinburgh: James Ballantye, 1810), Vol. I, p. 1.

6 *Cambridge Orlando: Women's Writing in the British Isles from the Beginnings to the Present*, ed. Susan Brown, Patricia Clements, and Isobel Grundy (Cambridge University Press, 2006–2015). http://orlando.cambridge.org.

7 Margaret Cavendish, Duchess of Newcastle, *CXI Sociable Letters Written by the Thrice Noble, Illustrious, and Excellent Princess, the Lady Marchioness of Newcastle* (London: William Wilson, 1664), p. 267. Subsequent references cited parenthetically in the text.

8 Ann Taylor Gilbert, *Autobiography and Other Memorials of Mrs. Gilbert*, ed. Josiah Gilbert, 2 vols. (London: H. S. King, 1874), Vol. I, pp. 128–9.

9 *Early Blossoms of Genius and Virtue: Including Maxims of Early Wisdom, Juvenile Memoirs, a Great Variety of Examples of the Moral Virtues, and a Selection of Moral Poesy Embellished with Engravings* (London: T. Heptinstall, 1797); *The Blossoms of Early Genius and Virtue: Containing a Great Variety of Juvenile Memoirs and Anecdotes* (Burslem: J. Tregortha, n.d. [1800?]).

10 Young Lady, *The Sorrows of Matilda: A Novel in Two Volumes: The Juvenile Attempt of a Young Lady* (London: Lee and Hurst, 1798), Vol. I, p. 6.

11 A Young Lady, *The Rock, or Alfred and Anna, A Scottish Tale, in Two Volumes* (London: Lee and Hurst, 1798).

12 Anna Maria Porter, *Artless Tales [1793]*, ed. Leslie A. Robertson, Lesley Peterson, Juliet McMaster, et al. (Edmonton, Alberta: Juvenilia Press, 2003), p. 4.

13 Anna Maria Porter, *Artless Tales, or Romantic Effusions of the Heart* (London: Hookham and Carpenter, 1796), p. 1.

14 Elizabeth Benger, *The Female Geniad: A Poem* (London: T. Hookham and J. Carpenter, 1791), n.p. Subsequent references cited parenthetically in the text.

15 Jane West, *Miscellaneous Poetry: Written at an Early Period of Life* (London: T. Swift, 1786).

16 Leslie Stephen, ed. *The Dictionary of National Biography* (New York: Macmillan, 1889). Vol. IX, p. 281.

17 Felicia Dorothea Browne [Hemans], *Poems* (Liverpool: G. F. Harris, 1808), p. vii.

18 "On the Small Advancement in Knowledge the Mind Makes after a Certain Age," in *The Female Preceptor, Containing Essays, Chiefly on The Duties of the Female Sex; with a Variety of Useful and Polite Literature, Poems, & c.*, ed. Mary Pilkington (London: B. R. Goakman, 1813–14), Vol. II, p. 157.

19 John Stedman, *Lælius and Hortensia, or Thoughts on the Nature and Objects of Taste and Genius, in a Series of Letters to Two Friends* (Edinburgh: J. Balfour, 1782), p. 187.

20 George Jerment, *Religion: A Monitor to the Middle-Aged, and the Glory of Old Men, in Several Discourses* (London: C. Buckton, 1796); John Townsend, *Three Sermons, Addressed to Old, Middle-Aged, and Young People* (London: Printed for the Author, 1797).

21 Thomas Gisborne, *An Enquiry into the Duties of the Female Sex* (London: T. Cadell, 1797), p. 397. Subsequent references cited parenthetically in the text.

22 Jane Austen, *Jane Austen's Letters*, ed. Deirdre Le Faye, 4th edn. (Oxford University Press, 2011), p. 261.

23 Robert Hooper, *Lexicon Medicum, or Medical Dictionary* (New York: J. and J. Harper, 1829), p. 283. Subsequent references cited parenthetically in the text.

24 Jane West, *Ringrove, or Old-Fashioned Notions* (London: Longman, Rees, Orme, Brown, and Green, 1827), p. 1. Subsequent references cited parenthetically in the text.

25 Jane West, *Letters to a Young Lady, in which the Duties and Characters of Women are Considered, Chiefly with a Reference to Prevailing Opinions*, 3 vols. (London: Longman, Hurst, Rees, and Orme, 1806), Vol. III, p. 392. Subsequent references cited parenthetically in the text.

26 Anne MacVicar Grant, *Memoir and Correspondence of Mrs. Grant of Laggan*, ed. J. P. Grant, 3 vols. (London: Longman, Brown, Green, and Longmans, 1844), Vol. II, pp. 320–1.

14

FIONA PRICE

National identities and regional affiliations

In Maria Edgeworth's novel *Belinda* (1801), Clarence Hervey, the hero, becomes involved in a rather dangerous performance. As he plays Sir Walter Raleigh to Lady Delacour's Queen Elizabeth, "the coquetry of the queen" conquers "prudery" and the actors become "fully possessed by their parts."[1] Narrowly escaping such sexual (and political) peril, Clarence Hervey responds to Dr X–'s desire to take Lady Delacour's pulse: "Look through the door at the shadow of Queen Elizabeth's ruff – observe how it vibrates; the motion as well as the figure is magnified in the shadow. – Cannot you count every pulsation distinctly?" (*Belinda*, p. 90).

In this scene, Edgeworth (1768–1849) has captured the sense of transition so strongly felt in the period following the French Revolution: at least momentarily, the technologies of modernity seem to replace the chivalric past. What takes place here is in fact as much rereading as removal: empiricism changes both the construction of femininity and the meaning of English history. Here, with Clarence's help, Dr X–'s method of detached observation allows him to begin to analyze the feverish illness that, lurking in courtly display, affects the body politic. Eventually able to make a diagnosis (concerning Lady Delacour's injured breast), he will transform Lady Delacour from flirtatious virgin queen to modern mother. In microcosm, we witness the alteration of the meaning of past and present to produce an improved model of the national family.

In *Nations and Nationalism* (1983) the social philosopher Ernest Gellner suggests that "in the post-agrarian, industrial age," the state and its related institutions inevitably arise, alongside an emphasis on rationality, as decoding and ordering mechanisms. In Edgeworth's text, empiricism seems to play this disciplinary role.[2] However, this is not merely a straightforward case of measuring what is already there. Gellner's account implies that, when the (apparent) social fixity that characterized agrarian society is eroded by modernity, a sense of national identity becomes necessary to support the new social order. To create this sense of identity, a narrative is necessary. To adapt Benedict Anderson's well-known phrase, the community must be "imagined."[3] As the historian Eric Hobsbawm puts it, there is an "element of artefact, invention and social engineering which enters into the making of nations."[4] When at the end of *Belinda* the happy family of aristocrats, sailors, and colonial representatives is assembled, Lady Delacour places them "all in proper attitudes for stage effect": Edgeworth cannot help but reveal that what is "quite pretty and natural" is constructed (*Belinda*, pp. 365–6). It is not only in the court of Elizabeth that power lies in performance; the modern nation is equally the product of invention – and part of what it must (re)invent is the past.

The Romantic period saw a struggle in Britain concerning the meaning – and boundaries – of the "nation." This was a struggle in which women writers played a key part. The ongoing movement toward a modern state formation, and the related patriotic demands of the wars with France, generated a need to define the political nature of community. Simultaneously, print culture, for all the diversity of its national imaginings, began to attempt to provide the mass education that Gellner finds essential to the development of state and nation (*Nations*, p. 28). During this period, when women's public and patriotic activities flourished, it was through print culture that women made some of their most important contributions to the concept of nation, frequently gaining authority by foregrounding print's educational function. In this process of national invention, history and historiography played a crucial role. Responding to the sense of historical breakage that emerged from the French Revolution, women writers reinterpreted the past in order to rewrite invented tradition. As they did so, they not only policed the concept of national identity; they also subjected it to vigorous critique, proposing competing models of the political community.

This interrogation was a consequence of women's strange position as at once central to and at the margins of the nation. Although the figure of Britannia suggested the symbolic importance of femininity to the political unit, the character of John Bull indicated that the imaginary, active, and often aggressive citizen was male: women were crucial to the nation in that they gave warmth and intimacy to an abstraction but their political position remained problematic. Equally, women were important in reproducing the nation, both in terms of their maternal role, and in relation to the diffusion of values through education. As a result, women's sexuality and the heterosexual relation were policed. Through the institution of marriage, women had the crucial role of facilitating the formation of new alliances and bonds. Nonetheless their ideal position within the (unstable) hierarchy of family was often assumed to be a subordinate one. Perhaps most significantly of all in terms of a developing discourse of nation, in Enlightenment historical discourse the treatment of women was taken as symbolic of a society's state of civilization, but the feminine (and effeminate) were seen as often undesirable markers of modernity.

Romantic women writers' position at the center and margins of their society caused an unease that can still be traced in contemporary writing on women and the nation. Aesthetically, women's writing that invents the nation is in danger of appearing dully representative, failing to meet the compulsory Romantic criterion of originality. Politically, imagining women writers as complicit in the growth of state and nation generates anxiety, not least because of the desire to trace a narrative of subversion that often accompanies the recovery of marginalized voices. To consider the treatment of Hannah More (1745–1833), although initially neglected by critics for her conservatism, the educational writer has more recently and rather oddly been reclaimed as liberal and subversive. It is as though such qualities are necessary for a woman writing nation to become a legitimate object of study. Once the fluidity of the separate spheres – private and public – is acknowledged, and women's entry into the arena of political propaganda becomes evident, the conservatism of some women's writing becomes problematic. This in turn generates a new interest in writing by women which positions itself as somehow outside of or marginal to nation. Having struggled to move women from a domestic to a public realm, critical discourse is compelled to place them back on the edge of the national unit.

As Romantic women writers were aware, the strange social position in which they found themselves shaped their contribution to the discourse of nation. Nation is in one sense a potentially egalitarian and inclusive concept, allowing political entities to claim notional equality, and requiring the people as a mass to identify with the political unit. At the same time, the nation is restrictive: how its borders are defined, and who belongs to it, are matters of contention. Thus women, simultaneously subject to inclusion and exclusion in relation to their own societies, are ideally placed not only to symbolize but also to interrogate the nation. This was particularly the case in the 1790s, when various definitions of femininity were used to speak to the problem of the formulation of nation, most markedly in relation to economic progress. The feminine could be associated with the luxurious, supposedly more mobile and threatening consumer culture of the late eighteenth century; equally, defined in terms of caring self-sacrifice, the feminine could provide a solution to the perceived individualism of modernity. Since nations, for all their connection to a new economic order, require the reinvention of history to claim authority, the problem of the definition of femininity was frequently tackled in historical terms.

For women writers responding to Edmund Burke's *Reflections on the Revolution in France* (1790), the need to redefine the position of women within the state and the drive to provide a new historical understanding of community and nation were profoundly linked. In addition, I contend, women writers were particularly concerned with how inclusive the national (or supranational) body might be. Hence Mary Wollstonecraft (1759–97) and Charlotte Smith (1749–1806) try to imagine a wider political community through a form of radical cosmopolitan historicism, only for more reformist and conservative writers to rework their emphasis on history, providing a more restrictive model of the nation as family. These conservative narratives in their turn also proved inadequate, both in relation to the competing nationalisms explored in the national tale and in terms of policing internal class divisions. Thus in the opening decades of the nineteenth century, historical fiction by Jane Porter (bap. 1776, d. 1850), Jane West (1758–1852), and Elizabeth Hamilton (c. 1756–1816) once more widens the idea of nation, recuperating radical and dissenting tropes to invite cross-class identification with the political unit. Unified through Christianity (that is, more problematically, through Protestantism), Britain can be at once inclusive *and* hierarchical. In this vision, women, as upholders of feminized and Christian values, have a key part to play.

Ernest Gellner defines nationalism as a desire for congruence between the political and national unit (*Nations*, p. 1). Yet the nature of the British political unit was problematic. Whereas an Act of Union had joined England and Wales in 1536, it was only in 1707 that England and Scotland became the United Kingdom of Great Britain, and not until 1800 that the United Kingdom of Great Britain and Ireland was created. The difficulty of producing coherence from such materials is suggested in *British Synonymy* (1796) by the writer Hester Lynch Piozzi (1741–1821). An educational "attempt at regulating the choice of words in familiar conversation" for foreign friends, Piozzi's book contains adjacent discussions of "War and Hostility" and "Warmth and Heat," which are revealing in relation to the discourse of nation. Under "War," Piozzi notes that she has "read somewhere" that a "state of hostilities with some neighbouring power may be considered as medicine for a state, rough no doubt and drastic, but possibly useful, whilst a civil *war* is little better than a domestic or ordinary poison."[5] Conflict with France could help Britain define itself. Nevertheless, this struggle for definition risks generating the internal tensions that Piozzi's source dreads – division not only between political factions, but between ranks, and even between Ireland, Scotland, Wales, and England.

Confronted by this vision of internal and external strife, in the next entry Piozzi compensates by describing the gentle "warmth of patriotism": "Visible amongst the happy subjects of our *British* empire," it "produces that solid texture in the constitution which its members so well know how to value, and that strong spirit of *cohesion* among individuals which alone can render it immortal" (*British Synonymy*, II: 351). Piozzi suggests that the individual define himself in legal or constitutional terms, terms that are at once generated and guaranteed by patriotism. According to Piozzi, "warmth" is "mild and friendly"; more threateningly, when it is intensified, the result is heat, "kindled into rage by violent motion, destructive in its nature, dreadful in its effects" (*British Synonymy*, II: 351). Both the constitution and national feeling are vulnerable to the heat of enthusiasm and neither language nor education (both extensively drawn upon to construct national identity in the French Revolution debate) seems capable of restraining such ferocity.

The politician and author Edmund Burke (1729/30–97) in the *Reflections* history – or, more particularly, tradition – forms a barrier against destructive enthusiasm. Burke argues for the (imaginary) continuity of the British constitution and of primogeniture, creating a kind of sublime of tradition that will protect Britain from revolution. In contrast, when he considers events in France, he draws upon stadial history. Stadial historians of the Scottish Enlightenment saw the development – or transformation – of society in relation to particular stages. Although the concept was "adaptively applied," such thinkers typically saw these "economic stages – hunter-gatherer, pastoral, the agricultural and the commercial" – in terms of social progress toward civilization.[6] Describing the March to Versailles (October 5, 1789), which ended in the royal family being brought back to Paris, Burke suggests that he is unable to imagine how "such disasters" could fall upon Queen Marie Antoinette "in a nation of gallant men": "the age of chivalry is gone. That of sophisters, economists, and calculators, has succeeded."[7] This shift between social stages is abrupt and symptomatic of decline. For William Robertson (1705–83) and other stadial historians (whatever their particular differences on the subject) chivalry, by improving relations between the sexes, had promoted social cohesion and progress in Europe and had shaped contemporary manners. As a result, as they saw it, the removal of chivalry might lead to social decay. Blurring the lines between nation and monarch, Burke's nostalgic apostrophe to chivalry renders not only the queen, but also the system of absolutism that she represents, more sympathetic.

Although Enlightenment historians had emphasized the importance of sensibility in historical discourse, Burke's invocation of the "manly sentiment" associated with chivalry was to prove problematic, particularly for women writers (*Reflections*, p. 170). In the epistolary novel *Desmond* (1792) Charlotte Smith critiqued Burke's account. Drawing on *The Rights of Man* by the radical Thomas Paine (1737–1809), Smith redirects sensibility toward the lower ranks, writing an alternative history of their pitiable exploitation under feudalism. Comparing French and American history with the English present, Smith exploits national feeling as a motivator for political change. At the same time, what she implicitly calls for is a sensibility that extends across ranks and borders. But Smith finds sensibility less adequate when applied to women's position within the state. Married to a corrupt exponent of aristocratic privilege, Smith's heroine, Geraldine, finds her agency compromised. The alternative, a match between Geraldine and the philosophical hero, Desmond, seems equally flawed.

To Wollstonecraft, Burke's historicized sensibility appeared even more suspect than to Smith. In her political treatise *A Vindication of the Rights of Men* (1790) Wollstonecraft feminizes Burke, suggesting his sensibility – and the chivalry she connects with it – connotes only an artificial desire for show, a desire that stems from the corruption of hereditary property. Drawing on her educational work concerning female behavior, in *A Vindication of the Rights of Woman* (1792) Wollstonecraft suggests that this form of behavior is not necessarily characteristic only of women but equally affects soldiers and clergymen, as well as politicians.[8] Building on the Enlightenment use of woman as symbol of historical and social development, Wollstonecraft's work suggests that instead of the condition of *women* being emblematic, the qualities and behaviors associated with *femininity*, as well as the effeminate, should now be seen as features of a particular social system, or stage.

Wollstonecraft's solution to such feminization becomes explicit in *An Historical and Moral View of the French Revolution* (1794). In her stadial narrative of "the advancement of communities, from a state of barbarism to that of polished society," the system Burke defends as chivalrous is instead seen in terms of the "idle caprices of an effeminate court," associated with inequality, insufficient progress, and the preservation of hierarchy "by the fraud of partial laws" (*Works*, 6: 19, 6: 18). In contradistinction to this, Wollstonecraft argues, the true purpose of government is to promote equality. In a more advanced social stage, "masculine ... philosophy" will replace Burkean feminized sensibility (*Works*, 6: 6). Such rational "exertions" will civilize "the grand mass, by exercising their understandings about the most important objects of enquiry" (*Works*, 6: 18). Significantly in view of Gellner's suggestion that mass education is essential to state and nation, what Wollstonecraft is hinting at here, and explicitly proposing in *A Vindication of the Rights of Woman*, is a national educational system which will be used to instantiate equality (*Works*, 5: 229–50). Wollstonecraft also notes in *An Historical and Moral View* that, certainly amongst the "ancients," "legislators" aimed at the "aggrandizement of their individual nation" and "trampled with a ferocious affectation of patriotism on the most sacred rights of humanity" (*Works*, 6: 15). In the feminized stage of unequal sensibility, nation is a dangerous concept, easily manipulated by the powerful. The rational, egalitarian community Wollstonecraft imagines reaches beyond conventional political boundaries.

As a result of the Terror and the French Revolutionary and Napoleonic Wars, such radical rewritings of gender, history, and nation became more problematic: it was increasingly difficult to imagine the reinvention of society. Hence in Smith's and Wollstonecraft's writings there are moments of retreat into alternative imagined communities, moments that themselves quickly come to seem inadequate or implausible. In Smith's later fiction, particularly the collection of tales *Letters of a Solitary Wanderer* (1800–2), the war-torn Europe of past and present seems to offer no space that is not ultimately tainted by oppression. Moments of retreat from social corruption seem equally precarious in Wollstonecraft's work. The isolation that makes the heroine a genius in Wollstonecraft's first novel, *Mary, a Fiction* (1788), also leads her to struggle to cope with social reality; in the author's last posthumously published and unfinished novel, *Maria, or The Wrongs of Woman* (1798), the temporary alternative community is located within the dubious space of the madhouse. In the "Essay on Poetry and our Relish for the Beauties of Nature" (1797) the moment of solitary wandering outside corrupt contemporaneity only lasts as long as the upper ranks are asleep. Wollstonecraft's portrayal of retreat is in fact part of her project of wider social improvement but such moments are, for her, problematic. The pre-social state of nature imagined by the French philosopher Jean-Jacques Rousseau (1712–78) cannot, even in an idealized form, be recreated. There is no escape from history.

The egalitarian political communities imagined by Wollstonecraft were subject to extensive challenge. Her emphasis on feminization as a sign of insufficient social progress was adapted by conservative women writers, who reconnected the "feminine" and the female, arguing that women were not only symptomatic of but also responsible for the health of the nation. In *Letters to a Young Lady* (1806) (a kind of epistolary conduct manual), for example, Jane West replies to radical historiography by using stadial history to justify, and to shape, women's "feelings of patriotic virtue."[9] West's suggestion that "the progress of any people toward civilization is uniformly marked by allotting increased degree of importance to the fair sex" is entirely standard (*Letters*, I: 56, I: 52). For West, this "progress" needs to be accompanied not only by Christianity but also by the institution of marriage: "wherever the institution of marriage is formally acknowledged, women become a branch of the body politic" (*Letters*, I: 54). From within this institution, West implicitly contends, women construct their own tradition, becoming "conservators of morals" (*Letters*, I: 70). They ensure that the "strong ties of nature or of choice" (the family and heterosexual relations) are dominant rather than the "pretended cosmopolites [sic]" of radicalism (*Letters*, I: 46). Claiming female centrality allows the egalitarian political community imagined by radical writers to be replaced by the more hierarchical trope of the family. As the mass education imagined by Wollstonecraft is replaced by women's pedagogic function within the home, the apparently inclusive maneuver of stressing women's importance ironically enshrines inequality.

West's fiction also suggests the importance of the correct attitude to history in facilitating this vision of the national family. Hence in the novel *A Gossip's Story, and A Legendary Tale* (1796) the inclusion of a narrative poem set in the time of the Crusades allows West to argue that marital happiness depends on women being educated enough to form the proper (royalist) interpretation of history. And in another of West's entries into the post-French Revolution debate, *A Tale of the Times* (1799), the Monteith family adopt an incorrect attitude to history, which leads to the neglect of their daughter, Arabella, and to the exposure of the heroine, Geraldine, to French philosophy. When radical intellectualism replaces true history, West suggests, the family and the community are threatened. In her novel *The Refusal* (1810) West underlines the political consequences of misreading both history and femininity even more strongly. Impatient with his retiring wife, the statesman Lord Avondel falls for the versatile historical displays of the Italian seductress Paulina, who mimics "the sober charms of Octavia," or becomes "Cornelia devoting her sons to the service of their country."[10] As the performance of patriotism replaces the reality, the proud aristocrat almost abandons public and private duty, thinking of leaving his blameless wife. Even as West uses the trope of family to challenge the broader political communities imagined by more radical thinkers, she remains aware that it requires extensive policing.

The instability of the domestic unit (and women's position within it) was particularly troubling because the metaphor of the national family was also used to describe the relationship between Ireland, Scotland, and England, and between Britain and the wider empire: if gender relations were unstable, so was the Union. Set in 10 AD, Ellis Cornelia Knight's epistolary novel and guide to ancient Rome *Marcus Flaminius* (1792) both analyses the causes of the French Revolution and suggests a growing concern regarding the British Empire and its relation to liberty. For Knight (1757–1837), this concern was expressed through the metaphor of family and the sexual relation. Drawing on stadial history, she argues that those from what she perceives as different stages of political and social organization should not marry. Knight suggests that Union and empire are impossible if there is combined and uneven development.

The same anxiety concerning the possibility of Union is another feature of Jane West's *A Tale of the Times*.[11] For West, the family is not only a locus for the misreading of history and gender but also a site of regional tension. Even if, in Wales, the heroine's father, Sir William Powercourt, possesses a more or less desirable approach to past and present, viewing himself as a "conscientious guardian," in Scotland the Monteiths have been corrupted by the "voluptuous court of that dissipated monarch," Charles II (*Tale*, I: 28, I: 17). And while the Scots have been tainted by Jacobitism, the English face even worse problems: London's modernity erodes history and promotes revolutionary philosophy. Viewed as a family, the Union is problematic, encompassing different attitudes to history and different stages of development.

The metaphor of the nation as family provided considerable purchase to writers of the national tale, allowing them to argue for more equality and better understanding between England and other parts of the United Kingdom. Moreover, if "historians have for a long time referred to the works of Edgeworth and ... Lady Morgan [Sydney Owenson], as 'historical evidence',"[12] they arguably do so in reply to the historiographic awareness and consequent rich use of history found in the national tale. Responding to the 1790s debate concerning nation, both Edgeworth and Owenson (bap. 1783, d. 1859) attempt to complicate historical understanding in order to improve Ireland's position within the Union. Yet Edmund Burke's reading of the French Revolution, which was so influential on the 1790s debate concerning the use of history, was disrupted for Irish writers by Burke's commentary on Ireland. Reacting to Burke's use of the metaphorics of the patriarchal family in the Irish context, both Edgeworth and Owenson found family and gender to be over-determined sites for the reworking of history.

Influenced by Adam Smith's economic thought, and by the doctrine of the association of ideas, as well as by Enlightenment stadial history, Edgeworth's project (for all its rich sense of the past and of social change) is essentially a modernizing one. Hence in *Castle Rackrent, a Hibernian Tale* (1800) (often recognized as the first regional novel), Edgeworth uses the history of four generations of the Rackrent family to explain the flawed development that seems to characterize the Irish past and present. Set before the Constitution of 1782 (which lifted restrictions on the Irish Parliament and led to a period of relative legislative freedom) but published in the same year as the Act of Union, *Castle Rackrent* explores how the Anglo-Irish feudal institution of the aristocracy has been corrupted, leading in turn to the corruption of the modern commercial and legal order.

Building on this unease concerning the precise form of modernity, the two series of *Tales of Fashionable Life* (1809, 1812) draw on the comparative tendency of stadial history to conduct a kind of experiment in historical causality: England, Ireland, and France are compared to allow Edgeworth to explore the dangers of luxury and to suggest that the best forms of commercial modernity rely on an established sense of reciprocal duties, a sense shared by both the lower and higher orders. In the most fully realized of these tales, *The Absentee* (1812) (written as a response to Sydney Owenson's *The Wild Irish Girl: A National Tale* [1806]), Edgeworth revisits the metaphor of the Irish family, shaping a more optimistic replacement for the ruined domesticity of the Rackrents. When the *Absentee*'s heroine, Grace, marries the Irish but English-educated Lord Colambre, a more ideal union is envisaged, at least between the Colambres and the land they are supposed to rule.

Maria Edgeworth's perspective is fundamentally Anglo-Irish. In contrast, Sydney Owenson implicitly argues that Irish national identity should be understood in terms of the glories of the Gaelic past (glories often contested in the historical writing of the late eighteenth century). In *The Wild Irish Girl* (1806), Glorvina, representative of what might be assumed to be the more primitive culture of Ireland but actually the inheritor of sophisticated cultural and historical knowledge, teaches the cosmopolitan Horatio, representative of England, to value Ireland more fully, simultaneously adjusting the heterosexual and national power relation. Further, Glorvina's harp-playing, the theatricals of *O'Donnel: A National Tale* (1814), and the manipulation of appearances expertly carried out by the heroine of Owenson's *Florence Macarthy: An Irish Tale* (1818) all point to the increasing importance of performance in Owenson's account of nation. Owenson is aware that the colonial center can exploit such spectacle. Nonetheless, in her works the stage-managing of performance increasingly becomes a source of power for subjects marginalized by gender or nation. Owenson's emphasis on performance subverts both the family as hierarchical unit and the relation between Ireland and England. Thus, although conservatives had attempted to use the idea of the national family to counter radical cosmopolitanism, the trope remained problematic, underlining the inequalities generated both within the "United Kingdom" and within the empire.

The national family was an equally problematic notion when it came to policing class divisions: while conservative thinkers were wary of the more inclusive vision of political life proposed by the radicals, the perception of mass political involvement in the French Revolution suggested that the lower ranks would, in some way, have to identify themselves with the nation, if revolution were to be avoided. Family was simply not an extensive enough metaphor and Edgeworthian narratives of peace through quasi-familial bonds of mutual obligation and gratitude remained unconvincing. Some other way of promoting a non-revolutionary identification with the nation was desirable and here Protestantism could provide some necessary ballast (even if the tactic was likely to aggravate difficulties in the context of Ireland).

Protestantism was a major force in the construction of British national identity throughout the eighteenth century. In the 1790s and 1800s it provided the basis of a conservative reply to the radical language of common humanity. For dissenters (like Richard Price [1723–91] in his *Observations on the Importance of the American Revolution* [1785]), the spiritual equality provided by Christianity had political implications in the present. But more reformist or conservative writers insisted that Christianity was on the side of the establishment. In the opening years of the nineteenth century, reformist and conservative writers recuperated elements of both dissenting and radical thought, incorporating them within a more establishment-orientated narrative of Christianity. Having reclaimed dissenting political energies, Protestantism could provide the egalitarian inclusivity that would allow mass identification with the nation, but still leave the social hierarchy intact. This approach allowed the radical stadial history proposed by Wollstonecraft to be replaced by a history that inculcated Christian values of selflessness and non-aggression, and that had a correspondingly defined femininity at its heart. In this process of recuperation, Elizabeth Hamilton, Jane West, and Jane Porter (despite the diversity of their political views) are particularly important.

Born in Belfast and brought up in Scotland by an Episcopalian uncle and Presbyterian aunt, Elizabeth Hamilton intervened in the post-French Revolution debate in order to reclaim the discourse of philosophy from the radicals. In her satirical novel *Memoirs of Modern Philosophers* (1800), Hamilton, a moderate reformist, critiqued the New Philosophy associated with the philosopher and novelist William Godwin. Linking radicalism with atheism, she emphasizes instead the philosophical, moral, and social efficacy of Christianity, which is crucial for women, family, and the nation. In her later works, instead of merely criticizing the new philosophy, Hamilton gives Christianity itself a modern philosophical underpinning. In *Letters on Education* (1801), Hamilton co-opts the doctrine of the association of ideas to suggest that the moral qualities that should be associated with femininity are at the core of the successful Christian nation. Constructing a brief history of misogyny, Hamilton suggests that the contempt for women in ancient Greece and Rome has had long-term effects. The use of classical rather than Christian values has led not only to contempt for femininity but "contempt for those moral qualities which are allowed to constitute the perfection of the female character. Meekness, gentleness, temperance, and chastity; that command over the passions which is obtained by frequent self-denial."[13] Here the biography *Memoirs of Agrippina* (1804) can be read as a kind of philosophical and religious case history. Hamilton exploits the growing popularity of the genre of female biography (a genre that provided a way of asserting and policing women's role within the state) to replace masculinist classical history with a narrative of women's agency. For Wollstonecraft, excessive feminization signaled the unhealthy inequality of the modern state. In contrast, Hamilton suggests that femininity, properly understood, brings a lack of self-interest that would support a Christian national community both in Scotland and beyond.

If Elizabeth Hamilton co-opts both history and philosophy to construct the nation, Jane West and Jane Porter call, respectively, upon (political) science and folk culture. In *The Loyalists, an Historical Novel* (1812), a fictionalized history of the civil war, West attacks dissent and retrieves its more Romantic qualities for the Church of England. The novel projects the characteristics of Joseph Priestley (1733–1804), a leading dissenter, political thinker, and natural scientist, onto an Anglican preacher: it is Anglicanism, not dissent, which is the truly progressive national force. In this narrative, history implicitly becomes a source of experimental political data, which, examined by women as well as by men, demonstrates the need for control and subordination. And for West this subordination can only be effectively provided by Church and King. Jobson, West's appropriately named representative of the loyal working man, learns, through an unpleasant experience of dissenting culture, that Anglican obedience (unleavened by independent thought) is the best way forward.

West (like Hannah More) imagines members of the lower ranks suitably emotionally chastened through their bad experiences of revolutionary politics. Jane Porter's approach is more evangelical. She attempts to harness the passions of the ordinary man. She envisages an engagement with nation that is egalitarian at least in that it requires the same passionate commitment from each individual. Here, the politically informed community imagined by Wollstonecraft is rendered unthreatening – the energies of the "mass" are no longer disruptive, but, through the recuperation of enthusiasm, are channeled to support the nation as a whole. Depicting Scotland's struggle against England in the late thirteenth and early fourteenth centuries, Jane Porter's historical novel *The Scottish Chiefs: A Romance* (1810) sites national conflict within Britain in the distant past, implicitly imagining a contemporary Britain unified through shared virtues and common culture. For Porter such culture does not include the tales of "troubadours" nor stories of "fairies, magicians, and the enchanting world."[14] Superstition and love are replaced by heroism, and ballads are supplemented by Bible reading: William Wallace, Porter's hero, is both Christian and feminized. In this feminized national space of *The Scottish Chiefs*, women are at once central and strangely diminished. Positioned as transmitters of folk culture and as educators, women are finally allotted a junior role within the national drama. In this reinvention of history, both they and the heterosexual relation are displaced by the feminized Christian hero.

Examining the possibility of an escape from social corruption to a more natural state, in her "Essay on Poetry" Wollstonecraft comments that "natural is a very indefinite expression" (*Works*, 7: 7). The same may be said of femininity. As something that seems essential and unchanging but is actually the product of invention, the feminine has an important role to play in supporting and naturalizing the equally artificial construct of the nation. In particular, during the 1790s, various definitions of the feminine were proposed in order to critique and to reshape national political life. Even though the position of women in British society was often seen as a reason for complacency by those influenced by Enlightenment historicism, the feminine could provide evidence not of social progress but of decadence. For commercial society to be reimagined and the modern nation to emerge, the feminine had to be redefined, a project that involved the appeal to the authority of (an often fictionalized) history. Women writers were heavily interpolated in this process. As both central and marginal to their own societies, they were in an excellent position to comment on the inclusivity (or otherwise) of the nation.

For Wollstonecraft and Smith, Burke's chivalric sensibility and the emotions associated with femininity were key barriers to modernity. Rewriting stadial history in response to Burke, Wollstonecraft argued that the negative behaviors usually associated with women were instead signs of an insufficiently advanced social stage. For modernity to occur, chivalric sensibility had to be replaced by an egalitarian rationality generated by mass political education. But this inclusive vision of political life (a vision that arguably goes beyond the national) proved troubling. Instead, more conservative writers challenged Wollstonecraft's ideas, reassociating the feminine and the female to create a moral nation with the hierarchical family at its core. Within this narrative, women act as conservators of a moral tradition: their education and ability to reproduce the appropriate values become central. This paradigm appears to give women importance but both restricts their behavior and provides a narrowed, less egalitarian model of the political community.

However, this conservative response was itself subject to challenge and adjustment. On the one hand, the idea of the nation as family provided a space for competing nationalisms to be explored, a project undertaken most notably in the national tale. On the other, the (apparent) mobility of consumer society required the mass of the people to have some identification with the nation. Hence in the opening decades of the nineteenth century, the tropes of radicalism and dissent, with their emphasis on egalitarian inclusivity, were recuperated by reformist and conservative writers and added to the narrative of Protestant femininity. In such reconstructions of history, the corrupt, society-wide femininity that Wollstonecraft attacks is replaced by a caring, self-sacrificing feminine. And even though the continued emphasis on Protestantism remained highly problematic in the Irish context, in terms of class the altruistic, Christian feminine still implicitly worked to limit the competition and social mobility of the consumer economy.

For this formulation of nation and national identity to do convincing political work, more threatening alternative narratives of the feminine and the historical had to be overwritten. In Jane Austen's *Emma* (1816) Mr. Knightley's Donwell Abbey and nearby Abbey Mill Farm signal the gentility and industriousness of nineteenth-century life. If the abbey's changed ownership contains any reminder of the religious and political struggles of the Reformation, the echo is extremely faint. The view of the mill is one of "English verdure, English culture, English comfort, seen under a sun bright, without being oppressive."[15] Through the unobtrusive use of the sun as symbol of kingship, governmental authority becomes as apparently unchallengeable and as mildly productive as the weather. Historical conflict becomes absorbed into the landscape that Emma overlooks. Nonetheless, the repetition of "English," so apparently celebratory, also contains a warning: the national unit and its history cannot be so easily fused with the environment.

The novels of Sir Walter Scott express a similar ambiguity toward both past conflicts and the interpretation of history. In *Waverley* (1814) female activism is associated, via the figure of Flora McIvor, with a passing age. In contrast, the present is embodied by the more congenial and domestic figure of Rose Bradwardine, associating the modern commercial nation not with consumer excess and political disorder but with tranquil production. It is only when Waverley remembers Rose with "more tender recollection" than Flora that the "real history" of "his life" commences.[16] But as Scott (1771–1832) indicates through the presence of "A Postscript which should have been a Preface," in narrative events do not always stay in place (pp. 339–43). Once the nation has been (even partially) invented, it is tempting to forget the invention, to consign other histories and alternative femininities to the realm of romance. To return to the troubled space of history in the post-French Revolution debate is to reveal alternative imaginaries of both femininity and the nation.

NOTES

1 Maria Edgeworth, *Belinda*, ed. Siobhan Kilfeather, Vol. II of *The Novels and Selected Works of Maria Edgeworth* (London: Pickering & Chatto, 2003), p. 89. Subsequent references cited parenthetically in the text.

2 Ernest Gellner, *Nations and Nationalism: New Perspectives on the Past* (Oxford: Blackwell, 1983), pp. 5, 20.

3 Benedict Anderson, *Imagined Communities: Reflections on the Origin and Spread of Nationalism* (London: Verso, 1991).

4 E. J. Hobsbawm, *Nations and Nationalism since 1780: Programme, Myth, Reality* (Cambridge University Press, 1990), p. 10. Subsequent references cited parenthetically in the text.

5 Hester Lynch Piozzi, *British Synonymy, or An Attempt at Regulating the Choice of Words in Familiar Conversation*, 2 vols. (London: Robinson, 1794), Vol. II: 350. Subsequent references cited parenthetically in the text.

6 Karen O'Brien, *Narratives of Enlightenment: Cosmopolitan History from Voltaire to Gibbon* (Cambridge University Press, 1997), p. 133.

7 Edmund Burke, *Reflections on the Revolution in France and on the Proceedings in Certain Societies in London Relative to that Event* (1790), ed. Conor Cruise O'Brien (Harmondsworth: Penguin, 1968), p. 170.

8 Janet Todd and Marilyn Butler, *The Works of Mary Wollstonecraft,* 7 vols., Vol. 5 (London: Pickering & Chatto, 1989), p. 86. Subsequent references cited parenthetically in the text as *Works*.

9 Jane West, *Letters to a Young Lady*, 3rd edn., 3 vols. (London: Longman, Hurst, Rees, and Orme, 1806). Subsequent references cited parenthetically in the text.

10 [Jane West], *The Refusal*, 3 vols. (London: Longman, Hurst, Rees and Orme, 1810), Vol. II, p. 318.

11 Jane West, *A Tale of the Times*, 3 vols. London. (Longman and Rees, 1799). Subsequent references cited parenthetically in the text.

12 Clíona Ó Gallchoir, *Maria Edgeworth: Women, Enlightenment and Nation* (University College Dublin Press, 2005), p. 3.

13 Elizabeth Hamilton, *Letters on Education* (Bath: Crutwell for Robinson, 1801), p. 241.

14 Jane Porter, *The Scottish Chiefs: A Romance*, ed. Fiona Price (Ontario: Broadview Press, 2007), p. 527.

15 Jane Austen, *Emma: A Novel*, 3 vols. (London: Murray, 1816), Vol. III, p. 98.

16 Sir Walter Scott, *Waverley Novels*, introd. Andrew Lang, 48 vols. (London: Nimmo, 1892), Vol. II, pp. 255–6.

15

JILLIAN HEYDT-STEVENSON

Sexualities

This essay considers the writings and lives of a variety of women writers of the Romantic period (1785–1832), who, when they wrote about sexuality, developed multiple rhetorical strategies to describe and celebrate physical love as one of the foundations for companionate unions, both traditional and non-traditional. They focused on the necessity of liberty in sexual unions, and they advocated a connection between sexuality and community, underscoring the consequences of isolation from social and political life. For these writers, sexual love has voltage, as Emma Courtney states: "darting from mind to mind, enlightening, warming, with electrical rapidity!"[1] Emma's poetic description of such currents reminds us of the era's understanding that sex unites brain, body, and spirit. Roy Porter observes that "censorship and repression work in subtle ways ... Carnal knowledge [was] desired, dangerous, denied all at once. And readers surely enjoyed playing with fire."[2] In writing about the body, women may have "played with fire," but their "play" was serious indeed.

"Expression" of sexuality as a term points to a key theoretical problem, since the word encompasses both sexual behavior (what did women do?) and sexually charged writing (what did women say?). Two centuries distant from these women writers, all we have is their discourse; thus, I focus on the specific forms of agency women take on in their writing and thought. Eliza Fenwick, Harriette Wilson, Mary Hays, Anne Lister, Maria Edgeworth, Charlotte Smith, Mary Wollstonecraft, and Mary Shelley's heroines explore spiritual, sexual, and intellectual self-awareness outside of traditional "courting" modes. Many of these authors offer examples of desires and circumstances that could be called non-normative but which were in fact common – sex before marriage, multiple sexual partners, embrace of extramarital passion, Sapphic love, and overdetermined attachments, where a lover is described as a father or brother or where unexpressed sexual vitality infuses a friendship. Finally, we observe post-marital or post-sexual courtship, where a single woman finds someone already married or, wedded herself, meets another with whom she could have been happy. These novels address all matters of love and sexuality, even when romantic discovery (generally) happens in a customary fashion, as in Jane Austen (1775–1817); thus even traditional authors infuse erotic vitality into their novels, illustrating how the heroine's happiness arises from expressing both mental and physical pleasure.

Many of these works operate outside or in defiance of a supposedly monolithic sexual repression and censorship. That women writers even privately, let alone in print, investigated sexuality may be surprising given that this was an era of "sex panic,"[3] one prompted by fears that the French Revolution would contaminate British women with freedoms that threatened to unsettle civic order and family life. In Britain, that meant a rise in publications (sermons, conduct books, periodicals) denouncing women's participation in political life and emphasizing their passive physical nature. In 1800, John Bowles (1751–1819) cautioned that as the nuptial "engagement is viewed with reverence, and observed with fidelity, an age may ... be denominated virtuous"[4] (135). While the fact of such publications is undeniable, scholars have assumed that because these ideas existed, they were universally accepted and practiced.

The stereotypical sexual repression associated with the Victorians, however, was not the standard in Romantic-era women's writings. The early nineteenth century was a time of blackmailing author–courtesans (Harriette Wilson), lesbian diarists (Anne Lister), and sexualized humorists (Jane Austen), as well as novelists who questioned such dogmas (Wollstonecraft, Hays, Edgeworth, and Fenwick). Older ideologies, such as the Judeo-Christian view of women as overly sexual, competed with that of physical passivity. Another, which provided a less negative model for both women writers and male scientists, was grounded in the belief that sexual pleasure was at the heart of courtship and joyful marriage. According to Samuel Solomon (1796), when "love is pure, the bliss is the greatest man can wish for"; physical love, in moderation, "raises and cheers the noblest faculty of the body and mind."[5] Many scientists and medical manuals, far from denying or pathologizing women's sexuality, saw it as natural and healthy. When sex is "united with the pleasures of love ... this joy aids digestion, animates circulation, accelerates all the functions, restores strength, and supports it."[6] *Aristotle's Master-Piece* (1684), a bestselling medical manual for newlyweds and midwives, explains that the clitoris, which is "the seat of the greatest pleasure in the act of copulation" heats the "coals" of the "*amorous fires, / youth and beauty to be quenched requires.*"[7] Such faith in the spontaneous overflow of sexual feelings contradicted ideas like natural passivity or an essential female materiality, given that the body, if healthy and unrestrained, knows itself as alive to sensation, which is connected to the brain.

We cannot know whether any individual woman's sexuality was non-existent, excessive, or normal, but we do know that it was a subject of intense importance and one that was rhetorically embodied in various ways, interwoven positively and negatively in everyday life. For example, picturesque travel, a "rational amusement" William Gilpin tells us, presents an analogue to body–mind co-mingling with erotic connotations insofar as it invites viewers to enjoy the healthy diversion of touring, pursuing pleasure, and increasing their visual literacy as they visit the countryside seeking scenes of grandeur that "burs[t] unexpectedly upon the eye."[8] The facts and imagery of sexuality-saturated botany appear in Erasmus Darwin's *The Loves of the Plants* (1789), where we find such metaphoric summons to human love: "With honey'd lips enamour'd Woodbines meet, / Clasp with fond arms, and mix their kisses sweet" – and even "icy bosoms feel the *secret* fire!"[9]

A third site of "rational amusement," the theater, functioned also as the site of assignations; infamous courtesan and memoirist Harriette Wilson (1786–1845), for example, had a box at the opera that was practically her business office. During this era, sites of public entertainment were often sexualized – whether theaters, the London Pantheon, and outdoor grounds, such as Vauxhall Gardens. In Frances Burney's novel *Evelina* (1778), for example, the eponymous character's walk through "the dark walks" of Vauxhall leads to momentary abduction and terror when "a large party of gentlemen, apparently very riotous,"[10] entrap her and her female companions, thinking they are actresses. Abolitionist texts, though rational in intent, exposed horrors that yet provided, inadvertently or not, an incendiary sexual rhetoric. Discussing the account of a slave revolt by John Gabriel Stedman (1744–97), Marcus Wood argues that the "eroticized vision of the tortured black female body [held] an obsessional power" that "hypnotically" fascinated him.[11] Other writings attributed sexual promiscuity and lasciviousness to black women, distorting their sexuality and creating a basis for establishing female "normality" as white and sexually passive; on the other hand, acknowledging that plantation owners forced sexual violence on slaves offered a rhetoric white women could use to protest forced marriage, marital rape, and sexual objectification.

Rational sexuality requires that the body and brain work together. Focusing on teaching sexual complexities rather than keeping them taboo, these writers concentrate on how identity formation depends on knowing the body, not rejecting it. Rhetorically, they link sexual liberty to natural freedom: women enjoy being outdoors and they resemble nature in their vitality and liveliness, and sometimes even in their wildness. The picturesque landscape, for example, offers women an outlet for their physical and intellectual energy, as well as a model of female manners given its aspiration toward a balance between nature and culture; it exhibits liberty, not anarchy; playfulness, not insipidity. The heroine of Mary Wollstonecraft's (1759–97) *Mary: A Fiction* (1788), "admir[ing] the various dispositions of light and shade ... rejoice[s] in existence."[12] Thus, whether the girl is a "romp," in Wollstonecraft's word – like Austen's Catherine Morland, "noisy and wild, hat[ing] confinement and cleanliness";[13] or a woman like Mary, artfully viewing the landscape's "dispositions" with a picturesque lens – nature offers a model union of body, psyche, and intellect that promotes happiness and encourages liberty and free will.

In following "Nature" and asserting inner, sacred promises – not sightlessly following arbitrary laws – another discourse emerges wherein a heroine makes sex, even premarital sex, ethical. This complicates the notion that sexual purity alone determines a woman's virtue. Thus some authors assert that women have a virtuous right to express desire, if it has been through the cleansing crucible of her morality, not the law's. Mary Hays's (1759–1843) character Emma Courtney (from the novel of the same name published in 1796) confesses to Harley, the married man she loves, that though living with him wouldn't "be pruden[t]," she would do so given that *"the individuality of an affection constitutes its chastity."* Her proposition – *"wholly, the triumph of affection!"* – does not violate "modesty," but does "involv[e] in it very serious hazards"(*Memoirs*, p. 123). In Eliza Fenwick's (1766–1840) *Secresy* (1795), Sibella has raised herself in the school of nature *and* had a boy's education: the liberty that has allowed her to walk and read unhindered lends "something wild" to her "air," while rendering her speech "simple" yet "eloquen[t]."[14] Nature's influence propels Sibella beyond social constructions: she writes to Clement, inviting him to join her in a sacred marriage, "to become my husband," for "'tis our hearts alone that can bind the vow ... Come to my apartments. With pure hearts and hands, we will plight our fervent unspotted faith ... You shall go the transported confiding husband" (*Secresy*, I: XII, 82; XIII, 84). Tragic consequences follow, not because she has had premarital sex but because both she and Clement are reacting to their guardian's authoritarian demands. Clement says he "love[s] her more than life" while admitting to his friend that he is meeting Sibella to enjoy a "secret triumph" over Valmont (*Secresy*, I: XII, 83). Artificial economies bind Sibella as well, for the desire to sacrifice herself to make him happy propels her. Here custom enchains sexuality, fueling it with oppression, not liberty.

Charlotte Smith (1749–1806) connects revolutionary and sexual energies via the rhetoric of things. In *Desmond* (1792), as the hero and heroine enter a vast, dark hall, a servant stumbles "over something ... [I]t was one of those caps to travel in of a night, used sometimes in England, but oftener in France; a bullet had pierced it, and it was on one side covered with blood. –"[15] This cap, shot through, bloody, and common in both countries, trenchantly links French and English politics and conjoins both nations' aristocracies, reproving them for their violence against human rights. When Geraldine sees the cap, she associates it with her husband, Verney: "the idea that the murdered body of some unhappy person to whom it belonged, might be concealed in the house, made me shudder as I surveyed it. – Suddenly the supposition that it was, perhaps, Verney himself, occurred to me. – … what horror accompanied that thought! –Involuntarily I caught the hand of Desmond" (*Desmond*, 398). The dutiful wife reaches for the hand of the man she loves while simultaneously envisioning her brutal husband shot through the brain. Shortly thereafter, she declares "that never have I, even in thought, transgressed the bounds of that duty" to Verney (p. 400). And yet, Geraldine has just revealed her passionate attachment to Desmond and her fantasy of Verney's death via a revolutionary cover, a bloody cap. The fantasy also suggests the hope that revolution will adjudicate the rights of both genders, ensuring that women like Geraldine can free themselves from the patriarchal privilege that forces them to internalize their subjugation as fair, as she does in pretending that she does not love Desmond and that her dutiful obedience is just, even though she knows her husband has sold her to another man to pay his gambling debts.

Women writers address the subject of sexual repulsion, communicating this in different lexicons. As in *Desmond*, Wollstonecraft's *Mary: A Fiction*, reveals how sexual life in a forced marriage renders the husband an anonymous monster and sexual union revolting. Mary leaves after the ceremony, and then, much later, when she sees Charles again, she faints. Physical repugnance takes on the vocabulary of illness: every time "her husband would take her hand, or mention any thing like love, she would instantly feel a sickness, a faintness at her heart, and wish, involuntarily, that the earth would open and swallow her" (*Mary*, pp. 147–148). Austen, in contrast, uses the language of dance in *Pride and Prejudice* (1813): heroine Elizabeth Bennet wants to avoid the odious Mr. Collins at the ball, for his mental stupidity is matched by his clumsiness, and in "often moving wrong without being aware of it, [he] gave her all the shame and misery which a disagreeable partner for a couple of dances can give. The moment of her release from him was exstacy."[16] In *Mansfield Park* (1814), when rakish suitor Henry Crawford's gift to heroine Fanny Price, a gold chain, will not "go through the ring of the cross,"[17] we understand that neither could there be a proper or happy fit – in the ternary sense of body, soul, and mind – between them. In the case of two more Austen heroines, *Sense and Sensibility*'s (1811) Marianne Dashwood and *Persuasion*'s (1818) Anne Elliot, both are passionately in love, and both experience a similar antipathy for competing suitors. Given Austen's persuasive portraits of the beauty and power of a woman's mind–body connection to a lover, readers feel pleasure in the marriage between Anne and Captain Wentworth, but doubt the "fitness" of Marianne's union with Colonel Brandon.

A pattern emerges in Romantic-era novels wherein female authors assert liberty as the foundation for sexual commitment, rendering the rhetoric of revolution an apt one for sexuality. Mary Shelley (1797–1851) affirms the relation between civil and sexual liberties in *Valperga* (1823), where Euthanasia's love for Castruccio rises from knowing that they share a faith in independence. She "wished also to read [Castruccio's] mind, to know if the love of liberty lived there," but once she discovers it does not, "the foundations of her very life seemed to give way";[18] later, his perfidy "unveiled at once the idol that had dwelt in the shrine of her heart, shewed the falseness of his apotheosis, and forced her to use her faculties to dislodge him" (*Valperga*, 261). In using her "faculties," she finds independence outside her love for him; she moves from believing that heterosexual love means everything, to grief, to knowing Castruccio's flaws, to an independence that allows her to befriend his former lover, Beatrice. When Euthanasia confronts Castruccio about his treatment of Beatrice, he responds by trying to seduce her: "you do not despise me, you love me, – be mine"; but her passions become her strength: "Never! Tie myself to tyranny, to slavery, to war, to deceit, to hate? I tell thee I am as free as air" (p. 338). In his attitude toward Beatrice, he simply admits that her sexual freedom "was a strange riddle to him. Without vow … without seeking the responsive professions of eternal love, she surrendered herself to his arms" (p. 230). This breed of woman who embodies an innocent sexuality is unknown to him because that category escapes those the era creates for women, which include only the innocently sexless, falsely sexless, or pathologically sexual.

These works incorporate an idiom that links sexual and personal liberation, but they do not advocate promiscuity, or what the twenty-first century would call "casual sex"; instead, a profound intimacy ideally propels sexual connections, though as I have suggested, these were not necessarily conventional. Even Darwin's *Love of the Plants* encourages a kind of polyamory when "Proud GLORIOSA led *three* chosen swains, / The blushing captives of her virgin chains" (lines 119–20). *The Memoirs of Harriette Wilson* offers evidence of unconventionality and of deep attachment insofar as she expresses pleasures that exceed moral dictates limiting sex to marriage, but she also conjoins the sexual and the liberated so as to ensure lasting happiness for herself and for others. Wilson's autobiography asserts that sexual connection should be a woman's choice, declaring to Frederick Lamb, her 'protector,' that is the man who pays for her services, that "I will be the mere instrument of pleasure to no man. He must make a friend and companion of me, or he will lose me."[19] Even after their "contract" is over, Lamb expects her body to be available, going so far as to attempt rape: "desperate" from her resistance, he proceeds from "brutal violence" to attempted murder (*Memoirs*, I: 129). As she recounts this event, she reminds Lamb that "He is … mistaken if he believes I have ever forgotten the agony of that moment" (I: 129). She declares her need for liberty and never again has sex with him – her body helps her remember "that moment" and avoid more violence.

The heroines of normative and non-normative, as well as radical and conservative, texts alike recognize the ways that ideological pressures disfigure women's sexual expression. Still, they strive for a comprehensive love. As Effie Deans says in Sir Walter Scott's (1771–1832) *The Heart of Midlothian* (1818), do you think a "love [such] as mine is lightly forgotten? –Na, na – ye may hew down the tree, but ye canna change its bend."[20] Samuel Solomon called the attraction between those in love a "sacred instinct" that "kindles the ethereal fire" and that "creates in them an idea of felicity not to be … compared to any thing except to heaven itself" (*Guide*, 102). Scott's Effie, like other Romantic-era heroines, longs to experience an intimacy Solomon's treatise describes in sublime terms, something that is more than just physical – something allied with sexual energy, articulated or not: an intermingling of soul, heart, and body.

Wollstonecraft's *Mary: A Fiction* initially expresses this yearning in religious ecstasy – a pantheistic rapture: "Enthusiastic sentiments of devotion at this period actuated [Mary]; her Creator was almost apparent to her senses in his works, but they were mostly the grand or solemn features of Nature which she delighted to contemplate" (*Mary*, 90). On her baptismal morning, "she hailed the morn, and sung with wild delight, Glory to God on high, good will towards men" (p. 91). Her ability to experience spiritual faith in nature provides both precedent and sanction for her ability to feel ecstasy, to derive happiness from inner motivation rather than external pleasures, and to taste unmixed delight, experiencing a union that provides a foundation for the desire she will later feel for Ann and Henry. Indeed, love fits more than just the body, the morals, or the income: it comprehends energy and potency, which trigger a sexuality women can ideally participate in fully.

Those "prettier musings of high-wrought love and eternal constancy" Anne muses on in Austen's *Persuasion* are, however, not only for the heterosexual or conventional.[21] In a (certainly) post-virginal courtship, Harriette Wilson falls in love with Lord Ponsonby, an affection she expresses in both the rhetoric of sexual passion, "our passion continued undiminished – increase it could not" (*Memoirs*, I: 124), and in the language of virtue as she strives to make herself "more worthy of him." Retiring to the country with a "carriage filled with books" (I: 110), she reads Voltaire, Racine, Boswell, Rousseau, and Shakespeare, thereby consummating their love intellectually. Once the relationship ends, her studies offer a model for a consummation more lasting: her writing.

Her "*début* in a tragic part" (I: 149) – losing Ponsonby's love – resembles the abolitionist rhetoric that emphasizes how the slave's ability to love her husband and family proves her humanity; here we see a parallel that verifies the "whore's" humanity. She may be a courtesan, and her witty reportage may sometimes diminish her emotions, but Wilson describes her brain as "absolutely on fire," her feeling of "bitter anguish" when the relationship ends (I: 153); she wants to see him, but thinks of his wife, and asserting the virtue Wollstonecraft expounds in the *Vindication*, Wilson prays for calm, reminding herself that "we are sent into the world to endure the evils of it patiently" (I: 153). She resists suicide: "I have a strong mind ... and I will exert it to consider where I shall look for help and consolation" (I: 154). Here romantic sexuality as an exercise in character emerges, for the lasting effect of losing Ponsonby's love is imprinted on her body in her desire to increase her virtue. She asks him to respect her, to give her his "approbation as a reward for my earnest endeavours to do right." Wanting "to reconcile myself to my God" (I: 160, 161), she channels her emotions into serving others by helping a friend in Newgate imprisoned for debt, and taking in an abandoned girl dying of tuberculosis.

These women writers acknowledged a universal problem but one this era's temperament intensified: how to avoid obsession – a sublime experience – while still employing the rhetoric of sublimity to describe sexual love. Martha Nussbaum writes that Greek notions of Erōs, seen as both "divine gift" and source of "madness and distraction, ... proved notoriously difficult to reconcile":

> the very madness and distraction in the lover that put virtue at risk are among the sources of his generosity to the beloved. The very passion that threatens virtue may also motivate virtuous actions ... [A]t stake in sex is not only one's own self-mastery, but also the well being, happiness, and ethical goodness of another. But if that is so, then one's own ethical goodness is on the line in a double sense. Not only the good of self-mastery, but also the good of being a responsible, decent, kindly social being ... In other words, sex is doubly, and inevitably, ethical.[22]

Likewise, Romantic sexual passion wants to idealize passion and virtue simultaneously. Anne Lister's (1791–1840) private journals show how she tries to achieve this, resisting an obsession that would be destructive both to her and her love, Marianne. Because she wrote her journals in code, Lister could be quite forthright (recording, for example, how many orgasms she experienced); thus she offers a less expurgated version of events than is typical of the era. In her daily encounters she was open about her affections for other women, but she never acknowledged to outsiders her sexual relationships with lovers, though many surmised.

Lister's narratives reveal the suffering she experiences as she yearns for a complete life – marriage – with Marianne, who has wedded for money. In describing her boundary-breaking love, she records the consequences of touching the sublime. After a year's separation, Marianne arranges a meeting with Anne. Lister's rhetorical strategies as she describes the meeting reveal a tangle of excitement, desire, and fear. Hoping to meet her on the road, having swallowed only "a draught of water & tak[en] 3 small biscuits,"[23] Anne sets off on foot, but "turn[s] back," worried that a coat she left behind won't be safe at a "2nd rate inn." Starting again, she realizes that her route might be wrong, so she "retraces" her steps, losing more time.

Although these events arise from her anxious but exhilarated state, they also recall the many "retracings" and "turnings back" she has already experienced in the unsteady relationship with her lover. Her emphasis on details of distance and route signifies her need to constrain her eager physicality/sexuality: she lists the milestones, and the distance of each from various villages. When she looks over the landscape she sees a "dreary mountain moor-scene," an artful insertion that foretells the coming catastrophe, but which also ties the scene to her own sublime emotions. Then her "wildness" returns, revealed when she spies the carriage and feels "a nameless thrill that banished every thought but of M – , & every feeling but of fearful hope" (*I Know*, 301). Having expressed that anxious optimism, she seems again to need to gain control through measurement, noting that "it was just 11:50 as I reached the carriage, having walked about 10 & ½ miles in 3 hours, 10 minutes, i.e. at the rate of a mile in 18 minutes." Her narrative records both the awe she felt upon seeing Marianne and the horror her lover and her servants experience upon seeing *her* passion: "unconscious of any sensation but pleasure at the sight of M – ... the astonished, staring eyes of the man & maid behind & of the post-boys ... were lost to me &, in too hastily taking each step of the carriage & stretching over the pile of dressing-boxes, etc. ... I unluckily seemed to M – to have taken 3 steps at once" (p. 301). She expresses some pride about her ability to arouse the sublime in others, but this is a pose she adopts to deal with Marianne's *"horror-struck"* reaction to her manic speech and her appearance, discomposed by her ten-mile walk (p. 301).

Reversing Elizabeth's arrival at Netherfield, in *Pride and Prejudice*, no pleased "Darcy" greets Lister, but rather a displeased lover: like Austen's Caroline Bingley, Marianne condemns Lister's passion, seeing physical activity as a sign of excessive sexual fervor. As Anne Lister repeats to herself Marianne's criticisms, she puts them in italics, which underscores the shock: "*Why did I come so far? Why walk? Why not come in the gig?*" No longer feeling pleased with performing Byronically, "petrify[ing] people," she submits to the sublime: "*I scarce knew what my feelings were. They were in tumult. 'Shame, shame,' said I to myself, 'to be so overcome.' I talked as well as I could. Yet it was evident, as M – said, that I was not right*" (pp. 302, 301, 302). Her journal works to frame and contain her emotion and sexuality via measurement and performance, a rhetorical strategy she tries to duplicate at the level of action: "*by the time we had reached King Cross I felt myself more easily under my own control* ... We were now all quite right & merry. Alas! I had not forgotten. The heart has a memory of its own, but I had ceased to appear to remember save in occasional joking allusions to '<u>the three steps</u>'" (p. 303). Her body knows the truth, though her actions might convince others, for she experiences a headache, nausea, and disassociation. She tries to joke about why she spends fifteen minutes retying her handkerchief, saying "it was the shock of 'the three steps'" (p. 303), but her threefold repetition of the "three steps" stands in poignantly for the terrible threesome she forms with Marianne and her husband as well as the threesome comprising Marianne, social convention, and herself.

Maria Edgeworth's (1768–1849) *Belinda* (1801) brings sexual transgression to light in order to educate readers that "proper" sexuality, as expressed in a traditional marriage, might ensure personal happiness, liberty, and social stability, and to show how marriages of alliance and aristocratic excess open the gate for "perverse" impulses. Though Harriet Freke may be a lesbian, a bisexual, both, or just a cross-dresser, we never see her express same-sex desire, except insofar as she deploys it through a will to power, capitalizing on the sexual chaos that emerges when heterosexual bonds deteriorate. The novel's desire to posit married heterosexual love as foundational for a functioning society arises from its critique of non-companionate marriage: when standards for wedded "bliss" are debased, society allegedly becomes degraded. Lady Delacour can forgive Harriet for remaining hypocritically loyal to her spouse, but not for abandoning her devotion to Lady Delacour herself: she understands that Freke "gives up her friend ... to make her peace with her husband ... Well! that I could have pardoned, if she had not been so base as to go over to Mrs. Luttridge."[24] Harriet seduces Lady Delacour, but her machinations end not in actual sex, but in enough apparent proof to destroy her friend's reputation. Even so, Lady Delacour never "reproached her" for "frighten[ing] [me] into fighting that duel with Mrs. Luttridge." Her friendship with Mrs. Freke, she says, has "cost me my peace of mind – my health – my life" (*Belinda*, 65). And yet it is *not* the loss of her life – or even her reputation – but the loss of her friend that makes Lady

Delacour cry out that Harriet "has no heart! She has no feeling for any living creature but herself" (p. 66). Such narcissism violates the sacred quest for a physical love the Romantics sometimes idealized.

Harriet's going "over to Mrs. Luttridge" reveals the triangulated desire forming the basis of the women's friendship. Mock-heroic battles (duels and cross-dressing) are fought over who gains possession of Harriet; love and possession have become one. The novel shuts down same-sex desire, implying that it leads to social degeneration; however, if not fulfilled, these desires evidently *will* be manifested, and in Lady Delacour's love for Harriet (transferred to Belinda) we infer the possibility. The novel diminishes same-sex love by illustrating it as mere displacement of heterosexual bonds into same-sex connections. Perhaps, more positively, it indicates that disarticulating sexual love from genuine affection and commitment trumps sexual heterodoxy.

These novels suggest that loneliness and isolation in unhappy marriages such as the Delacours' can lead to passionate obsession for one person, an idea that Austen parodies in her juvenilia. Her stories reveal the insanity of fixating on the "one," and the tyranny in having little or no choice in marriage: in "Jack and Alice," all the women vie for Charles Adams, whose heart is "cold and indifferent," except to the wealthy Lady Williams, leaving Alice with only one outlet – drink.[25] In a more serious register, Shelley dramatizes in *Valperga* how love led both Beatrice and Euthanasia to exalt Castruccio, a love that so separates both of them from larger social networks that they stand to lose their sense of self. In "placing him apart and selecting him from his fellows, [they] look on him as superior in nature to all others." In "the entrancing dream of love," Shelley philosophizes, "even as we idolize the object ... do we idolize ourselves: if we separate him from his fellow mortals, so do we separate ourselves" (*Valperga*, 231). In defining this singular love, Shelley demonstrates its adverse impact on identity rather than either idealizing or condemning it as merely carnal.

The problem is not sexuality, these texts argue, but passion without an outlet, sequestered passion felt but socially repressed. A scene repeats itself throughout the era: a woman falls in love with the subject of a portrait. Hays's Emma Courtney becomes fixated on a painting of Harley, "till, I fancied, I read in the features all the qualities imputed to the original by a tender and partial parent. Cut off from the society of mankind ... all the strong affections of my soul seemed concentrated to a single point" (*Memoirs*, 59). In these works, the sublime desire for the "one," still popular as a romantic ideal, is idealized, but also, paradoxically, identified as a symptom of larger social inequities that force women into social and political quarantine, rendering them ripe for erotic obsession. As Emma asserts, "[t]he social propensities of a mind forbidden to expand itself, forced back, pre[y] incessantly upon that mind, secretly consuming its powers" (p. 134). Social mores that isolate women must take some responsibility for obsessive passion.

These Romantic writers take chances with the public by writing about sexuality and daring to assert that women are not psychically or biologically "passionless," but neither are they excessively sexual by nature. They express an act of faith in society, literature, and science in hoping that their work could alter public opinion. Sometimes that gamble ends disastrously, given that politics and sexuality are inextricable. For example, when the renowned Catharine Macaulay (1731–91), at age forty-seven, married William Graham, aged twenty-one, it shook the foundations of her reputation as an eminent historian. When Anna Letitia Barbauld (1743–1825) published *Eighteen Hundred and Eleven* (1812), Southey condemned her for "dash[ing] down her shagreen spectacles and her knitting needles" to "sav[e] a sinking country."[26] Biographies and reviews of women who wrote about politics or sexuality, however well intended, tended to shut down the liberty necessary for sexual happiness.

As Hays wrote in her biography of Charlotte Smith, female authors are "arraigned, not merely as writers, but as *women*, their characters, their conduct, even their personal endowments become the subjects of severe inquisition: from the common allowances claimed by the species, literary women appear only to be exempted."[27] Given that women are vulnerable, as Hays says, "to the curiosity of the idle and the envy of the malicious," it has been a particular blow that such an "inquisition" arose after the publication of William Godwin's (1756–1836) *Memoirs of the Author of 'A Vindication of the Rights of Woman'* (1798), a recklessly optimistic display of honesty that exposed secrets his wife, Mary Wollstonecraft, would surely have kept from such an unsympathetic public. Godwin engages the topics this essay has addressed: woman and her sexualities – transcendent, nurtured and fostered by liberty, ripened in the natural world, and connected to friendship and community. When he published her secrets, though, he unleashed the condemnation that the novelists fought against. The right-wing press gloried in the gore and even the most liberal shuddered at the details of her love for Henry Fuseli and Gilbert Imlay; at Fanny, her illegitimate daughter with Imlay; and at her rejection of religious and civil law in two suicide attempts.

At the opposite end of this spectrum is the effect Austen's family had in their sanitizing biographies of her, published after her death, a legacy that continues to influence interpretations of her novels. The desire to rewrite and thus possess Austen seems as ubiquitous as the desire to dispossess Mary

Wollstonecraft. Harriette Wilson's *Memoirs*, also in the truth-telling business, illuminates open secrets by placing responsibility on those culpable, though she, like Wollstonecraft and other women writers, becomes the target of social injustice. Exposing how aristocracy works (it violates others while itself remaining inviolate), Wilson also unveils the networks of intimacy between men – so many sharing the same woman – an intimacy recreated in a public forum when they read about their own sexual lives. The "impact of the *Memoirs* was colossal. Nothing since compares with it; Profumo is a mere hiccup in comparison."[28] Whether the book, as Wilson's editor Thomas Little proclaimed in 1825, "produce[d] the greatest moral effect on the present and future generations" is debatable, but in baring British vice, it terrified and challenged prominent men.

In his Postscript to her *Memoirs*, Wilson's editor says she "drag[s] forth [another] monster from his most secret recesses" (*Memoirs*, II: 681) in the shape of Thomas Barnes, editor of the *New Times*, who attacks her writing; in doing so, she "drags" out another ghoul – the ideology that decrees that women are naturally innocent beings vulnerable to the "pollution" of sexual knowledge: Barnes calls "most earnestly ... on our fair countrywomen not to suffer such pollution [as] to approach" the *Memoirs* (II: 683). Wilson shrewdly points out that such bidding acts as a stimulant: "there were, no doubt, thousands of young ladies who had neither read [the *Memoirs*], nor dreamt of reading it, when this paragraph of the kind and judicious editor, like the apple upon Eve, so worked upon their imagination and excited their curiosity" (II: 682).

The subject of sexualities and Romantic women's writing resists a unifying argument. As I have shown in this essay, multiple plurals challenge us – women, sexualities, writing. Not one of these categories signifies a singular or stable object of study. Although women share the same gender, how they view their relationship to that gender, and how that relationship expresses itself sexually, and how those complex relations find form in writing from the most private to the most public, challenges our understanding. This topic also plays out against the ways in which women's sexualities were subject to the most rigid kinds of essentializing. Such long-held and entrenched ideas have unduly influenced our interpretations of women writers, their work, and their era. I have argued, instead, that writers often venerated, and even idealized, sexuality as an intellectual and spiritual love that sanctioned physicality as something inherently sacred; that they represented the elevation of the body itself as blessed in the exchange of sexual love; and that they characterized physical desire and attraction for the beloved as a necessary aspect of a sexual romantic partnership, even if unconsummated. In consecrating sexuality in this way, passion and power become allies.

NOTES

1 Mary Hays, *Memoirs of Emma Courtney*, ed. Eleanor Ty (Oxford University Press, 1996), p. 99. Subsequent references cited parenthetically in the text.

2 Roy Porter, "Literature of Sexual Advice before 1800," in *Sexual Knowledge, Sexual Science: The History of Attitudes to Sexuality*, ed. Roy Porter and Mikulas Teich (Cambridge University Press, 1994), p. 137.

3 This alludes to the title of Katherine Binhammer's article, "The Sex Panic of the 1790s," *Journal of the History of Sexuality* 6:3 (1996): 409–434.

4 John Bowles, *Reflections on the Political and Moral State of Society, at the Close of the Eighteenth Century* (London: F. and C. Rivington, 1800), p. 135.

5 Samuel Solomon, *A Guide to Health, or Advice to Both Sexes in a Variety of Complaints: With an Essay on the Venereal Disease, Gleets, Seminal Weakness; and that Destructive Habit Called Onanism; Likewise, an Address to Parents, Tutors, and Guardians of Youth*, 9th edn. (London, [1796?]), pp. 101, 102. Subsequent references cited parenthetically in the text.

6 Samuel Auguste David Tissot, *Three Essays: First, on the Disorders of People of Fashion. Second on Diseases Incidental to Literary and Sedentary Persons, with Proper Rules for Preventing their Fatal Consequences, and Instructions for their Cure. Third, on Onanism, or A Treatise upon the Disorders Produced by Masturbation, or The Effects of Secret and Excessive Venery* (Dublin, 1772), p. 73.

7 *Aristotle's Compleat Master-Piece, in Three Parts, Displaying the Secrets of Nature in the Generation of Man*, 31st edn. (London: The Booksellers, 1776), pp. 24, 17.

8 William Gilpin, *Three Essays: On Picturesque Beauty; On Picturesque Travel; and On Sketching Landscape: To which is Added a Poem, on Landscape Painting* (London, 1792), pp. 41, 44.

9 Erasmus Darwin, *The Botanical Garden, Part II: Containing The Loves of the Plants: A Poem: With Philosophical Notes*, Vol. II, 2nd edn. (London: J. Johnson, 1790), lines 19–20, 280. Subsequent references cited parenthetically in the text.

10 Fanny Burney, *Evelina* (Oxford University Press, 1982), p. 195.

11 Marcus Wood, "John Gabriel Stedman, William Blake, Francesco Bartolozzi and Empathetic Pornography in the *Narrative of a Five-Years' Expedition Against the Revolted Negroes in Surinam*," in *An Economy of Colour: Visual Culture and the Atlantic world, 1660–1830*, ed. Geoff Quilley and Kay Dian Kriz (Manchester University Press, 2003), p. 140.

12 Mary Wollstonecraft, *Mary: A Fiction and The Wrongs of Woman, or Maria*, ed. Michelle Faubert (Peterborough, Ontario: Broadview Press, 2012), p. 88. Subsequent references cited parenthetically in the text.

13 Mary Wollstonecraft, *A Vindication of the Rights of Woman and The Wrongs of Woman, or Maria*, ed. Anne K. Mellor and Noelle Chao (New York: Longman Cultural Edition, 2007), p. 63; Jane Austen, *Northanger Abbey*, ed. Barbara M. Benedict and Deirdre Le Faye, *The Cambridge Edition of the Works of Jane Austen* (Cambridge University Press, 2006), pp. 6–7.

14 Eliza Fenwick, *Secresy, or The Ruin on the Rock* (London: Pandora, 1989), p. I:III, 16. Subsequent references cited parenthetically in the text.

15 Charlotte Smith, *Desmond*, ed. Antje Blank and Janet Todd (Peterborough, Ontario: Broadview Press, 2001), p. 396. Subsequent references cited parenthetically in the text.

16 Jane Austen, *Pride and Prejudice*, ed. Pat Rogers, *The Cambridge Edition of the Works of Jane Austen* (Cambridge University Press, 2006), p. 101. (Vol. 1, Ch. 18). Subsequent references cited parenthetically in the text.

17 Jane Austen, *Mansfield Park*, ed. John Wiltshire, *The Cambridge Edition of the Works of Jane Austen* (Cambridge University Press, 2005), p. 314 (Vol. 2, Ch. 9).

18 Mary Shelley, *Valperga, or The Life and Adventures of Castruccio, Prince of Lucca*, ed. Tilottama Rajan (Peterborough, Ontario: Broadview Press, 1998), pp. 142, 250. Subsequent references cited parenthetically in the text.

19 Harriette Wilson, *Harriette Wilson's Memoirs* (London: The Folio Society, 1964), Vol. I, p. 33. Subsequent references cited parenthetically in the text.

20 Walter Scott, *The Heart of Midlothian* (New York: Holt, Rinehart and Winston, 1969), p. 219.

21 Jane Austen, *Persuasion*, ed. Janet M. Todd and Antje Blank, *The Cambridge Edition of the Works of Jane Austen* (Cambridge University Press, 2006), p. 208 (Vol. 2, Ch. 9).

22 Martha Nussbaum, "*Erōs* and Ethical Norms," in *The Sleep of Reason: Erotic Experience and Sexual Ethics in Ancient Greece and Rome,* ed. Martha C. Nussbaum and Juha Sihvola (University of Chicago Press, 2002), pp. 56, 58.

23 Anne Lister, *I Know My Own Heart: The Diaries of Anne Lister (1791–1840),* ed. Helena Whitbread (London: Virago, 2012), p. 300. Subsequent references cited parenthetically in the text.

24 Maria Edgeworth, *Belinda*, ed. Kathryn J. Kirkpatrick (Oxford University Press, 1994), p. 66. Subsequent references cited parenthetically in the text.

25 Jane Austen, "Jack and Alice," in *Juvenilia*, ed. Peter Sabor, *The Cambridge Edition of the Works of Jane Austen* (Cambridge University Press, 2006), p. 17.

26 Grace A. Ellis, *A Memoir of Mrs. Anna Laetitia Barbauld, with Many of Her Letters* (Boston: James R. Osgood and Co., 1874), p. 272.

27 Mary Hays, "Mrs Charlotte Smith," in *Public Characters of 1800–1801* (London, 1801), p. 60.

28 Rosemary Hill, "I am the Thing Itself," review of Harriette Wilson's *Memoirs,* ed. Lesley Blanch and *The Courtesan's Revenge: Harriette Wilson, the Woman who Blackmailed the King* by Frances Wilson, *London Review of Books,* 25:18 (September 25, 2003), pp. 19–20.

GUIDE TO FURTHER READING

Poetry

Backscheider, Paula R., *Eighteenth-Century Women Poets and their Poetry: Inventing Agency, Inventing Genre*, Baltimore, Johns Hopkins University Press, 2005

Bainbridge, Simon, *British Poetry and the Revolutionary and Napoleonic Wars*, Oxford University Press, 2003

Behrendt, Stephen C., *British Women Poets and the Romantic Writing Community*, Baltimore, Johns Hopkins University Press, 2009

Behrendt, Stephen C., and Harriet Kramer Linkin (eds.), *Romanticism and Women Poets: Opening the Doors of Reception*, Lexington, University Press of Kentucky, 1999

Bennett, Betty T. (ed.), *British War Poetry in the Age of Romanticism 1793–1815*. www.rc.umd.edu/editions/warpoetry/index.html

Bradshaw, Penny, "Dystopian Futures: Time-Travel and Millenarian Visions in the Poetry of Anna Barbauld and Charlotte Smith," *Romanticism on the Net* 21 (2001)

Curran, Stuart, "Romantic Poetry: The I Altered," in *Romanticism and Feminism*, Anne K. Mellor (ed.), Bloomington, Indiana University Press, 1988, 185–207

Dyce, Rev. A. *Specimens of British Poetesses: Selected and Chronologically Arranged by the Rev. Alexander Dyce*, London, T. Rodd and S. Prowett, 1825

Fay, Elizabeth A. *A Feminist Introduction to Romanticism*, Oxford, Blackwell, 1998

Feldman, Paula R. (ed.), *British Women Poets of the Romantic Era: An Anthology*, Baltimore, Johns Hopkins University Press, 1997

Jackson, J. R. de J. *Romantic Poetry by Women: A Bibliography 1770–1835*, Oxford, Clarendon, 1993

Knowles, Claire, *Sensibility and Female Poetic Tradition, 1780–1860: The Legacy of Charlotte Smith*, Aldershot, Ashgate, 2009

Mellor, Anne K., *Romanticism and Gender*, New York, Routledge, 1993

Price, Fiona, *Revolutions in Taste, 1773–1818: Women Writers and the Aesthetics of Romanticism*, Aldershot, Ashgate, 2009

Ross, Marlon, *The Contours of Masculine Desire: Romanticism and the Rise of Women's Poetry*, Oxford University Press, 1989

Shattock, Joanne (ed.), *The Cambridge Bibliography of English Literature, Volume 4: 1800–1900*, 3rd edn., Cambridge University Press, 1999

Waters, Mary, *British Women Writers and the Profession of Literary Criticism, 1789–1832*, Basingstoke, Palgrave Macmillan, 2004

Wu, Duncan, *Romantic Women Poets: An Anthology*, Oxford, Blackwell, 1997

Fiction

Batchelor, Jennie, *Women's Work: Labour, Gender, Authorship, 1750–1830*, Manchester University Press, 2010

Blakey, Dorothy, *The Minerva Press, 1790–1820*, London, The Bibliographical Society, 1935

Butler, Marilyn, *Jane Austen and the War of Ideas*, new edn., Oxford, Clarendon, 1988

Cambridge Orlando: Women's Writing in the British Isles from the Beginnings to the Present, Susan Brown, Patricia Clements, and Isobel Grundy (eds.), Cambridge University Press, 2006–15, http://orlando.cambridge.org

Chandler, James (ed.), *The Cambridge History of English Romantic Literature*, Cambridge University Press, 2009

Feather, John, *A History of British Publishing*, 2nd edn., London, Routledge, 2005

Fergus, Jan, *Provincial Readers in Eighteenth-Century England*, Oxford University Press, 2006

Gallagher, Catherine, *Nobody's Story: The Vanishing Acts of Women Writers in the Marketplace 1670–1820*, Oxford, Clarendon, 1994

Garside, Peter, "Walter Scott and the 'Common' Novel, 1808–19," *Cardiff Corvey: Reading the Romantic Text* 3 (Sept. 1999). www.romtext.org.uk/articles/cc03_n02

Garside, Peter, and Karen O'Brien (eds.), *The Oxford History of the Novel in English, Volume 2: 1750–1820*, Oxford University Press, 2015

Garside, Peter, Jacqueline Belanger, and Sharon Ragaz, *British Fiction, 1800–1829: A Database of Production, Circulation & Reception*, designed by Anthony Mandal, Cardiff University, 2004. www.british-fiction.cf.ac.uk

Garside, Peter, James Raven, and Rainer Schöwerling (eds.), *The English Novel, 1770–1829: A Bibliographical Survey of Prose Fiction Published in the British Isles*, 2 vols., Oxford University Press, 2000

Kelly, Gary, *English Fiction of the Romantic Period 1789–1830*, London, Longman, 1989

Lynch, Deidre Shauna, *The Economy of Character: Novels, Market Culture, and the Business of Inner Meaning*, University of Chicago Press, 1998

Mandal, Anthony, *Jane Austen and the Popular Novel: The Determined Author*, Basingstoke, Palgrave Macmillan, 2007

Maxwell, Richard, and Katie Trumpener (eds.), *The Cambridge Companion to Fiction in the Romantic Period*, Cambridge University Press, 2008

Pearson, Jacqueline, *Women's Reading in Britain 1750–1830: A Dangerous Recreation*, Cambridge University Press, 1999

Schofield, Mary Anne, and Cecilia Macheski (eds.), *"Fetter'd or Free?" British Women Novelists, 1670–1815*, Athens, Ohio University Press, 1986

Shattock, Joanne (ed.), *The Cambridge Bibliography of English Literature, Volume 4: 1800–1900*, 3rd edn., Cambridge University Press, 1999

Spencer, Jane, *The Rise of the Woman Novelist: From Aphra Behn to Jane Austen*, Oxford, Basil Blackwell, 1986

St. Clair, William, *The Reading Nation in the Romantic Period*, Cambridge University Press, 2004

Tompkins, J. M. S., *The Popular Novel in England, 1770–1800*, London, Constable, 1932

Turner, Cheryl, *Living by the Pen: Women Writers in the Eighteenth Century*, London, Routledge, 1994

Wiltshire, John, *Recreating Jane Austen*, Cambridge University Press, 2001

Drama

Bolton, Betsy, *Women, Nationalism, and the Romantic Stage: Theatre and Politics in Britain, 1780–1800*, Cambridge University Press, 2001

Burroughs, Catherine B., *Closet Stages: Joanna Baillie and the Theater Theory of British Romantic Women Writers*, Philadelphia, University of Pennsylvania Press, 1997

(ed.), *Women in British Romantic Theatre: Drama, Performance, and Society, 1790–1840*, Cambridge University Press, 2000

Burwick, Frederick, *Playing to the Crowd: London Popular Theatre, 1780–1830*, Basingstoke, Palgrave Macmillan, 2011

Bush-Bailey, Gilli, *Performing Herself: Autobiography & Fanny Kelley's "Dramatic Recollections,"* Manchester University Press, 2011

Crisafulli, Lilla Maria, and Keir Elam (eds.), *Women's Romantic Theatre and Drama: History, Agency, and Performativity*, Aldershot, Ashgate, 2010

Crochunis, Thomas C. (ed.), *Joanna Baillie, Romantic Dramatist: Critical Essays*, New York, Routledge, 2004

Crochunis, Thomas C., and Michael Eberle-Sinatra (eds.), *British Women Playwrights around 1800*. www.etang.umontreal.ca/bwp1800

Donkin, Ellen, *Getting into the Act: Women Playwrights in London, 1776–1829*, New York, Routledge, 1995

Engel, Laura (ed.), *"The Public's Open to Us All": Essays on Women and Performance in Eighteenth-Century England*, Cambridge Scholars, 2009

Mann, Susan Garland, and Camille Garnier, *Women Playwrights in England, Ireland, and Scotland, 1660–1823*, David D. Mann (ed.), Bloomington, Indiana University Press, 1996

Moody, Jane, *Illegitimate Theatre in London, 1770–1840*, Cambridge University Press, 2000

Moody, Jane, and O'Quinn, Daniel (eds.), *The Cambridge Companion to British Theatre, 1730–1830*, Cambridge University Press, 2007

Nelson, Bonnie, and Catherine Burroughs (eds.), *Teaching British Women Playwrights of the Restoration and Eighteenth Century*, New York, Modern Language Association of America, 2010

Shattock, Joanne (ed.), *The Cambridge Bibliography of English Literature, Volume 4: 1800–1900*, 3rd edn., Cambridge University Press, 1999

Essays and political writing

Abelove, Henry, Michèle Aina Barale, and David M. Halperin, *The Lesbian and Gay Studies Reader*, New York, Routledge, 1993

Badowska, Ewa, "The Anorexic Body of Liberal Feminism: Mary Wollstonecraft's *A Vindication of the Rights of Woman*," *Tulsa Studies in Women's Literature* 17:2 (1998): 283–303

Demers, Patricia, *The World of Hannah More*, Lexington, University of Kentucky Press, 1996

Eckroth, Stephanie, and Hawkins, Ann R. (eds.), *Romantic Women Writers Reviewed*, 9 vols., London, Pickering & Chatto, 2012

Elias, Norbert, *The Civilizing Process: The History of Manners*, trans. Edmund Jephcott, London, Urizen, 1978

Elliott, Dorice, " 'The Care of the Poor is Her Profession': Hannah More and Women's Philanthropic Work," *Nineteenth-Century Contexts* 19 (1995): 179–204

Johnson, Claudia L. (ed.), *The Cambridge Companion to Mary Wollstonecraft*, Cambridge University Press, 2002

Luria, Gina, *Mary Hays (1759–1843): The Growth of a Woman's Mind*, London, Ashgate, 2006

McCarthy, William, *Anna Letitia Barbauld: Voice of the Enlightenment*, Baltimore, Johns Hopkins University Press, 2008

Mellor, Anne K., *Mothers of the Nation: Women's Political Writing in England, 1780–1830*, Bloomington, Indiana University Press, 2000

Romanticism and Gender, New York, Routledge, 1993

Pascoe, Judith, *Romantic Theatricality: Gender, Poetry, and Spectatorship*, Ithaca, Cornell University Press, 1997

Sapiro, Virginia, *A Vindication of Political Virtue: The Political Theory of Mary Wollstonecraft*, University of Chicago Press, 1992

Silver, Anna Krugovoy, *Victorian Literature and the Anorexic Body*, Cambridge University Press, 2002

Stott, Anne, *Hannah More: The First Victorian*, Oxford University Press, 2003

Taylor, Barbara, *Mary Wollstonecraft and the Feminist Imagination*, Cambridge University Press, 2003

Wolfson, Susan, "The Poets' 'Wolstonecraft,' " *Romantic Interactions*, Baltimore, Johns Hopkins University Press, 2010

The Gothic

Chaplin, Sue, *Law, Sensibility and the Sublime in Eighteenth-Century Women's Fiction: Speaking of Dread*, Aldershot, Ashgate, 2004

Clery, E. J., *The Rise of Supernatural Fiction, 1762–1800*, Cambridge University Press, 1995

Women's Gothic: From Clara Reeve to Mary Shelley, Tavistock, Northcote House, 2000

Craciun, Adriana, *Fatal Women of Romanticism*, Cambridge University Press, 2003

Ellis, Kate Ferguson, *The Contested Castle: Gothic Novels and the Subversion of Domestic Ideology*, Urbana, University of Illinois Press, 1989

Gamer, Michael, *Romanticism and the Gothic: Genre, Reception, and Canon Formation*, Cambridge University Press, 2000

Hoeveler, Diane Long, *Gothic Feminism: The Professionalization of Gender from Charlotte Smith to the Brontës*, Liverpool University Press, 1998

Lynch, Deidre, "Gothic Libraries and National Subjects," *Studies in Romanticism* 40:1 (2001): 29–48
Miles, Robert, *Ann Radcliffe: The Great Enchantress*, Manchester University Press, 1995
Smith, Andrew, and Diana Wallace (eds.), "Female Gothic," *Special issue of Gothic Studies* 6:1 (2004)
  (eds.), *The Female Gothic: New Directions*, Basingstoke, Palgrave Macmillan, 2009
Townshend, Dale, and Angela Wright (eds.), *Ann Radcliffe, Romanticism and the Gothic*, Cambridge University Press, 2014
Williams, Anne, *Art of Darkness: A Poetics of Gothic*, University of Chicago Press, 1995
Wright, Angela, *Britain, France and the Gothic, 1764–1820: The Import of Terror*, Cambridge University Press, 2013

Travel writing

Amoia, Alba, and Bettina L. Knapp (eds.), *Great Women Travel Writers: From 1750 to the Present*, London, Continuum, 2005
Bohls, Elizabeth A., *Women Travel Writers and the Language of Aesthetics, 1716–1818*, Cambridge University Press, 1995
Buzard, James, *The Beaten Track: European Tourism, Literature and the Ways to "Culture," 1800–1918*, Oxford University Press, 1993
Campbell, Mary B., *The Witness and the Other World: Exotic European Travel Writing 400–1600*, Ithaca, Cornell University Press, 1988
Chard, Chloe, *Pleasure and Guilt on the Grand Tour: Travel Writing and Imaginative Geography, 1600–1830*, Manchester University Press, 1999
Dolan, Brian, *Ladies of the Grand Tour: British Women in Pursuit of Enlightenment and Adventure in Eighteenth-Century Europe*, New York, Harper Collins, 2001
Fay, Elizabeth A., *Fashioning Faces: The Portraitive Mode in British Romanticism*, Lebanon, NH, University Press of New England, 2010
  A Feminist Introduction to Romanticism, Oxford, Blackwell Publishers, 1998
Gilroy, Amanda (ed.), *Romantic Geographies: Discourses of Travel, 1775–1844*, Manchester University Press, 2000
Hooper, Glenn (ed.), *The Tourist's Gaze: Travellers to Ireland, 1800–2000*, Cork University Press, 2001
Kelly, Gary, *Women, Writing, and Revolution, 1790–1827*, Oxford University Press, 1993
Korte, Barbara, *English Travel Writing from Pilgrimages to Postcolonial Explorations*, trans. by Catherine Matthias, Basingstoke, Palgrave Macmillan, 2000
Melman, Billie, *Women's Orients: English Women and the Middle East, 1718–1918*, Ann Arbor, University of Michigan Press, 1992
Morrison, Lucy (ed.), *Women's Travel Writings in Post-Napoleonic France*, London, Pickering & Chatto, 2011
Moskal, Jeanne, "Politics and the Occupation of a Nurse in Mariana Starke's *Letters from Italy*," in *Romantic Geographies: Discourses of Travel, 1775–1844*, Amanda Gilroy (ed.), Manchester University Press, 2000, 150–64
Pratt, Mary Louise, *Imperial Eyes: Travel Writing and Transculturation*, London, Routledge, 1992

Robinson, Jane, *Wayward Women: A Guide to Women Travellers*, Oxford University Press, 1994

Siegel, Kristi, *Issues in Travel Writing: Empire, Spectacle, and Displacement*, New York, Peter Lang, 2002

Smethurst, Paul, and Julia Kuehn (eds.), *Travel Writing, Form, and Empire: The Poetics and Politics of Mobility*, London, Routledge, 2009

Teltscher, Kate, *India Inscribed: European and British Writing on India, 1600–1800*, Oxford University Press, 1995

Walchester, Kathryn, *Our Own Fair Italy: Nineteenth Century Women's Travel Writing and Italy 1800–44*, Bern, Germany, Peter Lang, 2007

History writing and antiquarianism

Bann, Stephen, *Romanticism and the Rise of History*, New York, Twayne, 1995

Ferris, Ina, *The Achievement of Literary Authority: Gender, History, and the Waverley Novels*, Ithaca, Cornell University Press, 1991

Goode, Mike, *Sentimental Masculinity and the Rise of History, 1790–1890*, Cambridge University Press, 2009

Hill, Bridget, *The Republican Virago: The Life and Times of Catharine Macaulay Historian*, Oxford University Press, 1992

Kasmer, Lisa, *Novel Histories: British Women Writing History, 1760–1830*, Madison, NJ, Farleigh Dickinson University Press, 2012

Kucich, Greg, "Romanticism and Feminist Historiography," *The Wordsworth Circle* 24 (1993): 133–40

Looser, Devoney, *British Women Writers and the Writing of History, 1670–1820*, Baltimore, Johns Hopkins University Press, 2005

Mellor, Anne K., *Mothers of the Nation: Women's Political Writing in England, 1780–1830*, Bloomington, Indiana University Press, 2000

O'Brien, Karen, *Narratives of Enlightenment: Cosmopolitan History from Voltaire to Gibbon*, Cambridge University Press, 1997

Phillips, Mark Salber, *Society and Sentiment: Genres of Historical Writing in Britain, 1740–1820*, Princeton University Press, 2000

Scott, Joan Wallach, *Gender and the Politics of History*, New York, Columbia University Press, 1988

Slagle, Judith, *Romantic Appropriations of History: The Legends of Joanna Baillie and Margaret Holford Hodson*, Madison, NJ, Farleigh Dickinson University Press, 2012

Woolf, D. R., *The Social Circulation of the Past: English Historical Culture, 1500–1730*, Oxford University Press, 2003

Writing in wartime

Bainbridge, Simon, *British Poetry and the Revolutionary and Napoleonic Wars*, Oxford University Press, 2003

Behrendt, Stephen C., *British Women Poets and the Romantic Writing Community*, Baltimore, Johns Hopkins University Press, 2009

Bennett, Betty T. (ed.), *British War Poetry in the Age of Romanticism 1793–1815.*
www.rc.umd.edu/editions/warpoetry/index.html

Brewer, John, *Sinews of Power: War, Money and the English State*, Cambridge, Harvard University Press, 1988

Craciun, Adriana, *British Women Writers and the French Revolution: Citizens of the World*, Basingstoke, Palgrave Macmillan, 2005

Craciun, Adriana, and Kari E. Lokke (eds.), *Rebellious Hearts: British Women Writers and the French Revolution*, Albany, State University of New York Press, 2001

Favret, Mary, *War at a Distance: Romanticism and the Making of Modern Wartime*, Princeton University Press, 2009

Guest, Harriet, *Small Change: Women, Learning, Patriotism 1750–1810*, University of Chicago Press, 2000

Hagemann, Karen, Gisela Mettele, and Jane Rendall (eds.), *Gender, War and Politics: Transatlantic Perspectives, 1775–1830*, Basingstoke, Palgrave Macmillan, 2010

Kelly, Gary, *Women, Writing, and Revolution 1790–1827*, Oxford, Clarendon, 1993

Shaw, Philip (ed.), *Romantic Wars: Studies in Culture and Conflict, 1793–1822*, Aldershot, Ashgate, 2000

Winn, James Anderson, *The Poetry of War*, Cambridge University Press, 2008

Enlightenment feminism and the bluestocking legacy

Backscheider, Paula R. (ed.), *Revising Women: Eighteenth-Century "Women's Fiction" and Social Engagement*, Baltimore, Johns Hopkins University Press, 2000

Chaplin, Sue, *Law, Sensibility and the Sublime in Eighteenth-Century Women's Fiction: Speaking of Dread*, Aldershot, Ashgate, 2004

Clarke, Norma, *The Rise and Fall of the Woman of Letters*, London, Pimlico, 2004

Clery, E. J., *The Feminization Debate in Eighteenth-Century Britain: Literature, Commerce and Luxury*, Basingstoke, Palgrave Macmillan, 2004

Eger, Elizabeth, *Bluestockings: Women of Reason from Enlightenment to Romanticism*, Basingstoke, Palgrave Macmillan, 2010

Franklin, Caroline, *The Female Romantics: Nineteenth-Century Women Novelists and Byronism*, New York, Routledge, 2013

Gleadle, Kathryn, *The Early Feminists: Radical Unitarians and the Emergence of the Women's Rights Movement, 1831–51*, Basingstoke, Palgrave Macmillan, 1998

Grenby, M. O., *The Anti-Jacobin Novel: British Conservatism and the French Revolution*, Cambridge University Press, 2001

Guest, Harriet, *Small Change: Women, Learning, Patriotism, 1750–1810*, University of Chicago Press, 2000

Jones, Steven E., *The Satirical Eye: Forms of Satire in the Romantic Period*, Basingstoke, Palgrave Macmillan, 2003

Kelly, Gary (ed.), *Bluestocking Feminism: Writings of the Bluestocking Circle, 1738–1785*, 5 vols., London, Pickering & Chatto, 1999

Major, Emma, *Madam Britannia: Women, Church and Nation 1712–1812*, Oxford University Press, 2012

Mellor, Anne K., *Mothers of the Nation: Women's Political Writing in England, 1780–1830*, Bloomington, Indiana University Press, 2000

Myers, Mitzi, "Reform or Ruin: 'A Revolution in Female Manners,'" *Studies in Eighteenth-Century Culture* 11 (1982): 199–216

Myers, Sylvia Harcstark, *The Bluestocking Circle: Women, Friendship, and the Life of the Mind in Eighteenth-Century England*, Oxford, Clarendon, 1990

Pohl, Nicole, and Betty A. Schellenberg (eds.), *Reconsidering the Bluestockings*, San Marino, CA, Huntington Library, 2003

Strachan, John, *Advertising and Satirical Culture in the Romantic Period*, Cambridge University Press, 2007

Taylor, Barbara, *Eve and the New Jerusalem: Socialism and Feminism in the Nineteenth Century*, London, Virago, 1983

The global context

Bradshaw, Penny, "Dystopian Futures: Time-Travel and Millenarian Visions in the Poetry of Anna Barbauld and Charlotte Smith," *Romanticism on the Net*, 21, February (2001)

Brewer, John, *The Sinews of Power: War, Money and the English State, 1688–1783*, Cambridge, Harvard University Press, 1988

Coleman, Deirdre, "Imagining Sameness and Difference: Domestic and Colonial Sisters in *Mansfield Park*," in *A Companion to Jane Austen*, Claudia L. Johnson and Clara Tuite (eds.), Oxford, Blackwell, 2009, 292–303

"Women Writers and Abolition," in *The History of British Women's Writing, 1750–1830*, Jacqueline M. Labbe (ed.), London, Palgrave Macmillan, 2010, 172–93

Craciun, Adriana, *British Women Writers and the French Revolution: Citizens of the World*, New York, Palgrave Macmillan, 2005

Gibson, Mary Ellis, *Indian Angles: English Verse in Colonial India from Jones to Tagore*, Athens, Ohio University Press, 2011

Leask, Nigel, "Romanticism and the Wider World: Poetry, Travel Literature and Empire," in *The Cambridge History of English Romantic Literature*, James Chandler (ed.), Cambridge University Press, 1999

Major, Andrea, *Pious Flames: European Encounters with Sati, 1500–1830*, New Delhi, Oxford University Press, 2006

Melman, Billie, *Women's Orients: English Women and the Middle East, 1718–1918*, Ann Arbor, University of Michigan Press, 1992

Midgley, Clare, *Feminism and Empire: Women Activists in Imperial Britain, 1790–1865*, London; New York: Routledge, 2007

Nussbaum, Felicity A. (ed.), *The Global Eighteenth Century*, Baltimore, Johns Hopkins University Press, 2003

O'Brien, Karen, *Narratives of Enlightenment: Cosmopolitan History from Voltaire to Gibbon*, Cambridge University Press, 1997

Park, You-Me, and Rajeswari Sunder Rajan (eds.), *The Postcolonial Jane Austen*, New York, Routledge, 2000

Rothschild, Emma, "Globalization and the Return of History," *Foreign Policy* 115 (1999): 106–16

Saglia, Diego, "National Internationalism: Women's Writing and European Literature, 1800–30," in *The History of British Women's Writing, 1750–1830*, Jacqueline M. Labbe (ed.), Basingstoke, Palgrave Macmillan, 2010, 268–87

Salih, Sara, "The Silence of Miss Lambe: Sanditon and Fictions of 'Race' in the Abolition Era," *Eighteenth-Century Fiction* 18:3 (2006): 329–53

Teltscher, Kate, *India Inscribed: European and British Writing on India, 1600–1800*, New Delhi, Oxford University Press, 1995

Tuite, Clara, "Maria Edgeworth's Déjà-Voodoo: Interior Decoration, Retroactivity and Colonial Allegory in The Absentee," *Eighteenth-Century Fiction* 20:3 (Spring 2008): 385–413

Turner, Katherine, "Women's Travel Writing, 1750–1830," in *The History of British Women's Writing*, Jacqueline M. Labbe (ed.), Vol. 5 of *The History of British Women's Writing*, Cora Kaplan and Jennie Batchelor (gen. eds.), Basingstoke, Palgrave Macmillan, 2010

Wilson, Kathleen, *The Island Race: Englishness, Empire, and Gender in the Eighteenth Century*, New York, Routledge, 2003

Wright, Julia M., *Ireland, India, and Nationalism in Nineteenth-Century Literature*, Cambridge University Press, 2007

Social, familial, and literary networks

Backscheider, Paula R. (ed.), *Revising Women: Eighteenth-Century "Women's Fiction" and Social Engagement*, Baltimore, Johns Hopkins University Press, 2000

Botting, Eileen Hunt, *Family Feuds: Wollstonecraft, Burke, and Rousseau on the Transformation of the Family*, Albany, State University of New York Press, 2006

Bush-Bailey, Gilli, *Performing Herself: AutoBiography & Fanny Kelley's "Dramatic Recollections,"* Manchester University Press, 2011

Carlson, Julie A., *England's First Family of Writers: Mary Wollstonecraft, William Godwin, Mary Shelley*, Baltimore, Johns Hopkins University Press, 2007

Crochunis, Thomas C. (ed.), *Joanna, Baillie: Romantic Dramatist, Critical Essays*, New York, Routledge, 2004

Levy, Michelle, *Family Authorship and Romantic Print Culture*, New York, Palgrave Macmillan, 2008

McCarthy, William, and Olivia Murphy (eds.), *Anna Letitia Barbauld: New Perspectives*, Lewisburg, Bucknell University Press, 2014

Mee, Jon, *Conversable Worlds: Literature, Contention, & Community, 1762 to 1830*, Oxford University Press, 2011

Mellor, Anne K., *Mothers of the Nation: Women's Political Writing in England, 1780–1830*, Bloomington, Indiana University Press, 2000

Rajan, Tilottama, *Romantic Narrative: Shelley, Hays, Godwin, Wollstonecraft*, Baltimore, Johns Hopkins University Press, 2010

Russell, Gillian, and Clara Tuite, *Romantic Sociability: Social Networks and Literary Culture in Britain, 1770–1840*, Cambridge University Press, 2002

The economics of female authorship

Batchelor, Jennie, *Women's Work: Labour, Gender, Authorship, 1750–1830*, Manchester University Press, 2010

Copeland, Edward, *Women Writing About Money: Women's Fiction in England, 1790–1820*, Cambridge University Press, 1995

Fergus, Jan, and Janice Farrar Thaddeus, "Women, Publishers, and Money, 1790–1820," *Studies in Eighteenth-Century Culture* 17 (1987): 191–207

Labbe, Jacqueline M. "Gentility in Distress: A New Letter by Charlotte Smith (1749–1806)," *The Wordsworth Circle* 35 (2004): 91–3

"Selling One's Sorrows: Charlotte Smith, Mary Robinson, and the Marketing of Poetry," *The Wordsworth Circle* 25 (1994): 68–71

Writing Romanticism: Charlotte Smith and William Wordsworth, 1784–1807, Basingstoke, Palgrave Macmillan, 2011

(ed.), *Charlotte Smith in British Romanticism*, London, Pickering & Chatto, 2008

(ed.), *The History of British Women's Writing, 1750–1830*, Vol. 5 of *The History of British Women's Writing*, Cora Kaplan and Jennie Batchelor (eds.), Basingstoke, Palgrave Macmillan, 2010

Levy, Michelle, *Family Authorship and Romantic Print Culture*, Basingstoke, Palgrave Macmillan, 2008

Poovey, Mary, *The Proper Lady and the Woman Writer*, University of Chicago Press, 1984

Robbins, Sarah, "Distributed Authorship: A Feminist Case-Study Framework for Studying Intellectual Property," *College English* 66:2 (2003): 155–71

Schellenberg, Betty A., *The Professionalization of Women Writers in Eighteenth-Century Britain*, Cambridge University Press, 2009

Stanton, Judith, "Charlotte Smith's 'Literary Business': Income, Patronage, and Indigence," *The Age of Johnson* 1 (1987): 375–401

Turner, Cheryl, *Living by the Pen: Women Writers in the Eighteenth Century*, New York, Routledge, 1994

Age and aging

Alexander, Christine, and Juliet McMaster (eds.), *The Child Writer from Austen to Woolf*, Cambridge University Press, 2005

Ariès, Philippe, *Centuries of Childhood: A Social History of Family Life*, trans. Robert Baldick, New York, Knopf, 1962

Botelho, Lynn, Susannah R. Ottaway, and Anne Kugler (eds.), *The History of Old Age in England, 1600–1800*, 8 vols., London, Pickering & Chatto, 2008–9

Botelho, Lynn, and Pat Thane (eds.), *Women and Ageing in British Society since 1500*, Harlow, England, Longman, 2001

Charise, Andrea, "Romanticism against Youth," *Essays in Romanticism* 20 (2013): 83–100

Gullette, Margaret Morganroth, "Age (Aging)," in *Encyclopedia of Feminist Literary Theory*, Beth Kowaleski-Wallace (ed.), New York, Garland, 1997, 9–11

Heath, Kay, *Aging by the Book: The Emergence of Midlife in Victorian Britain*, Albany, State University of New York Press, 2009

Looser, Devoney, "Old Age and the End of Oblivion," *Journal of Victorian Culture*
16:1 (April 2011): 132–7
"Why I'm Still Writing Women's Literary History," in *The Critical Pulse: Thirty-Six Credos by Contemporary Critics*, New York, Columbia University Press, 2013, 217–25
Women Writers and Old Age in Great Britain, 1750–1850, Baltimore, Johns Hopkins University Press, 2008
Mangum, Teresa, "Growing Old: Age," in *Companion to Victorian Literature and Culture*, 2nd edn., Herbert F. Tucker (ed.), Oxford, Blackwell, 1999
Menchi, Silvana Seidel, "The Girl and the Hourglass: Periodization of Women's Lives in Western Preindustrial Societies," in *Time, Space, and Women's Lives in Early Modern Europe*, Anne Jacobson Schutte, Thomas Kuehn, and Silvana Seidel Menchi (eds.), Kirksville, MO, Truman State University Press, 2001, 41–74
Ottaway, Susannah R., *The Decline of Life: Old Age in Eighteenth-Century England*, Cambridge University Press, 2007
Peterson, Lesley, and Leslie Robertson, "An Annotated Bibliography of Nineteenth-Century Juvenilia," in *The Child Writer from Austen to Woolf*, Christine Alexander and Juliet McMaster (eds.), Cambridge University Press, 2005, 269–303
Small, Helen, *The Long Life*, Oxford University Press, 2007
Sontag, Susan, "The Double Standard of Aging," *Saturday Review* 55 (23 Sept. 1972): 29–38
Stewart, Joan Hinde, *The Enlightenment of Age: Women, Letters and Growing Old in Eighteenth-Century France*, Oxford, Voltaire Foundation, 2010
Thane, Pat, *Old Age in English History: Past Experiences, Present Issues*, Oxford University Press, 2000
Troyansky, David G, *Old Age in the Old Regime: Image and Experience in Eighteenth-Century France*, Ithaca, Cornell University Press, 1989

National identities and regional affiliations

Anderson, Benedict, *Imagined Communities: Reflections on the Origin and Spread of Nationalism*, London, Verso, 1991
Colley, Linda, *Britons: Forging the Nation, 1707–1837*, 3rd rev. edn., New Haven, Yale University Press, 2009
Corbett, Mary Jean, *Allegories of Union in Irish and English Writing, 1790–1870: Politics, History, and the Family from Edgeworth to Arnold*, Cambridge University Press, 2000
Craciun, Adriana, *British Women Writers and the French Revolution: Citizens of the World*, Basingstoke, Palgrave Macmillan, 2005
Ferris, Ina, *The Achievement of Literary Authority: Gender, History and the Waverley Novels*, Ithaca, Cornell University Press, 1991
The Romantic National Tale and the Question of Ireland, Cambridge University Press, 2002
"Writing on the Border: The National Tale, Female Writing, and the Public Sphere," in *Romanticism, History and the Possibilities of Genre,* Tilottama Rajan and Julia M. Wright (eds.), Cambridge University Press, 1998, 86–108

Gellner, Ernest, *Nations and Nationalism; New Perspectives on the Past*, Oxford, Blackwell, 1983

Guest, Harriet, *Small Change: Women, Learning, Patriotism 1750–1810*, University of Chicago Press, 2000

Hobsbawm, E. J., *Nations and Nationalism since 1780: Programme, Myth, Reality*, Cambridge University Press, 1990

Keane, Angela, *Women Writers and the English Nation in the 1790s: Romantic Belongings*, Cambridge University Press, 2000

Kelly, Gary, *Women, Writing, and Revolution 1790–1827*, Oxford, Clarendon Press, 1993

Major, Emma, *Madam Britannia: Women, Church, and Nation 1712–1812*, Oxford University Press, 2011

Maunu, Leanne, *Women Writing the Nation: National Identity, National Female Community, and the British–French Connection, 1770–1820*, Lewisburg, Bucknell University Press, 2007

Mellor, Anne K., *Mothers of the Nation: Women's Political Writing in England, 1780–1830*, Bloomington, Indiana University Press, 2000

O'Brien, Karen, *Women and Enlightenment in Eighteenth-Century Britain*, Cambridge University Press, 2009

Ó Gallchoir, Clíona, *Maria Edgeworth: Women, Enlightenment and Nation*, University College Dublin Press, 2005

Price, Fiona, "'A Great Deal of History': Romantic Women Writers and Historical Fiction," *Women's Writing* 19:3 (2012): 259–72

Trumpener, Katie, *Bardic Nationalism: The Romantic Novel and the British Empire*, Princeton University Press, 1997

Watson, Nicola, *Revolution and the Form of the British Novel, 1790–1825*, Oxford University Press, 1994

Sexualities

Abelove, Henry, Michèle Aina Barale, and David M. Halperin, *The Lesbian and Gay Studies Reader*, New York, Routledge, 1993

Carlson, Julie, *England's First Family of Writers: Mary Wollstonecraft, William Godwin, Mary Shelley*, Baltimore, Johns Hopkins University Press, 2007

Clark, Anna, *Scandal: The Sexual Politics of the British Constitution*, Princeton University Press, 2004

Grosz, Elizabeth, *Volatile Bodies: Toward a Corporeal Feminism*, Bloomington, Indiana University Press, 1994

Guest, Harriet, *Small Change: Women Learning, Patriotism 1750–1810*, University of Chicago Press, 2000

Heydt-Stevenson, Jillian, *Austen's Unbecoming Conjunctions: Subversive Laughter, Embodied History*, New York, Palgrave Macmillan, 2005

"'Pleasure is now, and ought to be, your business': Stealing Sexuality in Jane Austen's Juvenilia," in *Historicizing Romantic Sexuality*, Richard C. Sha (ed.), Romantic Circles Praxis Series, Jan 2006. www.rc.umd.edu/praxis/sexuality/heydt/heydt.html

James, Felicity, "Writing Female Biography: Mary Hays and the Life Writing of Religious Dissent," in *Women's Life Writing, 1700–1850*, Daniel Cook and Amy Culley (eds.), New York, Palgrave Macmillan, 2012, 117–32

Johnson, Claudia L. (ed.), *The Cambridge Companion to Mary Wollstonecraft*, Cambridge University Press, 2002

   Equivocal Beings: Politics, Gender, and Sentimentality in the 1790s, Wollstonecraft, Radcliffe, Burney, Austen, University of Chicago Press, 1995

Kelley, Theresa M., *Clandestine Marriage: Botany and Romantic Culture*, Baltimore, Johns Hopkins University Press, 2013

McKeon, Michael, *The Origins of the English Novel 1600–1740*, Baltimore, Johns Hopkins University Press, 1987

Mandell, Laura, "Bad Marriages, Bad Novels: The Jacobin 'Philosophical Romance,'" in *Recognizing the Romantic Novel: New Histories of British Fiction, 1774–1824*, Jillian Heydt-Stevenson and Charlotte Sussman (eds.), University of Liverpool Press, 2008, 49–76

Moore, Lisa L., *Dangerous Intimacies: Toward a Sapphic History of the British Novel*, Durham, Duke University Press, 1997

Rajan, Tilottama, and Julia M. Wright (ed.), *Romanticism, History, and the Possibilities of Genre: Re-forming Literature 1789–1837*, Cambridge University Press, 1998

Trumbach, Randolph, *Sex and the Gender Revolution: Homosexuality and the Third Gender in Enlightenment London*, University of Chicago Press, 1998

Wilson, Frances, *The Courtesan's Revenge: Harriette Wilson, the Woman who Blackmailed the King*, London, Faber and Faber, 2003

Wiltshire, John, *Recreating Jane Austen*, Cambridge University Press, 2001

INDEX

abolition, *see* slavery
accomplishments
  female, 47, 120
actors
  female, 33
    as mistresses, 36
    as playwrights, 34
    as prostitutes, 37
Africa, 10, 74–75, 77, 86, 102, 131, 133, 135, 137, 142
age and aging, xv, xvi, 170, 178
  childhood, 47, 170–171, 173–174
  middle age, 175–177
  old age, 170, 176–179
  stages of life, 171
  for women, 177
  youth, 4, 106, 139, 170–171, 173–178, 180, 199
Aikin, John, 147
Aikin, Lucy, 9, 149
  and family literary relations, 146
  relationship to Anna Letitia Barbauld, 127
Akenside, Mark, 118
Alcock, Mary, 104
American Revolutionary War, 45, 48, 101, 107, 129, 193
Anderson, Benedict, 183
anonymous and pseudonymous publication, xv, 34, 50, 60, 63, 68, 77, 79, 119, 126, 173–174
anonymous publication, 84
anthologies, 1, *see* textbooks
antiquarianism, xvi, 11, 98–99, 117
  artifacts, 97
  Society of Antiquaries, 98
architecture, 58–59, 62, 66, 69, 74, 76, 85
Arctic, 75, 77, 137
Ariès, Philippe, 170–171

Ariosto, 62
art and artists, 88, 94, 98, 121, 126, 170
Asia, 77, 85
Astell, Mary, 50–51, 89, 94, 119
  Reflections upon Marriage, 119
Austen, Cassandra, 134
Austen, Jane, xiv, xv, 16, 20, 25–26, 60–61, 66–67, 70, 89, 91, 133–135, 145, 148, 163, 199, 202, 209
  on aging, 177
  as anonymous author, xiv, xv
  as canonical author, xiv
  Catharine, or the Bower, 133
  Emma, 115–116, 126, 140, 162, 196
  fathers in fiction of, 120
  juvenilia, 172, 208
  letters of, 20, 26, 67–68
  literary earnings, 27
  Mansfield Park, 134, 162, 202
  and money, 162, 167
  Northanger Abbey, 20, 60–61, 66–68, 70, 89–91, 201
  Persuasion, 133, 202, 204
  Pride and Prejudice, 11, 166, 202
  and publishers, 162, 166
  Sanditon, 135
  self-presentation as author, 134, 159
  Sense and Sensibility, xv, 124, 134, 162, 202
  as sexual humorist, 199
  on war, 133
authorship
  and age, 170, 178–180
  by children, 172–175
  copyright, 158, 160
  economics of, xv, xvi, 17, 26, 60, 63–64, 118, 158, 167
  by literary daughters, 156

professional, xv, 13, 20, 32–34, 38, 41, 116, 118, 126, 145–146, 152, 161–165, 170, 178, 180
publishing by subscription, 118, 158, 175

Backscheider, Paula, 2, 5
Baedeker, Karl, 80
Bage, Robert, 148
Baillie, Joanna, xv, 38, 40, 42, 68–71, 93–94, 96, 110, 118–119, 151–152, 154, 169
    Count Basil, 68
    De Monfort, 68–69, 152
    family relations, 152
    as friend of Barbauld, 156
    and history writing, 94
    and male characters, 94
    Orra, 69
    Plays on the Passions, 40, 68–69, 119, 151–152
    as playwright, 93–94, 151–152
    The Tryal, 68
Baillie, Marianne, 86
Baillie, Matthew, 152
ballad, see poetry, ballads
Ballard, George, 117
Bannerman, Anne, 4, 105, 110–112
Barbauld, Anna Letitia, xv, xvi, 2, 6, 9–10, 44, 55–56, 101, 103, 118, 121–122, 125–127, 129, 133, 137–138, 142, 149–150, 152–153
    Appeal to the Opposers of the Repeal of the Corporation and Test Acts, 55
    as abolitionist, 10
    as bluestocking, 116
    The British Novelists, 118
    criticisms of, 127
    and the critics, 118
    as Dissenter, 9
    as editor, 118
    Eighteen Hundred and Eleven, 9, 101–102, 112, 137, 148–149, 209
    Epistles on Women, 9
    and family literary relations, 146–147
    as friend of Baillie, 156
    Hymns in Prose for Children, 56
    Lessons for Children, 147, 150
    marriage, 147, 149
    on education, 56
    On the Origin and Progress of Novel-Writing, 55
    Sins of Government, Sins of the Nation, 56

on women's college, 121
Barnard, Lady Anne, 86
Barrett, Eaton Stannard, 61
Barrington, Daines, 98
Barrow, Sir John, 75
Batchelor, Jennie, 20
Battier, Henrietta, 12
Beauclerk, Diana, 126
Beddoes, Thomas, 152
Behn, Aphra, xv, 34
    The Forc'd Marriage, 33
Behrendt, Stephen C., xiii, xvi, 2, 5
Benger, Elizabeth, 174
Bennett, Anna Maria, 21
Bentinck, Margaret, Duchess of Portland, 117
Berry, Mary, 39, 123
Bible
    in literature, 97
    reading of, 117
bibliography, 2, 16
Big Six Poets (Blake, Wordsworth, Coleridge, Byron, Shelley, Keats), xiii, 16
biography and memoir, xvi, xvii, 2, 50, 75, 77–79, 83–84, 145, 148, 154, 172–173, 209
    popularity of, 89
Birkett, Mary, 10
Blake, William, xiii, 1, 16
Bloomfield, Robert, 1
Bluestocking Circle, xvi, 12, 120, 124, 126
    and French salons, 120
    national pride in, 117
    second generation, 116
bluestockings, 115–117, 119, 123, 125–128
    as authors, 118
    celebrations of, 121
    criticisms of, 116
    as critics, 121
    as hostesses, 127
    as literary critics, 118
    and marriage, 120
    as models, 119
    and money, 117
    origins of label, 115
    as patrons, 122
    and philanthropy, 117
    and publishers, 117
    representations of, 127
    satires on, 117
    and sociability, 121

book, history of, xviii, 3, 17–18,
    29, 164
booksellers and bookselling, 6, 17–18, 27,
    147, 164
Boothby, Frances, 34
Boscawen, Frances, 116, 120, 127
Bourke, Hannah Maria, 11
Bowes, Mary Eleanor, 38
Boyd, Diane, 165
Brand, Hannah, 40
Brewer, John, 102
Britannia, figure of, 7, 36, 184
British empire, 56, 73, 81, 93, 112, 121, 129,
    134, 137, 186, 190, 192
British Fiction, 1800–1829, xvii
Brontë, Charlotte, 172
Brooke, Frances, 40–41
Browning, Elizabeth Barrett, 169, 175
Bruce, James, 75
Brunton, Mary, 20, 24
Brydges, Sir Samuel Egerton, 4
Burke, Edmund, 44–45, 61–62, 132,
    187–188, 191, 195
    Reflections on the Revolution in France,
        61, 185
Burney, Frances, xv, 9, 16, 20–21, 26, 28, 56,
    118, 121, 126
    books about, 172
    Camilla, 20–21, 26
    Cecilia, 21
    Evelina, 21, 200
    and Hester Thrale Piozzi, 156
    The Wanderer, 21
Burns, Robert, 1
Burrell, Lady Sophia, 38
Burroughs, Catherine, xvi, xvii
Bush-Bailey, Gilli, 153–154
Butler, Judith, 123
Butler, Marilyn, 16
Byron, Lord George Gordon, xiii–1, 3, 16,
    29, 38, 70, 75, 77, 115–117, 125,
    127, 136
    and publishers, 163
    Childe Harold's Pilgrimage, 75, 77

Cadell, Thomas, 159–160, 165–166
canon, *see* literary canon
Carey, Frances Jane, 86
Carlson, Julie A., xvi
Carpenter, Mary, 116
Carrington, Edmund Frederick John, xv
Carruthers, Robert, 77
Carter, Anne, 84

Carter, Elizabeth, 117, 121, 123–124,
    126–127
Cary, Elizabeth, 33
castles, 59, 64, 66, 107
Cave, Edward, 117
Cavendish, Margaret, Duchess of Newcastle,
    33, 40, 173
celebrities and celebrity culture, 3, 37, 155
Centlivre, Susanna, 34–35
Chambers, Marianne, 39
Chambers, Robert, 77
chapbooks, 17
Chapone, Hester Mulso, 120, 126–127
Chapone, Sarah, 119
charity work, *see* philanthropy
Charke, Charlotte, 34
Charles I, 98
Charles II, 36, 191
Charlotte Smith
    as role model, 4
children's literature, 118, 124, 146, 150–151,
    155, 171
China, 75, 108, 134, 136
chivalry, 120, 187–188
Chorley, Henry, 96
Church of England, 52, 55, 117, 119, 121,
    124–127, 194
Cibber, Susannah, 34
circulating libraries, 19, 21, 73, 86
    perception of, 19
civil society, 44, 55, 120, 122
Clairmont, Mary Jane, 147
Clare, John, 1
class, *see* social class
classical tradition, 6, 8, 37, 62–63, 88,
    93, 108, 121, 125, 136, 170, 176,
    193–194
Clio, 88
Clive, Kitty, 34–35
Colburn, Henry, 19, 29–30, 163
Coleman, Deirdre, xvi
Coleridge, Samuel Taylor, xiii–1, 16,
    125, 160
    Christabel, 156
Coleridge, Sara, 155
Colley, Linda, 104
Collier, Mary, 118
Collins, William, 118
colonialism, xvi, 9, 23, 39, 44, 56, 101–102,
    129, 133–134, 142, 184, 192
comedy, 21, 34–35, 37–39, 151
Comenius, Johann, 171
commerce and commercialism, 185

community and communalism, 5, 9, 12–13,
    49, 53, 89, 183–184, 186, 189–190,
    194–195, 209
    and sexuality, 198
conduct books, 120, 122, 147, 176,
    178–179, 189, 199
Confessions of An Old Maid, xv
conservatism, 9–10, 17, 19–21, 30, 51,
    62, 76–77, 80, 116, 121, 124–126,
    133, 185–186, 189–190, 192–193,
    195–196, 204
Cook, James, 75
copyright legislation, 17–18, 21, 118
    Donaldson v. Becket, 18
correspondence, *see* letters and letter writing
cosmopolitanism, 83, 127, 130, 186, 192
Cowley, Hannah, xvii, 35–36, 39–41, 118
Crabbe, George, 1
Craven, Lady Elizabeth, 38–39, 76–77, 79
Crewe, Emma, 126
Croker, John Wilson, 118
Cromwell, Oliver, 98
Crouch, Anna Maria, 36
Curran, Stuart, 2
Currier and Ives, 171
customs, 73–74, 76, 78, 86,
    89, 138

Dacre, Charlotte, 69–71
Dark, Mariann, 4, 13
Darwall, Mary Whateley, 104, 106
Darwin, Erasmus, 127, 200
databases
    electronic, xvi, 173
Day, Thomas, 149
death and dying, 103
De Camp Kemble, Marie Therese, 39
de Gouges, Olympe, 122
De J. Jackson, J. R., 6
Della Cruscans, 37
democracy, 45, 48
De Quincey, Thomas, xiii
de Staël, Germaine, 23, 29, 75, 77, 118,
    125, 127
    Corinne, 23
de Talleyrand-Perigord, Charles
    Maurice, 45
Deverell, Mary, 38
Dickens, Charles, 3
Dissent and Dissenters, 9, 49, 55, 117, 126,
    148, 186, 193–194
    and Bluestocking Circle, 116
Dodsley, James, 3

domesticity, 13, 23, 29, 48, 51, 54–56, 60,
    75, 81, 84, 93, 101, 104, 108, 110,
    112, 117, 121, 126, 146, 150, 156,
    185–186, 190, 196
Drake, Nathan, 63
drama
    closet, 34–35
    Gothic, 69
    siege, 41–42
Duncombe, John, 117
Dyce, Alexander, 5

East India Company, 138
Eaton, Charlotte Anne Waldie, 77, 86
Eaton, Stannard Barrett
    The Heroine, 67
Edgeworth, Maria, xv, 16, 23–24, 26, 38,
    56, 91, 97, 125, 135, 147–148, 150,
    191–192, 198–199
    The Absentee, 23, 192
    Belinda, 125, 135, 147, 149, 183–184,
        207–208
    Castle Rackrent, 23, 191
    and family literary relations, 146
    on ladies' periodical, 122
    Ormond, 23
    Practical Education, 97, 147
    Tales of Fashionable Life, 192
Edgeworth, Richard Lovell, 97, 135, 147
education, 2, 25, 44–50, 52–56, 61, 64,
    73, 116–117, 124–125, 131, 147,
    184, 195
    for children, 97–98
    co-education, 122
    female, 123–124, 149–150
    male, 201
    national, 188, 190
    and national identity, 187
    religious, 123
    and theater, 152
    universities, 119
    women, 122
Eger, Elizabeth, 36
Egleton, Jane, 34
Egypt, 8, 80, 83, 102, 111, 135, 137
electronic databases, *see* databases,
    electronic
elegy, *see* poetry, elegiac
Eliott, General George, 106
Elizabeth I, 92
Ellis, Kate Ferguson, 59
Elstob, Elizabeth, 117
Engels, Friedrich, 120

Enlightenment, 45, 48, 88, 116
  and feminism, 119
  French, 48
  historiography, 96, 98, 184, 187,
    191, 195
  and philosophy, 117
  Scottish, 187
  and sociability, 121
  woman as a symbol of, 188
equality, 45–46, 48–50, 55, 129, 185, 188,
    191, 193
  class, 130
  sexual, 55, 125–127
Europe, 6, 18, 23–24, 41, 59, 61, 73–74,
    76, 79–80, 85, 102, 117, 130–131,
    134–138, 155, 170, 187, 189

Far East, 74, 77
Farren, Elizabeth, 36
fashion, 60, 83, 89
Favret, Mary, 103
Fay, Eliza, 79–80
Fay, Elizabeth A., xvi, xvii
Feather, John, 18, 29
Feldman, Paula, 2
female education
  and reform, 46
feminism
  history of, 50–51, 55, 116–117, 126,
    128, 133
  second-wave (1970s-80s), 123
Fenwick, Eliza, 21–22, 198–199
  and Mary Wollstonecraft, 156
  Secresy, 201
fiction writers
  numbers of, 16
Finch, Anne, 34
Fleming, Marjory, 175
Fleury, Maria de, 7
Forsythe, Joseph, 77
France, 7, 37, 39, 45, 48, 59–61, 64, 73, 76,
    79–81, 83–86, 101–104, 122, 125,
    129–132, 134, 136, 184, 186–188,
    190, 192, 201
  as effeminized, 121
  influence on Britain, 127
  and luxury, 121
  as threat, 103
Francis, Ann Gittins, 38
Franklin, Caroline, xvi
Fraser, Susan, 38
French Revolution, xvi, 21–22, 37, 44–46,
    52, 61–63, 76, 81, 84, 102, 111, 117,

121, 125, 127, 130, 142, 183–184,
    187–188, 190–193, 196, 199
Girondists, 84
  and the Gothic, 61
  Jacobins, 104
friendships
  among literary men, 155
  among women, 117
  among women writers, 156
Fuseli, Henry, 209

Garrick, David, 35, 38
Garside, Peter, 16, 22, 27
Gellner, Ernest, 183, 186
gender
  and genre, 5
  roles in wartime, 7–8
genre, xviii, 4–5, 61, 63, 65, 68, 70, 91, 136,
    149, 151
  and gender, 5
Gent, Thomas, 5
George I, 34
George III, 36, 79, 83
Germany, 37, 39, 58, 65, 68, 83, 86, 122,
    130, 136
  stereotypes of, 130
Gibbes, Phebe, 139
Gibbon, Edward, 88, 93
Gifford, William, 125, 127
Gilpin, William, 75, 200
Godwin, William, 116, 125, 132, 147–149,
    155–156, 193, 209
Goethe, 21, 85
Goldsmith, Oliver, 32, 95
Gore, Catherine, 42
gossip, 36, 115
Gothic, xvi, 10–11, 21–22, 24–26, 37,
    58–63, 65, 67–70, 92–94
  and architecture, 66–67
  definition of, 58
  female, 59–60, 119
  "Female Gothic," 60
  and French Revolution, 61
  and history, 91
  Irish, 10
  satires on, 61
  supernatural elements, 65–66, 91, 119
  in the theater, 69
governesses, 85, 117, 155
Graham, Maria, 86
Grand Tour, 73, 83
Grant, Anne MacVicar, 9–10, 180
Graves, Robert, 92

Gray, Thomas, 62
Greece, 6, 77, 193
Griffith, Elizabeth, 35, 39–40, 119
Gwynn, Nell, 36

Hamilton, Elizabeth, 22, 125, 186,
    193–194
    Memoirs of Agrippina, 194
    Memoirs of Modern Philosophers,
    125, 193
Hands, Elizabeth, 118
Hanson, Martha, 4
Hanway, Mary Ann, 22
Hastings, Warren, 80, 134
Hawkins, Laetitia-Matilda, 24
Hays, Mary, xvi, 21, 44, 49–51, 56,
    95, 124–125, 135, 148–149,
    198–199, 209
    *Appeal to the Men of Great Britain in
    Behalf of Woman*, 49
    and feminism, 51
    feminist writings, 126
    Memoirs of Emma Courtney, 149, 198,
    201, 208
    *Memoirs of Queens Illustrious and
    Celebrated*, 50
    as radical, 123
Haywood, Eliza, 34, 40
Hazlitt, Sarah, 155
Hazlitt, William, xiii
Helme, Elizabeth, 38, 135
Hemans, Felicia, 1–3, 6–7, 13–14, 41–42,
    96–97, 136–137, 163, 169, 175
    and audience, 163
    *The Domestic Affections, and Other
    Poems*, 7
    *The Forest Sanctuary and Other
    Poems*, 96
    The Grave of a Poetess, 14
    juvenilia, 175
    "Lays of Many Lands," 96
    and Lord Byron, 3
    and Maria Jane Jewsbury, 156
    Modern Greece: A Poem, 6
    and money, 167
    poetry about, 14
    and publishers, 163–164
    Records of Woman, 96
    reputation of, 3
    reviews of, 6
    self-presentation as author, 159
    and wartime, 137
Herder, Johann Gottfried, 96

Heydt-Stevenson, Jillian, xvi, xvii
Hill, Isabel, 38
historians
    and gender, 89
    histories of women, 121
historiography, xvi, 88–89, 91, 95–99,
    184, 189
    changes in, 88, 100
    as excluding women, 90
    feminist, 99
    and fiction, 92
    in literary genres, 90
    as male-addressed, 89
    as masculine pursuit, 89
    Romantic, 88
history
    reading of, 88
    stadial, 187, 189–193, 195
history of the book, *see* book, history of
history writing, *see* historiography
Hobhouse, John Cam, 77
Hobsbawm, Eric, 184
Hoeveler, Diane Long, 59
Hofland, Barbara, 12, 26, 29, 38
Holcroft, Fanny, 38, 106, 155–156
    as dutiful daughter, 155
Holcroft, Thomas, 148, 155
    as father, 156
Holland, 130
Hoole, Barbara, 7
Hornby, Mary, 38
horses, 37, 79
Hughes, Anne, 38
Humboldt, Charlotte de, 38
Hume, David, 88, 92
Hunt, Leigh, xiii–1

Imlay, Gilbert, 209
Inchbald, Elizabeth, 21, 39–40, 56, 118,
    134, 153
    The British Theatre, 118
    criticisms of, 125
    as translator, 136
India, 39, 56, 79–81, 85, 96, 102, 108,
    133–135, 137–139, 141–142
Ingrassia, Catherine, xvi
Ireland, 2–3, 6, 10, 12, 23, 35, 76, 78,
    99, 127, 133, 135, 147, 186,
    190–193, 196
    Edgeworthstown, 147
    politics, 147
Italy, 22, 66, 75, 77, 79–81, 83, 85–86, 125,
    136, 156, 190

Jamaica, 81
Jameson, Anna, 116
Jebb, Ann, 126
Jefferson, Thomas, 48
Jerdan, William, 163
Jewsbury, Maria Jane, 156
Johnson, Joseph, 4, 117, 161
Johnson, Samuel, 117
Jordan, Dorothy, 37, 153–154
juvenilia, 172–175, 208

Kairoff, Claudia, 105
Kauffmann, Angelica, 126
Kean, Edmund, 35, 40
Keats, John, xiii–1, 16
Kelly, Fanny, 153–154
  daughter of, 154
Kemble, Charles, 42
Kemble, Frances Anne, 42
Kemble, John, 35, 40, 146, 153
Knight, Ellis Cornelia, 190
Kucich, Greg, 40

L. E. L., see Landon, Letitia Elizabeth
Labbe, Jacqueline M., xv, xvi
Lacey, James, 4
Lake, Crystal, xvi
Lamb, Lady Caroline, 29
Landon, Letitia Elizabeth, xv–2, 140, 169
  as celebrity, 3
  as editor, 3
  and popularity, 3
  Stanzas on the Death of Mrs. Hemans, 14
Landor, Walter Savage, 1
Lane, William, 19, 29–30, 65
Lathom, Francis, 68
Leadbeater, Mary, 12
Leapor, Mary, 118
Lee, Harriet, 39
  as playwright, 69
Lee, Sophia, 24, 39, 65–66, 92
  as playwright, 41
  The Recess, 24, 65, 92
Lee, Vernon, 175
Lefanu, Alicia Sheridan, 39
Lennox, Charlotte, 39–40, 119
letters and letter writing, 12, 21, 26, 41,
  45, 49, 65, 73–74, 79–81, 84–86,
  105, 117–118, 127, 130–131, 138,
  159–161, 189
Levy, Michelle, 30, 146
Lewald, Fanny, 86
Lewis, Mary G., 38

Lewis, Matthew
  The Monk, 70
Lickbarrow, Isabella, 7
Lister, Anne, xvii, 198–199, 205–207
literary annuals, 3, 13, 17
literary canon, xiv–1, 32, 55, 62, 118, 145,
  150, 152
  male, 176
literary history
  feminist, 30
  male-centered, 1
  masculine, 118
  periodization, xv
  revisionist, 3
literary marketplace, xvi, 3, 13, 16–21,
  24–26, 29, 60, 74–76, 118,
  158–164, 166
  and gender, 159
  and profit, 30
literary relations
  and families, 146–147
  among women, 5
London, 17–18, 191
  and global trade, 138
  Pantheon, 200
  and radical politics, 147
  and theater, 151
Longman Publishers, 29, 160
Louis XVI, 44, 76, 102
Louis XVIII, 84
Luby, Catherine, 10–11
Lumley, Jane (Joanna), 33
luxury, 112, 121, 185, 192

McCarthy, William, 103
Macartney, Lord George, 75, 134
Macaulay, Catharine, 45, 50–51, 90, 122,
  126, 209
  Letters on Education, 45
Macready, William Charles, 42
Mandal, Anthony, xv, xvi, 16
Manley, Delarivier, 34
Manners, Lady Catherine Rebecca, 3
manuscript circulation, see scribal
  publication
Marcet, Jane, 125
Marie Antoinette, 45, 61, 187
marriage, 36, 38, 46–48, 52, 60, 69, 79, 81,
  119, 124, 133, 135, 139, 145, 147,
  184, 189, 201, 203, 206–208
  arranged, 120
  companionate, 120
  courtship, 120, 198–199, 204

criticisms of, 125, 147
forced, 200, 202
interracial, 135
legal aspects, 119
as market, 133
as oppression, 139
and sexuality, 198
unhappiness in, 208
Martineau, Harriet, 116, 125
Marx, Karl, 120
Mary, Queen of Scots, 92, 98
Masters, Mary, 103
Mathias, Reverend T. J., 6, 60, 62
Matthews, Charles, 154
medieval period, 10, 86, 88, 91, 96, 119, 170
Meeke, Elizabeth, 26, 29
Mellor, Anne K., xvi, 36
melodrama, 11, 38, 42, 151
memoirs, 37, 79–80, 84
Meryon, Charles Lewis, 83
Millar, John, 120
Miller, Lady Anna, 78–79, 86
Milling, Jane, 34
Milton, John
    Paradise Lost, 46
Minerva Press, 19, 27, 29, 68
Mitford, Mary Russell, 12, 42
Moers, Ellen, 59
Montagu, Elizabeth, 40, 115, 119–121, 124, 126–127
Montagu, Lady Mary Wortley, 34, 73–74, 83, 131, 172
    Turkish Embassy Letters, 73, 75, 131
Morgan, Lady, *see* Owenson, Sydney
Moody, Elizabeth, 4, 106
Moore, Sir John, 7, 136
Moore, Thomas, 10, 127
More, Hannah, xvi, 9–10, 23, 35, 41, 44, 52, 54–56, 118, 121, 123–124, 126–127, 133, 150, 185, 194
on bluestockings, 116
Coelebs in Search of a Wife, 24, 52–53
as conservative, 51
as feminist, 51
feminist criticisms of, 126
on the novel, 19
as patron, 118
Percy, 41
as playwright, 41
as role model, 126
Slavery, A Poem, 10
Strictures on the Modern System of Female Education, 52

motherhood, 111, 120, 125–126, 129, 146, 148
Mothers of the nation, 36, 54–55, 89
Murphy, Arthur, 36
Murray, John, 3, 80, 163
museums, 98
benefactors, 98
history of, 88

Napoleon, 23–24, 76, 84, 102
Napoleonic Wars, 9, 84, 94, 102, 104, 117, 125, 127, 189
nations and nationalism, xvi, xvii, 7–9, 11–12, 23–24, 36, 39, 45, 48, 52, 54–56, 96, 102, 104, 108, 112, 130, 138, 148, 183–187, 189, 191–196
and borders, 185
British, 52, 99
Christianity, 109
and citizenship, 142
development of, 184
and economics, 185
and education, 188
in fiction, 192
and gender, 189, 192, 196
and history, 184
meaning of, 184
morality, 109
patriotism, 121, 137, 186–188, 190
wartime, 109, 111
and women, 184–185
in women's poetry, 8
Navy, British, 102
Near East, 74–75, 83
Nelson, Horatio, Admiral, 7
New World, 3, 9, 138
Nooth, Charlotte, 38
North America, 9, 39, 45, 74
novels
anti-Jacobin, 125
Barbauld on, 56
epistolary, 21, 187, 190
Evangelical, 24
Gothic, features of, 60
historical, 24, 65, 90–91, 194
Jacobin, 21, 104, 148
national tale, 23
numbers of, 20, 26, 29, 118
women readers of, 88
Nugent, Lady Maria, 81

old age, 170–171, 176, 179
old maids, *see* single women

O'Neill, Eliza, 36
Opie, Amelia, 4, 8, 24, 26, 29, 105, 111,
    115–116
    Adeline Mowbray, 125
    The Father and Daughter, 11
    Poems, 8
    Temper, or Domestic Scenes, 24
    on war, 105
Owenson, Sydney, 10, 16, 23, 26, 29, 76–77,
    91, 118, 127, 191
    Florence Macarthy, 192
    The Missionary, 139
    O'Donnel: A National Tale, 23, 192
    The Wild Irish Girl, 23, 192
    Woman, 23

Pacific, 56, 75
Pacific Islands, 56
Paine, Thomas, 48, 117
    The Rights of Man, 187
paper, cost of, 18
Park, Mungo, 75
Parker, Mary Ann, 135
Parkes, Fanny, 139–140
Parry, Sir Edward, 75
Parsons, Eliza, 26–27, 59, 64
    The Castle of Wolfenbach, 65
patrons and patronage, 34, 118, 122, 153–154
peace and peacetime, 8, 109, 111–112,
    129, 192
Peacock, Thomas Love, 61
    Nightmare Abbey, 67
Periodical Press, 3–4, 6, 8–9, 13, 17, 36,
    60–61, 67, 90, 92, 104, 106, 117,
    125, 127, 135
    antiquarianism, 98
philanthrophy, 53, 116–119, 126
Philips, Katherine, 33
Pinchard, Elizabeth, 38
Piozzi, Hester Thrale, 125–127, 156,
    186–187
Pix, Mary, 34
plays
    licensing of, 35, 42
    numbers of, 34, 39, 41
Plumptre, Anne, 86
poetry
    anti-war, 5
    ballads, 97, 106
    canon of Romantic, 2
    Della Cruscan, 125
    elegiac, 13, 103
    and feminist critical theory, 2

non-canonical, 1
    popular reception of, 4
    sonnet form, 4–5, 13, 110
poets
    women, numbers of, 6
Polack, Elizabeth, 69
Polwhele, Elizabeth, 34
Polwhele, Rev. Richard, 6, 125–126
    The Unsex'd Females, 6
Poovey, Mary, 159
Pope, Alexander, 9, 174
    influences on women, 125
Porden, Eleanor Anne, 10
Porter, Anna Maria, 24, 29, 91, 174
Porter, Jane, 24, 29, 91, 186, 193–194
    The Scottish Chiefs, 24, 194–195
prefaces, 4, 39–40, 55, 58, 77, 118–119, 159,
    174, 179, 196
Price, Fiona, xvi
Price, Richard, 193
Priestley, Joseph, 97
Prince of Wales, 36
prose, non-fiction, 44
prostitutes and prostitution, 37, 45, 51,
    125, 205
public sphere, 14, 44, 51, 55, 74–75, 94,
    117, 121, 129, 185
publishers and publishing, xiii, xv, 3, 5–6,
    12, 17, 19–21, 29, 34, 76, 79, 104,
    117–118, 135–136, 158–160,
    162–165, 173, 178
publishing, history of, 18

Quaker, see religion, Quaker

race and ethnicity, 56, 115, 133, 135, 200
Radcliffe, Ann, xvi, 10, 22, 26, 28–29,
    56, 59, 62–67, 69–71, 75, 92–93,
    118–119, 126
    The Castles of Athlin and
        Dunbayne, 63, 66
    compared to Sophia Lee, 92
    The Italian, 22, 26, 66–67
    The Mysteries of Udolpho, 22, 26,
        62–67, 70, 93
    The Romance of the Forest, 63
    A Sicilian Romance, 63, 65
Radcliffe, Mary Anne, 51
radical politics, 76, 99, 186
radicalism, 22, 51, 55, 76, 104, 117, 121,
    123–125, 147, 186–187, 189–190,
    192–193, 204
    and men, 149

Raven, James, 16, 27
Rawdon, Elizabeth, Countess of
    Moira, 98–99
readers and readership, xvi, xvii, xviii, 3,
    5, 7–13, 18–21, 23, 25, 29, 33, 44,
    58–61, 63, 67–68, 70, 74–75, 77–78,
    80–81, 88–93, 95, 97, 118, 138, 147,
    158–159, 171, 176, 178, 180, 198,
    203, 207
reception, xvi, xvii, 63, 76, 79, 86, 176
Reeve, Clara, 58, 65, 91–92, 119, 121, 127
    The Old English Baron, 65
Regency Period, 9, 19, 23–24
religion
    Catholic, 61, 63, 93
    Evangelicalism, 23–24, 53, 116,
        125–126, 133
    festivals, 74
    Hindu, 138–139
    Presbyterian, 20, 193
    Protestant, 117, 119, 186, 193, 196
    Quaker, 12, 55, 124
    religious intolerance, 9
    Unitarian, 49, 55, 116
Restoration, 33–35, 37, 85
Reynolds, Sir Joshua, 36, 98
Riccoboni, Madame, 41
Richardson, Elizabeth, 39
Richardson, Samuel, 21, 39, 51, 117–118
Richardson, Sarah, 38
rights
    civil, 44–46, 48–49, 55, 84, 116, 122, 124,
        127, 133, 189, 202
    property, 141
    universal, 129
    women's, 44, 120, 122–123
Roberts, Emma, 140
Robertson, William, 92, 187
Robinson, Mary, xvi, 2–4, 6, 21–22, 36–37,
    51, 56, 59–60, 62–64, 66–67, 112,
    118, 125, 127, 160–162
    as Anne Frances Randall, 51
    criticisms of, 125
    daughter of, 127
    feminist writings, 126
    Hubert de Sevrac, 62, 67
    and indebtedness, 167
    as Perdita, 160
    as playwright, 36
    as poet, 3, 104
    as radical, 123
    self-presentation as author, 159
    Three Poems, 3

on war, 105–106, 112
Roche, Regina Maria, 22, 26, 28, 59, 64,
    66–67
    The Children of the Abbey, 66
    Clermont, 66–67
Rogers, Samuel, 1
Roland, Madame, 50
Romanticism
    definition of, xiii
    development of term, xiii
Ross, Captain John, 75
Rossetti, Christina, 175
Rousseau, Jean-Jacques, 21, 45–47, 123,
    149, 189, 205
    Emile, 47, 122
Rowe, Nicholas, 36
Royal Literary Fund, 27–28
Rundall, Mary, 97–98
Ryan, Eliza, 12

Samuel, Richard, 51
Sargant, Jane Alice, 7
satire, 89, 125
Scandinavia, 84, 131–132
science and scientists, 70, 75–76, 95, 116,
    127, 194, 199
Scotland, 6, 17, 40, 63, 73, 76, 186,
    190–191, 193–194
Scott, Jane, 38
Scott, Mary, 117, 119
Scott, Sarah, 119
Scott, Sir Walter, 1, 3, 16, 24–26, 29, 127,
    148, 175, 204
    The Heart of Midlothian, 204
    Waverley, 24–25, 90, 196
scribal publication, xiii, 12
sensibility, 21–22, 54, 56, 90–91, 97, 132,
    187–189, 195
sentimental tradition, 1, 5–6, 8, 12–13,
    21–24, 26, 29, 37, 64–66, 84, 88–92,
    94, 96–97, 125
Seward, Anna, 5, 103, 105–106, 108, 118,
    121, 123, 126–127
    juvenilia, 173
    on war, 109
Seward, Thomas, 117
sex and sexualities, xvi, xviii, 51, 120, 170,
    198–201, 203–205, 208–210
    bisexual, 207
    botanic imagery, 200
    female, 199–200
    heterosexual, 184, 190, 192, 195,
        203–204, 207–208

sex and sexualities (*cont.*)
    lesbian, xvii, 199, 206–207
    race and ethnicity, 200
    reputation, 37
Shakespeare, William, 33, 35–38, 40, 62–63,
    118–119, 151, 170, 205
Shelley, Mary Wollstonecraft, xiv, 26, 70–71,
    74, 86, 129–131, 145, 147, 156, 198
    and family literary relations, 146
    Frankenstein, xiv, 70, 147, 149
    The Last Man, 149
    Valperga, 203, 208
Shelley, Percy Bysshe, xiii, xiv–1, 16, 86,
    130, 147
    Zastrozzi, A Romance, 68
Sheridan, Frances, 35
Sheridan, Richard Brinsley, 32
Siddons, Sarah, 35–37, 39–40, 42, 146,
    153–154
Sidney, Mary, 33
single women, 14, 41, 119, 152, 198
sisterhood, *see* literary relations,
    among women
slavery, 9–10, 49, 56, 132–134, 141–142,
    200, 203, 205
    abolition of, 133, 135
    as analogy for women's oppression,
    46–47, 119–120, 140
    slave trade, 44
    in West Indies, 129
Sleath, Eleanor, 64
Sloane, Sir Hans, 98
Smith, Adam, 69, 191
Smith, Charlotte, xvi, 2–6, 20–22, 26, 58–63,
    65–67, 70, 94–96, 105, 118, 124,
    126, 158–159, 165, 186–189, 195,
    198, 209
    "Avis au lecteur," 63, 65, 67
    The Banished Man, 61
    Beachy Head, 95–96
    and business acumen, 166
    Celestina, 21
    correspondence, 165–166
    criticisms of, 125
    daughter of, 160
    Desmond, 21, 62, 187–188, 201–202
    Elegiac Sonnets, 3–4
    The Emigrants, 165
    Emmeline, 21, 62
    Ethelinde, 62, 66
    and historiography, 94
    influence of, 4–5
    Letters of a Solitary Wanderer, 189

Marchmont, 159
The Old Manor House, 21
    poems about, 4
    popularity, 167
    and publishers, 164–166
    and William Wordsworth, 4
    on writing as labor, 164
    The Young Philosopher, 21
Smollett, Tobias, 98
sociability, 121, 145–146
social class, xvii–1, 13, 17, 19, 24–25, 38,
    42, 47–49, 52–53, 73–74, 76, 79, 81,
    86, 111, 121–123, 130, 186, 196
    aristocracy, 34, 116, 121–122, 127,
    188, 207
    distinctions, 126
    divisions, 186, 192
    elite, 120
    middle class, 55, 149, 151
    oppression, 120
    privilege, 99
    working class, 44, 52, 104, 117–118, 151
sonnet, *see* poetry, sonnet form
South Africa, 74
South America, 9, 74, 85, 102, 135, 138
Southey, Caroline Bowles, 11
Southey, Robert, xiii, 4, 119, 125, 140
Spain, 7, 102, 106, 136–137
Spenser, Edmund, 62
Spivak, Gayatri, 140
Stage Licensing Act, 35
Stanhope, Lady Hester, 74, 77, 82–84
Starke, Mariana, 39, 75–76, 80–81
Stedman, John, 176, 200
Sterne, Laurence, 21
suicide and suicide attempts, 205, 209
Sutherland, Kathryn, 54
Switzerland, 23, 85, 96, 127, 130

Talbot, Catherine, 127
Tasso, 62
Taylor, Ann, 150, 173
Taylor, Jane, 6, 150
Taylor, John, 4
textbooks, xiv, xv, 2, 5, 32, 39
theater
    Covent Garden, 39, 41–42, 151
    Drury Lane, 35–36, 41–42, 151–153
    King's Theatre, London, 41
    London, 34
    managers, 34, 69
        women as, 37
    private theatricals, 35, 38

royal, 33, 38, 41, 151–152
and theatrical families, 146, 151
Thomas, Ann, 103, 108
Thomson, James, 18, 62
Tighe, Mary, 2, 13
Tory politics, 3, 76, 125, 127
tourists and tourism, 76
tragedy, 20, 36–37, 39, 41, 69, 93, 151
translators and translation, 6, 25, 32–33, 35, 41, 51, 122, 135–136, 155
travel narratives
numbers of, 135
travel writing, xiv, xvi, xvii, 73–79, 81, 84–86, 130
by men, 75
as nascent area of study, 78
Trench, Melesina, 12
Trimmer, Sarah, 38, 97, 124
Trotter, Catharine, 34
Tuite, Eliza, 105, 112
Turkey, 73–75, 79, 131
Turner, Cheryl, 19, 25, 29
Turner, Margaret, 38

United States
history of, 188
utilitarianism, 125
Utopianism, 119, 124–125

Vaughn, Iris, 172
Vauxhall Gardens, 200
Vesey, Elizabeth, 120, 126
Victorian period, xv, 14, 35, 42, 55, 116, 126, 128, 173, 175, 177, 199
virtue, 24, 46, 52, 88–89, 120, 123, 194
feminine, 52–53, 89
male, 121
masculine, 89
national, 89
Voltaire, 45, 48, 119, 205
von Hippel, Theodor Gottlieb, 122

Wakefield, Priscilla, 124
Wales, 76, 186, 191
Wallace, Lady Eglantine, 39
Walpole, Horace, 65, 79
The Castle of Otranto, 58, 65, 91
war and wartime, xvi, 4, 6–9, 13, 21, 62, 84, 101, 103, 105–107, 132, 137, 186, 194, 203
anti-war views, 5
British literature, 113

casualties, 102, 105, 107
classical imagery, 108
commercialism, 104, 108, 113
conservatism, 104
costs, 108
criticisms of, 105, 130, 148
economic impact, 103–104, 108–109, 113
effects on women, 102
emotional costs, 101
England, 103
everyday lives, 101
government policies, 104
grief, 111
military service, 102
moral consequences, 101
poetry of, 8
prisoners of war, 103, 108
returning soldiers, 101
soldiers, 103, 108, 110
in support of war, 8
and taxation, 149
victory, 106, 111
women, 105
Waterloo, 6, 102
Wells, Helena, 135
West Indies, 129, 133–135
West, Jane, 22, 24, 38, 124, 186, 193–194
A Gossip's Story, 124, 190
Letters to a Young Lady, 189
Miscellaneous Poetry, 174
Ringrove, 178–180
A Tale of the Times, 191
Wharton, Anne, 34
Wheatley, Phillis, 175
Whig politics, 121, 126
widows, 119
sati, 133, 138–141
Wilberforce, William, 10, 133
Wilde, Oscar, 32
William IV, 37, 153
Williams, Anne, 59
Williams, Helen Maria, 4, 76, 81, 84–85, 104, 116, 118, 121, 126–127, 130, 142
as Francophile, 130
Wilson, Ann, 38
Wilson, Harriette, 198–200, 203–205, 210
Wilson, Kathleen, 104
Winchilsea, Countess of, 34
Winscom, Jane Cave, 105, 107–108
Wolfson, Susan J., 136

Wollstonecraft, Mary, xiv, xvi, 21, 26, 44–56,
    61–62, 74, 84, 116, 121–127,
    131–133, 147–150, 155, 161–162,
    165, 186, 188–190, 193–196,
    198–199, 201, 205, 209–210
  absence from textbooks, xiv
  association with bluestockings, 116
  biography, 50
  career as author, 44
  compared to Hannah More, 51
  compared to Mary Hays, 49
  compared to prostitute, 125
  on education, 45, 122
  and Eliza Fenwick, 156
  and family literary relations, 146
  and femininity, 188
  An Historical and Moral View of the
    French Revolution, 188
  Maria, or The Wrongs of Woman, 189
  on marriage, 47
  Mary: A Fiction, 149, 189, 201–202, 204
  and money, 161
  Original Stories from Real Life, 124, 150
  on physical differences between the
    sexes, 46
  posthumous reputation, 50, 123, 126–128
  as radical, 123
  relationship with publisher, 160–162
  as reviewer, 4
  on revolution in female manners, 123
  self-presentation as author, 159
  on sexuality, 48
  as travel writer, 131–132
  A Vindication of the Rights of Men, 45,
    61, 188
  A Vindication of the Rights of Woman,
    45, 50–51, 116, 120, 122, 124–126,
    188, 209
women writers
  numbers of, xvii
Wood, Marcus, 200
Wordsworth, Dorothy, xiv, 75, 155
Wordsworth, William, xiii–1, 9, 13, 16, 96,
    158–159, 173, 176
  Preface to Lyrical Ballads, 119
  on women's writing, 4
Wright, Angela, xvi
Wu, Duncan, 2

Yearsley, Ann, 41, 105, 126, 133
  and Hannah More, 118
  as playwright, 41

Cambridge Companions to ...

AUTHORS

Edward Albee edited by Stephen J. Bottoms
Margaret Atwood edited by Coral Ann
   Howells
W. H. Auden edited by Stan Smith
Jane Austen edited by Edward Copeland and
   Juliet McMaster (second edition)
Beckett edited by John Pilling
Bede edited by Scott DeGregorio
Aphra Behn edited by Derek Hughes and
   Janet Todd
Walter Benjamin edited by David S. Ferris
William Blake edited by Morris Eaves
Jorge Luis Borges edited by Edwin
   Williamson
Brecht edited by Peter Thomson and
   Glendyr Sacks (second edition)
The Brontës edited by Heather Glen
Bunyan edited by Anne Dunan-Page
Frances Burney edited by Peter Sabor
Byron edited by Drummond Bone
Albert Camus edited by Edward J. Hughes
Willa Cather edited by Marilee Lindemann
Cervantes edited by Anthony J. Cascardi
Chaucer edited by Piero Boitani and Jill
   Mann (second edition)
Chekhov edited by Vera Gottlieb and Paul
   Allain
Kate Chopin edited by Janet Beer
Caryl Churchill edited by Elaine Aston and
   Elin Diamond
Cicero edited by Catherine Steel
Coleridge edited by Lucy Newlyn
Wilkie Collins edited by Jenny Bourne
   Taylor
Joseph Conrad edited by J. H. Stape
H. D. edited by Nephie J. Christodoulides
   and Polina Mackay
Dante edited by Rachel Jacoff (second
   edition)
Daniel Defoe edited by John Richetti
Don DeLillo edited by John N. Duvall
Charles Dickens edited by John O. Jordan
Emily Dickinson edited by Wendy Martin
John Donne edited by Achsah Guibbory
Dostoevskii edited by W. J. Leatherbarrow
Theodore Dreiser edited by Leonard
   Cassuto and Claire Virginia Eby

John Dryden edited by Steven N. Zwicker
W. E. B. Du Bois edited by Shamoon Zamir
George Eliot edited by George Levine
T. S. Eliot edited by A. David Moody
Ralph Ellison edited by Ross Posnock
Ralph Waldo Emerson edited by Joel Porte
   and Saundra Morris
William Faulkner edited by Philip M.
   Weinstein
Henry Fielding edited by Claude Rawson
F. Scott Fitzgerald edited by Ruth Prigozy
Flaubert edited by Timothy Unwin
E. M. Forster edited by David Bradshaw
Benjamin Franklin edited by Carla Mulford
Brian Friel edited by Anthony Roche
Robert Frost edited by Robert Faggen
Gabriel García Márquez edited by Philip
   Swanson
Elizabeth Gaskell edited by Jill L. Matus
Goethe edited by Lesley Sharpe
Günter Grass edited by Stuart Taberner
Thomas Hardy edited by Dale Kramer
David Hare edited by Richard Boon
Nathaniel Hawthorne edited by Richard
   Millington
Seamus Heaney edited by Bernard
   O'Donoghue
Ernest Hemingway edited by Scott
   Donaldson
Homer edited by Robert Fowler
Horace edited by Stephen Harrison
Ted Hughes edited by Terry Gifford
Ibsen edited by James McFarlane
Henry James edited by Jonathan Freedman
Samuel Johnson edited by Greg Clingham
Ben Jonson edited by Richard Harp and
   Stanley Stewart
James Joyce edited by Derek Attridge
   (second edition)
Kafka edited by Julian Preece
Keats edited by Susan J. Wolfson
Rudyard Kipling edited by Howard J. Booth
Lacan edited by Jean-Michel Rabaté
D. H. Lawrence edited by Anne Fernihough
Primo Levi edited by Robert Gordon
Lucretius edited by Stuart Gillespie and
   Philip Hardie

Machiavelli edited by John M. Najemy
David Mamet edited by Christopher Bigsby
Thomas Mann edited by Ritchie Robertson
Christopher Marlowe edited by Patrick
Cheney
Andrew Marvell edited by Derek Hirst and
Steven N. Zwicker
Herman Melville edited by Robert S. Levine
Arthur Miller edited by Christopher Bigsby
(second edition)
Milton edited by Dennis Danielson (second
edition)
Molière edited by David Bradby and
Andrew Calder
Toni Morrison edited by Justine Tally
Nabokov edited by Julian W. Connolly
Eugene O'Neill edited by Michael Manheim
George Orwell edited by John Rodden
Ovid edited by Philip Hardie
Harold Pinter edited by Peter Raby (second
edition)
Sylvia Plath edited by Jo Gill
Edgar Allan Poe edited by Kevin J. Hayes
Alexander Pope edited by Pat Rogers
Ezra Pound edited by Ira B. Nadel
Proust edited by Richard Bales
Pushkin edited by Andrew Kahn
Rabelais edited by John O'Brien
Rilke edited by Karen Leeder and Robert
Vilain
Philip Roth edited by Timothy Parrish
Salman Rushdie edited by Abdulrazak
Gurnah
Shakespeare edited by Margareta de Grazia
and Stanley Wells (second edition)
Shakespearean Comedy edited by Alexander
Leggatt
*Shakespeare and Contemporary
Dramatists* edited by Ton Hoenselaars
Shakespeare and Popular Culture edited by
Robert Shaughnessy
Shakespearean Tragedy edited by Claire
McEachern (second edition)
Shakespeare on Film edited by Russell
Jackson (second edition)
Shakespeare on Stage edited by Stanley
Wells and Sarah Stanton
Shakespeare's History Plays edited by
Michael Hattaway

Shakespeare's Last Plays edited by Catherine
M. S. Alexander
Shakespeare's Poetry edited by Patrick
Cheney
George Bernard Shaw edited by Christopher
Innes
Shelley edited by Timothy Morton
Mary Shelley edited by Esther Schor
Sam Shepard edited by Matthew C.
Roudané
Spenser edited by Andrew Hadfield
Laurence Sterne edited by Thomas Keymer
Wallace Stevens edited by John N. Serio
Tom Stoppard edited by Katherine
E. Kelly
Harriet Beecher Stowe edited by Cindy
Weinstein
August Strindberg edited by Michael
Robinson
Jonathan Swift edited by Christopher Fox
J. M. Synge edited by P. J. Mathews
Tacitus edited by A. J. Woodman
Henry David Thoreau edited by Joel
Myerson
Tolstoy edited by Donna Tussing Orwin
Anthony Trollope edited by Carolyn Dever
and Lisa Niles
Mark Twain edited by Forrest
G. Robinson
John Updike edited by Stacey Olster
Mario Vargas Llosa edited by Efrain Kristal
and John King
Virgil edited by Charles Martindale
Voltaire edited by Nicholas Cronk
Edith Wharton edited by Millicent Bell
Walt Whitman edited by Ezra Greenspan
Oscar Wilde edited by Peter Raby
Tennessee Williams edited by Matthew C.
Roudané
August Wilson edited by Christopher
Bigsby
Mary Wollstonecraft edited by Claudia L.
Johnson
Virginia Woolf edited by Susan Sellers
(second edition)
Wordsworth edited by Stephen Gill
W. B. Yeats edited by Marjorie Howes and
John Kelly
Zola edited by Brian Nelson

TOPICS

The Actress edited by Maggie B. Gale and
John Stokes

The African American Novel edited by
Maryemma Graham

The African American Slave Narrative edited
by Audrey A. Fisch

African American Theatre edited by Harvey
Young

Allegory edited by Rita Copeland and Peter
Struck

American Crime Fiction edited by Catherine
Ross Nickerson

American Modernism edited by Walter
Kalaidjian

American Poetry Since 1945 edited by
Jennifer Ashton

American Realism and Naturalism edited by
Donald Pizer

American Travel Writing edited by Alfred
Bendixen and Judith Hamera

American Women Playwrights edited by
Brenda Murphy

Ancient Rhetoric edited by Erik
Gunderson

Arthurian Legend edited by Elizabeth
Archibald and Ad Putter

Australian Literature edited by Elizabeth
Webby

*British Literature of the French
Revolution* edited by Pamela Clemit

British Romanticism edited by Stuart
Curran (second edition)

British Romantic Poetry edited by James
Chandler and Maureen N. McLane

British Theatre, 1730–1830 edited by Jane
Moody and Daniel O'Quinn

Canadian Literature edited by Eva-Marie
Kröller

Children's Literature edited by M. O.
Grenby and Andrea Immel

The Classic Russian Novel edited by
Malcolm V. Jones and Robin Feuer
Miller

Contemporary Irish Poetry edited by
Matthew Campbell

Creative Writing edited by David Morley
and Philip Neilsen

Crime Fiction edited by Martin Priestman

Early Modern Women's Writing edited by
Laura Lunger Knoppers

The Eighteenth-Century Novel edited by
John Richetti

Eighteenth-Century Poetry edited by John
Sitter

English Literature, 1500–1600 edited by
Arthur F. Kinney

English Literature, 1650–1740 edited by
Steven N. Zwicker

English Literature, 1740–1830 edited by
Thomas Keymer and Jon Mee

English Literature, 1830–1914 edited by
Joanne Shattock

English Novelists edited by Adrian Poole

English Poetry, Donne to Marvell edited by
Thomas N. Corns

English Poets edited by Claude Rawson

English Renaissance Drama edited by A. R.
Braunmuller and Michael Hattaway
(second edition)

English Renaissance Tragedy edited by
Emma Smith and Garrett A. Sullivan Jr.

English Restoration Theatre edited by
Deborah C. Payne Fisk

The Epic edited by Catherine Bates

European Modernism edited by Pericles
Lewis

European Novelists edited by Michael Bell

Fairy Tales edited by Maria Tatar

Fantasy Literature edited by Edward James
and Farah Mendlesohn

Feminist Literary Theory edited by Ellen
Rooney

Fiction in the Romantic Period edited by
Richard Maxwell and Katie Trumpener

The Fin de Siècle edited by Gail Marshall

The French Enlightenment edited by Daniel
Brewer

*The French Novel: from 1800 to the
Present* edited by Timothy Unwin

Gay and Lesbian Writing edited by Hugh
Stevens

German Romanticism edited by Nicholas
Saul

Gothic Fiction edited by Jerrold E. Hogle

The Greek and Roman Novel edited by Tim
Whitmarsh

Greek and Roman Theatre edited by
Marianne McDonald and J. Michael
Walton

Greek Comedy edited by Martin Revermann

Greek Lyric edited by Felix Budelmann
Greek Mythology edited by Roger D. Woodard
Greek Tragedy edited by P. E. Easterling
The Harlem Renaissance edited by George Hutchinson
The History of the Book edited by Leslie Howsam
The Irish Novel edited by John Wilson Foster
The Italian Novel edited by Peter Bondanella and Andrea Ciccarelli
The Italian Renaissance edited by Michael Wyatt
Jewish American Literature edited by Hana Wirth-Nesher and Michael P. Kramer
The Latin American Novel edited by Efraín Kristal
The Literature of the First World War edited by Vincent Sherry
The Literature of London edited by Lawrence Manley
The Literature of Los Angeles edited by Kevin R. McNamara
The Literature of New York edited by Cyrus Patell and Bryan Waterman
The Literature of Paris edited by Anna-Louise Milne
The Literature of World War II edited by Marina MacKay
Literature on Screen edited by Deborah Cartmell and Imelda Whelehan
Medieval English Culture edited by Andrew Galloway
Medieval English Literature edited by Larry Scanlon
Medieval English Mysticism edited by Samuel Fanous and Vincent Gillespie
Medieval English Theatre edited by Richard Beadle and Alan J. Fletcher (second edition)
Medieval French Literature edited by Simon Gaunt and Sarah Kay
Medieval Romance edited by Roberta L. Krueger
Medieval Women's Writing edited by Carolyn Dinshaw and David Wallace
Modern American Culture edited by Christopher Bigsby
Modern British Women Playwrights edited by Elaine Aston and Janelle Reinelt

Modern French Culture edited by Nicholas Hewitt
Modern German Culture edited by Eva Kolinsky and Wilfried van der Will
The Modern German Novel edited by Graham Bartram
The Modern Gothic edited by Jerrold E. Hogle
Modern Irish Culture edited by Joe Cleary and Claire Connolly
Modern Italian Culture edited by Zygmunt G. Baranski and Rebecca J. West
Modern Latin American Culture edited by John King
Modern Russian Culture edited by Nicholas Rzhevsky
Modern Spanish Culture edited by David T. Gies
Modernism edited by Michael Levenson (second edition)
The Modernist Novel edited by Morag Shiach
Modernist Poetry edited by Alex Davis and Lee M. Jenkins
Modernist Women Writers edited by Maren Tova Linett
Narrative edited by David Herman
Native American Literature edited by Joy Porter and Kenneth M. Roemer
Nineteenth-Century American Women's Writing edited by Dale M. Bauer and Philip Gould
Old English Literature edited by Malcolm Godden and Michael Lapidge (second edition)
Performance Studies edited by Tracy C. Davis
Piers Plowman by Andrew Cole and Andrew Galloway
Popular Fiction edited by David Glover and Scott McCracken
Postcolonial Literary Studies edited by Neil Lazarus
Postmodernism edited by Steven Connor
The Pre-Raphaelites edited by Elizabeth Prettejohn
Pride and Prejudice edited by Janet Todd
Renaissance Humanism edited by Jill Kraye
The Roman Historians edited by Andrew Feldherr
Roman Satire edited by Kirk Freudenburg

Science Fiction edited by Edward James and Farah Mendlesohn

Scottish Literature edited by Gerald Carruthers and Liam McIlvanney

Sensation Fiction edited by Andrew Mangham

The Sonnet edited by A. D. Cousins and Peter Howarth

The Spanish Novel: from 1600 to the Present edited by Harriet Turner and Adelaida López de Martínez

Textual Scholarship edited by Neil Fraistat and Julia Flanders

Theatre History edited by David Wiles and Christine Dymkowski

Travel Writing edited by Peter Hulme and Tim Youngs

Twentieth-Century British and Irish Women's Poetry edited by Jane Dowson

The Twentieth-Century English Novel edited by Robert L. Caserio

Twentieth-Century English Poetry edited by Neil Corcoran

Twentieth-Century Irish Drama edited by Shaun Richards

Twentieth-Century Russian Literature edited by Marina Balina and Evgeny Dobrenko

Utopian Literature edited by Gregory Claeys

Victorian and Edwardian Theatre edited by Kerry Powell

The Victorian Novel edited by Deirdre David (second edition)

Victorian Poetry edited by Joseph Bristow

War Writing edited by Kate McLoughlin

Women's Writing in the Romantic Period edited by Devoney Looser

Writing of the English Revolution edited by N. H. Keeble